The Working Class in American History

Books in the Series:

Worker City, Company Town: Iron and Cotton-Worker Protest in Troy and Cohoes, New York, 1855–84
Daniel J. Walkowitz

Life, Work, and Rebellion in the Coal Fields: The Southern West Virginia Miners, 1880–1922
David Alan Corbin

Women and American Socialism, 1870–1920
Mari Jo Buhle

Lives of Their Own: Blacks, Italians, and Poles in Pittsburgh, 1900–1960
John Bodnar, Roger Simon, and Michael P. Weber

Working-Class America: Essays on Labor, Community, and American Society
edited by Michael H. Frisch and Daniel J. Walkowitz

Eugene V. Debs: Citizen and Socialist
Nick Salvatore

American Labor and Immigration History, 1877–1920s: Recent European Research *edited by Dirk Hoerder*

American Labor and Immigration History, 1877-1920s

American Labor and Immigration History, 1877–1920s: Recent European Research

Edited by Dirk Hoerder

UNIVERSITY OF ILLINOIS PRESS

Urbana   Chicago   London

© 1983 by the Board of Trustees of the University of Illinois
Manufactured in the United States of America

This book is printed on acid-free paper.

LIBRARY OF CONGRESS CATALOGING IN PUBLICATION DATA

Main entry under title:

American Labor and immigration history, 1877–1920s.
  (The Working class in American history)
  Papers prepared for a conference at the University of
Bremen, Nov. 1978
  Includes index.
  Contents: Introduction: American labor history in
the United States and Europe / Dirk Hoerder—Workers,
scholars, militancy: Strikes and economics, working-
class insurgency and the birth of labor historiography in
the 1880s / Bruno Cartosio. W.E.B. Du Bois and the
proletariat in Black reconstruction / Ferruccio Gambino.
Workers' self-organization and resistance in the 1877
strikes / Marianne Debouzy. "Reefs of roast beef," the
American worker's standard of living in comparative
perspective / Peter R. Shergold—[etc.]
  1. Labor and laboring classes—United States—History—Congresses. 2. United States—Foreign population
History—Congresses. 3. European Americans—History—
Congresses. I. Hoerder, Dirk. II. Series.
HD8081.E93A45   305.5′6   81-23078
ISBN 0-252-00963-0   AACR2

Preface

DAVID BRODY and HERBERT G. GUTMAN

The essays in this volume are the result of a memorable conference that took place at the University of Bremen in November 1978. The conference was intended as a stock-taking of current European work in American labor and immigration history. The scholars presenting papers were from Australia, Finland, France, Great Britain, Ireland, Italy, Sweden, West Germany, and Yugoslavia. The American participants—David Brody, Alan Dawley, Herbert G. Gutman, William H. Harris, Daniel J. Leab, Rudolph J. Vecoli, and Alfred F. Young—served as commentators, as did a group of senior European scholars, including Charlotte Erickson of the London School of Economics and Political Science, Günter Moltman of Hamburg University, Bo Öhngren of Uppsala University, Longin Pastusiak of the Research Institute on Contemporary Capitalism in Warsaw, Tihomir Telišman of the Institute of Migration and Nationality in Zagreb, Arnaldo Testi of the University of Pisa, and Loretta Valtz-Mannucci of the University of Milan.

It would be hard to convey the heady atmosphere that prevailed during the week of meetings in Bremen. Any gathering of talented scholars is likely to generate lively discussion. And if the meeting is well planned, with provocative papers circulated and read in advance, the sessions cannot fail to be productive and stimulating. The extra ingredient here was, of course, the international character of the Bremen conference. The insularity of our historiography has long troubled American scholars. We have sorely missed the kinds of insights and perspectives accessible to students who stand outside the stream of our national history. Limited in the years after World War II mainly to "American Studies"—to literature and cultural history rather narrowly defined—European scholarship has in the past decade begun to strike out in new directions, and nowhere more vigorously than toward the history of American working people. The Bremen conference was an occasion for serious discussion of that new work, for the European authors to hear from seasoned American practitioners, for the Americans to discover what might be called European perspectives on American labor and immigration history.

Immigration, of course, forms a natural link between European and American history. The subject has drawn a good deal of research in recent years, especially in the countries of northern and eastern Europe that sent large populations to America. As is evident in the essays of David Doyle and Lars-Göran Tedebrand, European immigration scholars are more prone to ask themselves why people left, what they carried with them, than how they were integrated into American life. The European perspective is also likely to be sensitive to class relationships and economic dislocations in the homeland and, as at least four of the papers in this collection do, to see the immigration process as a part of American working-class history. Of the other contributors, all but one specifically credits the events of the 1960s with inspiring an interest in American working-class history. The connecting link for them evidently was the discovery of common elements of radical insurgency on both sides of the Atlantic during the Vietnam era and, out of that discovery, a curiosity as to the history of industrial conflict and radical movements in America. That they can throw fresh light on these topics is altogether clear in the essays of Bruno Cartosio, Marianne Debouzy, Ferruccio Gambino, and Hubert Perrier. And, not least important, there is the comparative perspective that European scholars bring to the subject, sometimes submerged as in Andrew Dawson's essay on American craft workers, sometimes explicit as in Peter Shergold's essay on comparative standards of living.

These essays can be taken as a first sign of an emergent European school of American working-class history. The Bremen conference has stimulated further activity. It led to a comprehensive survey of ongoing scholarship that has been published in two installments in *Labor History* during 1980. At Bremen, too, plans were made for a project to survey and microfilm the immigrant labor press in the United States. Professor Loretta Valtz-Mannucci organized a conference on American radical history the following year in Milan under the auspices of the Italian Society of American History. At the University of Munich another conference participant, Dr. Hartmut Keil, is heading a major project on German workers in Chicago with funding from the VW Foundation. Among European scholars in the field a network is emerging, and ongoing communication exists with colleagues in America.

Special note needs to be taken of Dr. Dirk Hoerder of the University of Bremen. He conceived and organized the conference, ran it with a firm and intelligent hand, and afterward shepherded the essays into this book. Only those familiar with the circumstances under which he worked will understand the magnitude of his achievement. Nothing could augur better for the future of American working-class history in Europe than the determination and energy shown by Dirk Hoerder.

We are proud to have this collection of essays in the Working Class in American History Series. We are confident that this volume represents only a first installment in the European study of the history of workers in America.

Contents

Introduction: American Labor History in the United
States and Europe   3
Dirk Hoerder

PART I: Workers, Scholars, Militancy   17

1. Strikes and Economics: Working-Class Insurgency and the
   Birth of Labor Historiography in the 1880s
   Bruno Cartosio   19

2. W. E. B. Du Bois and the Proletariat in *Black Reconstruction*
   Ferruccio Gambino   43

3. Workers' Self-Organization and Resistance in the
   1877 Strikes   61
   Marianne Debouzy

4. "Reefs of Roast Beef": The American Worker's Standard of
   Living in Comparative Perspective   78
   Peter R. Shergold

PART II: Organization   107

5. The Socialists and the Working Class in New York,
   1890–96   111
   Hubert Perrier

6. The Parameters of Craft Consciousness: The Social Outlook of the Skilled Worker, 1890–1920   135
   Andrew Dawson

7. The German Immigrant Working Class of Chicago,
   1875–90: Workers, Labor Leaders, and the
   Labor Movement   156
   Hartmut Keil

8. Yugoslav Immigrants in the U.S. Labor Movement,
   1880–1920   177
   Ivan Čizmić

PART III: Immigrants   191

9. Unestablished Irishmen: New Immigrants and Industrial
   America, 1870–1910   193
   David N. Doyle

10. Strikes and Political Radicalism in Sweden and Emigration
    to the United States   221
    Lars-Göran Tedebrand

11. Political Mobilization of the Workers: The Case of the
    Worcester Swedes   235
    Sune Åkerman and Hans Norman

12. For or Against Americanization? The Case of the Finnish
    Immigrant Radicals   259
    Auvo Kostiainen

    About the Authors   276

    About the Commentators   281

    Index   283

American Labor and Immigration History, 1877–1920s

Introduction: American Labor History in the United States and Europe

DIRK HOERDER

Why an anthology of essays on the American working class by European scholars at this time? Interest in American workers and the immigrant components of the class has been on the upswing for about a decade and a half now. Reasons for this interest vary from region to region and country to country. But the quality and quantity of the work published and in progress are now coalescing and warrant an effort to pull together the threads of the various national developments.

There were earlier periods of similar interest, the late nineteenth century and the twenties and early thirties of this century. Each time economic, social, and political developments influenced scholarly endeavors to understand North America—usually meaning the United States only. In the late nineteenth century reformers seeking solutions to the "labor problem" of their own country kept in close contact with reformers in other countries. They studied working conditions and collective bargaining procedures on both sides of the Atlantic in the hope of shedding light on their own society by describing and analyzing similarities and dissimilarities with other societies. This, we might add, was not only a scholarly concern. European diplomats in the United States sent home detailed reports about the labor movement and the condition of the working classes.[1] The Wisconsin and Illinois scholar-reformers exchanged ideas with their European colleagues:[2] the Settlement House movement established in Great Britain took roots in the United States.,[3] the German Kathedersozialisten and the Ely-Commons-Perlman group opened the columns of their journals to each other. Trade union and manufacturers' delegations from Europe visited the United States and sometimes Canada; they included a French delegation in 1876, the centennial year, followed by another in 1883, a British delegation in 1890, and a German economist in 1893. Americans collected information in Europe; witness, among others, the Department of Labor delegation in 1888.[4]

A similar wave of interest began at the end of World War I and lasted into the early thirties. The war had brought a general recognition of the power of the United States in world affairs. *American Studies—A Timely Demand* was the title of Friedrich Schönemann's programmatic essay concerning a curriculum that included economics and sociology.[5] Principles of Taylorism had been introduced into European factories on a large scale; to numerous influential European union and business leaders, scientific management and collective bargaining seemed to open avenues for peaceful industrial relations.[6]

The recent wave of interest among Western European scholars was sparked off by new questions being asked in the wake of the student rebellion, and we are now beginning to harvest the scholarly crop. The attention to the daily lives, activities, ways of thinking of the underdogs—working-class, artisan, ethnic—was accompanied by a search for their roots in American traditions other than the mainstream/consensus/silent majority tales.[7] Soon, however, it became obvious that the history of movements alone could hardly provide answers more satisfactorily than the stale diet of political history. The result was a shift to a history of society with emphasis on the lower classes.

In the socialist countries in Eastern Europe interest in the history of the American working class stems from other roots, the different position of the classes in socialist societies being perhaps the most obvious but certainly not the only reason. There is the question of and hope for international workers' solidarity: cooperation presupposes a detailed knowledge and analysis of the other national working classes, their organizations, and their respective socioeconomic environments.[8] Though the hope for international solidarity has suffered serious reverses during two world wars and the Cold War,[9] it is still a motivation for probing into U.S. working-class history, one shared by a number of younger West European scholars. While in the West Great Britain has the longest tradition of research into American labor history—the cultural affinity being the probable cause—in the East this distinction goes to the Soviet Union, where since 1945 scholarly publications on American unions, workers, governmental labor policies, and similar questions have redounded.[10] An important reason for the interest in American labor history in other socialist countries may be found in their pre–World War I history: their precarious political existence between the Ottoman and czarist empires on one side, the Habsburg and Hohenzollern monarchies on the other. Only after the dissolution of the Austro-Hungarian empire and the reestablishment of Poland as a nation with its own territory could any form of national scholarship re-emerge. By that time, after 1918, a considerable percentage of the ethnic stock of each of these new nations had emigrated to join the American labor force: millions left from the 1880s onward. For southern and East European historians, interest in the ethnic heritage of their nations' emigrants to the United States overlaps with American working-class history because the vast majority of the "new immigrants" joined the industrial labor force. Bulgarians and Greeks seem to be the exception to this rule. It is no coincidence that Yugoslav (i.e. South Slav) scholars working on immigrant socialists in the United States are affiliated with the Zagreb *Institute of Migration and Nationalities.*[11]

Whether from East or West, socialist, capitalist, or nonaligned countries, scholars shared one shortcoming: the lack of international cooperation and exchange of ideas. Language barriers and divergent ✓ ideological points of view as well as political difficulties in crossing some boundaries, whatever the direction may have been and may be, contributed to a kind of parochial outlook. If individual scholars looked beyond their nation's boundaries, it was toward the United States, where archival sources were to be found and where a host of highly specialized colleagues worked with whom they shared a common means of communication, the English language. Attempts to improve the situation by and large remained piecemeal. It is only now, with all the different motivations for studying American labor and working-class history, that an international scholarly discourse has become a meaningful possibility in our field.

A brief glance at the table of contents of this volume shows that Europeans seem not to have taken up the challenge posed by labor historians of the American New Left: there is little attempt to achieve ✓ a cultural history of the U.S. working class. Is this, then, a discourse between partners rejecting each other's approaches? It certainly is not. Historians on both sides of the Atlantic have been influenced by the working-class history as developed by E. P. Thompson and other British Marxists. But they have applied this approach mainly to their own societies. It is also apparent that minorities within the working class—blacks, Chicanos, migratory labor, women—receive less attention than they do in the United States. Aside from the pressures to select topics that will be acceptable to the doorkeepers of academia, there are other problems. It simply is more difficult to deal with U.S. minorities from a European base of operations: archives are far away, stipends for the study of oral history are nonexistent. In addition, while in the United States the "Old Left" with the exception of Philip Foner seems to have left the field of labor history, many European colleagues still share certain views of the "Old Left": emphasis on organizations, on an "avant-garde" in class struggles. Also, no demands for a nonorganizational history came from segments of the working classes until 1968, because AFL-CIO activities in rebuilding

European, especially West German, trade unions after World War II have muted all forms of workers' self-activities that sprouted immediately after liberation.

While the lack of a cultural history of the American working class is a shortcoming that cannot be denied, the European scene has brought forward the operaist approach and—documented in this volume—it has taken intensive note of intraclass friction between ethnic groups. To live in the culture of origin makes it possible to detect meanings that are lost on persons living in the new "amalgamated" culture. But again this is not an isolated development: the Immigration History Research Center at the University of Minnesota has become something of a mecca for scholars. Within Europe, scholars from the socialist countries are particularly active in this field, but it seems to me that the Nordic Emigration History Project, institutionally centered on Uppsala University, has been the largest effort to coordinate work in this field. Social composition of migrants, push and pull factors, spread of information, means and routes of travel, direct migration and migration in stages, precipitating factors and long-term economic developments, all have been included in this and other massive studies at the end of which a Finnish farmer, a Danish labor leader, a Norwegian shopkeeper, an Icelandic laborer have become American workers.[12] The focus of emigration or immigration history—depending on whence you look—has shifted from explaining assimilation processes and differences in speed of assimilation between several ethnic groups to analyses of what parts of their culture emigrants took with them, of how they influenced American beliefs, work structures, and institutions.

Another development is that for a long time many historians of immigration, blinded by the rhetoric about the poor huddled masses coming to the land of unlimited opportunities, never realized that what they were talking about was a complex of seasonal trans-Atlantic migrations of farmhands following the harvest cycles, of artisans working in America in the summer and staying in their home countries during the winter, of remigration movements that at times were larger than the in-migration movements. While economists today debate whether developed countries should pay for every worker and professional they drain off from developing countries, historians have not yet attempted to explain America's growth by the shifting of social costs to the countries of the Old World. In several European countries scholarly interest in American labor and immigrants still has to overcome resistance from many quarters. One frequently repeated argument is that minorities, e.g. the Wobblies or Polish immigrants, do not deserve attention in European university curricula because only the "basics" of American history are essential. They are, provided agreement can be reached about these "basics"; to take one example, unskilled immigrants and Taylorism played an important role in restructuring the American labor force and the production processes. The Industrial Workers of the World attempted to develop an ideology and an organization adapted to the new situation. Historians have to deal with questions like these unless they are willing to write a determinist history justifying the powers that are. Jesse Lemisch once pointed out in words geared to the rhetoric of the Western economic system that throughout American history alternative concepts of social organization were available in the marketplace of ideas and that historians have to bear the responsibility for buying only those concepts that suit their tastes. Of course, the Industrial Workers of the World were a minority. So was each immigrant group. But the unskilled, whom the Wobblies sought to organize, were a majority within the working class; and immigrants—to use Oscar Handlin's words—were American history.[13]

Today ethnic groups are claiming their place in history. Under a sociopolitical impetus—the black rebellion and the growing consciousness of the values of a black culture—nonblack ethnic groups began to search for their roots, and a host of ethnic studies programs followed. Congress, taking cognizance of these developments, passed the Ethnic Heritage Act[14] to provide for educational materials. For historians writing the history of the winners and of great white men, this came as something of a surprise. After having been told about homogenized and streamlined Americans by many political and social science texts, we are confronted by a vast variety of "unmeltable ethnics," rather outspoken ones at times. One example is the Ohio steel mills, once manned to a considerable degree by "huns," "slavs," "hunkies," "dagos," and the like: an internationally composed national working class. Just three years after having been imported, Polish workers struck for better wages at the Cleveland Rolling Mills Company's plant. Industrialists soon stopped talking about Americanization and instead had recourse to the National Guard, the U.S. Army, and the Mahoning Valley "formula," a combination of blacklists, labor spies, fake citizens' front organizations, vigilante groups, strike-breaking services, private armed forces, and arsenals. Among those applying the "formula" was the Youngstown Sheet and Tube Company mill in the 1930s, which made headlines recently when businessmen from the Lykes conglomerate employed a new corporate strategy—raiding the assets of a firm and then shutting it down without regard to the future of the workers. The workers attempted to take over the steel mill: second- or third-generation "hunkies" running a steel mill is not quite what employers expected when they imported laborers considered docile, submissive, and content with starvation wages.[15]

If consensus historians overlooked the ethnic components of American society, those historians writing about the American working class, about immigrants, women workers, and black slaves, are not immune to making mistakes or having narrow points of view either. Histories of workers' lives without attention to changes in the processes of production yield only one-sided views; so does a history of a left party or union leader that pays little attention to the mass of rank-and-file members. When Ely, Commons, and later Perlman began to study labor unions, this was certainly an achievement.[16] But what was a step ahead fifty or a hundred years ago is not necessarily progressive now. A more recent approach, history from the bottom up, however, does not automatically correct all the deficiencies of history from the top down. At first it was mainly concerned with periods of accelerated social change. In static periods those at the bottom were certainly not inarticulate but seemingly were invisible, so the argument went. This may result in a return to the spasmodic view of history which E. P. Thompson justly criticized. Also, the attempts to explain crowd action sometimes became somewhat apologetic about violence, and the rationalization of mass action by middle-class historians decked the participants out with nice and neat middle-class mentalities. The dean of this seminal approach, George Rudé, has pointed to these problems in a self-critical essay.[17]

Meanwhile, with the cultural history of the working class or history of everyday life, with history of the "other labor movement" and history of organized labor, with history of workers at the workplace and operaism, we have come to realize that those at the bottom of society need not be invisible if only we care to look. They influence historical developments as much as concentration of capital, technological change, or other classes.

The cultural history of the working class considers everyday life, i.e. the reproductive section of a working-class family's life, as an important factor in explaining working-class organization, class consciousness, and forms of self-organized action against employers. The argument—which is borne out by immigration history—is that a community with shared views and traditions is necessary if the individual worker is to assert his position. (Employers knew this all along; they mixed different nationalities in order to prevent communities of workers from developing.) Herbert Gutman is one leading proponent of this approach, Alfred Young has used it for the early national period, and Alan Dawley and Paul Faler have produced magnificent studies of the transformation of shoemakers' lives in Lynn, Massachusetts. Philip Foner, whose work was once considered the prototype of an organizational approach, is now editing documents on culture and consciousness of working-class men and women.[18]

Complementary to this approach is the emphasis on the workplace. What technological changes did workers face? How did they react? How did shared work experiences change into ways of thinking and seeing society? David Brody's study of steelworkers at the turn of the century is a good example of this approach.[19] Brody has recently argued that cultural history should not be overemphasized and he explains: "Informal work rules turn into the shop agreements of trade unions and, as the struggle with management intensifies, what Montgomery calls 'workers' consciousness' manifests itself in sympathy strikes and an impulse toward industrial unionism."[20]

While both these approaches are limited to well-defined units, the community that can be experienced by workers or the actual situation within a particular craft or unskilled job, several approaches attempt to treat the class, its organizations and capital, as a whole. The "old labor history" with its emphasis on organization, trade unions, or workers' parties, is far from having outlived its usefulness. Practiced in the United States and in Europe, particularly in the socialist countries, its interpretive framework ranges from those who argue that the proletariat can come into its own only under the leadership of an enlightened avant-garde, to those who consider union leaders the only acceptable and "responsible" spokesmen for labor, to those who are willing to include temporary "wildcat" organizations. It would certainly be one-sided to argue that labor organizations have little to do with working-class activity, though AFL policies sometimes do have a tendency to suggest this. But given the geographic mobility of American labor, stable organizations were an important prerequisite for collective bargaining successes. Bread-and-butter unionism, often decried as narrow and stale, does have perceptible effects on workers' everyday lives, as the term graphically makes clear.

The history of the "other labor movement" is concerned with spontaneous self-activity outside the well-established unions. It emphasizes the role of the unskilled, the recent immigrants, and women workers whether at home or in the factory. An excellent example of this is Gisela Bock's as yet untranslated study of the strike cycle of 1909–15 and the role of the IWW.[21] This is a vast field, difficult to toil, open to labor historians: not union archives but fleeting correspondences, not proceedings of conventions but oral traditions of mass meetings during strikes, not long-lasting union organs but short-lived news bulletins put out by striking workers whether organized or not. Like cultural and workplace history, the organizational and the "other labor movement" approaches complement each other.

The "operaist" approach, developed by Italian and West German scholars, attempts to link class consciousness and degree and form of organization to the development of the productive forces and the movement of capital.[22] It argues that forms of organization and of class consciousness do not simply follow the technical development of production, e.g. the increasing mechanization and automatization of work, the splitting up of jobs into increasingly repetitive tasks of finishing details. On the contrary, the organization of production, i.e. originally Taylorism, is also a reaction of those in control of capital and machinery to the strength of the craft or industrial unions, of the workers on the shop floor. When workers could stop production by withdrawing their skills,[23] from capital's point of view it was necessary to make skills obsolete. There was no teleological progress, no unmotivated advance of technology and science; it was a power struggle between classes. Operaism sees labor-capital relations as a continuous struggle, not as periods of calm followed by revolutionary upheavals. In these struggles trade unions may act as retarding factors as well as accelerating ones. In the English language the Italian scholar Bruno Ramirez—*When Workers Fight: The Politics of Industrial Relations in the Progressive Era, 1898–1916*—was the first to take up this approach.[24] But in this perspective the worker as an individual gets lost, just as the cultural approach sometimes neglects the larger forces that act beyond the community.

From the foregoing, I think, we may construct a Weberian ideal type of labor history. In this model the individual worker, male or female, white or black, should be visible as a person in his/her productive and reproductive work:

(1) Workers as a class have to be recognizable in their class consciousness and class composition; conflicts within the class have to be analyzed and related to the capability of the class as a whole to pursue common or fragmented, international, national, or local interests; the effectiveness of class organizations has to be assessed.

(2) The development of the means of production and the movement of capital have to be understood as a function of the class struggle and as independent variables governed, for example, by economies of scale in mass production; contradictions between different forms and sizes of capital have to be related to the outlook of the owners (e.g. big versus small business).

(3) The relations of business, industry, and commerce, of the unions,

and of the state—theoretically the mediating agency—have to be assessed as to their influence on each other.

A study measuring up to this model will have to be an interdisciplinary effort. Many labor historians lack the economic training to analyze movements of capital, few economists have acquired the
methodological tools necessary to reconstruct the life of an individual
worker. Historians of technology may understand the impact of
changing technology on the work process and the actual amount of
work a machine operator has to do, but often they are not capable of
studying the concomitant changes in the operator's thinking: does he
feel that elements of his craft are lost, or is he proud of the power
and output of the new machinery? Nor are historians of technology
able to look into the minds of the machine builders: was it a secluded
engineer that propelled technical knowledge a step further, or was he
told that more machines were necessary to break the union? While we
are approaching overall perspectives as postulated in our model—of
glassworkers in Carmaux, France, or of shoemakers in Lynn, Massa-
chuesetts—the step from a local or craft perspective to a national or
international one still has to be taken. But collaborators in the Nordic
Emigration History Project have had to face similar problems: how
do international migratory movements relate to village structures and
attitudes? As an offshoot of their work the problem of relating micro-
and macrohistory will hopefully be solved within the next few years.[25]

Two further points have to be mentioned in regard to a future
history of the working class, or, in fact, to all histories of alternatives
to mainstream developments. Many labor historians are somewhat
defensive about the radicalism of their subjects, unjustly so. Why explain, to take one example, that the Haymarket anarchists of 1886
were neither fanatics nor given to violence and then cautiously admit
that some had experimented with explosives? The whole focus of the
story is wrong—the police, the Pinkertons, the judges, the press are
left out of the picture. Were there not fanatics among the police, who
had just shot striking workers; were there not private armies hired to
protect property by taking lives; were not judges strangling justice,
politicians fanatically defending the status quo and the security not
even of private property but of large capital only? Businessmen were
in search of order. Whose order? And does paying Chicago police to
invent further anarchist conspiracies contribute to order?[26] To focus
on the "labor martyrs" is a narrow class history. To explain that politicians and businessmen were the extremist faction incapable of seeing
alternatives and of striking out in new directions, while the striking
McCormick workers and the speakers at the Haymarket meeting may

be seen as moderate men concerned about the dignity of life and just compensation for work, gives a fuller picture. Since no struggle of the oppressed ever took as many lives and maimed as many bodies as the preservation of what some call "law and order," there is no need to be defensive about the direct action of the oppressed.[27]

While many historians of the mainstream and its stagnant waters worship businessmen and order to a degree that they see no alternatives, some historians of the working class sometimes do the same with a middle-class German philosopher named Karl Marx. But workers had a labor theory of value before Marx penned his first word. They talked about wage slavery and the effects of mechanization without having to read sophisticated books. That a surplus value went into the pockets of the bosses whether small or large was the daily experience of each and every worker. The problem for us historians is that Marx's writings are more easily available than workers' newspapers and that the reach of his theory overawes us. Just as American "Indians" did not quite see what was so new about Columbus's "discovery," so workers probably did not regard Marx as altogether original. Is not the old "we-them" dichotomy of "unsophisticated" workingmen as comprehensive as highly complex analyses of capital-labor relations? It might be useful to listen more to what workers had to say.

Of course, no pretense is made that the essays in this volume measure up to the above model for a future working-class history, which really is an interdisciplinary history of society with emphasis on its majority. They provide stepping stones toward this goal. A final word about the limitation of our topic to the years from 1877 to the 1920s. Little work has been done on the pre–Civil War period; it is being coordinated by the International Study Group of Early American History at the University of Milan, Italy.[28] A considerable amount of work is being done on the working class after the 1920s, particularly during the Depression. Some of it is already known in the United States, but other important monographs and articles have not yet been translated. The influence of American labor unions on Europe immediately after World War II and during the Cold War is the subject of numerous studies by European scholars.[29] And if scholarly cooperation works out as planned, a volume on the twentieth-century working class will follow.

The essays presented here were specially commissioned for this volume and have not been published elsewhere. They were subjected to the criticism of other European and American specialists during a symposium held at the University of Bremen, West Germany, in November 1978. The need for cooperation was so obvious that several international projects and means of exchanging information were discussed. Thus a survey of the state of scholarship in the European countries has been published in *Labor History*, as has a directory of European scholars in American working-class history in *International Labor and Working Class History*, a newsletter.[30] Many knowledgeable specialists from all European countries are cooperating in a project to preserve labor newspapers published in the United States and Canada for and by immigrants in languages other than English.[31] Credit is due to those scholars who attended the symposium as commentators and to those who commented from afar.[32]

NOTES

1. Dirk Hoerder, ed., *Plutocrats and Socialists: Reports by German Diplomats and Agents on the American Labor Movement 1878–1917* (Munich, 1981). For other countries, particularly Italy, Austria, and Russia, which sent agents to America to spy on their emigrants, see the respective archives of the departments of foreign affairs, of the interior, and the police headquarters.

2. See F. Boese, *Geschichte des Vereins für Sozialpolitik, 1872–1932* (Berlin, 1939), and G. Wittrock, *Die Kathedersozialisten bis zur Eisenacher Versammlung 1872* (Berlin, 1939). Cf. also Herman Kröner, *John R. Commons: Seine wirtschaftstheoretische Schule und ihre Bedeutung für die sozialrechtliche Schule in Amerika* (Jena, 1930).

3. The first settlement house was founded in London in 1884 (Toynbee Hall). Stanton Coit, who had received a Ph.D. from the University of Berlin, was the first to take up the idea in the United States, moving into New York's Lower East Side in 1886. Allen F. Davis, *Spearheads for Reform: The Social Settlements and the Progressive Movement, 1890–1914* (New York, 1967), pp. 3–17.

4. See, among others, Philip S. Foner, "The French Trade Union Delegation to the Philadelphia Centennial Exposition, 1876," *Science and Society* 40 (1976):257–87; August Sartorius Freiherr von Waltershausen, *Der moderne Sozialismus in den Vereinigten Staaten von Amerika* (Berlin, 1890), pp. 229–30.

5. (Berlin, 1921).

6. Frederick W. Taylor, *Shop Management* (New York, 1912) and "A Piece-Rate System: Being a Step toward a Partial Solution of the Labor Problem," American Society of Mechanical Engineers, *Transactions* 16 (1895):856–83; see also Frank B. Copley, *Frederick W. Taylor: Father of Scientific Management*, 2 vols. (New York, 1923).

7. The French America Studies Association recognized the new developments at its conference at Pont-à-Mousson in 1976, the Italian Committee for American History at a conference in Milan in 1978,

8. The Polish Research Institute on Contemporary Capitalism in Warsaw is preparing a fundamental comparative work on trade unions in capitalist countries.

9. The International Federation of Trade Unions, founded in 1901, was defunct during World War I. The World Federation of Trade Unions,

founded in 1945, split in 1949, the unions of the industrialized countries in Western Europe and the United States founding a separate International Confederation of Free Trade Unions.

10. See Leo Okinshevich, comp., *United States History and Historiography in Postwar Soviet Writings 1945–1970* (Santa Barbara, Calif., 1976).

`11. There still is a sizable remigration from the United States to the socialist countries. Poland has a community of several thousand pensioners who worked in the United States but spend their retirement "at home." See also Ivo Baučić, *The Effects of Emigration from Yugoslavia and the Problems of Returning Emigrant Workers* (The Hague, 1972).

12. Harald Runblom and Hans Norman, eds., *From Sweden to America: A History of the Migration*, a collective work of the Nordic Emigration History Project (Minneapolis and Uppsala, 1976); Bo Kronborg, Thomas Nilsson, and Andres A. Svalestuen, *Nordic Population Mobility: Comparative Studies of Selected Parishes in the Nordic Countries, 1850–1900*, a collective work of the Nordic Emigration History Project (special issue of *American Studies in Scandinavia*, vol. 9, nos. 1–2, 1977).

13. Jesse Lemisch, "The Papers of Great White Men," *Maryland Historian* 6 (1975):43–50; Oscar Handlin, *The Uprooted: The Epic Story of the Great Migrations That Made the American People* (Boston, 1952).

14. *Congressional Record*, vol. 118, no. 168, 17 Oct. 1972.

15. U.S. Congress, Senate, subcommittee report, 1937, by Robert M. LaFollette, Jr.; Gerd Korman, *Industrialization, Immigrants and Americanization: The View from Milwaukee* (Madison, Wis., 1967); *Progressive* (Oct. 1978).

16. John R. Commons *et al.*, *History of Labour in the United States*, 4 vols. (New York, 1918–35).

17. George Rudé, "The Changing Face of the Crowd," in M. Curti, ed., *The Historian's Workshop* (New York, 1970), pp. 187–204.

18. Herbert G. Gutman, "Work, Culture, and Society in Industrializing America, 1815–1919," *American Historical Review*, repr. in Gutman, *Work, Culture and Society in Industrializing America* (New York, 1973); Alan Dawley, *Class and Community: The Industrial Revolution in Lynn, Massachusetts* (Cambridge, Mass., 1976); Paul G. Faler, "Workingmen, Mechanics, and Social Change, Lynn, Massachusetts, 1800–1860" (Ph.D. dissertation, University of Wisconsin, 1971); Philip S. Foner, ed., *American Labor Songs of the Nineteenth Century* (Urbana, Ill., 1975) and *The Factory Girls: A Collection of Writings on Life and Struggles in the New England Factories of the 1840s* (Urbana, Ill., 1977); Alfred F. Young, "From Ritual to Rebellion" (forthcoming).

19. David Brody, *Steelworkers in America: The Nonunion Era* (Cambridge, Mass., 1968).

20. David Brody, "The Old Labor History and the New," *Labor History* 20(1979):111–26.

21. Gisela Bock, *Die andere Arbeiterbewegung in den USA von 1909–1922: Die Industrial Workers of the World* (Munich, 1976).

22. Mario Tronti and Toni Negri in Italy, Karl-Heinz Roth, Elizabeth Behrens, and Eckhard Brockhaus in West Germany. See Brody, *Steelworkers*.

23. Joan Scott, *The Glassworkers of Carmaux: French Craftsmen and Political Action in a Nineteenth-Century City* (Cambridge, Mass., 1974).

24. (Westport, Conn., 1978).

25. Sivert Langholm, "On the Scope of Micro-history," *Swedish Journal of History* 1 (1976):1–22; Gudmund Hernes, "Structural Changes in Social Processes," *American Journal of Sociology*, 82 (1976).

26. Henry David, *History of the Haymarket Affair* (New York, 1958), pp. 482–84, speaks of an attempt by the so-called Citizens' Association, a combination of some businessmen, "to make Chicago safe for capitalism."

27. On violence and repression, see Dirk Hoerder, comp., *Protest, Direct Action, Repression: Dissent in American Society from Colonial Times to the Present: A Bibliography* (Munich, 1977), Introduction, pp. 1–15.

28. C/o Prof. Loretta Valtz-Mannucci, Cattedra di Storia Americana, Università degli Studi di Milano, via Conservatorio 7, 20122 Milano, Italy.

29. Dirk Hoerder, "American Labor & Immigration History: Reports on the State of the Historiography since 1945 in the European Countries," pts. I and II, *Labor History* 21 (1980):261–76, 392–419.

30. Dirk Hoerder, comp., "A Preliminary List of European Scholars in American Labor and Working-Class History," *International Labor and Working Class History* 17 (1980):29–37.

31. "Bibliography and Archival Preservation of Non-English-Language Labor and Radical Newspapers and Periodicals in North America, 1845 to 1976," *International Labor and Working Class History* 16 (1979):46–50. For further information contact Dirk Hoerder, Universität Bremen, Postfach 33 04 40, 2800 Bremen, West Germany.

32. We are grateful to the Stiftung Volkswagenwerk for a grant to conduct the symposium and to Andrew Winter and Bonnie Depp for copyediting the manuscript.

PART I

Workers, Scholars, Militancy

The 1871 Paris Commune in Europe and the 1877 railroad strike in America shocked businessmen, politicians, and scholars into awareness of the so-called labor problem. The formation of united socialist parties combining Lassalleans and Marxists in Germany (1875) and in the United States (1876), the British Trade Union Congress (1868), the Knights of Labor (1869), the German unions' General Commission (1892), and the French Confédération Générale du Travail all proved that the working class became articulate in such a way that the ruling middle classes were forced to listen. Scholarly reaction was lively, as international as the movement, and frequently geared to an improvement of (the situation of) the working classes. The Christian socialists in the United States, the Verein für Socialpolitik in Germany, and the Fabian Society in Great Britain emerged at this time. In 1891 the Vatican took note of the labor movement in its encyclical "Rerum novarum," and the international Association for Labor Legislation was established.

In the United States John H. Noyes published a *History of American Socialisms*, meaning utopian communities (1870); Richard T. Ely, Christian socialist and scholar, wrote on the *Labor Movement* (1886); and George E. McNeill, an active trade unionist, edited a history of trade unions (1887). By 1891 two Germans, Heinrich Semler and A. Sartorius von Waltershausen, and one Italian, S. Cognetti de Martiis, had published books on socialism in the United States. Attempting an early synthesis, William D. P. Bliss edited his *Encyclopedia of Social Reform* in 1898 and a guide to socialist developments all over the world, the *Handbook of Socialism*, in 1907.

From social reform a quest for knowledge about underlying societal problems developed that was the inception of our present-day sociology. Reform-minded economists turned to the labor question and founded the American Economic Association. Academic research and workers' education still intersected closely. The University of Wisconsin had a School for Workers, the London Mechanics Institute became

Birkbeck College of London University, John Ruskin from Oxford
taught at the Workingmen's College founded in London in 1852, a
Workers' Educational Summer School was held at Balliol College,
Oxford, and in 1895 Fabian socialists supported the foundation of
the London School of Economics and Political Science, whose aim was
to teach about reform and enlightened social policies.

Bruno Cartosio traces the connections between the origins of labor
historiography and working-class activity. Were scholars in the last
quarter of the nineteenth century less objective because they actively
supported reform causes? If they came to recognize the suffering of
the working class, how close were they to its actual thinking, feeling,
working, and eating? Induced by the Depression, another scholar-
activist, W. E. B. Du Bois, began to reflect on the black experience,
the transition from chattel to wage slavery. Ferruccio Gambino ana-
lyzes the interaction of Du Bois's experience in his study of the Reconstruction period and the trajectory black workers traveled from
emancipation and the long depression after 1873 to the Great
Depression beginning in 1929. What was the relationship between
free (white) labor and (black) slavery? What did it mean for black
workers to try to join a class large sections of which were hostile to
them? To what degree did black workers shape their own lives, to
what degree did capital force conditions on them? The refusal of
workers to be shaped is the theme of Marianne Debouzy's study of
militant self-organization of the railroad workers during the 1877
strikes. Why was this autonomy possible on the railroads? Did the
strike suggest a revolutionary outlook among workers, or were demands limited to the solution of immediate grievances, bread-and-
butter issues? If it was the latter, were not American workers better
off than their European brethren? Was not the whole stream of immigration eloquent testimonial to the validity of this hypothesis? Peter
R. Shergold has pursued these questions in a detailed comparison of
Birmingham and Pittsburgh working-class living standards.

The almost nationwide railroad strike of 1877 proved that workers
could handle the whole system without taking orders, just as the dock-
workers of the Boston Tea Party more than a century earlier needed
no avant-garde or bosses to explain to them how to open a hatch or
handle a winch. While John Commons pondered over questions of
reform from above, drawing on his experience in Germany and the
United States and his knowledge about other countries, workers pondered over the question of how to improve their situation—should
they emigrate or stay where they were, shuttle back and forth or fight,
or both? The complex calculations Shergold offers had to be made by
them, too; any miscalculation could prove disastrous.

1

Strikes and Economics: Working-Class Insurgency and the Birth of Labor Historiography in the 1880s

BRUNO CARTOSIO

A few weeks after the end of the great railroad strike in 1877, the *New York Labor Standard,* organ of the Socialistic Labor party, indicated what it felt was the main lesson to be derived from the upsurge: "The strike has taught the Government and the people that there is a labor question, a wage labor problem seeking solution." The article further asserted that "the strikes of the cotton operatives, locomotive engineers, trainmen and miners have forced a wider and deeper discussion of our question than all the political conventions of the past ten years."[1]

A similar opinion, even if in different terms and in a different spirit, was expressed by the *New York Times.* It admitted that "the workmen have here and there compelled compliance with their demands, and in other instances, they have attracted popular attention to their grievances, real or alleged, to an extent that will render future indifference impossible," and it later concluded that "the old world no longer faces alone the labor problem. It is here and it presses for a solution."[2]

The solutions proposed by the "capitalistic press"—defined as "the worst enemy we have" by the *Iron Molders' Journal* a week before the strike[3]—during and after the strikes had been remarkably few. They ranged from the sharp-shooters recommended by the *Nation,* to the "diet of lead for hungry strikers" advocated by the *New York Sun,* to the suggestion advanced by the *Chicago Journal* that "a strong force of regular troops be stationed in every city."[4] The latter suggestion, even if not accepted unanimously, was widely favored by the national press and welcomed by influential political circles, along with demands for a larger standing army.[5] It actually led very soon to the construction of numerous armories in the larger industrial cities and to the reorganization of the National Guard, to make it an effective means whereby the states' "laws may be enforced, social order maintained and [protection afforded] against the sudden violence of popular faction."[6]

The many strikes among industrial workers during the decade, the demonstrations of the unemployed in the big cities, and what became known during the depression as the "tramp question" had clearly aroused strong and widespread fears that "insane imitations of the miserable class warfare and jealousy of Europe"[7] might no longer be impossible or even unlikely.

We still lack comprehensive data on the number of strikes between the Civil War and 1881, but by collecting the pieces of information available for the 1870s it is possible to conclude that episodes of bitter and often long struggle were extremely frequent among railroad, mine, textile, and iron workers, and cigarmakers, and somewhat less frequent among other industrial workers such as printers, coopers, boatmen, etc. Apart from the railroads, where the numerous strikes of the early seventies were obscured only by the explosion of 1877, there are the well-known strikes at Fall River cotton manufacturers in 1874–75, and the 1873, 1874, and 1875 strikes among anthracite and bituminous coal miners. Among iron workers, 87 "legalized strikes" were recorded by John Jarrett in George E. McNeill's *The Labor Movement* for the period 1867–75, and 93 for the period 1877–85. Cigarmakers were also very restless in those years. Between 1871 and 1876 they organized 87 strikes, and in 1877 "over 7,000 men and women" were affected by a 107-day strike against "a powerful combination of 32 manufacturers." Demonstrations and meetings of the unemployed had been held in all the major cities since October 1873. It was in January 1874 that the savage police assault on the demonstrators took place at Tompkins Square in New York City.[8]

Violence was used against strikers, the unemployed, and vagrants during the depression years. Private and urban police forces and state and federal troops were called upon in various places to restore law and order.[9] Their intervention—and in a different sense that of scabs— was often unwelcome in smaller communities, where class solidarity and popular opposition to the domineering logic of manufacturing or mining or railroad interests were stronger. "Imported" workers could either be forcefully prevented from scabbing or persuaded to refrain from weakening the positions of fellow workers on strike, especially in mining. In certain cases during the 1877 strikes, militia forces fraternized with demonstrators in such communities. But in larger cities, as Herbert Gutman further points out, "unions and all forms of labor protest, particularly strikes, were condemned," and repression of the disruptors of "natural and moral laws" was widely urged.[10]

The episodes of open warfare of 1877 reinforced the already present view, which conceived of workers as social disruptors or of the "proletariat" as the "dangerous class," as the *Nation* wrote on 2 August 1877. Particularly frightening was the fact that, for the first time, a single strike action had developed into a wave on a national scale, becoming "a sort of epidemic of strikes running through the laboring classes of the country,"[11] and bringing into the open signs of militant solidarity among workers of different trades in different places, between employed and unemployed, and even between "good citizens" and "tramps."

But those views also revealed all the uncertainties of judgment to which fear and repression were tied. As Marianne Debouzy summarizes it: "As a matter of fact, in reading the press one does not know what they fear more: the unorganized working class, despisingly considered as mob, or the organized workers controlled by communists. They are equally concerned about the absence of leaders and the presence of agitators. They blame the mob both for its boldness and for its cowardice. And the position of the dominant class swings between two contradictory extremes: fear of the mob, fear that the insurrection might arouse the scum of the underworld, and fear of organization, of the Commune."[12]

The upsurge was a reaction against the harshness of the long depression, the disorderly transformation of the social and economic structure, and finally against the railroads' manpower and wages policies. Once the disorders were settled by the use of arms, it did not take long for the state legislature of Pennsylvania and the federal government to set up committees to investigate the recent labor uprisings and the relationship between the labor problem and the economic depression.[13]

The select committee set up by the House of Representatives in 1877 heard numerous witnesses of all tendencies—from William Graham Sumner, professor at Yale and a staunch advocate of laissez faire, to Adolf Douai, a socialist kindergarten teacher and vulgarizer of Marx; from George E. McNeill, the labor reformer and first deputy of the Massachusetts Bureau of Statistics of Labor, to Carroll D. Wright, successor of McNeill in that office and future National Commissioner of Labor, to Adolph Strasser, president of the Cigar Makers' International Union. It is not without importance that the committee's chairman, Abram S. Hewitt, himself a sort of enlightened iron manufacturer, could observe in 1878 that "a new power has entered into the industrial world, which must be recognized. . . . It must be heeded. . . . The great result achieved is that capital is ready to discuss. It is not to be disguised that till labor presented itself in such an attitude as to compel a hearing capital was unwilling to listen; but now it does listen."[14]

Hewitt's opinion was most probably not shared by the majority of American businessmen and manufacturers, who were still in favor of strong-arm tactics. Instead, his thought was in tune with those dawning reformist attitudes that were appearing within small circles of enlightened entrepreneurs and politicians and, on a different level, among some young intellectuals not directly involved with party politics or the labor movement. Hewitt's favorable attitude toward unionism and arbitration in labor-capital disputes is not far removed from that expressed by Wright or even McNeill or, more to the point for us, from that developed by Richard T. Ely and others a few years later.

On the whole, however, after 1877 capital, if not ready to listen to labor, had to be ready at least to take into new consideration its presence on the industrial scene. The strikes of 1877 appeared as the high point of a rising tide, but its first motions could be traced back before the depression. During the depressed years the tide had simply advanced more swiftly and boldly. Moreover, as subsequent inquiries in the mid-1880s would reveal, workers' unrest and labor organizations were to increase even after the return of economic prosperity in 1878, thus showing their relative independence of business cycles.

The Blair committee, set up in 1882 and so named after its chairman, embodied the alarm with which Congress viewed the persisting industrial conflicts and, particularly after 1883, the increase in the degree of workers' organization, represented by the growth of the membership of the Knights of Labor and of trade unions on a national scale. The committee, as Mark Perlman summarizes, heard "witnesses discuss the relations between capital and labor, the state of wages and hours, the conditions of the laboring classes in the United States as compared with those abroad, the causes of strikes, and the agencies behind the strikes." Of the more than 250 witnesses who appeared before the Blair committee, many were Knights of Labor or trade union officials. From their testimonies emerged all the typical demands of organized labor: federal collection of labor statistics, recognition of trade unions, the eight-hour day, labor legislation, monetization of wages as opposed to the truck system and company stores.[15]

In 1886, when Senator Blair announced the near completion of the fifth volume of testimony (which, in fact, was never to appear), the recently established National Bureau of Labor published its report on industrial depressions, which would make a qualified contribution to the understanding of the working mechanisms of the rapidly evolving situation in the American industrial and business world.[16]

It took one more year before the first systematic statistical research on strikes and lockouts was printed. But when it came out, the *Third Annual Report of the Commissioner of Labor* gave impressive quantitative evidence of the labor problem.[17] During the six years covered by the report (1881–86), 3,902 strikes occurred, affecting 22,304 establishments and involving 1,323,203 workers. The dimensions of the problem loom much larger when compared with the estimate of a total number of 1,440 known strikes and lockouts prior to 1881 in the United States as recorded in the same report. Its political dimensions, already clear after 1877, were made clearer in the first six years of the 1880s by more strikes in all the major industrial sectors—railroads, textiles, mining, iron, and steel—and by the agitation of the eight-hour movement of 1884–86.[18]

The year of Haymarket, with its 1,572 strikes and lockouts and 610,000 workers involved, and again with all its violence, marked a new high in the escalation of class warfare. After 1877 the wave had receded slightly, but in 1890 an English commentator could still write that "the future of the labor question in the United States is by no means determined."[19]

None of the various committees proved able to produce a theoretical or practical guideline for the effective handling of the situation. They ended up collecting volumes of the most widely divergent testimony. From those documents emerges to our eye a relatively obvious absence of theoretical unanimity and a degree of dilettantism in political and economic analysis, which the dramatic events on the industrial scene made all the more evident. Various shades of laissez fairism, greenbackism, socialism, labor reformism—even the first signs of "pure and simple" unionism—were recorded in an ineffective juxtaposition that left the federal and state governments with no clear indication of what was to be done about the labor problem.[20]

The first institutional signs of what Joseph Dorfman defines as "the communities' growing concern with improving the conditions of labor" were the bureaus of statistics established in a number of states to inquire into labor conditions.[21] These bureaus were created and essentially modeled after the Bureau of Statistics of Labor established by Massachusetts when "the eight hour men . . . succeeded in securing the passage of a resolve establishing [it] in 1869, the first of the kind ever established."[22] The influence of political agitation for the reduction of working hours and for labor legislation, and the contribution of well-known reformers like Wendell Phillips, George McNeill, and Henry K. Oliver, among others, were decisive in pushing the Massachusetts legislature to enact important labor laws in 1866 and 1867, and finally to give birth to the bureau.[23]

McNeill and Oliver were appointed respectively deputy and chief of the office, but after four years, under the attack of conservative forces within the legislature, business circles, and the press because of their connecting "investigation concerning the poverty of the working-classes" and militant reformism, they were forced out of the bureau.[24] They were replaced by Carroll D. Wright, a progressive economist who was not an enemy of labor and was a much more qualified statistician. Thus in 1873 the effort to bend a state agency to make it work actively for the promotion of labor reform and legislation came to an end. Having become an embarrassing embodiment of the political voice of labor in the most industrialized state of the nation, the bureau had to strip itself of its political connotations to survive. In broader terms, the whole stategy of involvement of the state and its agencies in operations on behalf of labor met with failure. What remained, under the direction of Wright, was the willingness to give a positive answer to the demands of the unions to have a bureau of labor statistics established and working. There is no doubt that with him the Massachusetts bureau produced its best achievements in terms of collecting, assorting, systematizing, and presenting "in annual reports to the legislature, statistical details relating to all departments of labor."[25]

By 1886, fifteen bureaus were in existence at state level. Significantly, thirteen of them were created after the eventful year of 1877. In 1884, moreover, a National Bureau of Labor was established in Washington, within the Department of the Interior, whose duty was to "collect information upon the subject of labor, its relation to capital, the hours of labor, and the earnings of laboring men and women and the means of promoting their material, social, intellectual, and moral prosperity."[26] Carroll D. Wright, who was to remain in charge of the Massachusetts bureau until 1888, was called upon to organize and direct it from the very beginning.

Except for the national and the Massachusetts ones, the various bureaus remained a long way from satisfying those expectations that their establishment undoubtedly had helped to create not only among unionists and reformers, who had a political stake in them, but also among economists of the new generation, who had learned to attribute much value to the use of statistics in economic research. Richmond Mayo-Smith, after reviewing the operations of the bureaus in 1886,[27] concluded his survey by stating that "the results are at first glance disappointing. The greater number of investigations are inadequate." Among the very few that at least tried to organize their research systematically, only the Massachusetts bureau seemed to achieve relatively "complete and satisfactory" results.

The main reasons for the general inadequacy were ascribed by Mayo-Smith to the difficulty "in this country . . . to find experts in any work of this sort," but also, more relevantly, to "the paucity of financial means placed at the disposal of these bureaus." The dramatic shortage of funds experienced by the majority of the bureaus revealed the slight importance assigned to them by state governments and, on another level, how slow the progress of statistics was within the fields of economic and social research. Mayo-Smith, himself an accomplished statistician and a progressive economist, while refraining from an overall discussion of state policies, did nonetheless express reservations about them. "When we consider the rapidity with which these bureaus have been established of late years," he wrote, "and at the same time the meagerness with which they have been endowed, the suspicion arises that legislators have not been altogether sincere in establishing them, or desirous that they could accomplish anything." The suspicion was legitimate that their establishment was intended only to give satisfaction to "demagogic clamors on the part of labor organizations or politicians."

There is a significant coincidence between Mayo-Smith's observations and Richard T. Ely's bitter remarks about how labor laws were enforced. Even while he was stressing the importance of an increased role of government, Ely resented the fact that "legislative bodies 'too often' passed labor laws without any intention of enforcing them. 'One might almost at times suspect [wrote Ely] a secret conspiracy with the administrative authorities that labor laws should remain a dead letter. Yet we talk of the moral depravity of the working classes!' "[28]

The story of the bureaus of labor statistics and to a lesser extent that of labor legislation in the 1880s contains the contradictory evidence of the growing weight of the working class and of organized labor within the political life of the community and, at the same time, of the conspicuous obstacles that stood in the way of the full recognition of workers as a social force. But it also reveals the existence of a new, scientifically and professionally oriented attitude that linked such intellectuals as Mayo-Smith, Wright, and Ely in tackling the new demands that the labor problem was raising. The fact that those who responded favorably to labor's requests belonged to an emerging intellectual group characterized by a pragmatic, reformist approach to the social and economic problems of their time then acquires particular relevance.

"Social and economic transformations in the seventies and eighties," summarizes a modern commentator, "resulted in a need for a new interpretation of social movement."[29] A group of young intellectuals, almost all trained at German universities, proved particularly sensitive to that need.[30] From within this group of "new economists" came the most original and innovative responses to the labor problem— "the problem of the day."

For them the labor problem was historically determined; it was the outcome of a deep moral, social, and institutional crisis. That basic assumption justified in the first instance their iconoclastic rejection of the politics of laissez faire, responsible for the existence of the problem, and of the theoretical apparatus of the classical school of economics, which proved useless in analyzing its dynamics. From that, the corollary followed that those institutions which had proved unable to prevent the shock of labor unrest and to keep the pace of industrial evolution under control were to be held guilty of grave defaults. New policies were needed. Institutions did not need to be revolutionized, as the socialists contended: rather, it was to prevent the spread of socialism that the emerging forces of organized labor ought to be recognized as legitimate institutional components of society.[31] It was a matter of social justice as well as of wise political economy and legislation. When Richmond Mayo-Smith wrote that "the burning question in political economy, at the present time, is that of the distribution of wealth, especially in respect to the so-called laboring classes," he was synthesizing in a sentence the reformist argument of the new economists vis-à-vis the labor problem.[32]

In 1884, a few years after his return from a four-year stay at the universities of Halle, Heidelberg, and Berlin, Richard T. Ely, in one of those bursts of missionary fervor that were not infrequent in him at that time, wrote that "this younger political economy no longer permits the science to be used as a tool in the hand of the greedy and the avaricious for keeping down and oppressing the laboring classes. It does not acknowledge *laissez-faire* as an excuse for doing nothing while people starve, nor allow the all-sufficiency of competition as a plea for grinding the poor."[33] But he had theoretical objections as well as ethical and political ones. Given certain premises, he wrote, the deductive political economy of the Manchester school proceeded "to evolve an economic system without any further recourse to the external world." While Adam Smith had made use of history and statistics, "this was not done by Ricardo, his most distinguished disciple, and the coripheus of English classical political economy." Another most objectionable tenet of the classical school was the certainty that the free play of natural forces would "arrange things so that the best good of all is attained by the unrestrained action of self-interest," from which it was deduced that "government should abstain from all interference in industrial life."[34]

The very existence of the labor problem was a contradiction to those assumptions and invited to question the "general conception of the naturalness of things as they existed in modern industrial society." According to the teachings of the German historical school,

> political economy is regarded as only one branch of social science, dealing with social phenomena from one special standpoint, the economic. It is not regarded as something fixed and unalterable, but as a growth and development, changing with society. . . . All *a priori* doctrines or assumptions are cast aside by this school, or rather their final acceptance is postponed until external observations have proved them correct. The first thing is to gather facts. . . . We must arrange and classify the facts as gathered, at least provisionally, to assist us in our observation. We must observe in order to theorize, and theorize in order to observe.[35]

A particularly "excellent service rendered to science" by the new school is a "more correct interpretation of economic history" that is based on the primacy of man, not wealth, and on the "organic nature of economic life of peoples." From the abandonment of individualism, from the accent on man and his welfare, and from the study of the historical laws of the economic development of the nation came the urge to go back to the sources of the labor problem. Knies's definition of political economy, which Ely quoted, amply justified its pertinence to the current social problems: "Political Economy examines the conditions, the processes, and the results of the economic life of men in communities."[36]

Even if it was not true that "the laissez faire policy has been knocked out of men's heads for the next generation," as the *New York Graphic* emphatically wrote,[37] it was certainly true that it was under severe attack and that German historicists had provided many of the weapons to sustain that attack.

Even such a moderate reformer as Carroll D. Wright, who had not been to Germany and who refrained from a complete severance of his connections with the English school, took a stance against it because of its responsibilities in relation to the labor problem:

> [Adam Smith's] followers, in their ambition have strayed far from the doctrines of their great master; and, with their departure from him, political economy has lost the sympathy and even the attention of the wage-workers of English and American communities, the very support it largely needs and should have. . . . It is because of this hard unsympathetic nature of the so-called science of political economy that the labor question has come to be considered as distinct from it; and, because of the departure from sound ethical features of the science by most of the leading writers, there has sprung up within a few years a new school, which bids fair to in-

clude on its roll of pupils the men in all civilized lands who seek by legitimate means and without revolution, the amelioration of unfavorable industrial and social relations wherever found as the surest road to comparatively permanent material prosperity.[38]

In Wright's or Ely's approach the moral imperative was dominant. For them the solution to the labor problem was first of all a moral duty for which the whole of society was responsible. The "moral approach" to the labor problem was widespread in the departments of ethics of various universities and theological seminaries,[39] but in such cases as those of Wright or Ely Christianity and ethics were functional to the demand that economic science recapture that sense of responsibility which had been lost in the growth of a competitive society.

Others of Ely's group, such as J. B. Clark or Henry C. Adams, looked even more closely into the dynamics of industrial evolution. In his highly discussed and influential *Relation of the State to Industrial Action*, Adams saw the labor problem essentially as the outcome of the inevitable ethical degradation produced by competition. He then called on the state not to "stand as an unconcerned spectator whose only duty is to put down a riot when a strike occurs" but, rather, to intervene actively upon the industrial scene as a concerned regulator of competition.[40]

Essentially through labor and factory legislation, Adams wrote, "the state can properly determine the conditions under which competition shall take place, and in this manner permit society to realize the best rather than the worst of the possible lines of action open to it. . . . In performing such a duty the state performs a moral function, for it regulates competition to the demands of the social conscience." But if monopoly was the consequence of undisciplined competition, the state was then called upon to realize for the public good the "peculiar privileges and unusual powers" that monopolies "perverted from their high purpose to serve private ends." "Society," continued Adams, "should be guaranteed against the oppression of exclusive privileges administered for personal profit, while at the same time it should be secured such advantages as flow from concentrated organization." According to his classification of industries, those which conformed to the law of "increasing returns"—that is, those where increased capital and labor brought progressively increased products—were the fittest for public control: railroads were the clear example he gave to illustrate what he meant. Public control of monopolies was to be founded on an extension of the administrative functions of the state and on a better paid civil service, so to avoid inefficiency or, worse, corruption.[41]

Relevant in Adam's theoretical scheme was the assertion that "the

labor problem must be worked out on the basis of freedom of contract," that is, as he pointed out in his address on "The Labor Problem" at Cornell, on the basis of collective bargaining. The full relevance
of the implicit recognition of the legitimacy of workers' organizations,
which went together with the advocacy of factory legislation, becomes
clearer if related to Adam's attitude toward monopolies: "These, it is
claimed, should be controlled by state authority."[42]

Adams was careful to make explicit that what he advocated was
simply an adjustment of the state to the new conditions, and not
socialism, but in the heated debate that his views aroused he was not
spared charges of "coquetting with anarchy" or of disguising socialist
positions under "a moderation which makes them all the more insid-
ious."[43] Bending the pole the other way, E. R. A. Seligman, in a
friendly review of Adam's book, wrote that "in this suggestive monograph the main point that strikes the reader is it essential conservatism. It is the best proof of the fact that an abandonment of *laissez
faire* does not connote socialism or anything materially approaching
socialism."[44]

Seligman himself, who was in almost complete agreement with Adams
and Ely on the increased role of the state and on the rejection of
individualism, but who sought a judicious combination of the methods of the classical and the historical schools, was an advocate of the
rights of labor and at the same time a staunch defender of capitalism.
Others of the group shared with him the opinion that the improvement of the conditions of labor was neither socialism nor even a
tendency toward socialism, but an essential move toward social peace
under capitalism, that factory and labor legislation was necessary to
prevent labor's violent action, that unions should be recognized because through collective bargaining it became possible to regulate and
control the wage question, which was the fundamental aspect of the
labor problem.

The emphasis upon the state's pivotal role in a modern economic
system came to the new economists from their appreciation not only
of the theoretical model they assumed but also of what seemed to be
the way theory found practical implementation within German society. Through the Verein für Sozialpolitik, founded in 1872, German
economists of the historical school scientifically investigated and discussed socioeconomic problems and played a significant role in shaping the economic life of their country. The opinion of Professor
Johannes Conrad, of Halle, as reported by E. J. James, was that the
experience of the Verein could be exported: "The old order was
passing upon the course of practical politics, it would be necessary to
take a new attitude toward the whole subject of social legislation, and

if the United States were to have any particular influence in the great
social legislation, and the great readjustment of society on its legal
side which seemed to be coming, an association of this sort would
have very real value."[45] According to such an opinion, shared by S.
N. Patten and Richard T. Ely as well as by E. J. James, an association
of economists, rallying point of ideas and individuals, and the state,
locus of political and legislative initiative, appeared as mediating
agencies between the intellectuals and society and constituted the ideal
ground for the new professional economists to experiment upon.

Moving from these premises, first James and Patten and then Ely
devoted their efforts to the organization of what was to become in
1885 the American Economic Association. Even if historians tend to
define it as a rather radical institution—as is the case with Mark Perlman—its radicalism is not to be overemphasized. In fact, the association as a whole demonstrated from the start an openness to
compromise with more "moderate" positions, "toning down"—as Ely
later wrote—the content of the original declaration of principles submitted to the assembled founders by Ely himself.[46]

Highly indicative of this disposition was the decision to elect Francis
A. Walker as its first president. He was not much older than the
majority of the new economists, but with his book *The Wages Question*,
published in 1876, he had already gained an "international reputation and was highly respected in almost all circles. He had been among
the first to speak well of the historical school, and he had stated in his
textbook [*Political Economy* 1883] that the classical school and the historical school were complementary."[47]

Ely, as the active secretary of the association during the first seven
years of its life, played a significant role, but it was the authoritative
figure of Walker which became the banner the whole association followed. Friction with economists outside of it did not cease at once,
but soon after its foundation the association itself helped to reduce
this by bending toward more moderate positions. In December 1887
the declaration of principles was "unanimously abolished because all
felt it had done its work."[48] And only a very few years later, when
most of the leading academic members of the "old school" were members of the American Economic Association—and most of the members of the association who had been ardent advocates of the "new
school" had gained academic positions—Ely could write to Seligman,
himself one of the founders, that "old issues which divided the economists a few years ago in this country are no longer so important as
they were and now is the time for a love feast!"[49]

This is not the place to discuss the progressive tendency of the
association as a whole and of some of its individual members—partic-

ularly Ely—toward less "radical" positions.[50] In any case, the progression of the association was more toward a pluralism of opinions, to which the internal evolution of economics as a scientific and academic discipline in itself contributed, than simply toward a new identification with more conservative policies. In the opinion of Joseph Dorfman, "The creation of chairs of economic history, sociology, and social ethics tended to remove from economics the issues that had made the Historical school a vital force, especially the concern with the moral problems presented by industrial changes."[51] However, the emergence of the new economists from the position of outsiders they held as a "tendency" in the late seventies and early eighties into often leading positions in the academic world during the nineties contributed to a less sectarian attitude on their part and consequently on the part of the association.[52]

In the United States labor historiography came into existence as a by-product of the wider concern for political and social problems that had already coalesced in the foundation of the American Economic Association. Scholarly research into the history of the labor movement, as conceived by its first practitioner, Richard T. Ely,[53] was to supply evidence for the demonstration of a thesis of an ideological nature according to which not only ethics but history as well would show the failure of competitive, individualistic political economy. That thesis, assuming the perfectibility of society through cooperation, had its groundings both in the contemporary society produced by the new economists and in Ely's relation of material extraneity but of intellectual identification with a sector of organized labor, the Knights of Labor. Thus written history of labor was neither simply a reflection of labor's strategies at a higher level nor a purely academic inquiry upon a particular aspect of reality. This character derived from the ancillary role that it had vis-à-vis that "reform of economics no less than of economic society," to put it in the words of Paul J. McNulty, that was the primary objective of the revolt against laissez faire.[54]

Between the two opposite extremes of socialism and competition, the middle road of reform was represented by cooperation. In that direction, according to Ely, pointed both the projection into the future of the rational and ethical certainties he had achieved through his analysis of contemporary conditions and what he saw as the historical evolution of the forces of labor. The strategies of the new political economy and of organized labor—undoubtedly represented in the mid-1880s by the Knights of Labor—seemed to coincide.[55]

In his essay on the labor movement Ely sketched out his point of view: "The laboring classes, through their unions, are learning discipline, self-restraint, and the methods of united action. . . . Thus the

labor movement is preparing the way for that goal which has for
many years been the ideal of the best thinkers on labor problems,—
the union of capital and labor in the same hands, in grand, wide-
reaching, co-operative enterprises, which shall embrace the masses."
Even if cooperatives had often met with "disastrous" failures in the
past, the novel strength of organized labor gave a new viability to the
cooperative perspective.[56] Thus cooperation was not only a distant
goal: "It begins within the framework of present industrial society,
but proposes to transform it gradually and peacefully, but completely,
by abolishing a distinct capitalist class of employers, the leading class
at present in that society, comprising those who are not inappro-
priately called captains of industries. Co-operation does not desire
fundamental change of law, for it hopes by means of voluntary association to unite labor and capital in the same hands—the hands of the
actual workers."[57]

The two crucial points in this perspective were those of peaceful
evolution and of voluntary association. Ely derived them from the
principles and teleology of the Knights of Labor; accordingly, he
strongly condemned violence, inviting workers to "imitate no violence," and emphasized the value of workers' unions as giving strength
and impulse to "the mighty stream" of organization.[58]

The theoretical model of organization he adopted reflected that
synthesis in the program of the Knights of Labor. This adhesion
supplied Ely with the criteria he needed to overcome the limited
scope of his historical research and to justify its ethical-political standpoint. "I have concerned myself," wrote Ely, "chiefly with the main
current of a main stream, and have not been able to find room for a
treatment of many separate lesser currents of social life, consequently
when I express approval of the labor movement, I do not approve
everything connected with it."[59] In fact, the parameters he adopted
were such as to leave broad margins for arbitrary judgment as to what
did or did not belong to the main stream. *A posteriori* rationalization
was not extraneous to his treatment of workers' struggles in recent
years. What he wrote about violence shows this clearly: "It is true that
workingmen have been guilty of violence, but it seems to be an established fact that the most of those who transgress the laws are outside
of the organizations."[60]

Thus the strikes of 1877, to give an example, did not find a place
in Ely's history, seemingly because they were spontaneous and violent—that is, outside and against the main stream. That approach,
more than deficiencies deriving from the limited historical documentation, accounts for the flaws of Ely's book. The relationship between
spontaneity and organization, between "the mob" and "the Com-

mune," which was at the heart of the upsurge of 1877, is not even posed as a problem. Consequently Ely does not analyze the divergent attitudes and behavior of the leadership and of the rank-and-file members of the Knights of Labor in connection with the eight-hour movement of 1884–86, particularly with its final stages.

Workers are never seen within those social and cultural contexts from which they derived sanction for their activities, violent or not, but reference is always made to abstract organizational platforms or ethical models of behavior that are, in fact, extraneous to their day-to-day experience. Ely's "main stream" approach ignored working-class self-activity as well as working-class culture. His hortatory approach to labor's history did not grant historical status and ethical dignity to what was not already formalized in organizational terms.[61]

That was Ely's way of stressing the need for workers to organize. Unorganized workers would be the counterpart of unorganized capital, but the denial of laissez faire implied that the confrontation between those two social groups takes place on a different level from that of individualism. And since capital had already organized its ranks, labor ought to do the same. Cooperation could succeed only if practiced by significant social groups, not by individuals. "Capital is one of the factors of production," wrote Ely, "labor is another, and it also must be massed together to stand on an equal footing, and this can be effected only by organization."[62]

Not alone in stressing the need to organize, Ely was also not the only labor historian. From within the ranks of the Knights of Labor came the book edited by McNeill and published in 1887, at about the same time as Ely's. The two books were different in their format and in their overall value but shared some common characteristics.[63] First, they shared an "admiration for the Knights of Labor," to use Ely's words, from which came the emphasis on cooperation. Then, in both of them the growth of the labor movement was interpreted as a succession of ever-widening organizational stages leading to the Knights of Labor, seen as the all-inclusive culmination of the process. However, McNeill's book devoted more space and detailed attention than Ely's to the history and to the declaration of principles of the Knights of Labor.

The Labor Movement: The Problem of To-Day was wider in scope and much more detailed than Ely's book in the sectorial analysis of the American labor scene. Moreover, while Ely seemed to make "his primary appeal directly to the upper classes rather than to the worker . . . [asking] the respectable middle class, the morally conscious industrialists, and the Christian ministers to recognize their true ethical obligations in the new industrial world,"[64] McNeill and his fellow contributors addressed themselves primarily to the workers. In McNeill's book the sense of labor as an independent force, capable of being politically active and of having a significant role in bringing about its own and society's betterment, is stronger, and the reality not only of the Knights of Labor but of the various trades' organizations is perceived in a more realistic way than in Ely's.

Even if they shared the main assumptions and the basic philosophy, the two books had a different fortune. McNeill's book had a briefer life than Ely's. It lost readers and influence following the decline of the Knights of Labor in the 1890s. Things went differently for Ely's book, and it was most probably not because of its greater intrinsic value. Ely's academic career, his position within the American Economic Association, and his being "an extraordinarily imaginative promoter" made for the difference.[65] Already at the publication of his book it was clear to Ely that to proceed from that initial stage, research of greater scope was necessary. But if, on the one hand, such work "was beyond the power of one man to accomplish,"[66] on the other hand, research into the history of the labor movement was far from being for him an exclusive field of activity. He was then—as he was before and even more afterward—devoting his interests to other subjects, principally within the field of economic theory. It was only in the second half of the 1890s that, probably to strengthen his academic position and his role within the University of Wisconsin, he came to conceive a project for the "organization of a society for industrial research, with a fund sufficient to cover the expense of investigation." Between 1902 and 1904 Ely succeeded in assembling the more than $30,000 he needed, and finally "in March, 1904, the American Bureau of Industrial Research was organized for the purpose of preparing a full and complete history of American industrial society."[67] John R. Commons, a former student of his at Johns Hopkins, was called to share with him the direction of the work. Eighteen years had passed since 1886. Since the year of its publication *The Labor Movement*— which had gone through three editions already by 1890—was to remain "the standard work on labor history and the contemporary labor movement for three decades," until Commons and his associates' first two volumes of their *History* appeared in 1918.[68]

The continuity between the initial steps by Ely and the final achievements of his immediate followers is summarized with revealing simplicity by David Saposs: "He initiated such scholarly research projects which resulted in *A Documentary History of American Industrial Society*, and the *History of Labour in the United States*. These monumental studies were edited by John R. Commons, giving John R. the opportunity to display his profound understanding and thinking in the social studies."[69] There is no need to stress the importance that the publication of those works, and particularly of the *History of Labour,* had in fixing the character of American labor historiography. "Thus far," a commentator wrote in 1971, "the history of American labor has been little more than a series of extended foot-notes and additional appendices to the work of the Wisconsin historians."[70]

Commons' presence at the University of Wisconsin after 1904 was decisive in establishing that university as the "leading center for the study of labor in the United States."[71] He had been attracted to Johns Hopkins and to the study of labor by Ely's ideas at the end of the 1880s, but in the definition of his approach to labor history and to labor problems in general, his later experiences with the National Civic Federation in the years between 1901 and 1904 were to have the utmost importance. From the close contact with the strategies of collective bargaining and of arbitration followed by the union, as well as by the capitalist element represented in the NCF, he derived his theory of collective bargaining and developed his idea of the history of the labor movement.

In his view, labor history was essentially the process of building and rebuilding organizations to adjust them to the changing dimensions of the markets and to the changes in workers' needs and conditions. In fully developing a theory of the labor movement, Commons moved away from Ely's path, taking the American Federation of Labor as the organizational model upon which to lay the foundations of his theoretical edifice. The differences between the Knights of Labor and the AFL made for the differences between Ely's cooperation and Common's collective bargaining. While the former was an end in itself, the latter was a means for the solution of industrial problems left unresolved by inept or corrupt legislators.

Commons borrowed heavily from Samuel Gompers his idea of collective bargaining and his perspective of an industrial government as a sphere relatively free from interferences by workers' politics as well as by political government. Commons gave theoretical status to what in Ely's formulation was scarcely more than a warning to workers to "beware of demagoguery, especially political partyism, which will give illusory triumphs, but leave to you only wretched failure."[72] He developed the conviction that politics only hampered the effective solution of industrial problems from the experience he had working for the NCF. His rejection was particularly strong with regard to labor politics—socialism, syndicalism, or any kind of revolutionary class perspective. He had an even clearer grasp than Ely of the dangers that an increased politicization of class conflict would represent for American capitalism and institutions.

Seeing the problem as one of deciding "whether the labor movement should be directed toward politics or toward collective bargaining," he stated that he wanted workers "to avoid politics and to direct
their energies toward what [he] knew was the policy for Samuel Gompers in building strong organizations on an equality, and freed from
the interference of politicians."[73] True, in the course of its history the
labor movement had swung "between the socialistic and anarchistic
doctrines," but "by a kind of natural selection a new pragmatic philosophy emerged taking form in the American Federation of Labor."[74]
Thus what American workers needed was help to further proceed
along the road they had already taken.

The two volumes of the *History of Labour* published in 1918 marked
the end of the journey that Commons had started twenty years earlier
toward the essential fusion of Gompers's philosophy of trade unionism and the theory of the labor movement developed at Wisconsin
after 1904. Commons assumed "employer-employee relations as essentially an act of exchange, as an 'economic' transaction whose character was 'politically neutral.' "[75] But in the "symmetrical institutional
framework" into which he forced industrial relations, both the complexity and radicality of class conflict as stressed by the revolutionary
industrial unionists and Gompers's business unionism philosophy and
Realpolitik were lost. Real power relations between labor and capital at
the level of production were pushed out of his theoretical horizon.
For Commons and for his followers, as for Ely, the history of labor
was the history of labor organizations. But while in the case of Ely his
"admiration for the Knights of Labor" meant the adoption of a reformist vision of society as a whole, in Commons's case the adoption of
the AFL's line of "pure and simple" unionism implied the reduction
of labor to a secondary role within American industrial and political
history.

And yet there was a direct and consistent thread running from Ely
to Commons, represented by their eagerness not to lose contact with
relevant social dynamics and by their determination to overcome the
limitations of a narrow academic life. However, Commons went further than Ely in that direction, keeping himself variously involved
with practical politics for most of his life. To the extent that it reflected
his politics—and it did so to a large extent—Commons's labor movement theory was a "highly political subject," to quote the words that
English labor historian Eric Hobsbawm uses to define labor history in
general.[76] Because of the particularity of class relations and of the
development of labor history itself in the United States, its political
relevance and orientation have not undergone any substantial discussion for years.

Only recently has it become evident that a critique of the Wisconsin school implied a critique of the political assumptions that were the basis of that historical tradition. As Robert H. Zieger wrote in 1972, "Refusing to accept the view of labor history established by University of Wisconsin scholars such as Richard T. Ely, John R. Commons, and Perlman, recent historians have been sharply critical of the American labor movement's national leadership and policies and the academic tradition which described and buttressed that tradition."[77] Significantly, he was making no distinction in his judgment between labor leadership policies and the academic school of labor history that traditionally "buttressed" those policies. Writing in different terms while reviewing Philip Taft's *Organized Labor in American History* in 1965, Hyman Berman pointed a way out of that tradition: "It is now time . . . to show that labor history is more than the rise and fall or the failures and successes of organizations—that it also consists of elucidating the role of the workers, both organized and unorganized in the course of this country's historical development."[78]

Since these words were written, much has been done in that direction. Research in working-class history has touched upon new questions, opened up new fields of investigation, and has started to give answers that undermine the conclusions reached by the Wisconsin historians. But what has been done in terms of empirical research to set labor history free from the institutionalism and the "mechanical economic determinism of the labor economists" is not enough.[79] What is also needed is further theoretical analysis, only sketched in this paper, that goes deep into the exploration of the social, political, and cultural conditions within which American labor historiography was born, and that puts in an adequate perspective both the ways by which Ely and the new economists and then Commons approached the labor problem, and the academic environment within which they made it grow.

NOTES

1. *New York Labor Standard*, 19 Aug. 1877.
2. Quoted in Robert Bruce, *1877: Year of Violence* (New York, 1959), p. 301, and *New York Labor Standard*, 2 Sept. 1877.
3. Quoted in Bruce, *1877*, p. 162.
4. See Philip S. Foner, *History of the Labor Movement in the United States*, 4 vols. (New York, 1972), 1:469 *New York Labor Standard*, 2 Sept. 1877. For an evaluation of the attitudes of the press, see Bruce, *1877*, p. 273, and Marianne Debouzy, "Grève et violence de classe aux Etats-Unis en 1877," *Le Mouvement Social* 102 (1978):44.

5. See Walter Millis, *Arms and Men* (New York, 1956), p. 143; Philip S. Foner, *The Great Labor Uprising of 1877* (New York, 1977), pp. 212–13; *New York Labor Standard*, 7 Oct. 1877; *Nation*, 2 Aug. 1877, pp. 68–69.

6. Millis, *Arms and Men*, pp. 144–45. See also Richard M. Brown, "Historical Patterns of Violence in America," in H. D. Graham and T. R. Gurr, *Violence in America: Historical and Comparative Perspectives* (Washington, D.C., 1969), 1:45. A special mention is due for the Pennsylvania "Coal and Iron Police," which increasingly functioned as a substitute for regular police forces in the last quarter of the nineteenth century; see Bruce, *1877*, pp. 39, 304–5.

7. Quotation from Herbert G. Gutman, "The Workers' Search for Power," in Henry W. Morgan, ed., *The Gilded Age* (Syracuse, N.Y., 1963), p. 36. "By 1876," writes Bruce, *1877*, p. 22, "the tramp seemed to have become a permanent institution in the United States, and demands were made for new laws to deal with him." See also pp. 20–23, 68–69.

8. Data and figures collected from: George E. McNeill, ed., *The Labor Movement: The Problem of To-Day* (Boston, 1887); Foner, *History*, vol. 1; Gutman, "Search for Power" and "Trouble on the Railroads in 1873–1874; Prelude to the 1877 Crisis?" *Labor History* 2 (1961); Joseph G. Rayback, *A History of American Labor* (New York, 1966), pp. 129–42.

9. See Jerry M. Cooper, "The Army as Strikebreaker: The Railroad Strikes of 1877 and 1894," *Labor History* 2 (1977):179–96. It is worthwhile noting that the compromise that ended the Reconstruction in the South allowed troops to be called on duty against strikers in the North and that a number of companies of the 9th and the 22nd Infantry, engaged in the war against the Indians in the West, were detached and sent east; cf. Foner, *Great Uprising*, pp. 42, 148, 155–56; Bruce, *1877*, pp. 219, 251, 259, 291; J. A. Dacus, *Annals of the Great Strikes in the United States* (Chicago, 1877), pp. 166, 171, 313–18, 428.

10. Gutman, "Search for Power," p. 50. See also his "The Buena Vista Affair, 1874–1875," *Pennsylvania Magazine of History and Biography* 3 (1964):251–93.

11. Pennsylvania Legislature, *Report of the Committee Appointed to Investigate the Railroad Riots in July, 1877* (Harrisburg, 1878), p. 40.

12. Debouzy, "Grève et violence," pp. 59–60.

13. The committee set up by the Pennsylvania legislature, the first to publish its conclusions, saw the epidemic of strikes as "caused by the great depression of business that followed the panic of 1873, by means whereof many men were thrown out of work, and the wages of those who could get work were reduced." *Report*, p. 40.

14. U.S. Congress, House, Select Committee on Depression in Labor and Business, *Causes of the General Depression in Labor and Business*, 45th Cong., 3d Sess. (1879). For a discussion of the works of this committee, see Mark Perlman, *Labor Union Theories in America* (Evanston, Ill., 1958), pp. 245–47; Joseph Dorfman, *The Economic Mind in American Civilisation*, 4 vols. (New York, 1949), 3:29–31, 44–46. Hewitt's words quoted from Allan Nevins, *Abram S. Hewitt, with Some Accounts of Peter Cooper* (New York, 1935), pp. 413–14.

15. U.S. Congress, Senate, Committee on Education and Labor, *Report of the Committee of the Senate upon the Relations between Labor and Capital, and Testimony Taken by the Committee*, 4 vols. (Washington, D.C., 1885). Perlman,

Labor Union Theories, pp. 247–64, discusses the content of many testimonies, pointing out their importance in showing opinions and strategies of labor leaders. See also Dorfman, *Economic Mind*, 3:125–30.

16. *First Annual Report of the Commissioner of Labor, March, 1886: Industrial Depressions* (Washington, D.C., 1886). For a discussion of its content, see Richmond Mayo-Smith, "The National Bureau of Labor and Industrial Depressions," *Political Science Quarterly* 3 (1886):437–48.

17. *Third Annual Report of the Commissioner of Labor, 1887: Strikes and Lockouts* (Washington, D.C., 1887). See also Carroll D. Wright, *The Industrial Evolution of the United States* (Meadville, Pa., 1895), pp. 297–300; T. S. Adams and H. L. Sumner, *Labor Problems* (New York, 1905), pp. 179–87.

18. An important aspect of the labor problem is already represented by immigration, which in 1882 reached its nineteenth-century peak with 788,992 entries. The relevance of immigrant labor in American industry is graphically given by Charlotte Erickson: "Aliens in 1870 constituted 53.3 per cent of the labor force in mining, 37.6 per cent in certain textiles, and 43.4 per cent in branches of the iron and steel industry. By 1890 the percentages were respectively 49.1, 42.8 and 37.9." *American Industry and the European Immigrant, 1860–1885* (Cambridge, Mass., 1957), app. 2, pp. 190–91.

19. W. H. S. Aubrey, "Labor Disputes in America," *Fortnightly Review* (n.s.) 284 (1890):246.

20. The Hewitt committee concluded its works with a majority report whose only recommendation was that Chinese immigration be restrained. The Blair committee, while expected to recommend ways and means to promote industrial harmony, ended up publishing 4,000 pages of testimony collected in four volumes and no recommendation at all.

21. Dorfman, *Economic Mind*, 3:29.

22. McNeill, *Labor Movement*, p. 137.

23. Wright, *Industrial Evolution*, pp. 269–76; Perlman, *Labor Union Theories*, pp. 1–3.

24. McNeill, *Labor Movement*, p. 145.

25. Wright, *Industrial Evolution*, p. 275.

26. Mayo-Smith, "National Bureau of Labor," p. 437.

27. Richmond Mayo-Smith, "American Labor Statistics," *Political Science Quarterly* 1 (1886):45–83.

28. Quoted in Benjamin G. Rader, *The Academic Mind and Reform* (Lexington, Ky., 1966), p. 78.

29. Perlman, *Labor Union Theories*, p. 15.

30. On the importance of university studies in Germany and of the German historical school in the formation of the "economic mind" of the new American economists, see particularly Joseph Dorfman, "The Role of the German Historical School in American Economic Thought," *American Economic Review* 2 (1955):17–28, and "Henry Carter Adams: The Harmonizer of Liberty and Reform," Preface to Henry C. Adams, *Relation of the State to Industrial Action* (1887; reprint ed., New York, 1954). On the reasons for the attraction of German universities for American students and on their importance as models for the reform of American colleges and universities, see R. Hofstadter and W. Smith, *American Higher Education: A Documentary History*, 2 vols. (Chicago, 1961), particularly vol. 2; R. Hofstadter and W. P. Metzger, *The Development of Academic Freedom in the United States* (New York, 1955), pp. 367–412.

31. While the new economists rejected any allegiance to socialism, they were often labeled as socialists by their opponents through the captious reference to their German models, known as "Katheder-Sozialisten." In the case of Richard Ely, his belonging to the movement of Christian Socialism made it easier to call him a socialist *tout court.* But even from within the group of the new economists there were those who "suspected" him of real sympathies for socialism; see Henry W. Farnam's review of his *Labor Movement,* in *Political Science Quarterly* 4 (1886):683–87. On his side, Ely more than once stated, and demonstrated, that he was for a "golden mean" that avoided both extremes, radicalism and reactionarism. See Rader, *Academic Mind,* esp. ch. 4, and Richard T. Ely, *Ground under Our Feet* (New York, 1937).

32. Mayo-Smith, "Labor Statistics," p. 45.

33. Richard T. Ely, *The Past and the Present of Political Economy* (Baltimore, 1884), p. 64.

34. *Ibid.,* pp. 8, 11, 12–13.

35. *Ibid.,* pp. 13, 45, 57.

36. *Ibid.,* pp. 47–49, 58.

37. Quoted in Bruce, *1877,* p. 314.

38. Carroll D. Wright, "The Relation of Political Economy to the Labor Question" (1882), in Wright, *Some Ethical Phases of the Labor Question* (Boston, 1902), pp. 31–32.

39. See Paul J. McNulty, "Labor Problems and Labor Economics: The Roots of an Academic Discipline," *Labor History* 9 (1968):248–49; Perlman, *Labor Union Theories,* pp. 18–20.

40. Adams, *Relation of the State,* p. 93. In his autobiography, p. 252, Ely recognizes the influence that Adams's ideas had on his thought on competition: "I was especially influenced, as were many of my contemporaries, by a monograph written soon after the American Economic Association was formed, by my friend Professor Henry C. Adams, called 'The Relation of the State to Industrial Action.' His idea was that through the agency of the state and other social forces, competiton should be placed constantly upon a higher and higher ethical level, but competition should be maintained."

41. It is possible that in this case it was Adams who was influenced by the heavy stress put on the civil service by Ely, who was still under the favorable impressions he gathered while studying the civil service in Berlin and, generally, in Germany. See Ely, *Ground,* pp. 60–63, 258–59.

42. Adams, *Relation of the State,* pp. 83–133 *passim.* See also Dorfman, "Adams," pp. 32–34.

43. Adams, *Relation of the State,* p. 125. Quotations from Dorfman, "Adams," p. 35.

44. E. R. A. Seligman, review of *Relation of the State,* in *Political Science Quarterly* 2 (1887):353.

45. Quoted in Ely, *Ground,* p. 134.

46. On the early history of the American Economic Association, see Ely, *Ground,* pp. 121–64, 296–99; Rader, *Academic Mind,* pp. 32–40; Dorfman, *Economic Mind,* 3:205–12; Perlman, *Labor Union Theories.*

47. Dorfman, *Economic Mind,* 3:207.

48. Lewis H. Haney, *History of Economic Thought,* 4th ed. (New York, 1951), p. 884. See also Rader, *Academic Mind,* p. 117.

49. Quoted in Rader, *Academic Mind*, p. 118.
50. On Ely's increasing conservatism after 1894, see *ibid.*, esp. ch. 6, "Retreat from Reform," and Dorfman, *Economic Mind*, 3:256–58.
51. Dorfman, "Role of German School," p. 28.
52. The new economists found their way into American universities, but not without opposition. Some of them were the target of attacks because of their prolabor attitudes or of their heterodoxy in matters of economic theory. Henry C. Adam's dismissal from Cornell in 1887 because of his views on the labor question; the trial of Ely at Wisconsin for heretical social and economic writings in 1894, the dismissal of Edward W. Bemis, a former student of Ely, from the University of Chicago in 1895 and that of James A. Smith from Marietta College in 1897 for their antimonopolist views; the *de facto* removals of John Commons from Indiana University in 1896 and from Syracuse University in 1899 for his economic heterodoxy; the forced resignation of Edward A. Ross, another former student of Ely, from Stanford University in 1900—these are some of the best-known cases of attacks on academic freedom in the name of orthodoxy. Hofstadter and Metzger discuss the cases just mentioned in ch. 9 of their *Development of Academic Freedom*. The case of Henry C. Adams is discussed in Dorfman, "Adams," pp. 32–42, that of Ely in Rader, *Academic Mind*, pp. 129–50. In some cases the wide solidarity within the academic world and the public attention these trials or dismissals aroused turned the attacks into triumphs for the attacked, as in the cases of Ely and Adams.
53. The only one among the new economists to enter the field of labor history proper was Ely, whose *The Labor Movement in America* (New York, 1886) was the first book of the kind published in the United States. The importance of the coexistence of history and economics in the definition of the role Ely had as the initiator of labor history is stressed by Perlman, *Labor Union Theories*, p. 55: "In point of fact, it is probably this book, written by a leading professional economist, that explains why the history of American unionism became associated initially with economics rather than with political science or history."
54. McNulty, "Labor Problems," p. 240.
55. In his *Labor Movement*, p. 75, Ely wrote of the Knights of Labor that they were "established on truly scientific principles, which involved either an intuitive perception of the nature of industrial progress, or a wonderful acquaintance with the laws of economic society."
56. *Ibid.*, pp. 136–37.
57. *Ibid.*, p. 6. After the decline of the Knights of Labor in the early 1890s, Ely admitted that "tendencies toward centralization of business have raised up new difficulties which have impeded the extension of co-operation." *Socialism: An Examination of Its Nature, Its Strength and Its Weaknesses, with Suggestion for Social Reform* (New York, 1894), p. 340.
58. Ely, *Labor Movement*, pp. x, 4.
59. *Ibid.*, p. 7.
60. *Ibid.*, p. 154.
61. This standpoint is exemplified in *ibid.*, p. 4: "socialism, communism, co-operation, trades-unions and labor societies, mutual benefit organizations of one kind and another, also, alas!, anarchy and nihilism, are different lines along which are directed the efforts of the masses to attain improved conditions and relations in industrial society."

62. *Ibid.*, p. 146.

63. While Ely's book was a one-man effort, McNeill's was a collection of essays written by various contributors. Some of them were labor leaders who wrote on their organizations, such as F. K. Foster (shoemakers), J. McBride (coal miners), J. Jarrett (iron workers), and others. Others were concerned economists such as Edmund J. James or F. H. Giddings; still others were well-known reformers, such as Henry George or the Reverend R. Heber Newton.

64. Rader, *Academic Mind*, pp. 76–77.

65. David Saposs, "The Wisconsin Heritage and the Study of Labor: Works and Deeds of John R. Commons," *School for Workers 35th Anniversary Papers* (Madison, Wis., 1960), p. 8.

66. Ely, Preface to John R. Commons *et al.*, eds., *A Documentary History of American Industrial Society*, 10 vols. (1910; reprint ed., New York, 1958), 1:21.

67. *Ibid.* See also Rader, *Academic Mind*, pp. 166–69.

68. Rader, *Academic Mind*, p. 72.

69. Saposs, "Wisconsin Heritage," pp. 8–9.

70. Thomas A. Krueger, "American Labor Historiography, Old and New: A Review Essay," *Journal of Social History* 3 (1971):277.

71. McNulty, "Labor Problems," p. 255.

72. Ely, *Labor Movement*, p. ix.

73. John R. Commons, *Myself* (New York, 1934), pp. 167–68.

74. John R. Commons, *et al., History of Labour in the United States*, 4 vols. (New York, 1918–35), 2:17.

75. Bruno Ramirez, *When Workers Fight: The Politics of Industrial Relations in the Progressive Era, 1898–1916* (Westport, Conn., 1978), p. 190.

76. Eric J. Hobsbawm, "Labor History and Ideology," *Journal of Social History* 7 (1974):371.

77. Robert H. Zieger, "Workers and Scholars: Recent Trends in American Labor Historiography, *Labor History* 1 (1972):250.

78. H. Berman, review of Taft's *Organized Labor*, in *Journal of American History* 4 (1965):741.

79. Paul Faler, "Working Class Historiography," *Radical America* 2 (1969):56.

2

W. E. B. Du Bois and the Proletariat in *Black Reconstruction*

FERRUCCIO GAMBINO

The conception and working out of W. E. B. Du Bois's *Black Recon-struction in America: An Essay toward a History of the Part Which Black Folk Played in the Attempt to Reconstruct Democracy in America, 1860–1880*[1] belonged to the period of the Great Depression. In reflecting on the events of the early 1930s, Du Bois found the motivation to write his major work. While the Great Depression was pushing the working class toward urban unemployment and rural subsistence, Du Bois was moving in the same direction as the radicalization prevalent in the ghettoes. The years 1903–6, 1914–19, and 1932–36 were crucial in the crisis of the black intelligentsia because they reflected crucial class experiences of blacks in the United States. The Great Depression exacerbated in black people the seismic tensions of the previous dec-ades. At this point Du Bois detached himself from any reform activity and paused to evaluate the meaning of another crisis, that Black Reconstruction which had preceded the New Deal by 60 years.

Until the beginning of 1933 not even white workers in the leading sectors of the U.S. economy appeared able to resist wage cuts, unem-ployment, and deterioration of living conditions in the main indus-trial centers. The unemployment that followed the Great Depression and the expulsion of blacks from the plantations combined their ef-fects in hitting the blacks' living conditions. In the thirties the growth of industrial employment among blacks was only 45% of that among whites, and the blacks were generally concentrated in declining sec-tors, such as coal, lumber, and tobacco. In this situation the National Association for the Advancement of Colored People (NAACP) was at least able to ensure a continuity of aid and publicization. But the ills were extreme. Before the Congress of Industrial Organizations im-posed its bargaining power, the Great Depression seemed to deepen the class divisions along racist lines. The group that accepted the battleground imposed on black people by the caste exclusions re-emerged in the ghettoes. In 1932 a laid-off Chevrolet worker in De-

troit, Robert Poole, became Elijah Muhammad, went to Chicago, and
established the Nation of Islam's headquarters there. The other line,
that of alliances with progressives, appeared unworkable unless the
terms of the alliance were sharply redefined in the light of the total
experience of black people in the United States.

The Reconstruction era constituted a central point in that experience. Revolutionary black activity and the white reaction, the blacks'
attempt to seize the levers of power in the South and the resistance to
it by northern and southern capital, looked as if magnetized in the
brief span of time of Reconstruction. Thus Reconstruction had elements of *déja vu* vis-à-vis the Great Depression. The pattern of black
people's attack and retreat had to be analyzed in depth in order not
to repeat history. In 1934 Du Bois decided to go his own way; he
returned to Atlanta University, leaving the NAACP and *The Crisis*. In
1933 he had started work on *Black Reconstruction*. Since for Du Bois
the discovery of the black proletariat, which is central to *Black Reconstruction*, was not easy, a survey of his previous work seems to be
necessary to evaluate the scope and meaning of *Black Reconstruction*.

Why was the discovery of the black proletariat not easy for Du Bois?
He had been enticed in the opposite direction by the education and
the intellectual milieu that recalled him to his youthful liberalism.
William James at Harvard and even Gustav Schmoller at Berlin taught
him the objectivity of the historical and psychological event. The wise
passage by Du Bois from philosophy to sociology in the Harvard years
occurred under the sign of "the empirical fact." "What we need," he
wrote in his notes during his Harvard years, "is not a philosophy of
history but such a gathering and . . . placing physical and mental data
so as to furnish material for a philosophy of man." Schmoller pointed
him toward empirical sociological work after the historian Du Bois
had selected a crucial "bit of history" and worked "hard and honestly"[2]
when writing his doctoral dissertation on "The Suppression of the
African Slave-Trade to the United States of America: 1638–1870,"
seventeen years before *The Economic Interpretation of the American Constitution* by Charles Beard.[3]

The re-emergence of the problem of control of urban concentrations after the defeat of populism in 1896 and the consequent academic opening to the method of "controlled experiment" and to the
"moral welfare of society" in the form of sociology allowed Du Bois to
carry out field research after his German years in 1894–96. Although
the ghettoes did not seem worthy of sociological study to the predom-
inant Social Darwinists, ghetto life and the southern plantation were
privileged fields of inquiry for Du Bois in the first decade of the
twentieth century. Thus he opened up new fronts to sociological ob-

servation. In such a process, those observed in the ghettoes and in the plantations forced Du Bois, the observer, toward a crisis.

Gunnar Myrdal wrote in *An American Dilemma* that if the sociological writings of Du Bois early in the twentieth century "sound much more modern than the writings of the whites," this "is a merely historical accident." Quite the contrary[4]—with *The Philadelphia Negro*,[5] a systematic study of one of the largest and oldest ghettoes in the United States, Du Bois proposed to lay down the basis of a long work of analysis of the conditions of blacks that he was able to carry on between 1897 and 1914 at Atlanta University with the publication of sixteen monographs. Sociological inquiry seemed to Du Bois the method suited to the objective conditions of blacks, as against Social Darwinism that still considered them untouchable. But beyond sociological objectivity, the urgency of reform was clearly manifested in *The Philadelphia Negro*. When Du Bois concluded that "the upper Negro class . . . embodies the idea of the group," he was assigning the job of leadership of the ghetto to the black professionals descended from the ex-slave urban artisans. In the proposal for a leadership of professionals Du Bois concentrated the frustration and ambivalence of the "Negro upper class." Excluded from industrial leadership, discriminated against in the professions, isolated from the black masses of the plantation South and of the ghettoes, the "Negro upper class" to which Du Bois referred was looking for an access to power in a social vacuum. On the Du Bois of *The Philadelphia Negro*, however, the daily contact with ghetto conditions was beginning to leave its mark, despite the uncertainties and doubts of the social stratum of which he felt part. In Philadelphia in 1896 he established himself in the worst part of the Seventh Ward, and lived there one year in an atmosphere of "dirt, alcoholism, poverty, and crime." He observed the destitution of a ghetto where "the police was our government, and philanthropy showed up from time to time with its usual advice."

The fourteen years that Du Bois spent at Atlanta University between 1897 and 1910 enabled him to understand the objective conditions of the blacks in the South. Their political leadership was in the hands of Booker T. Washington and his Tuskegee Institute, founded in the heart of rural Alabama and financed by the new industrial barons of the North. Booker T. Washington staked his bets on a program of agricultural modernization in the South, with the black sharecroppers and tenant farmers as its natural protagonists. Preliminary to this process was his acceptance of the power relations between black and whites that white terror had imposed after Reconstruction. Deserting the political terrain and accepting segregation as a form of defense against racist intimidation, Booker T.

Washington had shaped the Tuskegee Institute into a training school
for technicians who were to bring about the development of agriculture in the South. With these he tried to ally the thin stratum of black
artisans, above all in the construction industry left over from the era
of slavery. Together they were intended to form a nascent black middle class and to open up substantial breaches in the structure of power.
Du Bois voiced his agreement with Booker T. Washington's work in
1895, but in Atlanta he slowly realized that Washington's line was at
best inadequate to capitalist initiative in the South itself. In the North
there was a progressive strengthening of a class of black professionals
whose interests stemmed from the relationship between ghettoes and
the rest of the cities and who rejected the defensive posture represented by Booker T. Washington.

Slow changes disturbed the quiet even in the Cotton South. "An
outmigration of black labor from the Cotton South ultimately did take
place" and accelerated between the 1880s and the 1920s. The direction of the out-migration was clear. "Although the prospect of industrial employment must have seemed more uncertain, it was no
coincidence that when blacks did leave the South it was primarily to
northern cities, not to northern agriculture, that they went."[6] In 1903
Du Bois was already moving away from the defensive tradition that
most of the black intelligentsia of the previous generation had accepted as a necessity imposed by anti-Reconstruction reaction.[7] Du
Bois based the possibility of reforming U.S. society on the initiative of
that stratum of intellectuals and professionals of the North who could
use their secure positions to denounce the institutional equilibrium
founded on plantation politicians. For Du Bois it was time to relaunch
the alliance of the white radicals with the abolitionists through the
Niagara Movement—the first nucleus of the NAACP, founded five
years later.

The Niagara Movement's pilgrimage to Harper's Ferry was followed by Du Bois's biography, *John Brown*.[8] The book turned the
spotlight on the interaction between a developing young abolitionist
and the slaves who were catalyzing his development. They were the
"living, organized, combatant group." Now Du Bois was outlining a
historical arc on which his attention revolved. At one extremity Du
Bois had placed his *John Brown*. He defined the other extremity in a
first article confuting the reactionary historical approach to Reconstruction in 1910; "Reconstruction and Its Benefits"[9] was a first outline for analyzing the *presence* of slaves in their own liberation. Du
Bois's viewpoint still owed much to the Brahminic tradition, but the
interpretation of the Civil War broke the ground for the grand design
of *Black Reconstruction* 25 years later. Meanwhile, with the approach

of World War I a new wind in the black ghettoes helped change the direction of Du Bois's activity.

With the birth of NAACP as an affiliate of the Niagara Movement in 1910, Du Bois pushed its founders into stepping beyond mere legal defense of the blacks and the financial and moral support of white philanthropists. The result was the monthly *The Crisis*, which Du Bois was to edit until 1934 and which, within a decade, became a leading black newspaper. After leaving Atlanta University in 1910, he was able to concentrate his activity on the NAACP. These fruitful years for Du Bois were also the years of new impulse to the advancement of black people and of hard resistance by Jim Crow. With the accelerating black out-migration from the Cotton South during the Progressive Era, the black proletariat of the northern ghettoes was coming to the center of the class lineup in the United States. At last radical black intellectuals could reach out to a black proletariat stronger in number and readier to take opportunities from the growing demands of labor than at any time since the Civil War.

In terms of dimensions, mobilization, proliferation, and goals, the struggles waged by the working class during the Progressive Era led to an irreversible process of industrial unionism. This process must be judged not on the basis of the many defeats and the few victories during the Progressive era—or the 1920s—but on the basis of the definitive victories of the 1930s when capital was forced to collective bargaining, which had to be established in abstract during the Progressive era. It was the strength and the dimension of working-class organization that was the main terrain of struggle in those years. It was a terrain that U.S. capital had not yet experienced in the late nineteenth century. It did not expect the millions of immigrants from eastern and southern Europe to be more than "the river of human flesh which separated, and had to keep separated, the Southern blacks from the Northern factories."[10] As the European immigrants were not quiet, U.S. capital could as well take on the black immigrants from the South. As both groups had been deprived of technical skills and of land, their egalitarianism and internationalism could find expression in the IWW to a larger extent than in any previous labor organization, and with an increasing opposition from craft unionism. "The immense labor struggles in the years before World War I forced Du Bois to consider the importance of class divisions within the white world as no academic exercise could have done. Above all, the lynchings and racist brutality of the South fueled his intellectual motor as much as all the books he ever read."[11]

The start of World War I induced Du Bois to examine the class situation at the international level; it also enabled him to outline his approach to the mass of unskilled workers and to glimpse the political novelty of which the IWW had already given proof. His essay "The African Roots of War"[12] described the European democracies as "democratic despotism" resulting from a social pact concluded between capitalists and skilled workers, and he imputed the war more to the partition of Africa than to the partition of the Balkans. The war was a conflict between "national armed associations of capital and labor whose purpose is the exploitation of the world's wealth, above all outside the circle of the European nations."[13]

In 1915 the volume *The Negro*[14] pursued the discussion, analyzing the relationship between the "moral retrogression in social philosophy" in the Western countries and the development of imperialism. In Du Bois's view anti-egalitarianism and stratification according to color lines had been accepted by the craft unions. The AFL of Samuel Gompers gave the clearest example just because the contiguity of the black and white labor markets in the United States summed up a less clear but equally real division at the international level. The dimensions of the problem were not reducible to the United States; they were worldwide, and the war would aggravate them.

It was necessary to trace the roots of the divisions between the white and the black proletariat. Du Bois may have felt at that time how close he had come to a full understanding of the process of division as early as 1894, when he wrote his dissertation on the suppression of the African slave trade. In the preface to the 1954 reprint of his dissertation, Du Bois complained three times that he had missed the point because of ignorance of "the philosophy of Karl Marx."[15] But in 1915 Du Bois could establish a fruitful historical sequence: "The Negro slave trade was the first step in modern world commerce, followed by the modern theory of colonial expansion." The modern working class arose out of the profits of the slave trade, and thus the white and the black proletariat had gone through different processes of exploitation, even in the United States where they were closer than in any other part of the world. Modern colonialism was ready to treat darker workers more severely, and "the European and the white American working class were practically invited to share in this new exploitation." At the same time, in some African colonies the plantation economy was extending the system of forced labor; in the West Indies, the United States, and parts of Africa black workers were held in peonage. He concluded:

> The Pan-African movement when it comes will not however, be merely a narrow racial propaganda. Already the more far-seeing Negroes sense the coming unities: a unity of the working classes everywhere, a unity of the colored races, a new unity of men. The

proposed economic solution of the Negro problem in Africa and
America has turned the thoughts of Negroes toward a realization
of the fact that the modern white laborer of Europe and America
has the key to the serfdom of black folk in his support of militarism
and colonial expansion.[16]

Echoing Marx, he wrote: "He [the Negro] is beginning to say to these
workingmen that, so long as black laborers are slaves, white laborers
cannot be free."[17]

Thus Du Bois rejected the twofold formula: white working class/
black people. For him, as for the young radical historians who followed in his wake in the 1960s, the problem was not the construction
of an alliance between two sociologically defined forces but the identification of the prime mover of the struggle: ". . . in all that he wrote
he tried to ascertain the direction of historical movement and where
black people should look to find solutions to their real problems."[18]
In *The Negro* the black worker began emerging as the motive force of
class antagonism in the United States, although Du Bois vaguely sensed
the peculiar relationship between free labor and slavery that was to
become the central theme of *Black Reconstruction.*

With the United States' entry into the war, the wave of new out-
migration from the South was taking on biblical proportions. Could
it repeat the miracles of agitation and propaganda among the black
people, North and South, that the runaways had worked in the decades preceding the Civil War? Was it possible to establish a relationship between black immigrants to the northern ghettoes and the
rebellion of the "illiterate and repressed masses of the white workers"? Or was it better to give in to the Wilson administration's intimi-
dations against *The Crisis* and Du Bois in particular, to retreat from
the lines drawn by "The African Roots of War" and *The Negro* and
quietly help black workers get jobs in the expanding industries? Du
Bois hesitated. With the postwar recession, the blacks, "the first to be
fired," could not see much point in respecting the picket lines. When
the picket lines at the Chicago steel strike in 1919 failed to hold off
the pressure of the so-called black strikebreakers, the white workers
saw how difficult it now was to make gains if the ghetto was left to
one side. "Self-defense and survival," Du Bois wrote, could not be
bargained against "signing up with a revolution which we now do not
understand."[19]

The forces that Du Bois had to consider in assessing the chances of
a new style of political work were extremely varied, reflecting a class
situation exacerbated by the postwar depression. On the one hand,
there were the unionized blacks "holed up" in jobs that paid low wages
but were protected against troughs in the economic cycle. On the

other hand, there were the recently urbanized black masses in whom
Marcus Garvey's "back to Africa" movement and his Universal Negro
Improvement Association (UNIA) struck a responsive chord.

Du Bois glimpsed the new form of anticolonial resistance taking
advantage of intra-imperial rivalries following World War I, but at
home he was unable to draw political conclusions from the twenty or
more ghetto revolts in the years 1917–21, with the two great epicen-
ters in East St. Louis and Chicago. Yet the phenomena underlying the
revolts could not escape him.

In the decade between the censuses of 1910 and 1920, the black
population in the major cities had increased dramatically. As long as
the three sectors receiving most of the migration—the food, steel, and
auto industries—were pushed ahead by the needs of war, "the impossibility of obtaining competent white workers was the reason given in
virtually all cases to explain the large number of Negroes employed
as of 1914."[20] At the time of the revolt in the Chicago ghetto in 1919,
10,000 black unskilled workers had been laid off at a stroke. In 1921
the unemployment rate among blacks in Detroit was five times the
rate for whites born in the United States and twice that of whites born
abroad.[21] Among black immigrants in the large urban centers, the
"back to Africa" movement grew to mass dimensions between the end
of the crisis of 1919–21 and the start of the economic upturn of 1922–
24. During this last three-year period approximately another half-
million blacks left the South.[22]

Caught between the unionized black minority on the one hand and
the nonunionized majority (most of them recent immigrants) on the
other hand, the NAACP's black intellectuals, and Du Bois to start
with, dithered for some time over whether a rapprochement should
be sought with the UNIA or whether it should be attacked with the
press instruments they had available. The Garveyist movement had
taken Du Bois by surprise, since he had not made a careful assessment
of the depth of the crisis that hit the industrial ghettoes of the North.
For two years, in 1921 and 1922, he remained uncertain, evaluating
the various aspects and ambiguities of Garveyism from the heights of
The Crisis.[23] The solution to the dilemmas of both black unions and
Garveyism turned out to be a compromise of convenience. Du Bois
attacked the UNIA when it was entering into crisis[24] and failed to
criticize the black group working within the AFL. The result was to
reinforce the NAACP's defensive line and its link with *The Crisis* during the ebb tide of the 1920s.

In general, the black intelligentsia had not seen the implications of
the "back to Africa" movement. But with or without the black intelligentsia, there was no attempt to salvage the UNIA's national organi-

zational network when it entered into crisis in about 1925. Du Bois's
effort to answer Garveyism with the pan-African congresses of the
postwar period was not in line with the demands emerging from the
black proletariat.[25] The upshot was that the NAACP's relationship
with the ghettoes in the grip of the Great Depression was virtually nil.
This failure led Du Bois to consider the NAACP a blunted tool in the
final crisis of their relations during 1931–33. But the first flaws between them dated back to the 1920s. Under the indirect impulse of
the ghetto revolts and Garveyism, Du Bois had tried to defend the
independence of the black ghetto against white philanthropy. This
much he could do. But he had to leave much to others. The new black
immigrants were now supplying the propagandists and organizers,
who would have their biggest tests in the 1930s. However attentive he
may have been, Du Bois followed the new agitation from a distance;
he had more weight with the national leaders than the local ones, and
was better known in the North than in the South.

The South was virtually impervious to Du Bois's national and international initiatives. But in at least one of the strongholds of segrega-
tionism, the black universities of the South, Du Bois helped inspire
the first mass student strikes against white charity and its blackmailing
of black students: in 1925 a strike at Fisk University, and in 1927 at
Howard, Lincoln, and Hampton. His journey through the black universities of the South two years later confirmed his impression that
the revolts had created a generation which could hardly be black-
mailed by philanthropy—and had also prevented the relative deterioration of the black students' conditions. At the start of the 1930s
four-fifths of the blacks were still in the South. With the agricultural
programs of the New Deal, the expulsion of blacks from the cotton
plantations became a joint action of the landowner and the state. In
the South the number of agricultural day laborers and sharecroppers
fell by 650,000 units, equivalent to a third, between 1931 and 1940.[26]
Only the war would enable them to enter the factory, at least for a
few years.

The terrain of struggle of black people in the early 1930s appeared
as a closed space. With that seclusion Du Bois identified. He could
perceive how distant a proletarian perspective on the history of black
people in the United States was from a liberal perspective. Charles
Vann Woodward noted the black's inability to take a cold look at the
Reconstruction era.[27] This may appear to be an implicit criticism of
Du Bois. On the contrary, it should be taken as an appreciation of the
political meaning of *Black Reconstruction,* which is not just a mere
refutation of the then dominating antiradical historiography but intends to be the proof of the leading quality that the black people's

struggle took on during the twenty years of Reconstruction. The yardstick by which to judge *Black Reconstruction* is Du Bois's ability to find the motive forces of the struggles resulting in the Civil War and the trends in the slaves' attack against the slaveocracy, from an intensifying "mutiny" during the war through military victory down to a defensive posture as Reconstruction was coming to an end.

In Reconstruction Du Bois saw primarily the self-activity of the ex-slaves becoming a modern proletariat with arms and power in their hands—and also the "counter-revolution of property" and its postbellum state. He was able to capture the double motion of the self-activity of the ex-slaves trying to make the state malleable to their needs and of the acquisitive greed of the new men of power in the South. The new men of power did not linearly inherit the state levers of power from the slaveholders; they had to conquer them with what Du Bois called "disruption," or the "counter-revolution of property." At a time when "the Marxists" usually portrayed the working class as an appendage to progressive capital,[28] the structure of Du Bois's book left no doubt about his class viewpoint: first comes "The Black Worker" (Chapter 1), then "The White Worker" (Chapter 2), and only then "The Planter" (Chapter 3). This was a new sequence unheard of in the 1930s. The exception was *The Black Jacobins* by C. L. R. James, another black man who was deeply involved in the anticolonial struggles of those years.[29] Even more than after the publication of *The Negro* in 1915, after *Black Reconstruction* it has become proven nonsense for historians to talk about labor *and* black people: black people as working class, as the oldest and most experienced section of the working class against the U.S. state—that was the lesson to be drawn from the Reconstruction years, when labor and blacks were still regularly conceived of as two separate entities: "It was thus the black worker, as founding stone of a new economic system in the nineteenth century for the modern world, who brought civil war in America. He was its underlying cause, in spite of every effort to base the strife upon union and national power."[30]

Du Bois made the issue involved in emancipation clear at the beginning with an underlying assumption: "If all labor, black as well as white, became free—were given schools and the right to vote—what control could or should be set to the power and action of these laborers?" Having set the protagonist at the center of the stage, Du Bois described the social position of "the white workers," their social mobility, their opposition to slavery "not from moral as from the economic fear of being reduced by competition to the level of slaves." As to the planter, he was faced by slaves who "might be made to work continuously but no power could make them work well." The planter was squeezed between the daily struggle of the slaves and northern merchant capital. He resorted to the expansion of cotton production in the Cotton Belt, to the largest forced migration in the nineteenth century, and to the breakup of the slave families. The internal disruption to the social fabric that King Cotton brought about accounts for the planters' lot: ". . . they lost because of their internal weakness. Their whole labor class, black and white, went into economic revolt." The aftermath of the demise of American slavery was the substitution of industrial capital for merchant capital in the colonial world: "The abolition of American slavery started the transportation of capital from white to black countries where slavery prevailed, with the same tremendous and awful consequences upon the laboring classes of the world which we see about us today."[31]

In the first part of *Black Reconstruction* (Chapters 1 through 5), Du Bois focused on the black masses' ability to clash and win against the slaveholders in a crescendo of action culminating in what Du Bois called "The General Strike" and in the partial transformation of blacks "from laborers to soldiers fighting for their own freedom." Regularly the day-to-day struggle did not involve acts of desperation. It found its support in the slaves' community and managed to undermine the slave society irreversibly. Flight, collective disappearance from the plantations with return conditional on certain improvements in the unwritten "collective contract," joint resistance to workloads, passivity toward the plantation and its fortunes, absenteeism during periods crucial to production, a relentless pressure to increase the cost of "treatment"—these were forms of struggle that grew increasingly intense and paved the way for "The Coming of the Lord." In *Black Reconstruction* the accent falls not on impulsive, momentary action but on "this slow, stubborn mutiny of the Negro slave." This was not merely a matter of 200,000 black soldiers and perhaps 300,000 "other black laborers, servants, informers and helpers. Back of this half million stood 3½ million more. Without their labor the South would starve. With arms in their hands, Negroes would form a fighting force which could replace every single Northern white soldier fighting listlessly and against his will with a black man fighting for freedom."[32]

The slaves were the prime movers in the disruption of the South. "This action of the slaves was followed by the disaffection of the whites." Du Bois saw the new balance of forces in its making: "This attitude of the poor whites had in it as much fear and jealousy of Negroes as disaffection with slave barons. . . . If the Negro was to be free where would the poor white be? Why should he fight against the

blacks and his victorious friends? The poor white not only began to
desert and run away; but thousands followed the Negro into the
Northern camps."[33]

The beginning of the manipulation of the blacks' victories came
with the whites' perception of the ex-slaves as a threat: "The guns at
Sumter, the marching armies, the fugitive slaves, the fugitives as 'con-
trabands,' spies, servants and laborers; the Negro as soldier, as citizen,
as voter—these steps came from 1861 to 1868 with regular beat that
was almost rhythmic. It was the price of disaster of war, and it was a
price that few Americans at first dreamed of paying or wanted to
pay."[34] As Du Bois traced the process of manipulation of the blacks'
achievements during the Civil War and Reconstruction, he saw black
people as being "used," a key word in *Black Reconstruction* frequently
suggesting a wide range of forms of exploitation.[35] Blacks were "used
as much-needed laborers and servants by the Northern army," "used"
as troops, and "repeatedly and deliberately used as shock troops,
when there was little or no hope of success." Finally, ". . . most Americans used the Negro to defend their own economic interest and,
refusing him adequate land and real education and even common
justice, deserted him shamelessly as soon as their selfish interests were
safe."[36]

Thus while the blacks were the diamond point in the fight for their
freedom and for the general emancipation of the working class, when
they were left alone in their struggle against the state, they suc-
cumbed. Du Bois indicated the trend of that struggle in the second
part of *Black Reconstruction* (Chapters 7 through 13). Here he traced
"the organization of free labor after the war,"[37] when the black proletariat in the South came as close as no other section of the working
class in the United States had come to making use of the state for its
needs. Black people, now emancipated, could not wipe out centuries
of European and American racism, and therefore could not exert an
irreversible attraction on white workers. What were the distinct elements preventing a combination of forces along class lines? Du Bois
acutely suggested that they were a yet insufficient class differentiation
between poor white laborers and planters and a sedimented separation between the ex-slaves and the labor movement. During
Reconstruction,

> as in the case of slavery, there was a combination in which the poor
> whites seemed excluded; unless they made common cause with the
> blacks. This union of black and white labor never got a real start.
> First, because black leadership still tended toward the ideals of the
> petty bourgeois, and white leadership tended distinctly toward
> strengthening capitalism. The final move which rearranged all these

combinations and led to the catastrophe of 1876, was a combination of planters and poor whites in defiance of their economic interests; and with the use of lawless murder and open intimidation.

Thus the centrality of black labor was not the founding stone of the official labor movement after the Civil War: ". . . the labor movement, with but few exceptions, never realized the situation. It never had the intelligence or knowledge, as a whole, to see in black slavery and Reconstruction, the kernel and the meaning of the labor movement in the United States." The key element in that defeat was thus stated: "When white laborers were convinced that the degradation of Negro labor was more fundamental than the uplift of white labor, the end was in sight."[38]

How were white laborers "convinced"? Du Bois did not consider the process of "conviction" as an ideological dispute or as a mere deed of devilish propaganda. The defeat of the black proletariat in the South was a direct result of industrial capital's conquest of the state through the Civil War and its aftermath. It was achieved with sheer and wild violence, organized fraud, and the "dull compulsion" of imported and native labor. To crush the resistance of the blacks and set an example for the poor whites, the state had necessarily to reject the "40 acres and a mule" demand and to drive 40,000 black people off the Sea Islands and adjoining lands that they had occupied and cultivated as freedmen. However, this was not enough. The new men of power in the South seized a rising industry—coal and iron—and denied landownership to black people, thus moving rapidly to throw the black proletariat from a position of attack to a position of defense. On the plantations the mobility of ex-slaves was violently limited. In the rising urban ghettoes seclusion was the rule. The counterrevolution needed an ideology. Racism provided an easy one. Racism had been deeply ingrained in Western society, but now it took on a key importance. It did to the white population in terms of social consensus what the material chains of slavery had done before to control the black people. As Du Bois had written in *The Souls of Black Folks*, "the Negro suffrage ended a civil war by beginning a race feud."[39] Yet some of the black people's accomplishments during Reconstruction were irreversible: the right to geographic mobility in some areas of the South, the founding of a public school system throughout the South from scratch, the ferment produced in the northern working class by the fugitive slaves and their political heirs, especially among coal miners—all these new activities could not be stopped by armed property.

How to draw the white section of the working class into the terrain

of struggle that the ex-slaves had kept open for more than a decade?
How to divide that section from the state in all of its manifestations?
If it had been a problem of the 1860s and 1870s, it remained a
problem in the 1930s for Du Bois. At least for a short time the majority of the people in the United States had accepted political rights for
black people, and southern poor whites had looked for a black leadership. The scenario Du Bois described in his suggestive asides in
Black Reconstruction help reveal his political motivations in writing this
work:

> Suppose, for instance, there had been in the South in 1863 a small
> but determined and clear-thinking group of men who said: "The
> Negro is free and to make his freedom real, he must have land and
> education. . . ."

> Suppose for a moment that Northern labor had stopped the bar-
> gain of 1876 and maintained the power of the labor vote in the
> South; and suppose that the Negro with new and dawning con-
> sciousness of the demands of labor as differentiated from the de-
> mands of capitalists, had used his vote more specifically for the
> benefit of white labor, South and North. . . .

> Suppose a Southern leader had appeared at that time and had said
> frankly: "We propose to make the Negro actually free in his right
> to work, his legal status, and his personal safety. . . .

> How this interaction of former land monopolists, white peasants
> and Negro peasants, would have worked itself out if uncomplicated
> by other interests, is a question. But it seems almost inevitable that
> division would have had to take place along economic rather than
> racial lines. . . .[40]

For Du Bois the black masses in the South had been, momentarily,
a centripetal force to the rest of society. Du Bois came close to calling
this phenomenon "the dictatorship of the proletariat," perhaps without taking proper account of the conditioning constantly exercised by
the industrial North and its army. Radical historians have thus been
able to pour a stream of easy criticism on a shortcoming of the book—
the split between Du Bois's semiadoption of the idea of "the dictatorship of the proletariat" during Reconstruction and the effective relations of power in those years.[41] At the same time they have been able
to point to the decisive role played by the state in enlarging the space
for maneuver created for the capitalist initiative of the Redeemers,
who were hemmed in by the defeat of the slaveholders, on the one
hand, and the victory of slaves, on the other. But there is virtually
never any reference to the reasons for this perspective, which should

be ascribed to the special pleading of Du Bois, the politician, rather than the alleged schematism of Du Bois, the historian: the search for a moment, not so much of command by the ex-slaves over all U.S. capitalist growth as of leadership for the proletariat of North America. This determination to retrace a U.S. class movement that went beyond the use the bourgeoisie could make of it for its own reconsolidation induced him to voice a positive judgment on the Union and its moves in the first phase of Reconstruction: not because he failed to notice the relations of force between an armed Union and a now disarmed proletariat but, rather, because he judged those relations of force to be favorable to the blacks' exertion of some power of attraction on the white proletariat.

Since for Du Bois slavery and Reconstruction were "the kernel and the meaning of the labor movement in the United States," the centrality of the black proletariat's experience was maintained throughout the work against reactionary and radical historiography. With respect to the latter, which has tended to reduce the struggle of the blacks to a battle for formal democracy, Du Bois's allegiance went to the political trajectories of the ex-slaves.[42] In the first place, if the slave was capable of dragging the South and the North into war, it was democracy in America that should be measured against the struggle of the slaves rather than vice versa. If the black masses had been *used,* if "most Americans used the Negro," the times when black people refused to be used were also times of crisis of democracy. Second, for Du Bois, unlike the radical historians, the forces the black rebellion in the United States had unleashed were to be measured internationally. The centrality of the experience of the black masses in the United States therefore had to be reiterated with reference to the passage from what Marx had called absolute exploitation to relative exploitation, not only at the level of the United States but also at the world level.[43]

At the close of the crucial chapter of the third part of *Black Reconstruction* (Chapters 14 through 17), "Counter-revolution of Property," Du Bois wrote: "And the rebuilding, whether it comes now or a century later, will and must go back to the basic principles of Reconstruction. . . ." To Du Bois that rebuilding did not seem to be on the agenda of the 1930s. "The South, after the war, presented the greatest opportunity for a real national labor movement which the nation ever saw or is likely to see for many decades."[44] His pessimism was excessive. As the developments in the black community would prove a few years later, the black movement in the late 1930s was ready to prevent capital from using the black people's demands for its ulterior aims, and when the differentiation from white politics came sharply—as during the March on Washington Movement—being a safe distance from the power structure did pay.

And it paid in terms of industrial wages, at long last. In a sense one can agree with Robert S. Starobin: ". . . even if slavery is theoretically and practically incompatible in the long run with full industrialisation, the point at which this inconsistency would manifest itself had, apparently, not yet been reached between 1770 and 1861."[45] Capital and slavery, capital and wagelessness, could coexist, if not indefinitely, certainly for a long time, if it were not for the resistance and attack of the slaves against their masters. It took the black people slavery, Civil War, Reconstruction, peonage, ghettoization, and urban revolts in this century to put the two words "capital" and "wages" irreversibly together, and to open a new stage in the struggle of the wageless against the state as collective capitalist.

NOTES

This article was translated by Julian Bees.

1. The book was first published by Harcourt, Brace and Co. (New York, 1935). Here I shall refer to the first Meridian reprinting by the World Publishing Co. (Cleveland, 1964).

2. W. E. B. Du Bois, *The Suppression of the African Slave-Trade to the United States of America 1638–1870* (New York, 1969), "Apologia" (1954), p. xxxi.

3. Du Bois's dissertation was published as the first volume in the Harvard Historical Studies in 1896.

4. As pointed out by William Gorman, "W. E. B. Du Bois and His Work," *Fourth International* (May–June 1950), pp. 80–86.

5. W. E. B. Du Bois, *The Philadelphia Negro: A Social Study* (Philadelphia, 1899).

6. Roger L. Ransom and Richard Sutch, *One Kind of Freedom: The Economic Consequences of Emancipation* (Cambridge and New York, 1977), p. 195.

7. Du Bois's attack against Booker T. Washington is in his essay "Of Mr. Booker T. Washington and Others," in *The Souls of Black Folks* (Chicago, 1903), pp. 43–59.

8. W. E. B. Du Bois, *John Brown* (Philadelphia, 1909).

9. W. E. B. Du Bois, "Reconstruction and Its Benefits," *American Historical Review* 15 (1910):78–99.

10. Sergio Bologna, "Class Composition and the Theory of the Party at the Origin of the Workers-Council Movement," *Telos* 14 (1972):21.

11. Paul Richards, "W. E. B. Du Bois and American Social History: The Evolution of a Marxist," *Radical America* 4 (1970):62.

12. W. E. B. Du Bois, "The African Roots of War," *Atlantic Monthly* 115 (1915):707–14,.

13. *Ibid.*

14. W. E. B. Du Bois, *The Negro* (New York, 1915).

15. Du Bois, *Suppression of the African Slave-Trade*, p. xxxii: "There are some approaches, some allusions, but no complete realization of the application of the philosophy of Karl Marx to my subject. That concept came much later, when I began intensive study of the facts of society, culminating in my *Black Reconstruction*."

16. Du Bois, *The Negro*, pp. 233, 245, 242.

17. *Ibid.*, p. 242.

18. Richards, "Du Bois," p. 53.

19. *The Crisis* (July 1921), p. 104.

20. Chicago Commission on Race Relations, *The Negro in Chicago* (Chicago, 1922), p. 363.

21. These figures are presented by H. M. Baron, "The Demand for Black Labor: Historical Notes on the Political Economy of Racism," *Radical America* 5 (1971):1–46.

22. On the exodus from the South to northern cities, see L. V. Kennedy, *The Negro Peasant Moves Cityward* (New York, 1930), esp. pp. 35–36.

23. The major articles that Du Bois devoted to Garvey and the UNIA are: "Marcus Garvey, Part I," *The Crisis* (Dec. 1920), pp. 58–60, and "Marcus Garvey, Part II," *The Crisis* (Jan. 1921), pp. 112–15.

24. W. E. B. Du Bois, "Back to Africa," *Century* 105 (1923):542.

25. The four pan-African congresses promoted by Du Bois were held in Paris (1919, 1921, 1923) and New York (1927).

26. See Baron, "Demand for Black Labor," p. 26.

27. See his essay "The Political Legacy of Reconstruction," in *The Burden of Southern History* (Baton Rouge, La., 1960).

28. The book by James S. Allen, *Reconstruction: The Battle for Democracy* (New York, 1937), opened the series as a semiofficial reply from the viewpoint of the Communist party and the popular fronts. Allen regarded the Civil War and Reconstruction as a bourgeois democratic revolution. Once this thesis was asserted, all the elements of the interpretation were made to fit, as Noel Ignatin notes in his excellent comparison of Du Bois's *Black Reconstruction* and Allen's *Reconstruction*, in "Study Guide to Reconstruction," *Urgent Tasks* 3 (1978):27–29. For a discussion of the state of the studies on Reconstruction at the end of the 1930s, see H. K. Deale, "On Rewriting Reconstruction History," *American Historical Review* 45 (1940):807–29. Deale recognized the novelty of viewpoint and seriousness of analysis in Du Bois's book, though he criticized the little attention paid by the author to "the middle classes" and, in general, to the elements of power transmitted without break from the antebellum slaveholders to the Redeemers of power in the late 1870s.

29. *The Black Jacobins: Toussaint L'Ouverture and the San Domingo Revolution* was first published in 1938.

30. Du Bois, *Black Reconstruction*, p. 15.

31. *Ibid.*, pp. 13, 17, 18, 40, 47.

32. *Ibid.*, pp. 84, 80.

33. *Ibid.*, pp. 80, 81.

34. *Ibid.*, p. 83.

35. The negative connotation often given by Du Bois to the concept of "use" was in contrast with the idea of utility as adopted by functionalism in

the same years, when functionalism was arising as the new ideology of "acquisitive man" against the social upheavals of the 1930s.

36. Du Bois, *Black Reconstruction,* pp. 63, 53, 378.

37. *Ibid.,* p. 84. Part of the organization of "free labor after the war" was—as Du Bois noted—"the frantic efforts, before and after emancipation, of Negroes hunting for their relatives throughout the United States" (p. 44). On family ties in the black community after emancipation, see Herbert G. Gutman, *The Black Family in Slavery and Freedom, 1750–1925* (New York, 1976), pt. II, pp. 360–475.

38. Du Bois, *Black Reconstruction,* pp. 352, 353, 381.

39. W. E. B. Du Bois, *The Souls of Black Folks* (New York, 1961), p. 40.

40. Du Bois, *Black Reconstruction,* pp. 165, 367, 274, 609.

41. See in particular the summary judgment passed by K. M. Stampp, *The Era of Reconstruction, 1865–1877* (New York, 1965), p. 21: "Although rich in empirical data, the book offers a Marxist interpretation of Southern Reconstruction as a proletarian movement, which is at best naive."

42. An excellent discussion of the political problems buried under Du Bois's concept of the dictatorship of the proletariat is Lauso Zagato, *Du Bois e la Black Reconstruction* (Rome, 1975), pp. 80–100.

43. The care with which Marx reconsidered the question of the workday for the first volume of *Capital* in about 1866 (letter to Engels dated 10 Nov. 1866) should also be linked to the experience of the American Civil War.

44. Du Bois, *Black Reconstruction,* pp. 635, 353.

45. Robert S. Starobin, *Industrial Slavery in the Old South* (New York, 1970), p. 189.

3

Workers' Self-Organization and Resistance in the 1877 Strikes

MARIANNE DEBOUZY

The increasing number of wildcat strikes in the late 1960s and early 1970s, the vitality of rank-and-file movements, and the recent miners' strike in Appalachia have brought to the foreground of the union scene the right of locals to strike and the problem of workers' self-organization. These events have given a new impetus to the debate on union democracy and workers' initiative. Simultaneously a theoretical discussion on working-class autonomy has been going on in some circles, especially in Italy and Germany. These recent debates and developments may help us to see in a new light a mass movement that took place a hundred years ago in the United States: the railroad strikes of 1877. These strikes constituted a remarkable example of experimentation in the field of workers' self-organization. Two aspects of this movement appear to be particularly significant in this respect: the strike committees and the use of violence.

Originally caused by a series of wage reductions and launched by discontented freightmen, brakemen, and firemen, the railroad strikes of July 1877 became a tremendous labor uprising that involved hundreds of thousands of workers throughout the country, not only in railroads but also in manufacturing establishments of all types.[1] Labor unions had disintegrated in the economic depression of 1873, national federations of labor were nonexistent, yet in July 1877 workers managed to paralyze transportation throughout eleven states.[2] They battled with the police and the troops sent to crush them and succeeded in taking over whole railroad networks. Not only did they blockade traffic, set cities ablaze, and trigger strikes that in several places (St. Louis, Chicago, Pittsburgh, etc.) assumed the proportions of a general strike, but locally they organized the strikes in an autonomous way. To the present-day historian these strikes appear to be a brief experiment in which rank-and-file workers developed their own initiative and proved their inventiveness in a multicentered movement. Besides, the strikers secured mass support that enabled them to carry on a kind of "guerrilla warfare"[3] against the railroad companies, the military, and the police. And yet the paradox of this movement was that in spite of its very radical practices, it not only failed to achieve an overall strategy of any sort but remained devoid of any revolutionary outlook. How can we account for the fact that it was able, at least for some time, to subvert the social order and at the same time be apparently so limited to bread-and-butter issues?

The complexity of working-class action during these strikes remains a subject of amazement for present-day observers. Generally speaking, there are two main aspects to this complexity. One is related to the diversity of conditions and circumstances. The extent of the uprising made for great disparities in terms of local situations, regions, and types of population. The concentration of urban masses and the presence of ethnic groups with their national, political, and cultural traditions give a specific character to the uprising in big cities like Chicago, Pittsburgh, and St. Louis, to take only a few. The situation was quite different in small places like Terre Haute, Springfield, or Zanesville. The nature of industrial activities, the intricate web of relationships that existed between different categories of workers, the power relations inside the city—all such elements had an impact on working-class action and made for diversity. The second aspect of this complexity is linked with the inventiveness of the workers and their ability to improvise and coordinate diversified actions. Here patterns of behavior rooted in community traditions may have been combined with newer attitudes shaped by industrial society. Yet through this complexity there emerge common features that point to some sort of unified action and organization and make it possible to attempt some form of generalization.

In this article I will deal with aspects of class-conscious solidarity and working-class inventiveness that characterized the strikers' self-organization throughout the country. The strikers used old and traditional forms of crowd action[4] and at the same time developed new tactics of industrial struggle.

Though the economic situation of the workers had been critical for some time, the railroad strike came as a complete surprise. The initiative came from individual railroaders or groups of railroaders who refused to work after a new wage reduction has been enforced. At Camden Junction, Maryland, on 16 July, a number of firemen quit their engines and persuaded brakemen to join them. Clashes occurred between the workers and the railroad officials, who called in the police. The arrest of three strikers caused engineers to join the strike, followed by other workers in the city. In Martinsburg, West Virginia, trainmen refused to start a train and the arrival of the militia provoked a gathering of people supporting the strikers: even the men of the militia were on the side of the railroaders.

The action first developed through a series of moves and counter-moves. Once men had gone on strike, the company officials would try to find another crew or other workers to do the work, or would call in the police and the militia. Whether these devices were successful or not, the strikers' immediate answer was an attempt to widen the movement. To achieve this aim they had to involve other workers in the strike, in order to extend it and make it known. And since there was no union to take the responsibility for this strike, groups of workers or individuals had to persuade or force workers to join them. The railroaders visited other depots and yards and spread the word. For instance, in Kansas City on 24 July, "The employes of all the roads centered here have struck. A large body of men formed into a procession and marched to each round-house receiving new accessions as they went."[5] In other cities the railroaders visited manufacturing establishments. Thus in Columbus, Ohio, on 23 July, "About noon, the railroad strikers, to the number of 300, went to the rolling mill and compelled the employes to suspend work. They also went to the Pipe Works, the Wassell Fire Clay Company Works, Patton's Pot Works, Adams' Planing Mill, Franklin Machine Works, Peters' Dash Works and other factories the employes of which joined the strikers as they went along. The entire mob, who had dinners with them, went to the Union Depot to the number of 200 and took dinner."[6] Or it might be the other way around: manufacturing workers induced railroaders to strike, as in Peoria, Illinois, on 26 July: "The railroad men are at work, but there is a great strike among the coopers and miners. 500 or 600 of them assembled last night in the lower part of the town and organized themselves into a mob and took possession of train and railroad shops."[7]

These gatherings formed a true mass movement, having as participants people of widely different backgrounds and feelings. The terms used by contemporary accounts point to the mixed nature of these crowds. Once the strikers congregated and walked from one depot or factory to another, they turned into a "mob." The latter word was used by the press to speak of strikers "in action" and was, of course, fraught with connotations of blame. It often referred to a crowd that included workers, young people, and a number of unemployed. Needless to say, if the strikers were black or included blacks, the word used was "rabble."[8]

In fact, it is very difficult to determine exactly the make-up of such crowds. Once the strike was launched as a dynamic process, it moved all kinds of people to action, in ways that were often obscure. The reactions of people showed a mixture of contradictory feelings and attitudes. On the one hand, even small shopkeepers, property owners, and people who belonged to the "better classes" might be drawn into the movement, because of their hostility to the railroad companies, or of their sympathy for strikers, or of the excitement created by rioting, though they might later express disapproval of violence and riotous action. For the workers, on the other hand, the motivation for striking might be strong, yet there were obstacles to be reckoned with. Striking in those days involved a high risk: retaliation from the employers as well as severe punishment by the state was the rule, as drastic laws concerning railroad property and transportation had been passed recently by several states (Pennsylvania, Ohio, New York, New Jersey, etc.). In many places workers joined the strike spontaneously, while in other cases strikers had to exert pressure on them. Thus in Louisville "at an early hour this morning it was announced that a party of armed men had been visiting the different factories demanding that the men at work should stop, or if they didn't the places at which they were at work would be fired."[9] This was not the only place where workers' protests were met with the slogan "shut up or burn up." In many places the workers were ready to strike but were afraid of reprisals and therefore welcomed any pressure that might be put on them so as to absolve them in the eyes of their employers. In St. Louis workers from different shops and factories came to the Workingmen's party's headquarters at Turner Hall one day to request that committees be sent around to "notify them to stop work and join the other workingmen, that they might have a reason for doing so."[10]

"Crowds," "mobs," "rabble": these words point to another specific form of action, the demonstration. Simultaneously with forming processions to mobilize people, strikers could call meetings. These early meetings, consisting in the first place almost exclusively of railroaders or of workers in one sector, or of all workers in one area, could also be open to the population. They took place in yards or depots, in factories or public places (state house, Tammany Hall). Generally speaking, their size and importance depended upon the degree of tension at the time, on the activism of workers, and so on. Circulation of information also played a most important part. It must be mentioned that when these meetings were called, saloons were closed by the strikers to avoid drunkenness or diversions that might prove harmful to the strike. In some cases meetings initiated the strike: in Kansas City an enormous meeting of railroad workers declared a general strike to begin at noon on the next day.[11] Support of strikers coming from different quarters was also expressed in such gatherings: on 21 July the first strike meeting of East St. Louis railroaders passed resolutions expressing support of the strike in the eastern states.[12] Similar sympathetic meetings took place in Cincinnati on 23 July, Milwaukee and Mckeesport, Pennsylvania, on 24 July, and Toledo on 26 July. In this way meetings shaped the course of action, launching the strike or delaying it so that workers might see how things developed. Not only did they often elect strike committees but they wrote up demands and drafted programs of action.

Local strike committees, which sprang into existence at most railway centers, became the active nuclei of the strike. These committees are worth examining more closely because of what they reveal about the workers' self-organization and the nature of their movement. From what information we have concerning their composition and structure as well as their decision-making processes, one may assert that they were composed of delegates from different departments of the railroads (as on the Louisville and Nashville[13]), of railroaders from different points along one line (on the B. and O. in the Baltimore area, or on the Ohio and Mississippi in the Vincennes area[14]), or of railroaders from different lines in one area: in St. Louis on 22 July representatives of a number of lines assembled at Traubel's Hall. They elected an executive committee, which represented various roads and branches of railroad labor. It seems that "this broad committee chose a smaller committee of perhaps not more than five members, which actually directed the strike in East St. Louis."[15] Local strike committees might also be made up of workers of "all trades and industries," as was the case in Steubenville, Ohio. In big cities these committees had to take into consideration the representation of nationalities. In Pittsburgh "the laborers, coal yard men, dumpers etc. who struck . . . at the American Iron Works of Jones and Laughlin, on the South Side, held a meeting to hear the report of a committee appointed in the afternoon to interview Mr. Jones of the firm. . . . The committee was made up of five persons, four members representing each a different nationality: English, Welsh, Polish and German."[16] To sum up, the composition of such committees varied according to the criteria of professional, local, and national representation, and so did their function.

What was the function of a strike committee? Its original purpose was to meet employers and present the workers' demands: rescinding wage reductions, obtaining wage increases, or reinstating the strikers when the strike was over. In the course of action, its main function was to organize the strike, mobilize workers, and develop a strategy. Thus in Albany, New York, on 28 July a meeting was held and "a committee appointed to induce the men in the locomotive shops to stop work."[17] On the Fort Wayne line "the strikers resolved to send

out a committee to 'whoop 'em up' all along the line and stiffen the
backbone of the Western strikers."[18] Elsewhere the strikers ordered
the committee to stop all passenger trains, except those carrying U.S.
mails. In Columbus, Ohio, "railroad men seemed to have brought
about a systematic manner of proceeding, and every important move
taken had its proper committee for the transaction of the business
which was to be brought before the meeting."[19] Quite often the strike
committee would protect railroad property, as in Terre Haute, Indiana, in Mattoon, Illinois, on the Indianapolis and St. Louis, in Detroit
on the Michigan Central,[20] and in Harrisburg on the Pennsylvania
Railroad.

One of the most important aims of strike committees was to coordinate action. In Martinsburg the railroaders' committee of four
traveled to other points to cooperate with other divisions with a view
to launching a general strike.[21] In East St. Louis "no one was empow-
ered to settle with any road except the Executive Committee" and it
"refused to negotiate separately with the various lines." "Order No.
2," posted on the walls of the depot, declared the strikers' rule to be
"All or none."[22] In Cleveland, another important railroad center, the
committee had similar preoccupations: "A committee, consisting of
some dozen members, was formed for the purpose of visiting the
shops of the Lake Shore and Michigan Southern Road from Buffalo
to Norwalk and learn the proposed movements of the workmen at
different points, in order that they might work together as one body."[23]

Since attempts to obtain concessions from railroad managers and
other employers often failed, strikers' committees were delegated by
workers to confer with state authorities. They appealed to the governors for arbitration. In Baltimore on 26 July "a delegation of strikers
waited on the governor and asked his intervention on behalf of a
settlement."[24] He declined. In Newark, Ohio, the committee visited
Governor Young. They "reported the men would not accede to the
reduction and asked him to go over to the yard and talk to the strikers
directly in person."[25] This reflects the workers' belief that, because he
was elected, the governor could act as an impartial umpire in a conflict between employers and wage-earners, instead of being the sworn
defender of the established order. Small wonder if these visits obtained no results, the governors claiming they could not arbitrate
labor conflicts.

The variety of roles played by the strike committees was quite surprising. For instance, such a committee was used as an instrument to
influence the stockholders of the company: in Baltimore on 26 July
"the strikers' meeting to-night appointed a committee to confer with
the merchants and induce them to persuade the Baltimore and Ohio

stockholders to agree to the strikers' demands."[26] More in keeping with its attributions was maintaining liaison with the press. The strikers were extremely distrustful of the press but knew it could play an important part in the conflict as it shaped public opinion. This may be the reason why the Cleveland Lake Shore strikers appointed a committee "formed for the purpose of calling upon the press of the city and requesting that the papers be truthful in their statements concerning them."[27] Strike committees also occasionally collected funds, as in East St. Louis.[28]

An initial question arises: how efficient were the strike committees? To judge from the workers' action in big cities and smaller places, the committees seem to have met their purpose at the practical level: that is, they managed to coordinate action and organize the strike. Action was coordinated at the city level, for instance, to neutralize potential strikebreakers. Thus in Newark, Ohio, the strikers "have pickets posted all round town and watch the houses of all engineers and know of the arrival of all new men."[29] Strategic points in big railway centers were rapidly occupied by congregating strikers coming from different lines.[30] The strikers made up their own crews: on 30 July in Columbus "the Indianapolis passenger train was seized by the rioters. The conductor was removed and the train taken possession of. They backed the train into the depot, tendered it to the officers of the road, dictating that it could proceed, if they, the rioters, were permitted to place their own conductor in charge."[31] Later they took complete control of the Cleveland, Columbus, and Indiana Central yards. They then appointed a yardmaster and a freight conductor to run the passenger train on schedule.[32] They organized so well that they took over whole networks, like the Fort Wayne and Pittsburgh.

This leads us to raise another point: what authority did the strike committees have in their relationship to employers and to strikers? No single answer is valid in all cases. Everything depended on the local situation, the personalities involved, the tension in a given place, the power relationships, and so on. They did exert real authority in certain cities and even whole regions. In East St. Louis on 23 July, E. L. Jones, superintendent of the Transit Company, "rode across the bridge after his men had joined in the strike to ask the strikers the privilege of employing 8 men to manage the switches on the bridge approach. He was told that the Executive Committee would see that the switches were properly attended. They would pick the men and not he, as to hiring them that could not be done—no man on the strike could receive any pay until such time as the corporations withdrew their unjust reductions of salaries. . . ."[33] The committees wrestled power from railroad managers and used it to carry out the decisions of the strikers. In other words, power did not remain vested in the committees' hands but was controlled by the rank-and-file.

As long as they existed, the strike committees seem to have functioned in a very democratic way. If a committee was sent on a mission, it would report on it and consult the workers before making a decision. Thus the master mechanic of the Missouri Pacific said in a conference with the East St. Louis committee: "I think we may take this delegation as representing all the men. If they accept the terms they and others will." A machinist, who was one of the spokesmen of the delegation, replied: "We have not been authorized to accept any terms. All we have been deputed to is to get your answer and take it to a meeting of the men to be held this evening. . . ."[34] Meetings were frequent, and one can assume that the collective will could express itself. In Cleveland the strikers had two or three meetings a day, and from newspaper reports we can see that, in general, meetings were lively, discussions concerning tactics and strategy sometimes very heated. The action of the committees was submitted to rank-and-file criticism. In Terre Haute, Indiana, on 26 July the Indianapolis committee decided to let a passenger train run on the Indianapolis and St. Louis Railroad and on the Vandalia; immediately afterward that decision was discussed at length in a railroaders' meeting.[35]

Conflicts did occur, and the committees sometimes encountered no little trouble in persuading workers to respect their decisions. An incident in East St. Louis on 24 July is quite revealing in this respect. At the relay house, after a short halt of the Vandalia passenger train, a striker pulled the coupling pin behind the mail car and called to the conductor: "Go on with your U.S. mail. We have got nothing against the Government." "This act and declaration were greeted with loud shouts by the 500 strikers." The conductor then appealed to the honor of the railroaders, asking them to permit him to proceed, because he had been promised that strikers would not interfere with passenger travel. "The appeal of the conductor created a discussion in the ranks of the strikers, many of them contending that the train should be allowed to pass and others declaring that it should not. Nearly an hour was spent in wrangling among the men, and finally the Committee in charge decided to let the train go."[36]

At times committees had to deal with unexpected moves or situations. Thus we read that ". . . a Committee of 22 Wabash trainmen returned from Toledo, where they had been in conference with General Manager Hopkins. A meeting of the Wabash employes was at once called and the Committee stated the results of their conference. They reported a very satisfactory interview with Mr Hopkins, who had agreed to redress the real grievances and to advance their pay when the business of the company would admit. The meeting was very stormy, one element desiring to go to extremes. Better counsels finally prevailed."[37] Again we learn that on 30 July the Pittsburgh and Fort Wayne strikers refused to obey the order of the strikers' committee to return to work at once.[38]

Such conflicts over tactics occurred in a number of places but, generally speaking, committees seem to have played the role the workers expected of them. Their autonomous, often informal character was best adapted to the demands of a shifting situation. They appeared to be more adequate than a highly centralized organization like the Brotherhood of Locomotive Engineers, whose constitution was denounced by some strikers on the Ohio and Mississippi in Vincennes for "not permitting a strike without orders from Grand Chief Arthur."[39] It is interesting to note that some members of the brotherhood claimed their autonomy. The Kentucky Central engineers took the trouble to write to the editor of the *Cincinnati Enquirer:* "We notice in *The Commercial* of yesterday a statement to the effect there would be no trouble on the Kentucky Central, unless a portion of the employes who belong to a labor organization should receive orders from Cleveland to strike. The employes referred to are engineers. The headquarters of the Engineers' Brotherhood are at Cleveland, Ohio. We consider ourselves free men, possessed of enough common sense to decide for ourselves without advice from Cleveland or points nearer home."[40] On the whole, the strike was neither launched nor supported by any pre-existing organization, but a number of individuals who were or had been members of such organizations as the Knights of Labor, the Trainmen's Union, and the Workingmen's party played a part in strike committees and helped shape local strategy, especially in big cities.

At this juncture it is necessary to observe that although they sometimes worked hand in hand, these committees did not constitute a national organization in any proper sense and the strike never had a centralized leadership. Yet this free and even loose association of autonomous committees appears to have been remarkably effective and to have enabled strikers to react to complex isues with rapidity.

Of course, more research is needed to fully assess the role of strike committees, but already some observations can be made. It was the workers themselves and not the employers who defined the competency of these representative organizations. In the course of events the committees often had to depart from their original purpose (i.e. meeting employers to present the workers' demands), and they broadened their scope because of the specific and unexpected difficulties they met with or the new steps that might be taken. Enforcing citywide strikes, running trains, taking over depots, roundhouses, and yards, even managing whole networks implied a high level of collective action and decision making. As a result of the dynamic process of the strike, the committees modified their goals and diversified their activities. Thus they may have been the embryo of a conception of working-class organization that took shape gradually. These committees, which first had been loosely structured, then became tools of experimentation and allowed for explicit discussion of gains and discoveries in terms of strategy and tactics.

In their struggle the strikers had to contend with powerful enemies: the railroad companies, having all the money and the support of state as well as federal authorities, used their power to crush the growing organization of strikers. In the beginning they had no doubt that this would be quickly done. Having persuaded the governor of Pennsylvania to send two regiments of the state militia from Philadelphia to Pittsburgh, Thomas Scott, president of the Pennsylvania Railroad, declared: "*My* troops will see that the trains pass."[41] Soon, however, the authorities and railroad officials found out that the strikers were not only striking but waging a real war, indeed a "civil war,"[42] and a violent one.

The role of violence in the 1877 railroad strikes is historically significant, for violence always introduces a qualitative change in struggles. It alters their course and makes for unforeseen consequences. In 1877, violence was a source of innovation, of inventiveness among the strikers, and this creative outburst was rich in "discoveries" at the level of class consciousness.

The workers' use of violence is a complex issue. First, the word "violence" is ambiguous: it refers both to the violence the workers were victims of and the violence they consciously used. The two, of course, were often closely linked. In the 1877 strikes the most violent eruptions, in Baltimore, Pittsburgh, Reading, and Chicago, occurred after the militia had shot at the crowd. Though tempting, the distinction between defensive and offensive violence is quite artificial, for in the dynamic process of the conflict one form of violence turned into the other and vice versa. Second, the attitude of workers toward violence appeared to be quite ambiguous, even contradictory. This may be partly due to the way in which violence was reported by the press. Though masses of people were involved in riotous action, the press always tended to make a distinction between "rioters" and "strikers." It is true that the strikers themselves were careful to disavow violence publicly, to "deprecate the spirit of vandalism in any shape."[43] They sometimes even refused the help of miners and canal boatmen, who seemed to have been considered particularly rebellious.[44] They frequently offered to protect railroad property and in some cases declared themselves "willing to assist in putting down the mob."[45] Yet it is totally unrealistic to claim that strikers did not participate in "riots" and "disorders." Innumerable observations and testimonies and a careful reading of newspapers all show that strikers were part of "mobs" that attacked the military and the police.

In addition, they were obviously involved in sabotage and other destructive activities. In order to prevent railroad companies from breaking the strike and bringing in troops to crush strikers, railroaders practiced sabotage on a vast scale. There was something deeply scandalous, spectacular, and subversive about sabotaging the railways, which, at the time, were the quickest and most modern means of conveyance. This was also a blow aimed at the railroad kings, whose power was supposed to be greater than that of the president of the United States. Sabotage did much to create an atmosphere of civil war. The railroaders had no theory of sabotage but had engaged in the practice during the 1873–74 strikes.[46] It required collective initiative and organization. The extent to which strike committees were involved in such activities is, indeed, a question.

Sabotage took different forms: twisting or tearing up the tracks; locking or "misplacing" switches; obstructing the track by piling up coal, bricks, or iron rails; disabling engines; setting fire to trains, depots, yards, etc. Trains carrying troops frequently met with accidents. Thus when the last detachment of the 23d Regiment (New York), which had left Brooklyn for Elmira on 23 July, reached Corning, "it was found that a baggage car had been placed across the track, several engines disabled and rails torn, twisted and otherwise injured."[47] The lives of troops were threatened: on 27 July a "turned" switch at Cambria City wrecked a train of regulars. The next day four trains traveling over the Pennsylvania Railroad arrived from the East with state troops. "As a section of the train passed the depot of Johnstown, Pennsylvania, it was attacked by a great mob, armed with stones and pieces of metal, which were thrown at the windows of the car with telling effect. . . . Further on a switch had been misplaced and a car heavily laden with fire bricks placed on the switch for the fast approaching train." The train crashed and a number of soldiers were injured.[48]

To achieve their ends, strikers resorted to all sorts of means. On the Dunkirk Division of the New York Central, the strikers had placed a long oil train at the summit of a steep grade, and "gave notice that upon the attempt to send a passenger or freight train over this division they would fire the oil and start the train."[49] At a crossing near Hornellsville the track was covered with soft soap. The strikers frequently disabled engines, destroyed the hose pipes of the locomotives, or removed the bolts and pins from the couplings.[50] In Chicago and Cleveland water tanks were either burned or emptied and the water shut off so as to make it impossible to run the engines.[51] On 22 July the Lebanon Valley railroad bridge over the Schuylkill, at Reading, was set afire so as to keep troops from passing on the 23d. This type of operation was not simply done "on the inspiration of the moment." It was repeated if necessary: "A bridge was burnt at Spring Brook, Penn., promptly replaced and within three days it was again destroyed."[52] Near Cleveland, when the strike was supposedly over, "the Delaware, Lackawanna and Bloomsburg people only got their freights under guard. The track was obstructed and the wires cut nightly."[53]

Sabotage enabled strikers to achieve two main goals: preventing the companies from running trains and preventing troops from reaching their destination. They caused a real "blockade" that made Pittsburgh and its environs inaccessible to troops for some time. State troops were constantly stopped and obliged to march through the countryside. Marching, they ran the risk of being captured or falling into ambushes set by strikers. Besides, they met with such hostility from the population that they found neither food nor shelter.[54]

Sabotaging involved great risks and, as mentioned earlier, was very severely punished by recently passed state laws. The saboteurs took care not to be recognized. Thus the men who practiced sabotage in the Reading area had their faces blackened with coal dust to prevent recognition.[55] Near St. John's Run, Maryland, 25 masked canal boatmen, on strike, boarded a boat "with a cargo of coal loaded at 90 cents a ton—10 cents less than the rate demanded by the strikers,"[56] and set it on fire. Similar raids of disguised men took place in Pittsburgh and on the Lehigh Valley railroad line.[57] Secrecy was part of the strikers' "guerrilla warfare," as we can see from frequent secret meetings and the fact that strikers would hide out, and even have camps in the woods.[58] Such covert action was possible because the people were on their side, especially in the mining regions. There, as well as on the Baltimore and Ohio line,[59] they practiced "bushwhacking," i.e. the shooting of trainmen on passing trains from bushes. They sometimes did this with great cleverness: in the Scranton area on 8 August "the engineer on the Bloomsburg train saw, when about 2 miles from the city, what he supposed to be a woman lying across the track. He stopped and just as he did so a bullet went whistling through his hat, and he found the obstruction was merely a dummy, placed there to stop the train and give the assassin a chance for the deadly shot."[60]

This element of lawlessness pervaded the 1877 strikes. The strikers defied law and authority and refused to obey sheriffs' orders and the police. In a great many cities they resisted arrest, and their resistance received mass support.[61] Arrests were usually made after desperate struggles, which often turned into real fights or riots and were followed by attempts at rescue. The strikers' resistance was not simply a collection of individual rebellions. It resulted from the dynamic process of the strike, which drew whole groups into the struggle. One action became an inspiration to others: the strike was instrumental in the development of a unifying sense of working-class power and unity.

Regarding the rise of working-class consciousness under the specific circumstances of the 1877 strikes, one cannot fail to notice that the forms of contemporary technology greatly contributed to its quick growth. Information traveled fast and clear along railroads and telegraph wires. One important feature of the strikers' organization was their ability to travel about. Strikers and strike committees were constantly on the move. For example, strikers from Indianapolis were reported in Seymour spreading the strike, some from Harrisburg in Chicago, others from Martinsburg participating in a meeting at Columbus. When necessary they took possession of engines to transport committees and messages or to spy on troops. Whenever possible they took over the control of telegraph lines and had their own secret code. Rapid broadcasting of information helped to develop a consciousness of the identity of workers' claims, and thus of a common situation of exploitation. The paradox was that a quick unification of the demands of one profession resulted in an awareness that exploitation occurred in others. This the *Chicago Tribune* discovered with dismay when chambermaids and scrubgirls of several hotels and taverns in Fort Wayne quit work and demanded a 50-cent weekly wage increase: "before the strike of the brakemen, switchmen and wipers at Fort Wayne, it had not occurred to these young ladies that they were not receiving all the compensation they were earning."[62] Simultaneously, gradual awareness of the fact that the workers were capable of running the operations of a network or a business—in other words, of taking the power of the employers in their hands—was a major step in the rise of class consciousness. This no doubt appeared as the fundamental subversiveness of the 1877 strikes to the bourgeoisie, who could not stand "this style of men, without a dollar, giving permission to capitalists to use their own property under certain conditions."[63]

Yet it is also clear that though workers seized railways, depots, and yards and set up some sort of "civil war" organization, they had no revolutionary aims. However revolutionary their acts might look, revolution was not on the agenda. The fact that, as mentioned earlier, in many places strikers protected railroad property and, when they did

attack, carefully selected the targets of destruction, is indeed quite
remarkable. This may be taken as a sign of the will to avoid alienating
public opinion and to preserve the machinery that enabled them to
earn a living. It may also tell us something about the workers' respect
for the amount of work that had gone into building the railroads. But
the protection offered by workers to railroad companies and the taking over of networks may also point to their conception of the way in
which property should be used.[64] In this perspective the revolt of the
workers can be seen as an attempt at "setting limits to what the new
capitalists could do," to use Gutman's phrase. If we take into account
the fact that the strikers received mass support, the uprising may be
seen as that of the community standing against the predatory system
that was being set up, symbolized by the arrogance of railroad mag-
nates ready to enslave workers and reduce them to starvation. Thus
the workers were out to restore their former positions as wage-earners and to assert their rights as productive workers. But they were
also out to defend certain values.[65] To the superintendent of the
Transit Company, a man employed on the Wabash Road declared:
"This is a fight where we are united and we mean to stay united and
work together until the poorest and humblest of us gets his rights.
You will understand me when I tell you that the Wabash men who are
on this strike are the best paid railroad men who run into St. Louis.
We are striking not for a few cents, but for principles, and the spirit
of liberty, equality and fraternity so actuates us, that we will stay on
the strike till the last one of our brothers on the other roads receive
their rightful pay."[66] Workers were fighting not only for survival but
for the recognition of their dignity and a certain idea of social justice.
Through struggles, their class-conscious awareness of their common
situation developed, and the strike became an original experiment in
social solidarity. So it was more than a strike after all: an economic
struggle on bread-and-butter issues turned into a generalized conflict
between employers and employees, a labor uprising involving whole
communities, and gave rise to mass resistance against the predatory
order being set up by the new capitalists. Inevitably this conflict revealed a collusion between the ruling class of employers and the politicians, as it revealed the community of claims of the different sections
of the working class as well as the necessity of original modes of
organization corresponding to the nature of the movement.

   In the 1877 strikes the forms of resistance and organization displayed a unique combination of inventive behavior, subversive practices, and orderly spontaneity. Working-class resourcefulness and
capacities for self-organization at the rank-and-file level gave peculiar
strength to the workers' determination to oppose by all means the

domination of the new "aristocrats."[67] The forms of resistance and solidarity that developed during the conflict clearly showed that much more was at stake than purely economic gains. That is why the strikers' collective strength appeared so threatening. Thus everything was done to stifle the explosive creativity of the masses and bury the rebellious spirit of the working-class struggle not only in short-sighted reformism and political repression but also in historical oblivion. Labor historians waited nearly a century[68] before attempting to study the 1877 uprising and probe its significance as one of the most creative outbursts in the history of the American working class.

NOTES

1. In another article, "Grève et violence de classe aux Etats-Unis en 1877," *Le mouvement social* 102 (1978):41–66, I focus on aspects of violence during the strike in Pittsburgh and the state of Pennsylvania, and I raise the problem of the use of journalistic sources. It should be emphasized again that though the press provides us with a wealth of information, this information has to be sorted out and criticized because of the ideological bias inherent in each report.

2. The events are reported at length in Robert Bruce, *1877: Year of Violence* (1959; reprint ed., Chicago, 1969), and Philip S. Foner, *The Great Labor Uprising of 1877* (New York, 1977). Both books contain lengthy bibliographies.

3. The expression was used at the time. See *Chicago Tribune,* 27 July (all citations of newspapers are for the year 1877).

4. See George Rudé, *The Crowd in History: A Study of Popular Disturbances in France and England, 1730–1848* (New York, 1964).

5. *Cincinnati Enquirer,* 25 July.

6. *Ibid.,* 24 July.

7. *Ibid.,* 27 July.

8. A study should be made of the words used by the press to describe strikers, rioters, or the unemployed. These words enabled journalists to create artificial distinctions between strikers and rioters, and the indiscriminant use of such words as "thieves," "tramps," "riff-raff," "roughs," etc. obscured the real make-up of crowds.

9. *Louisville Commercial,* 26 July.

10. David Burbank, *Reign of the Rabble* (New York, 1966), p. 43.

11. *New York Sun,* 25 July.

12. *St. Louis Globe Democrat,* 22 July.

13. *Louisville Commercial,* 24 July.

14. *Cincinnati Enquirer,* 25 July; *Baltimore Sun,* 19 July.

15. Burbank, *Reign of the Rabble,* pp. 15–16.

16. *Pittsburgh Post,* 25 July.

17. *Cincinnati Enquirer,* 28 July.

18. *Ibid.,* 18 July.

19. *Daily Ohio State Journal,* 21 July.

20. *Chicago Tribune,* 26 July; *Detroit Evening News,* 25 July.

21. *Baltimore Sun,* 19, 20 July.

22. *St. Louis Globe Democrat,* 25 July.

23. *Cleveland Plain Dealer,* 25 July.

24. *Cincinnati Enquirer,* 27 July.

25. *Ibid.,* 22 July.

26. *Ibid.,* 27 July.

27. *Cleveland Plain Dealer,* 25 July.

28. *St. Louis Globe Democrat,* 23, 25 July.

29. *Cincinnati Enquirer,* 23 July.

30. *Chicago Times,* 26 July.

31. *Cincinnati Enquirer,* 31 July.

32. *Daily Ohio State Journal,* 31 July.

33. *St. Louis Globe Democrat,* 24 July.

34. *Ibid.*

35. *Chicago Tribune,* 27 July.

36. *Cincinnati Enquirer,* 25 July.

37. *Ibid.*

38. *Ibid.,* 31 July.

39. *St. Louis Globe Democrat,* 23 July.

40. *Cincinnati Enquirer,* 25 July.

41. Quoted in *ibid.,* 23 July (italics mine).

42. The expression was used by the contemporary press. See *Chicago Tribune,* 23 July; *Detroit Evening News,* 21, 23 July.

43. Declaration of Toledo strikers, *Daily Ohio State Journal,* 26 July.

44. *Ibid.,* 25 July; *Cincinnati Enquirer,* 22 July.

45. *Daily Ohio State Journal,* 24 July.

46. See Herbert G. Gutman, "Troubles on the Railroads in 1873–1874," in his *Work, Culture and Society in Industrializing America* (New York, 1976).

47. *Frank Leslie's,* 11 Aug. 1877, p. 386.

48. *Cincinnati Enquirer,* 29 July.

49. Edward W. Martin (J. McCabe, pseudonym), *History of the Great Riots* (Philadelphia, 1877), pp. 373–74.

50. *Cincinnati Enquirer,* 19 July.

51. *Ibid.,* 25, 28 July, 1 Aug.

52. J. A. Dacus, *Annals of the Great Strikes in the United States* (Chicago, 1877), p. 147.

53. *Cleveland Plain Dealer,* 4 Aug.

54. See George B. Stichter, "The Schuylkill County Soldiery in the Industrial Disturbances in 1877, or the Railroad Riot War," *Publications of the Historical Society of Schuylkill County,* Pa. 1 (1905):198–99, 201, 206.

55. *Reading Dispatch,* quoted in *Pittsburgh Evening Chronicle,* 26 July.

56. *Philadelphia Public Ledger,* 31 July.

57. *New York Sun,* 30 July; Martin, *Great Riots,* p. 194.

58. In the Scranton area and near Hornellsville; see Martin, *Great Riots,* pp. 231–32.

59. *Pittsburgh Post,* 2 Aug.

60. Samuel Logan, *A City's Danger and Defense, or Issues and Results of the Strikes of 1877* (Scranton, Pa., 1887), pp. 155–56.

61. For Pittsburgh, Chicago, and Cumberland, Md., see *Chicago Times,* 22 July; for Peoria, Ill., *Cincinnati Enquirer,* 28 July; for Fort Wayne, Ind., *ibid.,* 29 July.

62. *Chicago Tribune,* 27 July.

63. Letter to the *Daily Ohio State Journal,* 31 July.

64. This idea was suggested by Herbert Gutman in the discussion that followed the presentation of an earlier version of this paper at the Bremen Conference on American Labor History in Nov. 1978.

65. See Gutman, "Troubles," pp. 49–53.

66. *St. Louis Globe Democrat,* 24 July.

67. See the speech of a crowd leader in Chicago quoted in *Chicago Tribune,* 26 July.

68. Robert Bruce's *1877: Year of Violence,* the first serious academic book devoted to the uprising, was published in 1959 and stirred little interest at the time.

4

"Reefs of Roast Beef": The American Worker's Standard of Living in Comparative Perspective

PETER R. SHERGOLD

"On the reefs of roast beef and apple pie socialistic utopias of every sort are sent to their doom."

Werner Sombart, 1906

Preparing to celebrate the nation's bicentennial in 1976, and desirous of providing background information on a sector of American life that "visitors are invariably interested in observing," the U.S. Information Service sent a reporter to interview Thomas C. Cochran, elder doyen of American business history. It was not long before questions turned to the condition of the manual workers in the era in which American business developed its modern characteristics:

> Q: We have spoken about the new industries and the new technologies, but what about the new people—the immigrants who came to the United States in waves in the late 1800's and early 1900's, the "huddled masses" which the Statue of Liberty at the entrance of New York's Harbor welcomed?

> A: The United States had, of course, a scarcity of labor. Consequently, workers were paid better in the United States than elsewhere. . . .[1]

The reasons for the question, and implications of the answer, are clear. Analysis of industrial productivity, capital investment, technological prowess, and entrepreneurial ability is all very well, but for many the success of American capitalism, and the degree to which economic growth has created a greater society, may best be assessed in terms of the material benefits it has provided for its working population: the extent to which growth has increased per capita income

and resulted in a more equitable distribution of that income throughout society.

Assessment of labor's benefits—or costs—from the industrial revolution and/or the development of capitalism has most frequently depended upon temporal comparison. In contrast, this paper employs
a spatial yardstick in order, it is hoped, to "add a new dimension to
the flat perspective which the purely national view of living standard
reveals."[2] The central question posed in this paper is whether Cochran's claim that American labor enjoyed pre-eminent material conditions—an assertion that has by now attained the stature of a
historiographical truism—survives empirical investigation. More specifically, it is asked, did early twentieth-century Americans have a
standard of living superior to their British counterparts?

This question is not merely of intrinsic interest. Analysis of comparative living standards is crucial to many areas of historical research. Studies of migratory causation, and of the respective force of
push-pull factors in stimulating the vast movement of European peoples in the nineteenth and early twentieth centuries, inevitably incorporate assumptions as to the relative well-being of workers on both
sides of the Atlantic.[3] However, it should not be thought that even
the most accurate examination of comparable living standards can
provide easy historical answers. Clearly one might expect material
lifestyle in the industrial towns of Britain to have been superior to
that experienced in rural areas of southern Ireland or the Italian
Mezzogiorno from which so many American workers were recruited.
Even within a narrower context the leap from quantitative foundation
to qualitative conclusion must be undertaken with extreme caution.
Perhaps English migrants received inadequate information about Atlantic opportunities; perhaps such factors as superior social mobility
were more important than wage rates in stimulating migration. It
should be borne in mind, for example, that the migratory British
laborer possessed, within the ethnically heterogeneous work force of
early twentieth-century America, an immediate skill for which he could
expect financial reward: namely, the ability to communicate in English. Nevertheless, statistical interpretation may provide some insight
into the declining attractiveness of the United States to English migrants, and some explanation of why, by 1900, it was increasingly
workers with skills who found the lure of America most appealing.
There can be no doubt that similar comparative studies of other areas
would enhance the historian's understanding of the migration
experience.

Analysis of comparative real wages is also of significance in the
debate about the advance of American technology. Explanation of

American technological innovation has frequently been based upon relative factor prices. Habakkuk has suggested that nineteenth-century America, because of its abundance of land, and because of the scarcity and inelasticity of its labor supply, received a powerful stimulus to technological inventiveness. The advent of labor-saving machinery was hastened, capital intensity increased, and productivity mightily advanced. The theoretical debate on relative factor combinations, on the comparative prices of British and American manufacturing inputs, has become increasingly confused. It is singularly unfortunate that, by contrast, the presentation of more empirical evidence on relative rewards to labor has been largely neglected.[4]

More significant, in the present context, is the manner in which labor historians have incorporated assumptions about comparative living standards into their analysis. Philip Taft, John Laslett, and Howard Quint, among others, have suggested that because the United States was a high-wage economy, and because its workers enjoyed superior material welfare, American unionism developed its peculiar nature: conservative, pure-and-simple, pragmatic, business-oriented, apolitical, and voluntaristic.[5] Yet few statistical data have been presented to establish that America was, by contemporary standards, a high-wage economy in the period in which the AFL came to possess its allegedly distinctive philosophy.

The aim of this essay is to provide a quantitative—if tentative—estimate of comparative living standards, and to construct a preliminary statistical base from which to assess the degree to which the American worker received superior material benefits vis-à-vis his counterpart in Britain. The definition of standard of living employed will be the real *hourly* wages paid to adult male manual workers in the mid-1900s. To achieve this measure, money wages have to be calculated; retail prices—for food products, rent, fuel, lighting, furniture, and clothing—estimated; expenditure schedules compiled; and a cost of living index constructed by weighting prices in accordance with family expenditure patterns. Money wages then need to be assessed in terms of the comparative cost of living, and real wages thereby derived: that is, real wages measured in terms of a common composite unit of consumables, the "basket of goods," bought in Britain and the United States. At the theoretical level this is a relatively straightforward cliometric exercise. At the practical level it rapidly reveals itself to be a complex historical problem, fraught with statistical complications and bedeviled with the need for qualificatory remarks.[6]

The standard of living here defined, an estimate of material welfare derived from an hour's employment, may well appear too narrow. Its major strength is its relative lack of ambiguity. In contrast, the calculation of weekly wage rates, or of family income, raises difficult theoretical issues.[7] At the same time the geographical limitations of the study—essentially a tale of two cities—may appear too restrictive. The justification is that living standards can only be satisfactorily compared at a far greater level of disaggregation than is normal. It is clearly ludicrous, a mere statistical deception, to talk of the wage paid to "American" or "British" workers. Wages varied according to the level of skill required of the manual employee, according to the region of the country in which he worked, and perhaps according to his ethnic origin. In order to minimize the problems presented by aggregated data, wages will be presented for a variety of comparable occupations, and information will be derived from two specific areas of comparable economic and demographic structure, namely Pittsburgh in the United States and Birmingham in England.[8]

Table 1 presents money wages for 21 occupations in Pittsburgh and Birmingham, including data from workers in the building, engineering, steel, printing, and baking industries and from municipal employment.[9] In each instance the American rate was substantially greater than that for the equivalent occupation in Britain, but the degree of monetary superiority varied. Pittsburgh's construction workers were far better off, compared with their counterparts in Birmingham, than were bakery workers. More significant was the fact that it was the skilled manual worker who gained most comparative advantage: in every case the Birmingham unskilled employee received a larger percentage of the wage of his skilled colleague than was the case in Pittsburgh. Although the mean hourly rate of the specified occupations in Birmingham was only 43.8% of the mean rate in Pittsburgh, there was considerable occupational deviation from the mean. In general, lower-paid employees in Birmingham were in a less disadvantaged position vis-à-vis their Pittsburgh counterparts than were higher-paid employees.

This fact is presented even more forcibly in Figure 1, where the rates paid to Birmingham occupations are plotted as percentages of the rates paid to the same jobs in Pittsburgh. If the wage spectrum had been identical in the British and American cities, the derived percentages would have remained constant no matter whether the comparison were made between bricklayers or engineering laborers. Such was not the case, yet it is apparent that the statistical distribution about the mean was not random. There was a trend: the higher the Pittsburgh wage, the lower was the Birmingham wage in percentage comparison. The Birmingham bricklayer (observation s) received only 30.6% of the rate of his Pittsburgh counterpart; in contrast, the en-

Table 1. *Hourly Wage Rates for 21 Occupations in Pittsburgh and Birmingham,*
1905–7.

	Hourly Wage Rate in Cents		
Occupation	Pittsburgh	Birmingham	Birmingham ÷ Pittsburgh
(A) Steel mill laborer	15.5	9.9[a]	0.635[a]
(a) Engineering laborer	15.8	9.2	0.582
(c) Baker, third-hand	18.5	10.3	0.557
(d) Baker, second-hand	21.5	11.5	0.535
(B) Public laborer	21.9	11.7[a]	0.534[a]
(h) Baker, first-hand	27.7	13.7	0.495
(b) Foundry blacksmith	29.0	16.5	0.569
(k) Building laborer	29.9	13.7	0.458
(i) Bookbinder	30.6	15.0	0.490
(e) Machinist	31.6	16.5	0.522
(g) Compositor, book and job	32.7	16.2	0.495
(f) Boiler maker	33.4	17.5	0.524
(j) Pattern maker	36.3	17.5	0.482
(l) Machine woodworker	39.2	17.3	0.441
(n) Painter	42.6	17.3	0.406
(m) Carpenter	43.8	19.3	0.441
(p) Plumber	50.0	19.3	0.386
(q) Stonemason	55.0	20.3	0.369
(r) Plasterer	56.3	20.3	0.361
(o) Compositor, newspaper	58.6	22.8	0.389
(s) Bricklayer	63.1	19.3	0.306

[a]Sheffield wage.

gineering laborer (observation a) obtained 58.2% of the hourly payment earned by a worker engaged in similar work in "Iron City." In
between these two extremes a fairly obvious pattern emerges, a negative relationship, with the Birmingham wage ratio falling as the Pittsburgh wage rose.

In short, in the early twentieth-century all Pittsburgh workers received money wage rates substantially superior to those paid in Birmingham, but the higher the financial status of the American manual
worker (a status that reflected, at least to some extent, superior skill)
the greater was his comparative wage advantage. Within the American city wage differentials were, in all industries, wider than in Britain, and the overall wage range substantially more extended.

Thus statistical evidence suggests that there was a far more affluent

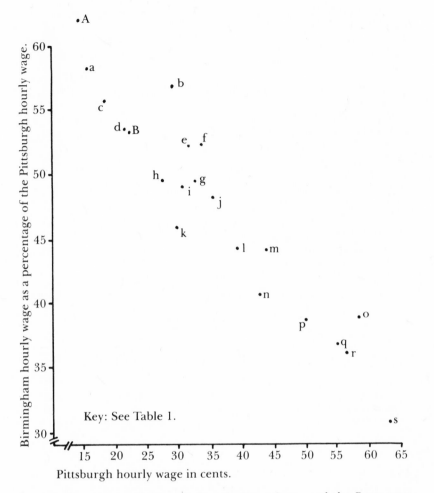

Figure 1. Twenty-one Pittsburgh Hourly Wage Rates and the Percentage of Those Rates Earned by Equivalent Occupations in Birmingham, 1905–7.

"aristocracy of labor" in the United States. In contrast, evidence from the first half of the nineteenth century has generally indicated the opposite. Victor Clark's study of American manufacturing estimated that wage differences between that country and Britain were much greater in *unskilled* occupations.[10] And much of Habakkuk's account of British and American technology in the nineteenth century was postulated upon the premise that "an increased demand for labor

raised the wages of skilled labor *less* than the wages of unskilled labor
. . . (and) that the premium on artisan skills was generally lower in
America than in England."[11]

Explanation of this apparent reversal in the latter third of the nineteenth century must be sought in the mass entry of immigrants into
the United States. An increasing percentage of America's work force
consisted of "new" immigrants, functionally illiterate, generally unable to speak English, and frequently nonacculturated to industrial
life. In consequence there may have been a deterioration in the degree of elasticity of substitution between the skilled and unskilled
sections of the American labor force. Certainly the overall supply of
labor was increased proportionately faster than the supply of skilled
labor late in the century, and most contemporaries agreed that the
wider range of wages in Pittsburgh by 1900 reflected the city's more
elastic supply of unskilled, migrant labor.

The comparatively low level of wages among the city's unskilled
workers reflected not only the relative abundance of such labor but
also a competition between such employees greater than in the more
homogenous and stable structure of Birmingham. The psychology of
immigrant laborers, already mobile in the spatial sense, seems to have
been different from that of relatively settled British workers. Uprooted from what was quite probably a rural environment, and primarily in America for economic gain, Pittsburgh's East European and
Italian workers were more willing to undertake whatever jobs happened to be available, and more ready to change occupations in response to the demand situation: they represented, in John Commons's
phrase, "a restless, movable, competitive rank-and-file."[12]

The contrast apparent in the Birmingham labor force is exceptional. The city's trades did not experience entirely concurrent seasonal depression, and observers were convinced that "in a properly
organized labor market it was probable that most of (the temporarily
unemployed) would have worked for several employers each year,
instead of working for only one master during his busiest season."[13]
Such did not occur, however, for the Birmingham worker seems to
have been far more willing to "play" until employment in his particular field returned.

The Pittsburgh laborer, in short, appears to have been a far less
specialized factor of production than he was in Birmingham, and the
greater competitive activity within the Pittsburgh work force may well
have been partially responsible for the comparatively low wages earned
by the city's unskilled employees.

Analysis of occupational wage dispersion about the mean thus indicates not only that the differential among skill levels in Pittsburgh

was substantially greater than in Birmingham but also that the overall wage spectrum was much wider in the American city. The common assertion (or implicit assumption) of historians that the American worker experienced a standard of living superior to his counterpart in England must therefore be considerably qualified. This is especially true in the light of contemporary observation that the manual labor force of the United States contained an abnormally large proportion of unskilled and semiskilled workers in the community.[14] Clearly this fact "would affect appreciably any general 'weighted' comparison between the level of wages in the two countries."[15]

Hourly wage rates having been estimated, it is now necessary to gauge retail prices in Pittsburgh and Birmingham. Table 2 presents food prices for a range of key commodities in the two compared cities. Although the price of pork was lower in Pittsburgh than in Birmingham, in general the British city was considerably cheaper. In Birmingham beef and mutton varied between 60–75%, dairy products were roughly 80–90%, while bread and potatoes sold for only about 50% of the Pittsburgh retail cost.

The cost of rented accommodation in Pittsburgh was far greater

Table 2. *Food Prices in Pittsburgh and Birmingham, 1905.*

Food Commodity		Retail Price in Cents		
		Pittsburgh	Birmingham	Birmingham ÷ Pittsburgh
Beef ribs	lb.	16.8	10.2	0.607
Beef round	lb.	15.1	11.2	0.742
Beef sirloin	lb.	18.9	14.3	0.757
Mutton leg	lb.	14.5	10.2	0.703
Pork chops	lb.	15.1	16.3	1.079
Bacon	lb.	17.9	16.3	0.911
Eggs	dozen	26.6	24.5	0.921
Cheese	lb.	17.5	14.3	0.817
Butter	lb.	31.5	26.9	0.854
Milk	Am. qt.	7.1	5.9	0.831
Bread	lb.	5.0	2.4	0.480
Flour	7 lbs.	21.7	20.4	0.940
Potatoes	15 lbs.	20.6	10.9	0.529
Tea	lb.	55.0	34.7	0.631
Sugar	lb.	6.5	4.1	0.631

Table 3. *Rent Levels in Pittsburgh and Birmingham, 1909.*

Rented Rooms	Rent Range		
	Pittsburgh	Birmingham	Birmingham ÷ Pittsburgh[a]
3	$2.08-3.00	$0.85-1.22	0.407
4	$2.76-4.16	$1.22-1.46	0.387
5	$3.46-4.62	$1.34-1.83	0.392
6	$4.16-5.08	$1.58-2.31	0.421
Mean[b]			0.402

[a]Based upon mid-point of price range.
[b]Each category weighted equally: Pittsburgh rents became relatively higher between 1899 and 1913.

than in Birmingham. Table 3 indicates that rents in Pittsburgh were almost two and a half times those in Birmingham: the median rent for three rooms in Birmingham was only 40.7% of the cost of similar accommodation in Pittsburgh, the cost of four rooms 38.7%, that of five rooms 39.2%, and that of six rooms 42.1%. The difference between the level of rent in the two cities was therefore far wider than that between the level of food prices, and in many cases the increased money wage received in Pittsburgh would not have been sufficient compensation for the higher cost of rented accommodation. A Birmingham building laborer, for example, would have had to work 9.8 hours to pay the median rent for a four-room house in 1909, while his counterpart in Pittsburgh would have been obliged to work 11.6 hours to provide a similar residence; a third-hand baker would have had to labor 11.8 hours in Pittsburgh in order to pay rent on three rooms, but only 9.0 hours in Birmingham.

In an era in which open fires and iron cooking ranges predominated, the cost of coal was a key factor in determining domestic fuel expenditure, and Pittsburgh, surrounded by bituminous coalfields 14,000 square miles in area, experienced a strong locational advantage; retail prices were—by contemporary American standards—extremely cheap. Pittsburgh consumers were abundantly supplied with the various grades of coal "at average prices as low or lower than were current in any other consuming market in the United States."[16]

Birmingham, however, experienced similar locational advantages in respect to coal supply. Consequently workers in that city paid prices for coal far lower than those prevailing in the English capital or in many provincial towns. The crucial question for this study is the comparative cost of coal to the domestic consumer in such "cheap" towns on different sides of the Atlantic.

In Pittsburgh workers commonly bought bituminous coal labeled "Pittsburgh Gas" or 1¼ inch, a quality comparable to "Class 2" bituminous in Birmingham. Table 4 presents statistical data on the price of these grades in both cities in 1907, which suggests that coal fuel was more than 50% more expensive in the British town than in the American.

Coal, then, was cheap for the Pittsburgh consumer, relative both to contemporary American and British standards. Nevertheless, most of that city's workers did not use coal for cooking purposes. Not only was Pittsburgh located close to some of the finest coal reserves in the United States, but the city also lay adjacent to another great fuel resource, natural gas. Substantially cheaper than manufactured gas (being only 25% of the cost in 1907) yet possessing a higher heat content, piped natural gas provided a source of inexpensive fuel and lighting for the majority of Pittsburgh's domestic consumers. By 1900 there existed "but few households . . . which [used] coal, since natural gas [was] generally used for all domestic purposes," and "almost every dwelling in Pittsburgh's densely populated district was furnished with pipes to supply the gas."[17]

In Birmingham, in contrast, consumers had to depend upon manufactured gas for their fuel and lighting requirements.[18] By the first decade of the twentieth century fishtail gas jets had become standard fixtures in most houses in the city, and an increasing proportion of Birmingham's manual workers used gas cookers to supplement their coal ranges.

The cost of gas fuel remained substantially lower, in absolute terms, to the Pittsburgher. Table 4 indicates that in 1907 the price was 134.2% higher in Birmingham. It is true that the provision of cookers, installation of fittings, and servicing of equipment was cheaper in the British city: whereas Birmingham's workers could acquire a gas cooker and fittings free if they were supplied via pre-payment meters, workers in Pittsburgh had to pay for such services and equipment. But against this must be weighed the fact that the natural gas used in Pittsburgh had a greater heat content than the manufactured gas supplied in Birmingham, so that if comparison were made of thermal units (rather than of cubic feet of gas), the difference in price would appear even greater.[19]

Although coal and gas provided the mainstay of heating and lighting requirements in both cities, paraffin (known as kerosene in the United States) remained an important item in the fuel bill. Table 4 indicates that the cost of paraffin/kerosene was almost identical in the two cities.

Of all items, clothing and home furnishings are the hardest com-

Table 4. *Fuel and Lighting Prices in Pittsburgh and Birmingham, 1907.*

Fuel		Retail Price Range		
		Pittsburgh	Birmingham	Birmingham ÷ Pittsburgh[a]
Coal, bituminous	2,240 lbs.	$3.51	$5.23-$5.35	1.507
Gas, natural (Pittsburgh) manufactured (Birmingham)	1,000 cu. ft.	26.0¢	60.9¢	2.342
Kerosene[b]	gallon	17.4-21.6¢	18.3-20.3¢	0.990

[a]Based upon mid-point of price range.
[b]Price in Pittsburgh, 1909; price in Birmingham, 1910.

Table 5. *Clothing Prices in Pittsburgh and Birmingham, 1900–1910.*

Article	Quality	Retail Price		
		Pittsburgh	Birmingham	Birmingham ÷ Pittsburgh
Man's suit/overcoat	ready-to-wear, lowest quality	$ 7.50	$ 2.90	0.387
	ready-to-wear, medium quality	$10.00	$ 4.22	0.422
	ready-to-wear, good quality	$20.00	$ 8.12	0.406
	excellent quality	$40.00	$19.47	0.487
	made-to-measure, lowest quality	$11.75	$ 4.87	0.415
Man's underwear	wool, cheapest	$ 1.00	$ 0.467	0.467
	wool, good quality	$ 1.50	$ 0.609	0.406
Man's shirt	cotton, cheapest	$ 1.00	$ 0.467	0.467
Man's socks	mercerized cotton	$ 0.50	$ 0.365	0.730
Woman's suit	medium quality	$15.00	$ 5.60	0.373
Woman's skirt	medium quality	$ 5.00	$ 2.17	0.434
Woman's shoes	medium quality	$ 3.50	$ 2.56	0.731

ponents of a cost-of-living index to incorporate successfully. Both spatial and temporal comparisons are extremely difficult to undertake, for it is virtually impossible to estimate the extent to which manufacturers restrained price increases by decreasing the quality of the materials used and/or by reducing the degree of workmanship employed in producing an article. Consequently the comparison of retail prices for clothing is less reliable than the data previously presented in this study, a problem compounded by the lack of adequate documentation. Yet "it is better to include an informed guess than exclude a value altogether, since omission may distort the index even more than an approximation."[20] The following analysis consists essentially of "guesses," as educated as one may make them from the fragmentary evidence available: evidence which, for Birmingham at least, has had to be derived from nationwide data.

The overall picture that emerges is confused. Clothing, there can be no doubt, was substantially less expensive in Birmingham. As Table 5 reveals, shoes and cotton socks were only about 73% of the retail price customarily paid in Pittsburgh, and most other clothing items could be purchased for between 40 and 45% of the equivalent Pittsburgh price. With respect to other goods, one can only present an informed "guesstimate" of price differences. In summary form the comparative cost of furnishings and domestic hardware in England and the United States may be presented as in Table 6: while British wooden utensils cost only 25–35% of the retail price of American goods, British cotton bedding and toweling were 50–60% more expensive than similar American items.

It is probable that additional, more sophisticated analysis would

Table 6. *English and American Prices for Home Furnishings, 1907.*

Commodity Range	English Price ÷ American Price
Domestic utensils, wooden	0.25-0.35
Furniture	0.40-0.50
Bedding, mattresses	0.40-0.50
Crockery, china, earthenware	0.45-0.55
Bedding and toweling, linen	0.45-0.55
Light fixtures	0.50-0.60
Glassware	0.70-0.80
Domestic utensils, metal	0.95-1.05
Cutlery, silver-plate	0.95-1.05
Floor covering, oil-cloth	1.10-1.20
Bedding and toweling, cotton	1.50-1.60

improve the accuracy of these educated estimates. Nevertheless if, as seems likely, "national" prices for furnishings fairly represented prices in the cities of Pittsburgh and Birmingham, then the figures do provide a satisfactory basis for comparative investigation.

The comparative expenditure schedules of Birmingham and Pittsburgh manual workers in the first decade of the twentieth century are presented in Table 7.[21] In both cities purchase of food comprised the most substantial item in family budgets. On both sides of the Atlantic Engels's law appears to have prevailed: that is, the lower the expenditure of the individual family, the greater the proportion of its total budget devoted to the provision of food. However, the mean food expenditure of Pittsburgh families, expressed as a percentage of their total budget, was substantially less than that of their Birmingham counterparts—44.3% compared with 54.4%. In contrast, they devoted a slightly greater share to paying rent and local taxes—18.4% compared with 17.7%. In brief, to feed and house a family required just over 60% of the Pittsburgher's purse, whereas it took approximately 75% of the British Midlander's.

Fuel and lighting together accounted for 5.1% of expenditure in Pittsburgh, the total annual purchases bearing a 4:1 relationship. In Birmingham fuel and light required 5.9% of the total budget.

Workers in both cities devoted similar portions of their expenditure to the purchase of clothing—approximately 12%. Total expenditure was larger in the American city and, in consequence, the absolute sum spent upon clothing would have been greater, but such additional disbursement would not have compensated for the comparative expensiveness of clothing. Thus the statistical evidence indicates—surprisingly—that British workers were buying more and/or superior quality clothing.

Comparative hourly rates of pay, commodity retail prices, and expenditure schedules having been presented, it is a straightforward task to calculate relative real wages or, more specifically, to estimate the real cost of a common composite unit of consumables in the British and American cities, expressed in terms of the hours of labor required to purchase it.

The major unresolved question involves the most satisfactory budgetary profile to select as the foundation upon which to construct the composite unit of consumables—a unit which, in turn, dictates the respective weights to be attached to commodity prices. Should one use the Pennsylvania worker's expenditure schedule as the guide to the comparative cost of living in Pittsburgh, or would it be more valid to base analysis upon the Birmingham pattern?

The theoretical issue is complex. It is unlikely that the Birmingham worker who migrated to Pittsburgh would have expended exactly the same percentage of income upon items as he had previously done at home: no matter how strong the force of unconscious habit, and no matter how great his commitment to previous lifestyle, the difference in relative price levels would probably have changed his consumption behavior, albeit slowly, toward a purchasing profile more akin to that of the native Pittsburgher.[22]

Yet even had the Birmingham worker been willing to alter his expenditure pattern in response to his new price environment, the question remains as to whether it is justifiable to use the Pittsburgher's budget as a guide to comparative living costs. It could be argued, for instance, that the Birmingham employee derived greater satisfaction from his Midlands diet than he did from the American diet to which the change in prices persuaded him to adapt. If so, then the transference incurred a real (nonquantifiable) psychic cost, and in consequence it might be fairer to base the comparative cost of living upon the assumption that the immigrant retained his previous expenditure pattern in his adopted country.

It is fortunate, given these difficulties, that practical application of the alternative weighting technique results in remarkably similar estimates. The calculations in Table 7 reveal that the monetary cost of living, based upon a composite unit of consumables derived from Birmingham budgetary behavior was 67.1% greater in Pittsburgh than in the English Midlands city in 1905, whereas the cost based upon a composite unit of consumables derived from Pennsylvania expenditure practice was 65.3% higher.

These relative cost-of-living indexes may now be compared with the relative money wage indexes paid to various occupations in Pittsburgh and Birmingham in 1906. By dividing the latter index by the former, a relative real wage index may be estimated for each job category. The derived quotients are presented in Table 8: for example, the relative cost of living in Pittsburgh was (as column 2 reveals) 65.3–67.1% greater than in Birmingham, while the relative hourly money wage in Pittsburgh for an engineering laborer was (as column 1 reveals) 71.7% higher. Thus the relative real hourly wage of the engineering laborer was (as column 3 shows) only 2.8–3.9% greater.

While all Pittsburgh occupations gained hourly rates of pay superior, in real terms, to those in Birmingham, the difference at the unskilled level was small. Laborers engaged in Pittsburgh's engineering and bakery trades, and those in public employment, all had real

Table 7. *Estimates of the Comparative Cost of Living in Pittsburgh and Birmingham.*

	1	2	3	4	5
	Percentage Expenditure			Weighted Price Index	
Item	Birmingham Budget (1914)	Pittsburgh Budget (1901)	Pittsburgh Price Index 1905 (Birmingham = 100.0)	For Birmingham Budget (col. 1 × col. 3)	For Pittsburgh Budget (col. 2 × col. 3)
FOOD	54.4	44.3			
Beef	6.7	6.8	143.9[h]	964.13	978.52
Pork	1.8	1.2	92.6[i]	166.68	111.12
Mutton	3.3	1.2[f]	142.2[j]	469.26	170.64
Bacon	3.0	2.0	109.8	329.40	219.60
Other meat[a]	3.4	1.9[g]	126.2[k]	429.08	239.78
Eggs	1.3	3.0	108.6	141.18	325.80
Milk	3.4	2.8	120.3	409.02	336.84
Cheese	1.3	0.4	122.4	159.12	48.96
Butter	3.4	4.3	117.1	398.14	503.53
Potatoes	2.3	1.9	189.0	434.70	359.10
Flour	0.9	2.3	106.4	95.76	244.72
Bread	7.8	1.9	208.3	1,624.74	395.77
Tea	2.8[e]	0.7	158.5	443.80	110.95
Coffee	0.5[e]	1.6	54.2[l]	27.10	86.72
Sugar	2.6	2.3	158.5	412.10	364.55
Other food	9.9	10.0	134.3[m]	1,329.57	1,343.00
RENT	17.7	18.4	252.7	4,472.79	4,649.68

	Birmingham budget	Pittsburgh budget	Price index	col. 1	col. 2
FUEL/LIGHT	5.9	5.1			
Coal[b]	3.5	3.0	66.4[n]	232.40	199.20
Gas[b]	1.5	1.3	42.7[n]	64.05	55.51
Paraffin[b]	0.9	0.8	101.0[n]	90.90	80.80
CLOTHING	12.0	12.4			
Clothes[c]	9.0	9.3	212.8[o]	1,915.20	1,979.04
Shoes[c]	3.0	3.1	136.8[p]	410.40	424.08
FURNITURE[d]	1.3	1.3	222.2	288.86	288.86
HOME UTENSILS[d]	1.3	1.3	129.0[q]	167.70	167.70
SUBTOTAL	92.6	82.8		15,476.08	13,684.47

Relative cost of a composite unit of consumables

	Based on Birmingham budget	Based on Pittsburgh budget
	Birmingham = 100.0 subtotal col. 4	Birmingham = 100.0 subtotal col. 5
(formula)	subtotal col. 1/92.6	subtotal col. 2/82.8
(calculations)	15,476.08/92.6	13,684.47/82.8
(final estimate)	167.1	165.3

[a]Includes fish and poultry. [b]Assumes fuel and lighting expenditure divided among coal, gas, and paraffin in the ratio 60:25:15. [c]Assumes clothing expenditure divided between clothes and shoes in the ratio 75:25. [d]Assumes furniture and home utensils expenditure divided between the two in the ratio 50:50. [e]Based upon food expenditure in Midland towns, 1904. [f]Assumes that "other meat" category referred to mutton. [g]Expenditure for salt beef, poultry, and fish. [h]Based upon relative prices of beef ribs, round, and sirloin. [i]Based upon relative prices of pork chops. [j]Based upon relative prices of mutton leg. [k]Mean unweighted price index for beef, pork, and mutton. [l]Based upon price charged for ground mixed and French coffee in "high"- and "medium"- class Birmingham stores. [m]Mean unweighted price index for all ten listed (nonmeat) food items. [n]Based upon the relative prices of coal, gas, and paraffin, 1907. [o]Based upon mean unweighted price index for man's suit, overcoat, underwear, shirt, and socks, and woman's suit and skirt. [p]Based upon relative prices of woman's shoes. [q]Based upon mean unweighted price index for wooden domestic utensils, mattresses, crockery, linen bedding and toweling, light fixtures, glassware, metal domestic utensils, cutlery, floor covering, and cotton bedding and toweling.

Table 8. *Comparative Real Hourly Wages in Pittsburgh and Birmingham, 1906*[a] *(categorized by occupation).*

Occupation	Pittsburgh RMWI[b] (Birmingham = 100.0)	Pittsburgh RCLI[c] (Birmingham = 100.0)	Pittsburgh RRWI[d] (Birmingham = 100.0)
Steel mill laborer	168.7	165.3	102.1
Engineering laborer	171.7	165.3-167.1	102.8-103.9
Foundry blacksmith	175.7	165.3-167.1	105.1-106.7
Public laborer	178.7[e]	165.3-167.1	106.9-108.1
Third-hand baker	179.6	165.3-167.1	107.5-108.7
Second-hand baker	187.0	165.3-167.1	111.9-113.1
Boiler maker	190.8	165.3-167.1	114.2-115.4
Machinist	191.5	165.3-167.1	114.6-115.8
Book and job compositor	201.9	165.3-167.1	120.8-122.1
First-hand baker	202.2	165.3-167.1	121.0-122.3
Bookbinder	204.0	165.3-167.1	122.1-123.4
Pattern maker	207.4	165.3-167.1	124.1-125.5
Public Rammer	207.5[f]	165.3-167.1	124.2-125.5
Building laborer	218.2	165.3-167.1	130.6-132.0
Machine woodworker	226.6	165.3-167.1	135.6-137.1
Carpenter	226.9	165.3-167.1	135.8-137.3
Painter	246.2	165.3-167.1	147.3-148.9
Morning newspaper compositor	257.0	165.3-167.1	153.8-155.5
Plumber	259.1	165.3-167.1	155.1-156.7
Stonemason	270.9	165.3-167.1	162.1-163.9
Plasterer	277.3	165.3-167.1	165.9-167.8
Bricklayer	326.9	165.3-167.1	195.6-197.8
Public pavior	347.2[f]	165.3-167.1	207.8-210.0

[a]Data for bakers refer to 1907; data for engineering laborers and public rammers refer to 1905; data for public paviors refer to 1909; data for steel mill laborers refer to Sheffield, based upon mean hours worked (54.7).
[b]RMWI: Relative money wage index.
[c]RCLI: Relative cost-of-living index, defined as the relative cost of a composite unit of consumables. The minimum figure refers to the relative cost of a composite unit based upon a Pennsylvania budget; the maximum figure refers to the relative cost of a composite unit based upon a Birmingham budget.
[d]RRWI: Relative real wage index, i.e. 100 (RMWI/RCLI).
[e]Assumes that Birmingham public laborer worked 48.0 hours.
[f]Assumes that Birmingham and Pittsburgh paviors/rammers worked the same number of weekly hours.

hourly rates less than 10% in advance of their counterparts in the British city. (Comparison of Pittsburgh and Sheffield indicates the same to be true in the steel industry. Laborers in Pittsburgh's blast furnaces and steel mills earned a real hourly wage less than 5% better than their Sheffield counterparts.) At the other extreme certain skilled workers gained rates very much higher: morning newspaper compositors, for instance, were paid more than half again as much in Pittsburgh as in Birmingham, bricklayers and paviors twice as much.

In general, then, Birmingham's unskilled workers tended to be better off, vis-à-vis their Pittsburgh equivalents, than were the city's skilled employees. Unskilled laborers in the American city's engineering, baking, and building trades, and those engaged in public employment, earned mean real hourly wages only 12–13% greater than their Birmingham counterparts; skilled manual employees in the same industrial sectors, namely pattern makers, first-hand bakers, bricklayers, and public paviors, gained real rates 62–64% higher than similar occupations in Birmingham.

The implications of this analysis are evident when the comparative wage data are placed within an extended chronological framework. If the real hourly wage ratios are linked to national indexes of real wage rates, it is possible to view the final estimates for 1906 within a wider historical perspective.[23] Time series, presented in Table 9, are based upon the premise that the wage paid to the engineering laborer represents the minimum comparative rate paid in Pittsburgh, and that of public pavior the maximum. The data, presented in summary form in Figure 2, suggest that 1906 was the *first* year in the post-1890 period in which the real wage of the engineering laborer rose higher in the American than the British city. The statistical evidence forcibly suggests that in most unskilled occupations real wages were as low in Pittsburgh as they were in Birmingham, and in many instances lower. The conclusion that Phelps Brown found "most remarkable," namely that "not until after 1900 . . . did the real wage in the U.S.A. draw ahead of the British," appears to be substantially correct.[24] For a considerable period unskilled laborers received real hourly rates of pay in Pittsburgh that were not much superior, and quite probably inferior, to those their counterparts received in Birmingham. At the other end of the wage spectrum skilled manual workers in the American city were paid real rates up to twice as high as those British employees received.

Thus far investigation has been confined to comparative hourly rates of pay. It is also necessary to estimate real weekly earnings.[25] This involves a subtle re-emphasis in analytical framework, insofar as interest is centered no longer on the difference in real earnings for a given (timed) amount of work but on the variance in real income irrespective of the hours of labor required to gain it. For this reason it seems sensible to incorporate within the calculations of weekly earnings estimates of the income derived from wives and children, for the

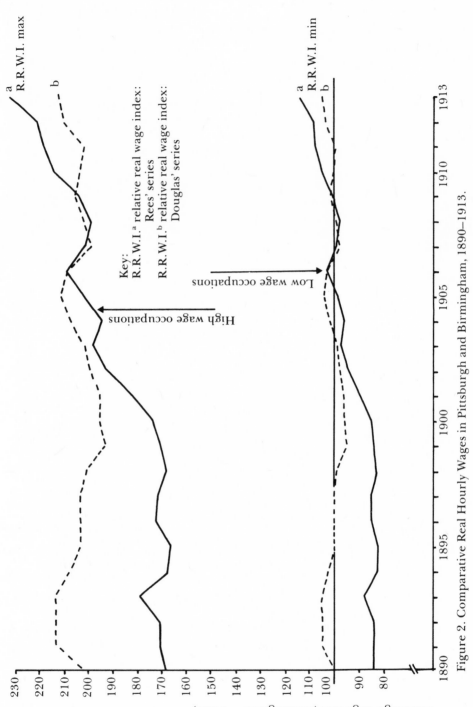

Figure 2. Comparative Real Hourly Wages in Pittsburgh and Birmingham, 1890–1913.

Table 9. *Comparative Real Hourly Wages in Pittsburgh and Birmingham, 1890–1913.*

Year	U.K. RWI[a]	U.S. RWI[b]	U.S. RWI[c]	Pittsburgh RRWI[d]		Pittsburgh RRWI[e]	
				min Birmingham = 100.0	max Birmingham = 100.0	min Birmingham = 100.0	max Birmingham = 100.0
1890	95	77	92	84	169	100	202
1891	94	77	96	84	171	105	213
1892	94	77	96	84	171	105	213
1893	96	82	98	88	179	105	213
1894	100	80	99	82	167	102	207
1895	102	81	99	82	166	100	203
1896	102	84	99	85	172	100	203
1897	100	82	97	85	171	100	203
1898	101	81	97	83	168	99	201
1899	106	86	98	84	170	95	193
1900	105	87	98	85	173	96	195
1901	104	90	97	89	181	96	195
1902	103	94	98	94	191	98	199
1903	101	95	97	97	197	99	201
1904	99	92	98	96	194	102	207
1905	99	95	100	99	201	104	211
1906	100	100	100	103	209	103	209
1907	103	99	98	99	201	98	199
1908	103	98	99	98	199	99	201
1909	102	99	100	100	203	101	205
1910	100	102	97	105	213	100	203
1911	99	103	95	107	217	99	201
1912	99	104	99	108	220	103	209
1913	99	110	100	114	232	104	211

[a]U.K. RWI: United Kingdom real wage index, based upon average earnings for a normal week of all wage-earners in the United Kingdom, divided by a cost-of-living index (Bowley).
[b]U.S. RWI: U.S. real wage index (estimate a), based upon average hourly earnings in all manufacturing industries in the United States, divided by a cost-of-living index (Rees).
[c]U.S. RWI: U.S. real wage index (estimate b), based upon average hourly earnings in all manufacturing industries in the United States, divided by a cost-of-living index (Douglas).
[d]Pittsburgh RRWI: Pittsburgh relative real wage index (estimate a)—(U.S. RWI (a)/U.K. RWI) × 103 (minimum) or 209 (maximum).
[e]Pittsburgh RRWI: Pittsburgh relative real wage index (estimate b)—(U.S. RWI (b)/U.K. RWI) × 103 (minimum) or 209 (maximum).
min = Minimum relative real wage (engineering laborer).
max = Maximum relative real wage (public pavior).

financial accruements thereby derived would have improved the material standard of living, just as would increases in the hours of employment.

This concentration upon the "end" standard, rather than upon the "means" by which it was achieved, begs key questions. The relative weekly earnings of many Pittsburgh workers were increased (vis-à-vis Birmingham employees) by the longer hours demanded of them, but it is uncertain whether the widening of the resultant earnings gap indicated a genuine advance in the American's comparative standard of living. It is at least possible that the manual worker in the British city placed a higher value upon leisure time than upon the ability to consume more material goods and/or to accumulate greater savings. Conversely, the Birmingham employee's earnings were, to a much greater extent than in Pittsburgh, bolstered by the wage labor of his wife, and this reduced the Anglo-American differential in family income. But did this signify a narrowing of the difference in family standard of living? Might it not be just to view longer hours of labor and the greater employment of working wives as alternative means of increasing material lifestyle?

It is questions such as these, which require that levels of contentment and degrees of satisfaction be assessed, that can least satisfactorily be resolved by quantitative analysis. All one can assert is that, given the longer hours worked in most Pittsburgh industries, and given the greater propensity for wives to enter the paid work force in Birmingham, the difference in comparative weekly real earnings that resulted was—for most occupations—less substantial than the difference in hourly rates.[26]

Table 10 suggests that the Birmingham unskilled worker in full-time employment received a weekly family income which allowed him to enjoy a standard of living almost as high as his colleague in Pittsburgh in 1906. Laborers employed by the Birmingham Council or engaged in the city's engineering industry actually had at their disposal greater real earnings, while building laborers had only a 3–4% superiority in Pittsburgh, and third-hand bakers 8–9%. The families of Sheffield's steel mill laborers also received larger real earnings than did Pittsburgh workers.

A major objection to this conclusion might be that the opportunity for the weekly income of household heads to be supplemented by the earnings of other family members was directly related to the existence of a surrounding family. The implicit assumption of many history texts has been that the unskilled labor force of early twentieth-century American cities was largely comprised of unmarried immigrants: while they saved a high proportion of earnings for remittance to extended

Table 10. *Comparative Real Weekly Family Earnings in Pittsburgh and Birmingham, 1906 (categorized by occupation of husband).*

Occupation	Weekly Earnings (inc. family contribution)[a] Birmingham:Pittsburgh		Pittsburgh RMEI[b] (Birmingham = 100.0)	Pittsburgh RREI[c] (Birmingham = 100.0)
Engineering laborer	$ 6.95	$11.41	164.2	98.3- 99.3
Foundry blacksmith	12.50	22.20	177.6	106.3-107.4
Public laborer	8.40	13.19	157.0	94.0- 95.0
Third-hand baker	8.35	15.10	180.8	108.2-109.4
Second-hand baker	9.40	17.54	186.6	111.7-112.9
Boiler maker	13.25	24.31	183.5	109.8-110.0
Machinist	12.50	23.20	185.6	111.1-112.3
Book and job compositor	12.02	22.16	184.4	110.4-111.6
First-hand baker	11.14	22.60	202.9	121.4-122.7
Bookbinder	11.14	20.73	186.1	111.4-112.6
Pattern maker	13.25	25.51	192.5	115.2-116.5
Public rammer	9.08	16.57	182.5	109.2-110.4
Building laborer	10.57	18.20	172.2	103.1-104.2
Machine woodworker	13.34	26.57	200.7	120.1-121.4
Carpenter	14.05	26.38	187.8	112.4-113.6
Painter	13.95	25.66	183.9	110.1-111.3
Morning newspaper compositor	15.65	35.30	225.6	135.0-136.5
Plumber	14.88	30.12	202.4	121.1-122.4
Stonemason	14.78	33.13	224.2	134.2-135.6
Plasterer	15.65	33.91	216.7	129.7-131.1
Bricklayer	14.88	38.01	255.4	152.8-154.5
Public pavior	12.50	38.13	305.0	182.5-184.5

[a]Family contribution estimated at 0.428 of adult male wage for each Birmingham occupation, and at 0.255 for each Pittsburgh occupation.
[b]RMEI Relative money earnings index.
[c]RREI Relative real earnings index:—100 (RMEI/165.3) or 100 (RMEI/167.1).

families in the "old country," they were generally unable to enjoy the financial contribution made by wives and children in the United States. If this were true in Pittsburgh, and if—in consequence—the conjugal status of workers differed considerably from that in Birmingham, then comparison of estimated family earnings represents a statistical illusion, an artificial creation divorced from historical reality. Such does not appear to have been the case. The proportion of single men was similar in the two cities: in 1910–11, 38.4% of Birmingham males aged fifteen years or over were unmarried, compared with 42.8% in Pittsburgh. Far more surprisingly, the proportion of married males was greater among Pittsburgh's foreign-born workers. In 1910, 62.6% of immigrant white adults were married, compared with only 46.7% for native-born whites and 54.1% for blacks. In part this reflected the fact that a greater share of foreign-born males was represented in the age categories in which rates of marriage were highest (25–64 years), but in every single age group (until 65 years and over) there existed a higher incidence of marriage among foreigners. Nor does there exist much evidence that rates of marriage were substantially lower among unskilled workers. A census investigation in 1900 revealed that 52.2% of Pittsburgh's male workers were married, compared with 49.0% for unspecified laborers: in the city's steel mills the equivalent figure was 55.2%.[27] Here, surely, is an area worthy of greater investigation.

In conclusion, whether comparison be made between hourly rates of pay or weekly family earnings, and regardless of whether the American or English budgetary schedules be used to determine the cost-of-living index, the statistical picture that emerges is remarkably similar. The American manual worker's standard of living was not as much in advance of the English worker's as most contemporary comment suggested. The skilled Pittsburgh tradesman, it is true, received an income which, judged by the composite unit of consumables it could buy, was 50–100% greater than that received by an equivalent occupation in Birmingham. But, in stark contrast, the unskilled Pittsburgh worker gained a real wage that was the same as, or very little better than, that paid to the laborer in Birmingham.

And if the definition of standard of living were extended, one might make a forceful argument that the Birmingham laborer was decidedly better off, experienced a significantly higher quality life, than did his counterpart in Pittsburgh. It is true that the opportunity for upward social mobility was probably greater in the American city. But the extent of annual unemployment was probably as great in the

United States as in Britain, and in nearly all other respects evidence—both quantitative and qualitative—indicates that the British worker experienced more substantial benefits. He generally had longer leisure time, enjoying (as did few Pittsburgh workers) a half-day on Saturday; he was far less likely to be killed or maimed while at the workplace; he labored under less pressure: and he was provided with superior social services and facilities—hospital accommodation, city-based unemployment benefits, garbage collection, park space, and so on. It is areas such as these to which future historians might usefully turn attention.

NOTES

1. Dorothy Crook, "Perspectives—An Interview with Thomas Cochran," *Economic Impact* 3 (1975):60.

2. J. Potter, " 'Optimism' and 'Pessimism' in Interpreting the Industrial Revolution: An Economic Historian's Dilemma," *Scandanavian Economic History Review* 10 (1962):259.

3. The most recent text to suggest that "it was high wages . . . that constituted America's main appeal," especially after the Civil War, is Maldwyn A. Jones, *Destination America* (London, 1976), p. 18.

4. See, by way of introduction, H. J. Habakkuk, *American and British Technology in the Nineteenth Century* (Cambridge, 1962) and "Second Thoughts on American and British Technology in the Nineteenth Century," *Business Archives and History* 3 (1963); Peter Temin, "Labour Scarcity and the Problem of American Industrial Efficiency in the 1850s," *Journal of Economic History* 26 (1966). For some empirical investigation of the early nineteenth century, see Nathan Rosenberg, "Anglo-American Wage Differences in the 1820s," *Journal of Economic History* 27 (1967); Donald R. Adams, Jr., "Some Evidence on English and American Wage Rates, 1790–1830," *Journal of Economic History* 30 (1970).

5. See, for example, Philip Taft, *The A.F. of L. in the Time of Gompers* (New York, 1957), p. xvii; John H. M. Laslett, *Labor and the Left: A Study of the Socialist and Radical Influences in the American Labor Movement, 1881–1924* (New York, 1970), p. 302; Howard H. Quint, *The Forging of American Socialism: Origins of the Modern Movement* (Columbia, S.C., 1953), p. 5; Henry Pelling, *American Labor* (Chicago, 1960), p. 216.

6. I am well aware that the necessary brevity of this paper results in gross simplification of a complex comparative analysis, in which assertions are too cavalier and in which necessary qualifications are sometimes absent. In defense I can only plead the existence of a far more substantial body of evidence upon which my abbreviated conclusions are based: see my dissertation, "The Standard of Living of Manual Workers in the First Decade of the Twentieth-Century: A Comparative Study of Birmingham, U.K., and Pittsburgh, U.S.A." (Ph.D., London School of Economics, 1976), for 125 supporting tables and 500 pages of detailed explanation and tortuous qualification.

7. The final section of the paper deals with weekly breadwinner earnings and family income, and notes the interpretative difficulties posed by such indexes.

8. Shergold, "Standard of Living," also compares Pittsburgh with Sheffield in England, a check that confirms the conclusions presented here. Two important comparisons, for which there existed no equivalent Birmingham wage data, are included in Table 1. Even though Pittsburgh is believed to "match" Birmingham/Sheffield, the problem remains of whether the selected cities are "representative" of conditions prevailing in their respective countries. While it is difficult to measure "typicality," Great Britain, Board of Trade, *Report of an Enquiry . . . into Working Class Rents, Housing, Retail Prices and . . . Wages in the U.S.A.* (1909) and *Report of an Enquiry . . . into Working Class Rents, Housing, Retail Prices and . . . Wages in the U.K.* (1905 and 1912), suggest the choice is fair. All were cities in which, by comparison with other towns investigated, food prices were high, fuel prices were low, and high monetary wages prevailed. Birmingham and Sheffield rents were relatively less expensive.

More important, the variation in wages and prices between the selected cities and possible alternatives was small. Of the 28 American towns studied, in 1909 only six had a combined price index differing more than 10% from that in Pittsburgh; of the 73 English and Welsh towns studied, in 1905 only seven had a price index varying more than 10% from that in Birmingham. Wages varied slightly more. Nevertheless, an index based on rates paid in the building, engineering, and printing industries suggests that only seven of 26 cities had wages that diverged more than 10% from those paid in Pittsburgh: the only towns with significantly better money wages were Chicago (20% higher), Milwaukee (6% higher), and New York (5% higher). Of 56 English and Welsh towns for which a similar index could be constructed, only eight had money wages that varied more than 10% from those paid in Birmingham: the only town with a significantly better pay rate was London (10% higher), but Hull and Manchester (1% lower), Newcastle (2% lower), Nottingham (3% lower), and Stockport (4% lower), also enjoyed high money wages.

9. The sources of the statistical data that comprise the core of this analysis are presented in the Appendix.

10. Victor S. Clark, *History of Manufactures in the United States* (Washington, D.C., 1929), 1:392.

11. Habakkuk, *American and British Technology*, pp. 21, 23, 151–52 (author's italics). For a recent analysis which assumed that British real wages were substantially less, and skill differentials significantly wider, than in America, see James Holt, "Trade Unionism in the British and U.S. Steel Industries, 1880–1914: A Comparative Study," *Labor History* 18 (1977): 17–20.

12. John R. Commons and William Leiserson, "Wage-Earners of Pittsburgh," in Paul Kellogg, ed., *Wage-Earning Pittsburgh* (New York, 1914), pp. 116–17.

13. E. V. Birchall, "The Conditions of Distress," *Economic Review* 20 (1910):39. He notes, p. 35, "that even the lowest grades of labor in Birmingham are more or less professional: the filers and polishers in the metal trades remain filers and polishers; if there is no filing or polishing to be done they are unemployed, and they do not to any great extent take up

other lines of work: every branch of trade has its own stagnant reservoir."

14. As a rough guide it may be noted that approximately 48% of Pittsburgh building workers were laborers, contrasted with 36% in Birmingham; in the Pittsburgh district steel industry approximately 50% of workers were unskilled, compared with 30% in Yorkshire mills. Shergold, "Standard of Living," p. 149.

15. Great Britain, Board of Trade, *Report of an Enquiry . . . into Working Class Rents, Housing, Retail Prices and Standard Rates of Wages in the U.S.A.* (1909), p. v.

16. J. H. Hillman, Jr., "Coal—Basis of Pittsburgh's Industrial Supremacy," in Pittsburgh Chamber of Commerce, *Pittsburgh and the Pittsburgh Spirit* (Pittsburgh, 1928), p. 35.

17. Pittsburgh Chamber of Commerce, *Year Book and the Directory* (Pittsburgh, 1900), pp. 62–63; Harry Huse Campbell, *The Manufacture and Properties of Iron and Steel* (New York, 1903), p. 660.

18. Charles Anthony Vince, *History of the Corporation of Birmingham*, 4 (Birmingham, 1923):410.

19. Albert Rees, *Real Wages in Manufacturing, 1890–1914* (Princeton, N.J., 1961), p. 108.

20. Sidney Pollard, "Real Earnings in Sheffield, 1851–1914," *Yorkshire Bulletin of Economic and Social Research* 9 (1957):61.

21. The budget profile for the state of Pennsylvania has been substituted for the city of Pittsburgh, for which no separate expenditure schedules exist.

22. It is assumed here (and this appears to be borne out by empirical study) that the native worker would have had an expenditure schedule more attuned to prevailing price differentials than the transposed budgetary profile of the immigrant.

23. The national series selected are A. L. Bowley, *Wages and Income in the United Kingdom, since 1860* (Cambridge, 1937), Table VII, p. 30; Rees, *Real Wages in Manufacturing,* Table 44, p. 120; and Paul Douglas, *Real Wages in the United States, 1870–1926* (Boston, 1930), Table 24, p. 108. All were converted to base year 1906.

24. E. H. Phelps Brown and Margaret H. Browne, *A Century of Pay: The Course of Pay and Production in France, Germany, Sweden, the United Kingdom, and the United States of America, 1860–1960* (London, 1968), p. 163.

25. Real earnings for a standard week.

26. Standard weekly hours ranged from 48.0 (morning newspaper compositors) to 60.0 (bakers) in Birmingham, the median being 53.0; hours ranged from 48.0 (building workers) to 72.0 (steel mill workers) in Pittsburgh, the median being 54.0. Estimates suggest that Birmingham wives added a mean 9.3% to family income, compared with 2.3% in Pittsburgh; that sons added 19.2% compared with 15.5%; and that daughters added 14.3% compared with 7.7%: in short, family earnings increased husband's income by 25.5% in Pittsburgh but by 42.8% in Birmingham. See Shergold, "Standard of Living," Table 3.9, pp. 153–56, and Table 4.15, p. 228.

27. U.S. Bureau of the Census, *Census, 1900,* vol. 2, Table 32, and Special Report, "Occupations at the Twelfth Census," Table 43; *Census, 1910,* vol. 1, Table 38; Great Britain, *Census, 1911,* vol. 7, Table 9. Sizes of family were also similar in Pittsburgh and Birmingham: in 1910–11 both cities averaged 5.4 persons per family.

Appendix

Details on wages, hours of labor, family earnings, retail prices, and expenditure schedules—the statistical bases of Tables 1–10—are derived from the following sources:

Great Britain, *Annual Abstract of Labour Statistics; Annual Report on Changes in Rates of Wages and Hours; Report on Standard Time Rates of Wages; Report on Wholesale and Retail Prices in the U.K. in 1902; Report of an Enquiry by the Board of Trade into Earnings and Hours of Labour* (the "Wage Census of 1906"); *Report on an Enquiry . . . into Working Class Rents, Housing, Retail Prices and . . . Wages in . . . the U.S.A.* (1909); *Report of an Enquiry . . . into Working Class Rents, Housing, Retail Prices and . . . Wages in the U.K.* (1905 and 1912).

United States, Commissioner of Labor, *Eighteenth Annual Report* (1903) and *Nineteenth Annual Report* (1904).

United States, Bureau of Labor, *Bulletin* nos. 59, 65, 71,77 (1905-8).

United States, Bureau of Labor, *Report on Conditions of Employment in the Iron and Steel Industry,* 4 vols., 62d Congress, 1st session (1913).

United States, Bureau of Labor Statistics, *Bulletin* nos. 105, 106, 108, 110, 113, 115, 121, 130–32, 136, 138, 140, 143, 156, 171 (1912–14).

United States, Select Committee on Wages and Prices of Commodities, *Report,* 61st Cong., 2d Sess. (1910).

United States, Senate, *Wages and Prices Abroad,* 61st Cong. 2d Sess. (1910).

Pennsylvania, Department of Internal Affairs, *Annual Report.*

Allegheny Council, *Municipal Reports.*

City of Birmingham, *Council Proceedings.*

Philadelphia Company, *Annual Reports.*

Pittsburgh Railways Company Arbitration, *Reports* (1914).

John T. Holdsworth, *Economic Survey of Pittsburgh* (Pittsburgh, 1914).

Margaret Byington, *Homestead: The Households of a Mill Town* (New York, 1910).

Edward Cadbury, *et al., Women's Work and Wages: A Phase of Life in an Industrial City* (London, 1906).

A. E. Carver, *An Investigation into the Dietary of the Labouring Classes of Birmingham* (Birmingham, 1914).

John R. Commons and William Leiserson, "Wage-Earners of Pittsburgh," in Paul Kellogg, ed., *Wage-Earning Pittsburgh* (New York, 1914).

Martha Cutler, "The Cost of House Furnishing—A Review," *Harpers Bazaar* 41 (Aug. 1907).

John A. Fitch, *The Steel Workers* (New York, 1911).

Joseph M. Gillman, *Rent Levels in Pittsburgh, Pennsylvania, and Their Causes* (New York, 1926).

William H. Matthews, "A Discussion of Housing Conditions in Pittsburgh," *Kingsley House Record* 10 (1907).

R. S. Smirke, *Report on Birmingham Trades, Prepared for Use in Connexion with the Juvenile Employment Exchange*, 10 pamphlets (1913–14).

Trades Union Congress, Joint Committee on the Cost of Living, *Final Report*, (1920).

Sears, Roebuck Co. *Catalogues.*

Army and Navy Stores, *Catalogues.*

Advertisements placed in the *Pittsburgh Dispatch, Pittsburgh Post, National Labor Tribune,* and *Iron City Trades Journal.*

PART II

Organization

The study of labor organizations has for many decades dominated the historiography of the American labor movement and working class. Neither unions nor parties followed European models. None of the several socialist parties grew to match the comparative influence of the British Labor party, the German Social Democrats, the French socialists or, later, communists. Similarly the American Federation of Labor never matched the radicalism of some of the European national federations. While many scholars have deduced from this development that socialism had no chance in the United States, there were socialist movements, both native and immigrant, in parties and in unions, and the leadership was as international as the working class itself.

What were the reasons for the lack of large-scale success of the Socialist Labor party? Hubert Perrier examines the problems party leadership faced when deciding to emphasize political action to the detriment of economic struggles. Was a uniform stand taken at all echelons of party leadership? What was the relation of the immediate surroundings, the New York economic life, and the national scene? There trustification was already giving way to the formation of holding companies, financially integrated rather than production-oriented. Here the striking cloak makers' union, negotiating for about 40,000 striking workers of several languages, had to deal with 1,800 bosses. How does an analysis of monopoly capitalism enter into the strategy and tactical moves of a struggle like the cloak makers? Was the bread-and-butter unionism of the American Federation of Labor the better answer? Andrew Dawson explores the possibilities for skilled workers concerning consciousness and conditions to unite for political action to achieve "social democracy." Did the exclusiveness of craft unionism vitiate attempts for united political action? Did the official AFL strategy associated with President Gompers—"reward your friends and punish your enemies"—work to the advantage of the established parties and, if so, to what degree? Were workers intent on forming their own separate organization, or did they take their cues from the middle class?

The ethnic dimension of union as well as political organization is taken up by Hartmut Keil. After the antisocialist law of 1878 many German labor leaders had to leave. At the same time—within the context of the proletarian mass migration from the 1880s to World War I—German workers moved in larger numbers to the United States. Immigrants from Germany have so customarily been lumped together with the "old immigration" that few take into account that it took fifty years for 2.9 million Germans to arrive (1820–79) and only another fifteen years during the industrialization process for a further 2 million to come (1880–95). They joined the ranks of the industrial workers as any other group of new immigrants. Did they improve their lot faster than southern or East European immigrants? Were exiled German socialist labor leaders displaced persons in the American context, or could they continue their work with little change? Did the economic context in the United States differ from German conditions to a considerable degree? Four German labor activists shared with their Swedish-American comrade Joe Hill and their Italian-American brothers-in-spirit, Sacco and Vanzetti, the dubious distinction of being singled out for legal murder, to serve as deterring examples to the rising masses at the beginning of the eight-hour struggle. In each case international movements protested national class justice. In each case immigrant radicals adapted with little difficulty to U.S.-specific forms of the working-class struggle.

While German immigrants moved from one industrializing country to another in a similar stage of development, the case was different for East European immigrants coming from peasant societies. They, too, began to organize. But more than other immigrants, those from the Balkans, still under Austrian domination, were also engaged in a process of forming their own ethnic and national identity. Thus a considerable amount of organizational energy was directed toward other goals than working-class ones. To what degree did the process of creating a new community that stood between the homeland and the strange new world keep immigrants tied to traditional values rather than facilitating their solidarity with other workers? Ivan Čizmić shows how developments in the Old World made Serbians, Croatians, and Slovenes join in a common South Slav (Yugoslav) movement. The multiplicity of organizations they formed, the different interests and ideologies that pulled them in different directions, are surveyed. This shows where future research has to begin: did the remaining ties to the culture of origin, the avowed interest not to form a diaspora but to shape national destiny by struggling for a nation-state, interact with the integration into the working class in terms of consciousness? Was the experience at the workplace or the creating of a new community more important?

5

The Socialists and the Working Class in New York, 1890–96

HUBERT PERRIER

In the last few years a series of new studies have considerably enriched our knowledge of American socialism. One may find it odd, therefore, that there should remain striking deficiencies in this knowledge. The Socialist Labor party (SLP), for instance, virtually embodied socialism in the United States during the last quarter of the nineteenth century. Yet, concerning even the period of the 1890s, which has received the most attention, our understanding of this movement remains in many ways inadequate. In the first place, the tendency persists to overlook the distinction between official party doctrine and policies on the one hand and the underlying and further-spreading realities of the movement on the other. Likewise, the tradition of paying almost exclusive attention to the role of one leader, Daniel De Leon, still prevails. Historians have also focused too narrowly on the SLP's activities at a national level, and especially on its alleged endeavors to "capture" national organizations of labor, while case studies of local situations are sadly missing, as are attempts to reinterpret the movement as a whole in the light of recent research in labor history from a social historical perspective.[1] Moreover, ideological biases have, to a large extent, predetermined historians' conclusions. On one side the SLP serves as an illustration of the general thesis that socialism was fundamentally irrelevant to American conditions; on the other side it is suggested that the SLP might have swept the labor field in the 1890s, had it not been for De Leon's disastrous policies.[2] In both cases, however, studies present a similar picture of impotence and irrelevance, which is mainly explained in terms of "internal" factors, i.e. factors allegedly inherent in the nature either of socialism in general or of the De Leonite version of it.[3]

The following case study is an attempt to re-examine some of these conventional ideas. Two related hypotheses will serve as guidelines here: (1) it would be useful to obtain a better understanding of the forces that were really at work within the socialist movement, and out of whose interaction actual policies developed; and (2) such an understanding cannot be achieved unless one examines the multilayered relationships that existed between the movement and the larger context in which it operated. Ideally, it is within the full context of American social history in the Gilded Age that the unfolding of the movement should be viewed, if one is to arrive at a satisfactory interpretation of what happened to, and particularly what went wrong with, American socialism at that time.

Such an ambition, of course, is beyond the scope of this paper. However, a study of socialist activities in New York between 1890 and 1896 will, we hope, allow us to disentangle some of the intricately interwoven threads with which party history was spun. New York seems a legitimate choice, since nowhere else were socialists so strong or influential throughout the period. The emphasis on the relationship between socialists and the working class is justified by the fact that for people who regarded themselves as part of a larger labor movement as well as the bearers of a specific revolutionary program, essential aspects of both theory and practice hinged upon this major problem: the relationship between economic and political action in general, and that between their own central organization (a *political* party) and the working class and its institutions in particular. Finally, this study focuses on the period from 1890 to 1896 because, even though SLP tactics varied during these years, there was a distinct continuity in the socialists' approach to the issue—which remained their central aim—of imparting to American labor an orientation in keeping with their own revolutionary perspective.

The problem is addressed here from three angles. First, an examination of the currents of opinion coexisting within the New York SLP's sphere of influence at the turn of the 1890s suggests that the victory of an original "New Trade Union" line can be traced to the tireless quest for relevance to important developments on the New York scene by a new, English-speaking group of socialists. Second, a case study of socialist activities in the Central Labor Federation of New York, a labor body dominated by SLP-oriented trade unionists, deals with the dialectic of theoretical assumptions and concrete practice in the day-to-day task of organizing workers. Third, a study explores the ways in which socialists dealt with the "ethnic" and immigrant texture of New York life, and with the repercussions of the changing composition of the city's working class on the movement's life as well as strength. This leads to a discussion of the relative importance of "internal" as opposed to "external" factors for an assessment of SLP achievements and failure: a first step, one hopes, in a re-evaluation of a poorly understood period in the history of American socialism.

The conventional view of De Leon's rise to leadership as a great divide in SLP history has blurred the significance of earlier developments in this history. It has also obscured the fact that "De Leonism," far from developing in a vacuum, was rather a further elaboration upon a strategy that had already been outlined by late 1890, i.e. before De Leon became the actual (if unofficial) leader of the SLP. It will not detract from the specificity of De Leon's contribution but, rather, help put it in proper perspective, to determine what the main lines of this strategy were and, most of all, to what concrete circumstances they can be traced.[4]

The revolutionary program shaped during the crucial year 1890 can be regarded as a synthesis between two orientations that had in the two preceding years given rise to two successive and also antagonistic programs: (1) to "Americanize" the SLP, i.e. rid it of its most glaringly Germanic aspects and make its message heard by a larger and more representative cross-section of the American population than heretofore, and (2) to strengthen its links with the labor movement as a preliminary condition for making the party its recognized vanguard. The first objective was the essence of the party's national line in 1888–89, under the secretaryship of W. L. Rosenberg. The Rosenberg or "political" faction denied the ability of labor organizations to play a significant, progressive role in a context of accelerated industrial concentration and mechanization, and regarded the loosening of the party's ties with labor as a necessity in order to increase its relevance to American conditions. They also advocated shifting the fulcrum of party activity to electoral campaigning in conformity with the national political tradition. In that, they could not help but antagonize a majority of New York socialists, essentially the city's "German Section," which combined an overwhelming superiority in numbers and the support of the *New Yorker Volkszeitung*, an influential socialistic daily with close relations with powerful craft unions.[5] The rebellion of the *Volkszeitung* or "economic" faction led to the ousting of Rosenberg and his friends from the SLP National Executive Committee in September 1889. A month later in Chicago a party national convention legalized the coup d'état and gave official recognition to the policy of active socialist involvement in working-class economic action. On the other hand, the convention's resolution on politics boiled down to abandoning "independent political action" in the near future and tying up socialist politics in the long term with the progress of organization in the economic field.[6]

The overhauling of the party that accompanied the victory of the economic line of action gave all the reins of the New York party structure to supporters of this line. Among them was Lucien Sanial, a member of the American section who had sided with the majority on the issue of the party's vital links with labor. It was mainly through his brilliant editorship of the *Workmen's Advocate,* the SLP's English-language official organ, that the next advance in party strategy was made.[7] By mid-1890 New York socialists had again embarked on a course of immediate as well as systematic electoral action.[8] This was less of a paradoxical turnabout than it might seem, if one views it in the context of their search for relevance to rapid developments on the city's labor and radical scene.

At the outset several stands taken by the American Federation of Labor leadership caused the *Advocate* to question the foundation for the socialists' faith in the federation's willingness to implement its declared dedication to far-reaching, anticapitalist goals.[9] Simultaneously, the active role played by New York socialists in the eight-hour movement met with significant successes, including their undisputed leadership in the demonstrations of May Day 1890.[10] This stimulated their confidence in their ability to spearhead what Sanial increasingly came to define as the "progressive" (as opposed to "conservative") camp within the labor movement, and combined with their mounting disgust with the Central Labor Union to persuade them to break away from it and re-form the Central Labor Federation (CLF) in June.[11] At the same time, the *Advocate* hailed the steps toward political action then being taken by a number of "Nationalist Clubs." Its support for SLP participation in the fall election actually had much to do with the general convergence it saw between its own views and those of the more "advanced" of Edward Bellamy's followers, whom it deemed capable of reaching a significant number of English speakers.[12]

This decision, in turn, played a major part in the degradation of the relationships between SLP and AFL, which materialized in the controversy that followed Samuel Gompers's refusal to return to the re-formed CLF the AFL charter it had formerly held. Socialist tactics in this respect were related to the global strategy the *Advocate* was busy giving shape to during those months. This strategy expressed the socialists' determination to avail themselves of the ideological effervescence characterizing their environment in order to bear more effectively on the policies of American labor.[13] The objective was simultaneously to open channels of influence for socialist labor activists within the AFL and to give the party as such direct access to these channels. This accounts for the formal admittance of SLP delegates to the CLF (July 1890) as well as for the attempt to secure the official affiliation of the CLF to the AFL, which lasted until Sanial lost the final battle on the AFL convention floor in Detroit (December). The "principle of unity between the political and economic organizations," which was the cornerstone of the socialists' argumentation during the quarrel, meant in practice that they were at that time willing to consider a division of roles between AFL and SLP. This was upon one condition: that the trade unions accept the necessity of political action as an indispensable complement to industrial action, and that they identify the SLP as the legitimate "political arm" of labor. While Gompers, alarmed at such a challenge to his efforts to justify "pure and simple" economic action, cleverly chose to fight it out with Sanial on the formal issue of the SLP's direct representation in the CLF, the real division was between two antagonistic programs for American labor.[14]

After the Detroit convention there remained one more step to be taken for the next and definitive shift in analysis to take place. This consisted in declaring the AFL unfit for a positive role even as an economic organization, and characterizing its leaders as stumbling-blocks (and, increasingly, the *main* stumbling-blocks) in the march of American workers toward socialism. Although this view received its most memorable formulations in De Leon's speeches and *People* editorials, it can already be found in embryo in Sanial's statements after the AFL 1890 convention.[15] After this decisive change from Sanial's earlier interpretation of the labor scene was made, the general formula concerning the relationship between economic and political action remained in all essentials the same until 1896. In order to attack capitalism simultaneously on two fronts, it was necessary to establish organic ties between the political party and the "bona fide" segment of organized labor. This was the theoretical foundation on which successive tactical moves were based until the founding of the Socialist Trade and Labor Alliance ushered in a new era.[16]

In practice, however, the party leadership envisaged these two "arms of the labor movement"—the "economic" and the "political"—in unequal terms. The political was in fact the superior weapon. Necessary in the short term to secure through legislation advantages for workers more durable than those economic action could ever achieve, it was also to be the means of "full emancipation" through the "voting out" of capitalism and the "voting in" of the Co-operative Commonwealth or Socialist Republic. On the other hand, economic organizations, although the "natural outgrowth" of workers' need for self-defense, had a value as agencies for socialist education rather than for their own merits in the anticapitalist struggle. Indeed, the relevance of the strike and boycott to modern conditions was questionable. As the chasm between AFL and SLP leaderships widened, the federation's hostility to independent political action further stimulated party lead-

ers to extol the political and slight (or at least take for granted) the
economic side of the movement. In their eyes the controversy took
the shape of a war to the finish between two mutually exclusive conceptions: that of "pure and simple" unionism, this "duck flying with
one wing," and that of "New Trade Unionism," as from 1891 on the
SLP dubbed its own plan of attack, which it viewed as the only sufficiently comprehensive one to be able to lead the proletariat to its final
(political) victory over capitalism.[17]

Such was, in its essentials, the concept of action propounded by the
SLP leadership in countless press editorials as well as speeches, man-
ifestoes, pamphlets, and the like. Too little attention has been given
to the relationship between these theoretical assumptions and the
involvement of diverse categories of socialists in the concrete conditions in which they operated. The connection between general doctrine and the day-to-day activities of socialist working-class militants
is of special interest here.

The meetings of the Central Labor Federation, as recorded in the
Workmen's Advocate and later the *People*, constitute a rich source of
information on the practices of and debates among the pro-SLP delegates from a large number of organizations that met weekly at its
sessions.[18] To describe them as "pro-SLP" is not overstating the case:
not only were there numerous avowed party members and sympa-
thizers among them, but even after the SLP discontinued its formal
participation in CLF meetings, the latter still acknowledged its privileged ties with the party.[19]

On a number of points there were clearly discrepancies between
the leaderships' interpretation of American reality and the lay of the
land in New York as it might have been seen through a labor activist's
eyes. A first difficulty was that the leadership's claim that the age of
"fully monopolized" economy was fast approaching simply did not
apply to New York's characteristic pattern of production. There, as
opposed to the national tendency of combination, concentration, and
the related growth in scale and size of firms, the number of businesses
increased and their size dwindled. Some industries that were to play
a key role in terms of socialist influence, like the clothing industry,
were notably organized on a small-scale basis and characterized by a
lesser degree of capital concentration than other trades.[20] A related
challenge to socialist theory lay in the fact that while the SLP placed
its confidence in the historical role of the united working class, New
York rather conveyed the picture of a labor mosaic. The conjunction
of a fragmented production apparatus and the disruptions resulting
from rapid technological developments fostered extremely diverse as

well as changing working-class conditions.[21] In addition, inextricable jurisdictional disputes constantly set Knights of Labor assemblies against AFL trade unions, CLF against CLU affiliates, workers of long-union-ized crafts against recently created unions that would encroach on their jurisdiction. In many cases ideological differences intermingled with occupational and also ethnic divisions.[22] The net result of these combined factors was to make the task of building economic organi-zations of labor an extremely arduous one for all working-class orga-nizers in New York.

As far as they were concerned, socialist organizers could expect little assistance from party headquarters. As already noted, the lead-ership increasingly came to pay lip service to the problems of eco-nomic organization, while putting a premium on political education, organization, and struggle. Besides, it was comparatively indifferent to the particulars of the New York labor scene: characteristically, when they pleaded for the retention of their city as the seat of the executive of the party in 1893, New York socialists reviewed its advantages as a center for political activity but hardly mentioned its specific features as an industrial metropolis.[23] Such deficiencies left bona fide labor cadres with substantial room for initiative, if only to bridge the gap between theory and practice, and sometimes even to bend theory so as to make it fit with the requirements of field action.

Indeed, at the grass-roots level, CLF delegates gave an immense amount of attention to the concrete circumstances and problems of affiliated organizations. Nor did they begrudge their fighting com-rades assistance. New York's small and middle-sized employers bit-terly fought workers' organizations. Intense competition between enterprises, compounded with business instability, "required cutting variable costs to the bone, especially the wage bill." Even the older organizations of skilled workers were concerned with employers' at-tempts to depress wages and status by taking advantage of technolog-ical innovations, the changing composition of the labor force, or their own combined efforts. At the turn of the 1890s the campaign against "pool" beer and "pool" bread crystallized much of the fighting energy of the CLF. In those years the boycott was still a much-used weapon, but its effectiveness was lessened by the divisions within organized labor: indeed, the CLF's efforts to enforce "legitimate" boycotts among its own affiliates raised endless practical problems.[24] But even more characteristic, perhaps, of CLF practice were the "greenhorn" unions' struggles to obtain boss recognition. The strike of the Pearl Button Makers' Union, a minor member of the pro-SLP United Hebrew Trades and a CLF affiliate, in 1893 presented features that could be found in a great number of conflicts fought under the auspices of the CLF.

It started in January as a protest against boss intimidation of workers. Four hundred workers walked out and picketed the shops but suffered continued harassment by police. CLF assistance—a pattern that was repeated in inumerable strikes—included issuing subscription lists for strikers; visiting police headquarters to protest against brutality; holding a mass meeting to denounce the same; and, when after a month strikers badly suffered from want, setting up an entertainment committee so as to obtain funds through concerts, and holding more mass meetings in the "Hebrew district" in the Lower East Side. Despite fierce resistance by some of the employers, by the end of March the union reported the fight "nearly won," the product, it seems, of the combination of workers' endurance and unfailing CLF assistance.[25]

Thus it appears that the CLF by and large lived up to its mission of coordination and mutual assistance between its diverse members. To a certain extent it did so despite, rather than in accordance with, the party leadership's negative evaluation of the strike and boycott under modern capitalism, not to speak of its barely masked impatience with labor delegates' concerns about their union labels and other paraphernalia of economic action. It is no less clear, however, that staunch involvement in struggles for "immediate demands" could coexist not only with the deep-seated conviction among delegates that nothing short of the voting in of the Cooperative Commonwealth would bring "final emancipation," but also with the unabated efforts of most of them to "educate" workers to that realization, which constituted another and major side of the activities of both individual unions and the CLF.[26]

On one level SLP-oriented labor organizers seemed, indeed, to be satisfied with a situation where socialist activities proper were carried out on top of trade union chores. Thus union as well as CLF meetings would frequently comprise a discussion on how to increase the circulation of the party press, a lecture on some political topic, exhortations to acquire citizenship so as to participate in elections, and other "consciousness-raising" efforts. Members were also urged to attend additional meetings of a clear-cut political character. It was not exceptional to see an organization interrupt its proceedings and march in a body behind its banner to some SLP occasion. However earnestly economic issues were dealt with, the broader educational and political perspective dear to the hearts of all socialists was therefore never lost sight of.[27]

It is possible, however, to detect a more fundamental link between socialist philosophy and CLF practice than the rather empirical coexistence of economic action and political concerns, with socialist education as a precarious bridge between them. The concrete circumstances of its affiliates called for the CLF to play the role it did. But into the very shaping of these circumstances a measure of policy choice, inspired by socialist doctrine, might have entered. For instance CLF intervention as a negotiator with employers or public authorities was required because in many cases individual unions could not rely on the central bodies of their trades in New York, which were often weak, if they existed at all. In addition to the central fact that many unions were recent, unstable, and even sporadic institutions, this may have reflected a characteristically socialist inclination toward placing one's fate in the hands of a central, cross-organization body like the CLF (the embodiment of a socialist ideal of labor solidarity) while deprecating administrative hierarchies for individual organizations. Similarly, if most unions had weak treasuries (a factor that called for financial solidarity), this was mostly because of their intrinsic weakness but also because the longer-established ones shared in the socialist view of paying little attention to the financial aspects of trade union policy. The originality of SLP labor activists therefore lay not only in the fact that they combined revolutionary with immediate goals but also in the way their long-range aims affected their practice in the field. This explains why, at the same time as they addressed themselves to specific trade problems, they opposed sheer "job consciousness." They were in fact at one with the leaders of the party in their conviction that what mattered most was to "unionize" workers, leading them in the process into the broad "movement" of their class, rather than to build up such and such a union as an end in itself.[28]

When taken to task for this approach, they denied—rightfully, it seems—that it made them poorer defenders of labor than their "pure and simple" counterparts. However, their concern with giving struggles a conscious direction against the capitalist order made them a different kind of activist, while it pointed to a more subtle convergence between the *People's* editorials and their own ideas than might have been perceptible at first sight. If, from leadership to labor organizers, the concept of socialist action varied on some points, it was a different position in the field (the rostrum and the editorial room on the one hand, the workshop and the union meeting hall on the other), rather than major ideological disagreements, that gave rise to these differences. Their familiarity with workers' concerns caused union leaders to disregard in practice the most extreme views of SLP newspaper editors on, say, the futility of strikes. Conversely they welcomed the notion that their efforts fitted into the framework of a great, approaching social revolution. There are signs that a similar broad accord with the party's general pronouncements on today's and tomorrow's society extended in some measure to the rank and file:

given the rarity of significant material rewards, class-conscious sympathy between members was the main source of solidarity with the union as well as of collective strength. It originated in a shared, deeply felt concern with the "labor movement" as united by a common cause and mission, which SLP influence helped make part of the consciousness of thousands of workers.[29]

Such convergences, more than anything else, welded the various parts of the SLP together. However, they left a major problem unsolved. Despite systematic educational efforts, the dynamics of industrial action did not evidently point to the SLP ballot as the solution to the social problems that they brought to the surface. Here again, various levels of SLP response should be considered. Hailing industrial struggles as tokens of discontent with the existing order, socialist orators would rush to the scenes of disturbances and, in the best of cases, bring heart-felt encouragement and even material contributions. At worst, however, their insistence that the struggle must be not only carried over to the political plane as well, but actually removed from the industrial field to the electoral one, was seriously inconsistent with the workers' primary concern, i.e. to win the struggle.[30] On the level of labor cadres, it is possible (taking the CLF as an example again) to draw a distinction between those delegates who were primarily SLP officials, and who therefore were mainly busy adjusting the party's official views to the CLF setting, and those delegates who, whether party members or not, were mostly concerned with instigating shop-floor action and spreading struggles, even if they did not neglect the battle for socialist consciousness. For the latter category, at least, a tension must have arisen at times between the dynamics of working-class mobilization on its own terrain (the shop floor, factory, working-class neighborhood) and with its own weapons (the walkout, self-organizaton against bosses and police, and other experiments in democracy), and the socialist demand that such radical potential be expressed in a totally different form and at a different point of time, i.e. votes for the SLP in regular elections. Yet the potential contradiction between these two different logics did not result in any clear, articulated challenge to the prevailing concept of socialist politics. Whatever this owed to the party leadership's privileged position in terms of policy making, or to the common dependence of all socialists upon the traditional equation between politics and electoral activity, or to any other cause, the fact remains that in these years there emerged no alternative, from socialist ranks, to the pattern of subservience of industrial to electoral struggle, and of economic to political organization, which prevailed in party doctrine.[31]

If anything like an alternative to "New Trade Unionism" was sketched during these years, it took shape outside the party's orbit rather than within it. This does not mean, however, that for all the continuity in the CLF's career from June 1890 to the time when it participated in the founding of the STLA (December 1895), no conflict took place among its members. At some critical points the CLF encountered severe problems in connection with some of its most influential affiliates. Such was the case with the crisis that, in 1891, saw the loss to the CLF of Bakers and Confectioners Local 7, German-American Typographia, and Brewers 1, all prominent organizations within their trades. In 1895–96 took place another exodus of CLF stalwarts, including Cigarmakers 90, formerly a leading exponent of "New Trade Unionism." The dates and circumstances of the crises (the escalating confrontation between AFL and SLP in 1891, the founding of the STLA five years later) point to one glaring cause for such losses: all refused, at different points, to endorse a belligerent attitude toward the AFL.[32] However, the fact that all were organizations of German craftsmen suggests another type of cause. If, indeed—and it is the contention of this paper that a good deal of the opponents' argumentation was sheer ideological garb for their vested interest in opting against party policy—one probes below the surface of political controversy, one hits upon a fundamental social phenomenon: that of the changing composition of the working population in New York, notably the increasingly rapid, mass influx of "new" immigrants. This evolution expressed itself in the form of major changes in the ethnic and social base of the SLP in the first years of the 1890s. On this level, too, it is interesting to observe the dialectic between SLP theory and strategy (i.e. the "subjective" perception socialists had of these developments and the responses they evolved) and the practical requirements of situations whose complexity tended to present insuperable difficulties.

To a certain extent, at least, socialists identified and set out to address the problem raised by the arrival of wave after wave of "new" immigrants. While the *People* carried headlines that it was "time to drop the cry against the foreign workingman," CLF delegates refused to go along with calls for the restriction of immigration, as illustrated by the AFL and, in New York, the CLU.[33]

However, while a nonexclusive philosophy resulted in a nonexclusive membership, the ethnic composition of both SLP and CLF inevitably reflected the particular histories and outlooks of the "old" and "new" immigrant groups. Thus, if the Irish among the "old" and Italians among the "new" provided few recruits, Germans on the one hand and East European Jews on the other (with a sprinkling of

Scandinavians and of Poles, Bohemians, Hungarians, and other East Europeans) were the pillars of the New York SLP between 1890 and 1896. In addition, groups did not occupy the same position at the same moment. At the turn of the nineties the Germans virtually embodied socialism. Jewish immigration, on the other hand, was still a recent phenomenon. But as early as 1889 the party press hailed the rapid development of socialist influence among Yiddish-speaking workers. The shift from German hegemony to Jewish active participation is, in a way, a summary of the SLP's evolution during those years.[34]

Facing a common class enemy, socialists of all backgrounds effectively practiced mutual solidarity. On the other hand, the specific terms of each group's relationship to the larger society was bound to affect its outlook. Such contrasts expressed themselves, in particular, in differing attitudes toward the AFL. The "new" immigrants, who were excluded from many established unions in the first place, had far less trouble adhering to the *People's* view that the AFL was a fraud than did long-standing members of the federation, for all their socialist proclivities. The latter's continued attachment to the AFL is, in fact, mainly to be understood in the context of the role the federation played as an agent of social integration for its "aristocracy of labor" membership during the 1890s. This process, in part a product of the alleged threat to skilled workers' status and jobs constituted by the mass arrival of new immigrants, was already underway in the early years of the decade. This situation presented radically oriented craft unionists with a dilemma. On the one hand, they tried to open their organizations to the newcomers, and opposed the conservative unions' policies of exacting high membership dues on the grounds that they kept poorer workers out of unions. On the other hand, the union strength achieved through more conservative policies became increasingly attractive to them. This may explain why, as the conflict between AFL and SLP escalated, an increasing number of craft unionists— most of them German-Americans—made uneasy allies for full-fledged "New Trade Unionists," until they balked or even seceded.[35]

The logical result of such an erosion of its traditional working-class base might have been, in the case of the SLP, to develop into an organization of "greenhorn" workers. There lay an immense field for future development, as socialists recognized it, especially as these workers were largely ignored by the mainstream of American labor. But the SLP's record in this respect remained a mixture of significant successes and ultimate failure to cope with all the complexities involved. On the one hand, it is a fact that years before the golden age of Yiddish socialism in New York (1910–18) a significant proportion of Jewish immigrants were attracted to the SLP, owing mostly to the determinant role Jewish socialists played in founding economic organizations of Yiddish-speaking workers.[36] On the other hand, it is possible to trace some of the limits of the socialists' influence among these workers to their theoretical approach to the issue of race and ethnic affiliation. Genuine as it was, the socialist concept of working-class solidarity owed much to the SLP's view of the worker as "Political Man," wielder of the potent weapon of the ballot, rather than "Social Man," as specified along ethnic, linguistic, and cultural lines. Significantly, when the *People* or the delegates to the CLF broached the subject of ethnicity, it was, in truth, sometimes to refute charges against immigrant labor. But just as often the emphasis was on ethnicity as a negative factor, an obstacle to the full expression of working-class unity as socialists saw it, i.e. political unity behind SLP electoral tickets. This was particularly true of the party's leaders, who sometimes expressed impatience with the union rank and file's slowness in acquiring citizenship. But even for Jewish socialist cadres, although helping Yiddish-speaking workers to improve their concrete conditions was an ever-present concern for them, organizing workers into unions (and this, given the overlap of occupational and ethnic lines in the case of Jewish workers, implied taking ethnic specificities into account) was only a first step in the proposed fusion of all workers into a vast proletarian army along *political* lines, in which ethnic affiliations would hopefully have been transcended.

In other words, while the masses' ethnic identity forced itself upon the attention of politically minded, but also labor-devoted, cadres, the latter were reluctant to give up the assimilationist outlook that accorded with their own "cosmopolitan" rather than strictly Jewish view of the world. A typical statement in the Yiddish *Arbeiter Zeitung* claimed that the Jews of America "do not consider themselves God's chosen people; they come as workers, as members and allies of the American working class. Therein lies the solution of the entire Jewish question in America." This was a brave statement for a movement with hardly a foothold in the field as yet, and which aspired to organize immigrants fresh from the world of "shtetl" and synagogue. One may nevertheless wonder whether the view of the national question underlying this statement was not oversimplified. Expressing, in Morris Schappes's words, "disdain for anything not directly concerned with the class struggle in the narrowest sense," it may even have been an obstacle to a durable socialist influence among Jewish workers. Although the program of "erasing all divisions between Jew and non-Jew in the world of the workers" clearly appealed to Yiddish-speaking toilers, it is possible that their leaders' insistence that the only reason for building up distinct Jewish organizations was a pragmatic and linguistic one had a negative result in terms of rank-and-file solidarity with these organizations. For instance, this may have been an additional reason for Jewish workers becoming indifferent to their unions as soon as a strike had been won—only an *additional* reason, however, because clearly the characteristics of Jewish radicalism (the sudden flares of industrial unrest, followed by periods of apathy and lack of interest in the unions, the marked interest in political theory but also the urge to work one's way out of the working class, and other tendencies that have been noted by many observers) derived from a set of factors many of which reached far beyond the sphere of socialist political intervention, i.e. "objective" factors rooted in the Jewish community's traditions, cultural experience, and relationship to its new American environment.[37]

It is possible to make similar observations concerning the SLP's response to the unrest that shook New York's Lower East Side in 1893–94. Following a crash on the New York Stock Exchange, a financial panic developed into a major industrial and business depression in the summer of 1893. In New York as in other cities, unemployment and distress were severe, and the most cruelly affected were "new" immigrants, especially Jewish workers on the Lower East Side. In August demonstrations and hunger marches broke out there, followed by more than a week of unrest. These events created a sense of emergency among all radical and labor elements. In a context of ruthless competition between conflicting views about remedies and, particularly, the issue of "immediate" relief, all factions vied in their efforts to relate to popular discontent and to channel it into the modes of action they favored.[38]

The SLP's initial reaction was to issue statements blaming the crisis on the "planless and unjust" system of capitalism and urging working-class political action as the only way out. But the condemnation of all attempts to seek relief from capitalists and their "political agents," which went along with this reassertion of basic SLP principles, soon placed socialists in an uncomfortable situation: in a contradiction-ridden one, insofar as the socialist United Hebrew Trades quite naturally bore the brunt of relief-giving in the tenements; and also in a dangerous one, because this stand left Gompers and other antisocialist labor leaders room to capitalize on the existing unrest by promoting their brand of "practical" unionism through a tireless succession of labor conferences, mass meetings, and delegations to pressure mayor and governor for relief work.[39]

In the last days of December, however, a sudden tactical turnabout bore witness to the SLP leaders' realization of the perils involved in this divorce between theory and concrete developments. This turnabout quickly brought the New York party to the forefront of a new coalition movement for relief work. The whole episode (January–March 1894) was to a large extent a repetition of the scenario of the previous months. Only this time the socialists were inside the movement, and increasingly influential in it. This was manifest at the "monster meeting" of 30 January at Madison Square Garden—"the greatest indoor labor meeting which New York has seen for a decade," wrote the *Sun*—which was dominated by SLP orators. The weeks that followed probably marked the highest tide of socialist confidence and expectations during the whole period.[40]

Significant as it was, this socialist triumph left the problem of relief for the unemployed intact, and therefore offered no guarantee as to the depth and durability of SLP influence on a recent and fragile coalition. In particular, it was not certain whether it was worth placing the party in contradiction with its earlier analyses and even, potentially, with the whole SLP tenet that no real solution to the problems of workers under capitalism could be found outside the "ultimate" socialist one. The answer to this question seems to have been a negative one, for shortly after difficulties developed within the coalition, a SLP manifesto declared the movement for the unemployed adjourned *sine die*.[41]

It would be tempting to argue here that the SLP's rigid theoretical assumptions (its dogmatic approach to social amelioration under capitalism, or its ingrained tendency to reduce the field of working-class politics to socialist campaigning) caused it to lose the best chance it may ever have had of meeting the needs of the poor, unorganized, and alienated masses. Yet it would be misleading to see, in the retreat that socialists beat in March 1894, *only* the mark of their own "subjective" deficiencies. When they grappled with the problem of the unemployed, SLP activists, owing to their tireless energy but also to the outposts Jewish socialists had built up in new immigrant territory, were for a short while rather more successful than their opponents in providing popular protest with leadership and orientation. But eventually they stumbled on the same obstacles as did their rivals. In those stirring months of 1893 and 1894 no organization, whatever its ideology, really managed to relate deeply or durably to such an inchoate and amorphous social force as was then constituted by the destitute, alienated unemployed of New York: another reminder of how heavily "objective conditions" weighed on the efforts of all the contenders for working-class allegiance.

It should be clear even from this limited study that the conventional emphasis on the SLP's "internal" limitations, and notably on the weaknesses embodied in De Leon's leadership, has resulted in a distorted picture of the movement in that period. The ups and downs of the SLP's fortunes, and ultimately its failure to fulfill its self-appointed role as leader of a great social revolution, rather partook of a more complex combination of "internal" and "external" causes than has heretofore been acknowledged.

A case in point is the evolution of the merciless struggle between SLP and AFL both during the period we have examined and in the later 1890s. In both periods the fortunes of the SLP were dialectically related to the progress of the federation: the former's predictions of victory of "New" over "pure and simple" unionism made sense, in the judgment of a significant segment of the New York working class, in direct relation to the AFL's slow and uncertain growth in the first years of the decade; on the other hand, the same expectations were emptied of much of their substance as it became clear to all that the federation was irrevocably and quickly expanding from 1897 onward. It would be as misleading, however, to characterize the SLP's defeat as only the product of inept tactics inspired by a stubborn, self-isolating, and self-destructive hostility to the AFL, as it would be to interpret it as the logical consequence of some intrinsic superiority of "business" over "ideological" unionism.[42] Pending a much-needed reexamination of the Socialist Trade and Labor Alliance, it appears from the available evidence that all kinds of factors combined to bolster the AFL while leaving the socialists stranded.

First, the SLP found itself in a strategic impasse. Faced with the continued erosion of its traditional German and craft unionist base, it was neither ideologically prepared nor practically able to take the decisive steps toward attracting a radically new type of following. It therefore fell back on a pattern of competing with the AFL as to which had the more successful model of organization vis-à-vis a substantially overlapping constituency, while toying with several formulas concerning the nature of the national body which should bear the colors of the socialist crusade in the economic field. In the process the socialists faced a second and major obstacle. The depression of the mid-1890s gave a formidable boost to the economic policies of conservative craft unions. While the SLP was striving to assume the leadership of the unemployed, socialist unions reported increasing difficulties. Indeed, by 1897 the line was irrevocably drawn between the stabler, conservative unions, which had weathered the crisis thanks to their ability to pay high unemployment benefits out of rich treasuries, and those organizations (including a considerable number of pro-

SLP ones) that were weakened or simply went under. When, in view of these results, the AFL's pattern of labor organization started encroaching on the till then almost exclusively socialist field of Yiddish unionism, the die was virtually cast in favor of the conservative versus socialist labor program. By the turn of the century AFL craft unions emerged as the undisputed leaders of the organized fraction of the American working class, their increased strength reflecting "a rising prosperity, a willingness by employers to treat skilled labor with equity, and the fusing of 'old' immigrants and second generation Americans into a privileged working class."[43]

This fateful evolution was accelerated by developments in the political field. While the first electoral setbacks of the SLP did not take place until the end of the decade, its progress in this field remained slow—too slow, indeed, to offset the temptation then presented to trade unions by the first tangible successes of political activity of the "reward your friends, punish your enemies" type. It became clear even to some formerly SLP-oriented union leaders that it would be a long time until socialists by themselves would be strong enough in state legislatures to enact badly needed legislation on behalf of the working class.[44]

In sum, from 1896 on, most objective trends snowballed to produce a divisive effect on the camp of "New Trade Unionism" and to make its program of political unity between all workers on a revolutionary socialist platform an increasingly impractical one. The response of the SLP leadership is well known but not necessarily well understood. Assailed from all quarters by developments that checked its advance and even undermined its positions, it chose to cling to its revolutionary stand whatever the prevailing odds. If the masses could not be won immediately, at least the "enlightened" minority should be preserved from ideological contamination. Since capitalism was heading toward its own demise in any case, numbers should not count so much as revolutionary preparedness. Such a mode of reasoning was self-admittedly at the root of the STLA. It testified to the peculiar blend of "voluntarism" and historical determinism that increasingly characterized the SLP in post-1896 years.[45]

This much must be granted. Yet one would feel less uneasy about the amount of scorn heaped upon De Leon and the SLP if a more successful approach to the strategic difficulties of organizing a revolutionary working-class movement in the United States had emerged at that time (or, indeed, at any time). But given the failure of alternative socialist lines, from that of the *Volkszeitung* group in the late 1880s to that of the Socialist party in the Progressive Era, to shape a real alternative to the hold of business unionism over the American

working class, one may wonder whether the historian's favorable pre-
disposition toward this more "moderate" brand of socialism is really
founded. There are signs, after all, that some of its successes—which
remained, needless to say, relative ones—should be attributed to cir-
cumstantial factors as much as to any superiority of its views. As to
their ultimate failure, De Leon, for one, may have shown some insight
when he warned his opponents that "the trade union leaders will let
you bore from within only enough to throw you out of the hole bored
by you."[46] Many historians would, of course, argue that De Leon must
be blamed in the first place for the divorce between socialism and the
mainstream of labor that was consummated in the 1890s and could
never be made up for in later years. However, this view conveniently
ignores the AFL leadership's shared responsibility in the belligerence,
while the widespread assumption that a "real cohesion would have
existed between the socialists and the trade union movement had De
Leon never appeared on the scene" simply begs the question. It would
be just as legitimate, in fact, to view the De Leonites as the acute, if
isolated, analysts of the AFL as a vehicle thoroughly inadequate to
the pursuit of socialist goals.[47]

The problem remains, of course, of the SLP's failure to give life to
a successful alternative of its own to class-collaboration unionism. Although we hope this study has thrown some light on the context in
which this failure took place, further studies will be necessary to ex-
plore this context more fully. Such exploration will have necessarily
to take into account the instruments of social analysis available to De
Leon and his friends. Certain of their political limitations are glaringly obvious, such as their inadequate distinction between the imper-
atives of long-term strategy and the flexibility required by tactics: for
instance, the principle of having "the contemplated step square with
the ultimate aim," although an acceptable test of union policy in terms
of general strategy, became a tremendous liability when translated by
the party convention of 1900 into the exclusion of any officer of a
nonsocialist labor organization.[48] As far as the inadequacy of their
social analysis is concerned, an important point remains to be interpreted. It is clear—if we confine ourselves to the weaknesses brought
to the fore in this study—that the reduction of politics to electoral
campaigning resulted from a short-sighted analysis of the capitalist
state, and the limited understanding of crucial subdivisions within the
working class was a consequence of a messianic conception of this
class's role in history. Likewise, it is possible to see in the deterministic
optimism still prevalent with De Leon and his companions (for all
their vigorous militancy) a token of "the opium of optimism and
certitude" that Gabriel Kolko sees as a particularly negative dimension

of the Marxist tradition. But we have yet to clarify, in each case, the relative importance of the interpretation of Marxism in vogue within the Second International, and of the fashion in which the De Leonites themselves handled this heritage.[49]

We run the risk, however, of granting, once again, too much importance to "subjective" factors. In the party's steady march to ideological rigidification, each step can be traced in terms of a corresponding setback in its confrontation with outside reality. What one needs to do, in fact, is to have at every moment both aspects of the problem in view: on the side of subjective factors, there was that disastrous tendency to trust in the "logic of events," the supposedly predetermined direction of history, to transform today's defeats into tomorrow's victories; but just as disastrous for the socialist cause were the "objective" dynamics of the *real* logic of events, which in every way contradicted their expectations. Ultimately, perhaps, the distinction between "external" and "internal" factors becomes an artificial one. Whatever their origins, subjective limitations acted just as other material factors, and indeed combined with actual objective developments in American society, to render the questions posed to revolutionary thought, at least in that time and place, practically insoluble.

NOTES

1. See John Laslett's valuable methodological comments in John H. M. Laslett and Seymour Martin Lipset, eds. *Failure of a Dream? Essays in the History of American Socialism* (New York, 1974), pp. 200–201, 221–22, 244–49.

2. For an instance of the first view, see Daniel Bell, *Marxian Socialism in the United States* (Princeton, N.J., 1967); for an instance of the second, see Philip S. Foner, *History of the Labor Movement in the United States*, 2 (New York, 1955):278–96.

3. Laslett and Lipset, *Failure.* For a useful review of literature on the SLP, see L. Glen Seretan, "The Personal Style and Political Methods of Daniel De Leon: A Reconsideration," *Labor History* 14 (Spring 1973):163–201. Since this paper was written in 1978, Seretan has added an important piece to that literature with his biography, *Daniel De Leon: The Odyssey of an American Marxist* (Cambridge, Mass., 1979).

4. De Leon joined the SLP on 1 Oct. 1890, at the head of a delegation of Nationalists after the failure of their attempt to build a political organization that would have acted in close association with the SLP without merging with it. His rise in the SLP was rapid, but did not reach its peak until he was given the editorship of the *People* in Aug. 1891. However, as a Nationalist luminary and an orator whose services were in great demand, he may have exerted some influence on the party even from the outside. *Workmen's Advocate (WA)*, 15 Mar. 1890, p. 3; 4 Oct. 1890, p. 1. On the other hand, it is a mistake to make him responsible for key party policies in 1890, as does Foner, *History,* 2:279–86. Even after he became the leader of the

party, there were, of course, counterforces to his influence. The myth of De Leon as "Pope" of the SLP in these early years is part of the rewriting of party history by his ideological foes, who have done much to obscure the issue of the true balance of power in the SLP, as well as of the real causes for dissension—questions which historians have subsequently by-passed. See Morris Hillquit, *History of Socialism in the United States* (New York, 1910), pp. 295–96; Hillquit, *Loose Leaves from a Busy Life* (New York, 1934), p. 45; *Volkszeitung*, 13 May 1914, quoted by Henry Kuhn in *Daniel De Leon: The Man and His Work* (New York, 1969), 1:24–25.

5. The rift was precipitated by the discouragement that seized socialists in late 1887, following the failure of their efforts to revive the labor-political movement of 1886: Hillquit, *History* pp. 256–57. Although most protagonists on both sides were German-Americans, they addressed themselves to different constituencies. The *Volkszeitung* stood for the tradition of working-class organization, which accounted for the strong socialist influence on the New York labor movement. The German section, 700 to 800 members strong, was also supported by the small Jewish section. On the other side, Rosenberg and his group derived their main support from the small American section, which deserved its name not so much because of the national origins of its members as because they were intent on reaching English speakers. *WA*, 30 June 1888, p. 2; 29 Sept. 1888, p. 2; 24 Nov. 1888, p. 1; 7 Sept. 1889, p. 2; *The Education of Abraham Cahan* (Philadelphia, 1969), pp. 344–48, 407–8, 412.

6. *WA*, 26 Oct. 1889, p. 3; 2 Nov. 1889, p. 2.

7. Among those who seconded Sanial were Hugo Vogt and Abraham Cahan, both examples of first-generation immigrants who, although they were active among German- and Yiddish-speaking workers respectively, put a premium on the development of the American section. *Education of Abraham Cahan.*

8. *WA*, 14 June 1890, p. 1; 13 Sept. 1890, p. 1.

9. *Ibid.*, 21 Dec. 1889, p. 2; 19 Apr. 1890, p. 2; 17 May 1890, p. 2. See also *ibid.*, 12 Dec. 1889, p. 1, for Sanial's views on the Knights of Labor.

10. *New York Sun*, 1 May 1890, p. 3; 2 May 1890, p. 2; *WA*, 10 May 1890, p. 1.

11. *WA*, 31 May 1890, p. 2; 28 June 1890, p. 1. The CLF had first been formed in Feb. 1889 following a split in the CLU, which was subsequently reunited (Dec. 1889). It is an important fact that SLP objections to the CLU were not only political ones but had also much to do with the fact that in its eyes the union was not active enough in the economic field. *WA*, 19 July 1890, p. 2.

12. *WA*, 5 July 1890, p. 2; 9 Aug. 1890, p. 1. See above, n. 4.

13. At that time boundaries between socialists, Nationalists, and other radical and reform groups were not sharply drawn. The interest in "socialistic" ideas, which had been stimulated by Edward Bellamy's *Looking Backward*, was growing rapidly at the turn of the decade and made such ideas as the nationalization of industry, an expanded role for the government, and social justice widely discussed themes in New York reform-oriented circles. There was a considerable degree of overlapping in membership and a good deal of mutual influence between diverse groups. De Leon himself was a good example of this ideological and organizational fluidity. As the decade opened, he was not only one of Bellamy's lieutenants in New

York but also a member of various groups of radical intellectuals and a member of L.A. 1563, a "mixed local" of the Knights of Labor. *WA*, 22 Feb. 1890, p. 1; 31 May 1890, p. 2; Rudolph Katz in *Daniel De Leon*, 2:28. See also Henry Bedford, *Socialism and the Workers in Massachusetts, 1886–1912* (Amherst, Mass., 1966), chs. 1, 2.

14. *WA*, 15 Nov. 1890; *Proceedings of the 10th Annual Convention of the AFL* (Detroit, 1890), pp. 12, 17, 23–26.

15. *WA*, 20 Dec. 1890, p. 1; 27 Dec. 1890, p. 2; *People*, 6 Dec. 1891, p. 2; 24 Dec. 1893, p. 2.

16. The ruling out of the AFL as an adequate national structure for socialist action did not entail the end of the SLP labor activists' work within affiliates of the federation. To avoid confusion concerning the SLP's labor policies before 1896, socialist activities on the local and shop-floor level should be carefully distinguished from the debate among them as to what national structure should either be supported or created in order to oppose the discarded AFL. Historians seem to have overlooked an early SLP attempt to build a "dual" national organization: the United Central Federations, a grouping of city central bodies organized along the lines of the New York CLF. *People*, 23 Apr. 1893, p. 2; 14 May 1893, p. 2; 11 June 1893, p. 2. This endeavor took place simultaneously with the attempt to permeate the Knights of Labor, which has been well studied; see, for instance, Howard Quint, *The Forging of American Socialism* (Columbia, Mo., 1953), pp. 153–60. This relatively open situation lasted until the De Leonites were expelled from the Knights in Nov.–Dec. 1895. The subsequent founding of the Socialist Trade and Labor Alliance represented a radical departure from the previous course of action on two counts: (1) all existing organizations of labor were now declared unfit for socialist action, unless they be controlled by the SLP in the first place; and (2) the logic of the STLA, if not its explicit purpose, was toward "war" with existing organizations at all levels, no longer only with their national "misleaders." It is therefore legitimate to see 1896 as a watershed in terms of the SLP's labor policies. *Proceedings of the 9th Convention of the SLP* (New York, 1896), pp. 25–30; Quint, *American Socialism*, p. 164; David Herreshoff, *The Origins of American Marxism* (Detroit, 1967), p. 126.

17. *WA*, 21 Dec. 1889, p. 2; 17 May 1890, p. 2; *People*, 26 July 1891, p. 5; 28 Aug. 1892, p. 2; 24 Sept. 1893, p. 1; De Leon, *Reform or Revolution* (New York, 1974), pp. 20–21, 31. This strategy was related to the socialists' analysis of late Gilded Age capitalism. Specifically they thought that it was approaching an ultimate stage of development when "fully monopolized" capital would confront a mass and largely undifferentiated proletariat, with the voting in of the Socialist Commonwealth the next and "logical" stage of historical evolution. Although Sanial and De Leon called for activism and criticized political passivity, they did not discard the legacy of historical determinism, influenced by the positivist evolutionism of the natural sciences, which seems to have been a feature common to all the "socialistic" tendencies of the age. See Richard T. Ely, *The Labor Movement in America* (New York, 1969), p. 213.

18. D.A. 49 of the Knights of Labor was another SLP-led body in New York in the early 1890s. Nevertheless, it did not become central to party strategy until 1893. Largely an English-speaking body, it seems to have regrouped a less representative cross-section of labor organizations than

did the CLF, although socialist Yiddish organizations joined it in 1893–94. Kuhn in *Daniel De Leon*, 1:10; Quint, *American Socialism*, p. 153; "Summary of Members D.A. 49, July 1, 1895," SLP Collection, Additions of 1974, Wisconsin State Historical Society (WSHS).

19. *People*, 10 Jan. 1892, p. 3; 11 June 1893, p. 2.

20. Melvyn Dubofsky, *When Workers Organize: New York City in the Progressive Age* (Amherst, Mass., 1968), pp. 5–6; Alexander C. Flick, ed., *History of the State of New York* (New York, 1935), pp. 10, 42–48, 51–53, 71.

21. *Social Economist* 5 (Nov. 1893):281–84; *ibid.* (Dec. 1893):353–58; Lucy W. Killough, *The Tobacco Products Industry in New York and Its Environs* (New York, 1924), pp. 20–26; Robert Christie, *Empire in Wood: A History of the Carpenters' Union* (Ithaca, N.Y., 1956), pp. 79–90.

22. Thus the antagonism between CLF and CLU was based upon a series of overlapping factors. The latter body was dominated by the building trades, and its members, to a large extent English-speaking, were predominantly affiliated with the KOL. Some of its leaders were charged with being "Tammany Hall heelers." Economic solidarities, compounded by ethnic affiliations, tended to prevail upon ideological inclinations, so that socialists were frustrated in their efforts to win over militant members of the CLU. *WA*, 13 Sept. 1890, p. 1; 20 Dec. 1890, p. 3. In addition, the "Board of Walking Delegates" whipped organizations in the building trades into line, depriving the CLF of any influence in this sector. *WA*, 3 Sept. 1890, p. 1; 20 Dec. 1890, p. 3.

23. *People*, 20 Aug. 1893, p. 3.

24. Dubofsky, *When Workers Organize*; *WA*, 4 Jan. 1890, p. 1; 1 Mar. 1890, p. 4; *People*, 16 Apr. 1893, p. 2; U.S. Industrial Commission, *Reports of the Industrial Commission on Immigration*, 15 (Washington, D.C., 1901):385–89; Hugo Miller, "Deutsch-Americanische Typographia," in George Tracy, *History of the Typographical Union* (Indianapolis, 1913), p. 1087; Hermann Schlüter, *The Brewing Industry and the Brewery Movement in America* (Cincinnati, 1910).

25. *People*, 29 Jan. 1893 to 2 Apr. 1893.

26. Katz in *Daniel De Leon*, 2:25–27; *People*, 23 July 1893, p. 3.

27. See, for instance, *People*, 29 Oct. 1893, p. 3.

28. Christie, *Empire*, pp. 61–74; John H. M. Laslett, "Reflections on the Failure of Socialism in the American Federation of Labor," *Mississippi Valley Historical Review* 50 (1964):635–51. See also Will Herberg, "The Jewish Labor Movement in the U.S.," *American Jewish Year Book* (n.d.), pp. 10–11.

29. Christie, *Empire*; *People*, 11 Oct. 1891, p. 5; 21 May 1893, p. 2; 25 Feb. 1894, p. 3. See also David Montgomery, "Spontaneity and Organization: Some Comments," *Radical America* 7 (1973):70–80.

30. *WA*, 17 Jan. 1891, p. 1; see De Leon's address to striking workers at Paterson, N.J., *People*, 25 Mar. 1894, pp. 1, 2.

31. Katz in *Daniel De Leon*, 2:31; Louis Fraina, "Daniel De Leon," *New Review* 2 (1914):393.

32. *People*, 16 Aug. 1891, p. 4; 13 Sept. 1891, pp. 4, 5; 8 Nov. 1891, p. 5; "Call from Confectioners and Bakers 7 and Clothing Cutters 4," 8 Aug. 1891, SLP Collection, WSHS; Katz in *Daniel De Leon*, 2:49; L.A. 1141 to Secretary of D.A. 49, 23 Jan. 1896, SLP Collection, Additions of 1974, WSHS.

33. *People*, 29 Jan. 1893, p. 2; 8 Oct. 1893, p. 1; 29 Apr. 1894, p. 4. The

foreign-born population of New York City made up 42.23% of the total. Taking into account native-born children of foreign parentage, the foreign element made up four-fifths of the population. It is necessary to bear these figures in mind for a correct evaluation of the "foreignness" of the SLP. U.S. Industrial Commission, *Reports*, pp. 261–63, 465–92.

34. *New York Sun*, 2 Sept. 1890, p. 2; *Education of Abraham Cahan;* Fraina, "De Leon," pp. 391–92; *WA*, 16 Mar. 1889, p. 1; Ezechiel Lifschutz, "Jewish Labor Movement: Discussants," *American Jewish Historical Quarterly* 52 (1962):135–41.

35. William M. Leiserson, *Adjusting Immigrant and Industry* (New York, 1924), p. 171; Laslett, "Reflections"; Moses Rischin, "The Jewish Labor Movement in America: A Social Interpretation," *Labor History* 4 (1963):228–33.

36. *WA*, 19 July 1890, p. 2; Abraham Menes, "The East Side—Matrix of the Jewish Labor History," *Judaism* 3 (1954):366–80.

37. *People*, 30 Aug. 1891, p. 2; 30 Apr. 1893, p. 2; 26 Nov. 1893, p. 3; Morris U. Schappes, "The Jewish Question and the Left—Old and New," *Jewish Currents* (June 1970), pp. 5–9; quotation from *Arbeiter Zeitung* in *ibid.*, p. 7; quotation from Aaron Antonovsky, *The Early Jewish Labor Movement in the United States* (New York, 1961) pp. 333–34; U.S. Industrial Commission, *Reports*, p. 327.

38. *New York Sun*, 17 Aug. to 5 Sept. 1893; *Herald*, 20 Aug. to 5 Sept. 1893; *Times*, 18–21 Aug. 1893.

39. *Sun*, 22 Aug. 1893, pp. 1, 2; *Herald*, 26 Aug. 1893, p. 8; 27 Aug. 1893, p. 15; *People*, 27 Aug. 1893, p. 2.

40. *People*, 31 Dec. 1893, pp. 2, 3; 7 Jan. 1894, p. 1; 25 Feb. 1894, pp. 1, 3; *Sun*, 14 Feb. 1894, p. 7; *Outlook* 49 (1894):354.

41. Leah M. Feder, *Unemployment Relief in Periods of Depression* (New York, 1936), pp. 71–188; *People*, 11 Mar. 1894, p. 4.

42. John H. M. Laslett, *Labor and the Left: A Study of Socialist and Radical Influences in the American Labor Movement, 1881–1924* (New York, 1970), pp. 288, 305 n. 3.

43. Moses Rischin, *The Promised City: New York's Jews, 1870–1914* (Cambridge, Mass., 1962), p. 185. The typographers and the capmakers, the two Jewish unions that successfully weathered the crisis, bore witness to the process of integration of Yiddish unionism to the AFL. *Ibid.*, pp. 186–88.

44. Laslett, "Reflections," pp. 648–49.

45. *Proceedings of the 9th Convention of the SLP* (New York, 1896), p. 29.

46. See Melvyn Dubofsky, "Success and Failure of Socialism in New York City, 1900–1918: A Case Study," *Labor History* 9 (1968):361–75; quotation from Thomas Wagstaff, "The People," in Joseph Conlin, ed., *The American Radical Press, 1880–1960* (Westport, Conn., 1974), 1:310. Wagstaff calls this statement an apt summary of the fate of the left in the American labor movement.

47. Quotation from Quint, *American Socialism*, p. 168. See also Foner, *History;* Herreshoff, *Origins*, p. 180. Laslett pointedly remarks that the view of anti–De Leonite socialists that there was no necessary conflict between revolutionary political goals and a conservative outlook in the economic field "involved an admission about the ability of the trade unions to co-exist with, and indeed to prosper from, the capitalist system" that took the

edge off socialist propaganda itself. "Reflections," p. 651. Indeed, this view boiled down to capitulating to the AFL's hegemony over the American working class, while defining the field of socialist political initiative in even more limited terms that was the case with De Leon and his followers. *Proceedings of the Seventh Convention of the Bakers' and Confectioners' International Union* (Buffalo, 1892), p. 4; Laslett, "Reflections," p. 641.

48. *Proceedings of the 10th National Convention of the SLP* (New York, 1901), p. 211; Kuhn in *Daniel De Leon*, 1:27; Katz in *ibid.*, 2:83.

49. Kolko, "The Decline of American Radicalism in the Twentieth Century," *Studies on the Left* (Sept.–Oct. 1966), pp. 10–11. Cristiano Camporesi's essay on De Leon in Aldo Zanardo, ed., *Storia del marxismo contemporaneo* (Milan, 1974), includes valuable comments on De Leon's interpretation of Marxism. So does James D. Young, "Daniel De Leon and Anglo-American Socialism," *Labor History* 17 (1976):329–50. An in-depth discussion of Marxism in the SLP of the 1890s should start with the real situation in the movement rather than its leaders' pronouncements. Not only was the party in 1890 not immune from the influence of other radical tendencies, but in subsequent years Nationalists, populists and reformers of all stripes threatened to inundate the party. Bedford, *Socialism;* Paul Buhle, "Marxism in the United States," in Bart Grahl and Paul Piccone, *Towards a New Marxism* (St. Louis, Mo., 1973), p. 195. As De Leon insisted on the superiority of Marxism, much of the *People*'s contempt for middle-class reform ideas, much of its intellectual arrogance, had to do with a sense of urgency concerning the ideological "reconstruction" of the party in order to make it a full-fledged member of the International. Finally, how deep and authentic was De Leon's Marxist culture? Confining this question to the early 1890s, several signs point to the necessity of a more accurate examination of De Leon's ideological contribution, in the context both of his own pre-SLP training and experience and of the ideological make-up of the SLP in those years. Until this is done, assertions that he had "a tremendous intellectual grasp of Marxism" (Quint, *American Socialism,* p. 145) or even that his thought is best subsumed under the term "Marxist," will remain unsubstantiated.

6

The Parameters of Craft Consciousness: The Social Outlook of the Skilled Worker, 1890–1920

ANDREW DAWSON

To European eyes the working-class movement in the United States is a curious thing; it is seen with only a few notable exceptions as conservative and hidebound—though periodically extremely militant—with its trade union leadership associated with corruption and support for American military involvement in various places around the globe. The major focus of attention for outside observers has been, for the most part, upon the whole question of a labor party, or rather the lack of one, in the United States. In most advanced countries of the West such parties already exist: in Britain and Canada there are labor parties, in West Germany the SPD, and in France and Italy the respective Communist parties essentially fulfill a similar role.

The absence of such working-class political institutions in the United States has been almost uniformly ascribed to a lack of class consciousness among American workers, which, depending on the particular source consulted, is variously accounted for by the plentiful supply of cheap land, high material rewards, the divisive effects of race and ethnicity, high rates of occupation and spatial mobility, and the lack of a feudal past and the concomitant unrestrained nature of bourgeois liberalism.[1] Without wishing here to directly question any of these explanations—though clearly some cannot now be, if they ever were, of overriding importance—their one unifying feature is a tendency to account for the low level of consciousness in terms of forces that act upon the working class in some broad, undifferentiated manner, against which the working class is powerless, as if it were merely a cork bobbing upon an ocean of broad, unstoppable social tides. The actual *structure* of the American working class, the particular political views that flow from its various constituent parts, and their contribution to overall consciousness are often overlooked or not examined in any detail. Such an aggregative approach fails to adequately document or comprehend movements within specific sections of the work-

ing class and how the differentiated responses of substrata contribute
directly to the level of class consciousness. It is taken as given that
once working-class consciousness is proven low, then a labor party
could not form, in spite of the fact that this glosses over the actual
experience of the European labor movement, especially the British
case—in many ways the closest parallel to that of the United States—
where the crucial social group behind the establishment of a viable
labor party was not, at least initially, the *whole* class acting in unison
but rather the skilled workers, or "labour aristocracy," forming about
one-tenth of the total.[2] Therefore, if we are to better understand the
labor party question, we have to examine the consciousness of the
skilled workers during the years 1890 to 1920, the major period of
sustained socialist political upheaval. Such an assignment is made all
the more complex when we remember that the outlook of the skilled
workers cannot easily be described as conservative or immature; indeed, they among all other strata in the United States were the major
vocalizers of social democracy[3] in the period up to 1920, and in many
cases beyond.[4]

So long as the line between those who worked for a wage and those
who were self-employed, or employed others in small numbers, remained blurred, a uniquely working-class consciousness could not
emerge. What we do see, rather, from the third decade of the nineteenth century on, is a rising artisan consciousness derived predominantly from groups of independent workers in close association with
farmers and small businessmen. Given America's relatively late start
in industrialization, compared with Britain or Belgium, and the continued importance of agriculture, there remained a viable place for
the independent artisan and small producer well into the 1890s, if
not later.[5] The similarity in status between artisans and the lower
middle class was such that both could combine as "producers of wealth"
against those who were seen merely as consumers or misusers of that
wealth—particularly financiers, land speculators, monopolists, and the
like. The popular movements that this political consciousness fostered
attempted to preserve a place for the self-employed and the small
employer in the face of spreading urbanization and industrialization.
In one sense such movements were reactionary; they sought to push
back particular social and economic developments in order to preserve or return to an idealized golden age; they wished to regain the
supposed competitive equality between producers and as a result,
paradoxically, establish a set of older and more harmonious social
relations. The only way to achieve this was to remove the manifestly
unequal competition between increasingly large-scale business and
the small producer. The focus of attention tended to vary between

the earlier and later parts of the nineteenth century but concentrated particularly upon monopolies in land, finance, railways, and parts of manufacturing.

While the wealth-producing class formed a sufficiently united group on most issues during the years 1820–80, it is in the final two decades of the nineteenth century that this consciousness begins to fragment. First, it is in the 1880s, an immensely important watershed, that we see the outlines, at least in occupational terms, of an American working class in the modern sense emerging out of the continued decline in the proportion of self-employed, both urban and rural, as large-scale production extends outside a narrow range of industries.[6] Simultaneously, at its birth the emerging class found itself fragmented into different strata as a result of imperialism, continuous and rapid internal industrial expansion, and differential rates of technological advance. With the development of a relatively distinct skilled stratum within the working class, no unified consciousness could emerge. The skilled workers, represented by the now permanent trade union movement, soon developed their own particular perspective— one of craft consciousness—which found only a small echo within the wider and more ethnically heterogeneous reminder of the working class. The modern American middle class, which also emerged as a result of the same process, split into an urban and a radical rural form; in political terms the farmers were represented by populism, while the urban middle class found expression in progressivism.

The transformation of sections of the artisan mass into a solidified craft stratum did not, in political terms, herald a parallel shift from radicalism to conservatism, even though the artisan movement had been more open, particularly in its attitudes toward the admission of women, ethnic groups, and laborers, than the exclusive craft unions. Artisan consciousness itself must have in some fashion influenced the outlook of the skilled industrial worker, though exactly which ideas were carried forward into the 1890s and which were filtered out by the new craft workers still remains to be determined. As long as the philosophy of the small producer continued to be antimonopoly, then a strong radical critique of capitalism endured among the populace, although the artisans' backward glances toward a golden age proved increasingly irrelevant to the working class in towns and cities. By the 1890s the great hope of the producer class—access to the land or individual self-employment—was a doubtful possibility. Romanticism or even reaction, then, was also becoming a strong element of artisan consciousness by the end of the nineteenth century.[7] In contrast, the splitting of the craft stratum away from the wider producer class also took with it the modern political ideology of social democracy—a much more cogent criticism of advanced capitalism than artisan radicalism had ever been. Social democracy sought not to modify capitalism but to transform it, and within large sections of the craft stratum, and other parts of the working class, it replaced artisan radicalism—particularly populism—as the major twentieth-century reforming ideology.

Numerically the craft stratum represented 12–14% of the working class as a whole; far from shrinking in size with the advance of mechanization, the group was actually maintaining its position, thriving off the dynamism of the American economy and the constant expansion in new processes and new products that offered the possibility of "skill creation." Despite the concern of contemporaries and the later assertions of labor historians, there is considerable evidence to suggest that the simplistic relationship between innovation and skill dilution among artisan groups needs drastic revision. Certainly the unevenness of technological change allowed particular artisans to maintain a comfortable living, in certain cases into the early years of the twentieth century; nevertheless the emerging modern craft group of the 1880s represented a clear break with the past.

The craft stratum was no longer primarily drawn from self-employed artisans but from those existing under wage labor in the dynamic sectors of the economy—such as engineering, printing, construction, and railroads—and to a lesser extent from boots and shoes, textiles, and mining. Such laborers as carpenters, bricklayers, machinists, printers, and railroad engineers formed the core of the emerging modern labor aristocracy. In spite of mechanization, the new skilled group, collectively, never found itself threatened by the depredations of rapid innovation. Slow transformation did occur; new occupations were added to the privileged few, while others, sometimes quietly and unnoticed or more often amid cacophonous last-minute protest, slipped into the greater mass of the working class. The political, social, and economic reflexes of such a body were not ones of submissiveness (though trade unionism always contained defensive facets) but a more self-confident assertiveness tempered as a result of the salutary warning afforded by the infrequent disappearance of particular long-standing crafts. The experience of the skilled workers in the iron and steel industry—the one major example of craft decline in this period—must have acted as an important reminder of the fate that awaited all workers if management entirely gained the upper hand.[8] By the closing two decades of the nineteenth century the modern craft stratum had formed itself into a cohesive "social bloc," with barriers restricting working-class entry from below and an antipathy toward mingling with the white-collar middle class above.[9] The strategic location at the interface between the two major classes in modern society gave the skilled worker a bifocal gaze: on the one hand the craftsman looked at the employing middle class with hostility, since the latter sought to circumscribe industrial freedom; just as crucially, he observed the activities of the nonskilled trades and sought to maintain his own position within the work process. Thus, contained within craft consciousness are two tightly interwoven and contradictory threads: the one a laborist outlook (which we may define as the fusion of aspects of trade unionism with social democracy) acting as a counterweight to employers' pressure, and the other, "exclusivity," the barring of entry to the rest of the working class.

The bonds tying workers together within a particular craft and the several crafts under the umbrella of trade unionism acted in a directly contradictory manner to the prevailing form of bourgeois individualism in America, a stronger and more tenacious ideology than that of its British counterpart, late nineteenth-century liberalism, which already contained within itself the seeds of doubt as to its own continued ascendancy. In part, bourgeois ideology in America acquired its particular force through the possibility, albeit a diminishing one, of working-class entry into the self-employing middle class, or, more generally, through the dynamism of the American economy in being able to create and, for many, satisfy an expectation of continued material advancement. The fact that the craft stratum, and indeed the working class as a whole, often found itself outnumbered in rural areas and small towns gave bourgeois ideology a further sound material base. The collectivist response on the part of the skilled workers, regardless of its particular weaknesses, posed a striking alternative to the social outlook of individualism: improvement for the skilled worker was to come not via solitary progress but through united action, through social rather than atomistic self-help. The other major component of craft consciousness articulated itself through "exclusivity." From the 1880s on the emerging craft stratum became underlain by a larger mass of semiskilled and unskilled workers, often immigrant and increasingly black. In order to maintain and improve their social status, the skilled workers had now to focus their attention upon two fronts: toward not only the employer but also the lesser skilled below them. The attempts to denigrate, reject, or control the employers' property rights produced a form of social democratic outlook within the labor aristocracy, while its exclusivity toward the unskilled created a new form of reaction based not only upon attitudes toward acquisition of skills but also upon conceptions of racial and national inferiority. The two elements of craft consciousness, the laborist and the exclusive, blended together to form a particularly unique, tangled, and contradictory consciousness, an outlook that was for all practical purposes impossible to reduce to its constituent components without doing an injustice to the overall view.

The early form of craft consciousness—still with slight vestiges of artisan influence—embodying an optimistic outlook and a belief in a mission for labor, laid great stress upon the morally detrimental aspects of the increasing division of labor and the adverse effects this had upon the crafts. T. J. McConnell, in his presidential address to the 1891 convention of the Pattern Makers' League, outlined the major components of this consciousness.

> During all the ages since the creation of mankind, humanity has been laboring in the mighty throes of a constant and unequal struggle—a struggle of the toiling masses to free themselves from the misery and thraldom they have endured from the crushing powers of oppression and persecution, that has been so cruelly exercised upon them by the wealthy and ruling classes of society.

> These great struggles for the emancipation of labor are now being waged with irresistible force in all parts of the civilized world. And to the great labor organizations of our time has been assigned the mission of securing to the toiler all the blessing of liberty and progress, which should characterize the close of this wonderful nineteenth century—the grandest and most eventful in the world's history. Let us therefore strive with all the ability at our command to place our organization well to the front, and there take a gallant part in the glorious battle for the triumph of organized labor.[10]

Such an outlook, shared as it was by the whole of the Second International—indeed, the address could have been written by a constituent socialist party—saw the crafts' claim to the fruits of modern industrial society as being morally unstoppable; theirs was a cause whose justice and righteousness were visible to all. The polarization of society, while it was bringing great riches to a few, degraded the worker. As the 1888 constitution of the Brotherhood of Painters, Decorators and Paperhangers pointed out:

> The wealthy capitalists, combined and consolidated, monopolize and control the wealth of the world, while the rapid concentration of wealth and power in the hands of the moneyed classes has had an extremely injurious effect upon all branches of honourable toil. . . .

> Year by year our various crafts have been reduced from their rightful position among the mechanical callings. Our wages are much lower than in other trades requiring no greater proportionate share of skill or manual effort.[11]

The contrast between work, an honorable activity, and those who

control capital is made explicit; the latter seek only to degrade the
skilled worker.

At the turn of the century a new strand, and to modern eyes a
much more decipherable consciousness, makes a general appearance.
The stress upon morality and the need to uplift the craft is replaced
by a more overtly political perspective:

> We, the International Association of Machinists, believing it to be
> the natural right of those who toil to enjoy to the fullest possible
> extent the wealth created by their labor; and realizing that under
> the changing industrial conditions of our time and the enormous
> growth of syndicates and other aggregations of capital, it is impos-
> sible for us to obtain the full reward of our labor except by united
> action;

> And believing that the organization based on sound principles as to
> the wisest use of our citizenship, based upon class struggle, upon
> both economic lines, with a view of restoring the common wealth
> of our government to the people, and using the natural resources
> and means of production and distribution for the benefit of all the
> people.[12]

The earlier "craft uplift" element within consciousness, which hardly
knew any particular boundaries or readily accepted criteria by which
success could be judged, was replaced by the more worldly and, in
trade union terms, the much more attainable demand of ". . . the
natural right of those who toil to enjoy *to the fullest possible extent* the
wealth created by their labor. . . ." No absolute demand was made for
all the wealth produced by labor but rather some acceptable, negoti-
ated level. The socialist and populist influence in the machinists' constitution is clear, but even in more conservative trades the general
trend was the same: away from nineteenth-century craft uplift toward
a more instrumental and pragmatic approach; tangible and measur-
able demands were to be made with fairly specific indications as to
the method by which they were to be achieved.

The constitutions of the craft unions occupied the attention of a
large proportion of the active membership and can often be used as
useful barometers of the particular mood of influential sections of the
skilled stratum. What may appear to later observers as an incon-
gruous clash between organization on "sound principles" on the one
hand and a recognition of class struggle on the other—that is, a combination of conservatism and radicalism—was hardly viewed as such
by the skilled workers. This kind of juxtaposition encapsulates the
duality contained within the stratum: on the one side, craft workers
could see the unequal distribution of wealth within society and through
economic action constantly seek to reclaim a greater share for them-

selves—this at a time when the small farmer and the residuum of the
artisan mass were chasing after monetary panaceas or cooperatives
and blaming their economic plight upon Jewish domination of eastern and European finance. It was the skilled workers, as a group,
above all others among those living off moderate property holdings
or from wage labor, who clearly understood the workings of the
American political economy and proposed remedies both in their own
best interests and also, to an extent, in the interests of the semi- and
unskilled workers. But, paradoxically, it was precisely because the
crafts perceived only too clearly the nature of an urban industrial
society and their relative position within it that they favored a form
of stable unionism. This contradiction, between a recognition of the
class nature of society and a remedy of conservative unionism, can
only be understood in terms of the particular and unique location of
the skilled workers within American society.

Organization based on sound principles facilitated the erection of
barriers around the social and economic life of craft workers; it sought
to contain or at least deflect the full imposition of bourgeois values.
While the rise of business unionism around 1900 can be seen as an
aping of the middle class by sections of workers (indeed, the phrase
is used to evoke precisely such a connotation by the Wisconsin school
of labor historians), craft unionism built upon centralized control and
financial propriety—high dues, benefits, and strike funds—was rather
a defense mechanism and institutional framework against the incur-
sion of capital, a springboard to retaliate against such penetration.
With the increasing stabilization of capitalism after 1900 and the skilled
workers' move further away from the rest of the class, the early focus
upon craft uplift gave way to a commitment to sound trade union
organization. The emphasis upon business unionism and "voluntarism"[13] reflected an actuality that the skilled workers were only too
well aware of: that the stratum had become divorced from immediate
points of ecomomic contact with the rest of the working class and,
further, that there existed no possibility of forming a mass reformist
party of the working class—something that had been confidently looked
forward to during the nineties.

With increasing fragmentation the skilled workers had recourse to
social and institutional tools for their own defense that lay immediately to hand: a sound economic organization and a refusal to become
embroiled with the state. Voluntarism meant a confident belief on the
part of the crafts in an ability to achieve their goal in a hostile environment through the voluntary institution of trade unionism. In the
period up to 1920 business unionism provided a bulwark against the
intrusion of private capital. Voluntarism, on the other hand, endowed

craft consciousness with its suspicion of, or indeed hostility toward, government; it recognized the extent of craft economic strength and also its major weakness, that labor's demands could not be substantially rectified by an appeal to an unsympathetic state (both federal and state governments, and the judiciary) without the backing of a mass working-class party. The crafts had toyed with the idea of direct political activity during the period up to about 1910, especially around such issues as nationalization, minimum hours of work, and state provision of old age pensions, but in the first decade of the twentieth century the AFL—and we must presume this represented, in some mediated way, the interests of large sections of the craft membership—increasingly opposed social legislation. Of course, voluntarism was never applied in any absolute sense, since wherever craft workers met sympathetic state and local governments they participated in politics to the full.[14] In fields of interest to labor within which it had little direct economic control, especially child and female labor, the unions proved willing to seek some legislative restraint. Of course, the major focus of the AFL's limited lobbying in Congress, for the enactment of a law forbidding the use of court injunctions during labor disputes, was itself the apotheosis of voluntarism.[15]

At the end of the nineteenth century economic instability and the increasing monopolization of industry forced a number of social groups to face directly the issue of economic reform and regulation. To an extent, the populists favored government control, though, given the particular class and sectional base of populism's support, it could never really extend its interests beyond the farmers' immediate concerns for railroad charges, grain elevators, and the like—and only then as consumers of those services. Urban middle-class progressivism also identified similar problems, particularly increasing monopolization, but its remedy was limited essentially to trust *regulation* rather than control for social purposes. From the start craft consciousness saw the trusts in a totally different light: like social democracy, it recognized the "progressive" nature of size, that the old form of competitive capitalism was giving way to seemingly more efficient, highly concentrated units of production. As Henry White of the Garment Workers put it:

> Workingmen are all too familiar with the disheartening reply when asking for an increase in wages: "Can't afford it on account of competition." The trust method at least changes the situation so far as the ability to concede better conditions is concerned.
>
> . . . .
>
> The trade unions, the creature of modern social evolution, have no quarrel with the progressive forces of society. . . . What will the

policy be toward union labor when the trusts are more fully established? Will the unions have to meet a more unyielding force? That
is the question which a million organized mechanics are asking, and
an answer cannot be given by word alone.[16]

At the 1899 AFL convention in Detroit, Max Hayes successfully
moved an amendment to the committee on the president's report,
calling ". . . upon the trade unions of the United States, and workingmen generally, to carefully study the development of trusts and monopolies with a view to nationalizing the same."[17] While the craft
workers never lost their faith in the efficacy of industrial action to
achieve their ends—indeed, this sentiment proved overriding in this
period—it was the skilled stratum more than any other in American
society that supported the idea of extensive government intervention
in industry for social as well as economic objectives.[18] In the 1890s a
number of crafts had realized that while their immediate economic
position seemed as secure as possible, the wider situation abounded
with difficulties; in any battle with corporations the major loser would
be the workers. It was this simultaneous recognition of their strengths
and weaknesses that propelled the stratum, both radical and conservative, into demanding the nationalization of large sections of American industry. Much of the focus rested upon streetcar lines and gas
and electric plants—the municipal public utilities—but also on more
all-embracing schemes such as public ownership of the mines and
railroads. Alternatively, some crafts voiced fairly narrow proposals
related specifically to conditions within their trade: the printers, for
example, actively sought the nationalization of the telegraph service,
also an old populist demand, in order, among other things, to break
the news monopoly of the Associated Press.[19]

Both for the crafts and social democracy the call for nationalization
rested upon a belief in some form of collective social justice, in particular that industries ought to be run not just for narrow sectional or
class interests but according to some wider, if ill-defined, criterion.
Social democracy, particularly of the middle-class intellectual variety,
saw in increased state control the possibility of minimizing the waste
caused by irrational competition. The two elements were such that
they fused to produce a common demand for increased state intervention at all levels. The municipal programs of the Socialist Labor
party and the Socialist party of America identified the same group of
industries for nationalization as did the skilled workers.[20] The right
wing of social democracy saw the gradual extension of government
ownership as the fulfillment of revolutionary objectives, while the
center and left accepted the need for immediate reformist demands

for electioneering purposes. The crafts, but more particularly social democracy, never faced up to the overriding problem and failed to identify the rationale for government ownership. Was nationalization to be for the sake of efficiency, to rescue an unwilling capitalism from its own competitive excesses, or in order to introduce an element of industrial democracy? The tensions embodied within the demand for nationalization—just as in the British case—were never resolved. Both features, Fabian-style, "efficiency socialism" and social justice, surfaced at particular times.

During World War I American trade unionists and many socialists had expected far-reaching concessions to be made to labor in return for supporting the war effort, but these wishes went unfulfilled. Certainly top AFL officials were taken into the wartime administration and attained positions of power never before achieved, but the extent of long-term readjustment in favor of increased state intervention proved minimal. United States participation in the war was too brief to allow such a situation to develop, and American capitalism emerged at the end not weakened but invigorated by the experience. Alternative stategies involving the incorporation of certain aspects of skilled workers' demands within the state's political apparatus, while they were called for in France, Germany, and Britain, were unnecessary in America. The laborist alternative, with its stress upon efficient planning and some form of social justice, was not required and, like the Plumb plan, could easily be brushed aside. During the war years the right and center of the Socialist party, along with some of the left wing, became increasingly confused over the difference between state capitalism and socialism; the strand of social justice became stripped away from social democracy leaving only the elements of central planning and efficiency, and even those were not required by an increasingly dominant American economy.

Stemming just as naturally from the same social elements within the work process as those that created a social democratic strain within craft consciousness, there also sprang the other, antithetical facet of the skilled worker's existence: exclusivity and reaction. Since the strength of the stratum lay in maintaining a short supply of its own labor—the raison d'être of craft unionism—the skilled workers constantly sought to distance themselves from those groups of workers existing below them in social and occupational terms. The economic rationale was the stated motive for exclusion, but since lesser-skilled workers were predominantly women, children, recent immigrants, and, after World War I, migrant rural blacks, the barriers that grew up were inextricably intertwined with racialism and a particular attitude toward the role of women in the family. The semiskilled and the unskilled were barred because of apprentice qualifications; immigrants, especially at ports of entry, were often charged higher initiation fees; blacks, where they were allowed to become union members, could only join separate locals confined to certain districts of northern cities; women were prevented from joining a number of unions, and in others their position was severely circumscribed.[21]

But exclusivity itself was not confined just to the outlook of the skilled worker; it also found an echo within social democracy. Indeed, how could it be otherwise when craftsmen, often white native Americans or immigrants from Western Europe, formed the backbone of the working-class membership of the Socialist party? Social democracy was an ideology in essence hardly more advanced than that of the craft workers, from which it ultimately drew a large portion of its strength and vitality. The socialists reflected the same ambivalence and fracturing on the question of race and ethnicity as the skilled workers themselves—part reformist and part reactionary. In all essentials the Socialist party failed to differentiate itself from prevailing assumptions on race; in relation to the question of immigration, the SPA found itself unable to adopt a clear, unambiguous nonracial position. While general restructions upon immigration were opposed, barriers to "artificially" stimulated immigration for the purpose of weakening American unionism or lowering living standards were favored.[22] It is not difficult to interpret such a sentiment as being against immigration from the economically backward countries of eastern and southern Europe, since they were the most likely to affect the living standards of the highly paid skilled worker. The position of the SPA legitimized the line of argument that looked upon immigrants as a "threat" to the high incomes of the American working class—a view that could find a parallel in craft consciousness. Thus the premises of social democracy could be used to support exclusivity, to keep immigrants out of the skilled trades by whatever means necessary. On the subject of the black's position within society, the first pronouncement, and indeed virtually the only formal statement, came at the Socialist party's unity convention in 1901. It recognized the particular position of black workers within America and, by appealing to them to join the party, placed itself in a more advanced position than the Republicans or the Democrats, but because of hostility by a portion of the membership who feared electoral unpopularity, the party could not bridge the chasm of racial antipathy. Even those who were sympathetic refused to call for positive measures to attract blacks or ethnic groups, preferring instead to make only blanket appeals to the *whole* of the working class, irrespective of the problem faced by individual groups. This position reflected the views of Morris Hillquit and Eugene Debs, representing the dominant strains within the party.[23]

Given the possibility and, indeed, increasing necessity of influencing government during the depressed nineties as a supplement to economic activity, two possible routes lay open: on the one hand, there was pressure-group politics, the obtaining of maximum concessions from those parties with greatest control over the state apparatus, presenting the alluring possibility of playing the Republicans off against the Democrats. The other approach, that of forming an independent party of labor, was largely but not exclusively advocated by the social democrats within the craft stratum. That the first alternative was eventually accepted in 1906 under Samuel Gompers's slogan of "reward your friends and punish your enemies" should not blind us to the fact that a genuine choice existed in the last decade of the nineteenth century, perhaps even as late as 1910.

The major incentive for skilled workers to enter politics stemmed from the tensions created by the depression of 1893–98. Long hours of work in certain occupations, stationary or only slowly rising wages for those in a job, high unemployment, and the marked hostility of employers, the judiciary, and the federal government meant that existing forms of purely economic activity were called into question. Some issues were amenable to direct negotiation with employers, but others, particularly the use of court injunctions, were not. Lobbying of Congress on a minor scale had already been tried, but now something more robust and wider in scope was required. To Gompers, writing in 1894, the AFL had set itself upon a path broadly similar to that of the British TUC, which in political terms ". . . endeavor[s] to defeat those who oppose, and elect those who support, legislation in the interest of labor, and wherever opportunity affords elect *bona fide* union men to Parliament and other public offices."[24] At the 1897 convention of the AFL the American approach was spelled out more clearly: ". . . that the A.F. of L. most firmly and unequivocally favors the independent use of the ballot by the trade unionists and working men, united regardless of party, that we may elect men from our own ranks to make new laws and administer them along the lines laid down in the legislative demands of the American Federation of Labor."[25]

This approach found a large measure of support from all sections of the craft stratum; L. R. Thomas, general president of the exclusive Pattern Makers' League, had this to say: "I also firmly believe that we must go further than has been ventured before by organized labor. Organized labor must enter the arena of political action, and there must wrest from our adversaries and oppressors, with the weapons of the constitution, the ballot, which is ours by rights."[26] The socialist D. Douglas Wilson expressed a view, if we remove the rhetorical gloss, not markedly different: "Let every worker throw off the yoke of the old party thraldom and cast a class-conscious ballot that makes him a freeman and puts him beyond the reach of the scheming scoundrels who have betrayed him again and again."[27] Thomas's line of approach lacked a degree of clarity; clearly, it meant something a great deal more than merely the old practice of lobbying Congress, but did it mean the formation of a labor party, or rather the election of trade unionists to Congress without any party affiliations? On balance it would seem that labor, if a consensus could be established, tended to the latter approach. But in practical terms it would seem hardly possible that a group of politically unaffiliated trade unionists could collect in a legislature without forming some kind of working alliance. Even if we accept that the aim of the skilled workers during the 1890s was to send workingmen irrespective of party to Congress, an independent labor party could not in the long term have been ruled out—bearing in mind British labor's experience in Parliament.

Paradoxically, at the precise moment the labor aristocracy found itself considering overt political action, those conditions that had in part brought the initiatives to the forefront began to move in the opposite direction. The development of heavy industry in the 1870s, continued urbanization, mass migration and immigration, crises in agriculture, and the periodic fluctuations in business prosperity since the Civil War all heightened social and political awareness within large sections of both the urban and rural middle and working classes. The resurgence of the economy in 1898 following the severe depression of the previous five years must have seemed at the time just like any other upturn, but from a longer-term perspective this was not the case. If it were possible to select a particular year to represent the dividing line between the earlier and essentially immature growth of American industrial capitalism and the later, relatively more developed period, then 1898 is such a year. For the American economy the years 1898 to 1929 were to be relatively stable, especially compared with those immediately preceding and those that followed. To be sure, after 1898 the trade cycle did not disappear, since there were periodic recessions—following 1903, a short sharp depression after the financial panic of 1907, and a more sustained depression during 1914–16—but nothing to match the cataclysms of the seventies and the nineties. The absence of a general social and political crisis can, in all essentials, be ascribed to three factors: from 1898 the price level began to rise for the first time since the Civil War, helping to remove at least some of the pressures on farmers and other small entrepreneurs. More crucially, the chronic instability of the late nineteenth-century economy, with its tendency to produce more than could be consumed, was *partially* solved for the time as a result of increasing monopolization of industry and America's developing involvement in overseas markets as an outlet for her surplus goods and capital.

But other economic forces connected with the increasing stabilization of American capitalism were also acting to deflect craft workers away from their stated goal of independent political action. According to Clarence Long's study of wages, occupational differentials between skilled workers and the remainder of the working class had shown some tendency to widen in the period 1860–90;[28] this trend dramatically accelerated in the early twentieth century, especially after 1907 (see Table 1). While average money wages for all workers in manufacturing increased by 54% during 1890–1914, the skilled workers increased theirs by 74%. Wages of the unskilled, in contrast, increased by at best only 31%.[29] But for a laborist or a social democratic consciousness to fully develop, precisely the opposite needed to occur: only through the erosion of craft strength vis-à-vis the remainder of the working class would the skilled workers throw themselves wholeheartedly into political action. A narrowing of differentials, bringing with it a greater political and social intermingling and the provision of a mass base for craft political action, did occur in Britain to an extent before 1914, but more especially after the steep decline in her hold over world markets following World War I.[30] The accentuation in America of craft privilege after 1900, in association with the stabilization of the economy, rapidly circumscribed craft unionism's expanding political commitment; what had been a policy of independent political action in the nineties soon became interpreted by Samuel Gompers, himself moving with the general political tide within the stratum, as nonpartisan politics. As a result, craft consciousness, far from breaking out of its sectional boundaries, in all essentials felt no impelling need to alter its status. With the social barriers on both the upper and the lower margins of the craft stratum intact, unlike its British counterpart, the political outlook of the skilled worker, while still retaining the duality of laborism and exclusivity, turned in upon itself to stress opposition to employers and the state via business unionism and voluntarism, and an antipathy to the lesser skilled.

Despite the maintenance of a degree of economic stability, of rising real incomes and falling unemployment, which effectively blunted though never entirely destroyed moves toward independent political action, nonetheless, some form of involvement became necessary as a result of the intermittent resurgence of employer hostility toward trade unionism. Consequently, what emerges during the formative

Table 1. *An Index of Money Wages for Certain Groups of Workers, 1890–1914 (1890–99 = 100).*

	Average for All Manufacturing (1)	Skilled Workers (2)	Unskilled Workers	
			Coombs (3)	Hurlin (4)
1890	100.84	99.35	101.99	100.00
1891	100.84	99.88	101.99	101.36
1892	101.54	101.77	101.99	100.68
1893	105.74	100.36	101.99	100.68
1894	97.34	98.16	97.01	99.31
1895	96.64	98.25	99.50	98.63
1896	100.84	99.69	98.26	99.31
1897	98.04	99.74	97.01	99.31
1898	95.94	100.28	99.50	100.00
1899	102.24	102.53	100.75	100.68
1900	105.75	106.55	101.99	101.36
1901	110.64	110.42	104.48	104.76
1902	115.55	115.67	106.97	106.12
1903	119.05	120.75	110.70	108.84
1904	118.35	120.89	111.94	109.52
1905	120.45	123.37	111.94	110.88
1906	128.85	128.52	116.92	114.28
1907	133.75	132.17	121.89	118.36
1908	128.85	137.87	115.67	117.68
1909	130.25	146.57	116.92	121.08
1910	138.66	158.54	120.65	121.08
1911	141.46	159.48	116.92	121.76
1912	144.96	164.50	118.16	124.48
1913	154.76	164.50	124.38	129.93
1914	154.06	173.73	124.38	130.61

Source: Column (1)—Albert Rees, *Real Wages In Manufacturing 1890–1914* (Princeton, N.J., 1961), p. 72.

Column (2)—The skilled occupations are: engineman, fireman, bricklayer, carpenter, machinist, blacksmith, compositor, and pressman. Except for engineman and fireman, which are daily earnings, all are hourly earnings for the job. Census data have been used to weight the occupations except for engineman and fireman, where Interstate Commerce Commission statistics have been preferred. Since BLS "payroll" wage data in many industries end in 1907, when splicing the series together, a comparable union rate from a northeastern or midwestern urban center has been selected.

For railroads, see Interstate Commerce Commission, *Fourteenth, Twenty-third,* and *Twenty-seventh Annual Report on the Statistics of Railways in the United States* (Washington, D.C., 1902–15), pp. 32, 37; 33–34, 38; 26–28.

For construction, see Bureau of Labor Statistics, *Bulletin, no. 77, pp. 28, 66; ibid.,* no. 604, pp. 158, 165–66.

period 1898–1906 is not the election by trade unionists of fellow workingmen, a policy that had found a good deal of sympathy in the nineties, but a particular hybrid nonpartisanship. In the congressional election of 1906 the AFL entered the political arena directly for the first time after the rejection of its "bill of grievances" by the Republican administration. Instead of the election of men drawn from the ranks of labor, ". . . sincere, progressive and honest men . . ." from either of the two main parties were to be voted for; only as a last resort were labor candidates to be nominated.[31] It is not so much that the AFL leadership actually "betrayed" its craft members—as Philip Foner at times suggests[32]—or that they conspired to effect a change in policy behind workers' backs, but that the strategy of "reward your friends and punish your enemies" emerged out of the crafts' social experience in the years after 1898. The skilled workers had always believed in the primacy of economic action (hardly something unique but found also in the British trade union movement even after the establishment of the Labour party), nor did industrial or social conditions move in such a way as to force them to reconsider. Thus, with the return of prosperity and the increasing stabilization of American capitalism, thoughts of independent action could be conveniently rejected. The shift in craft consciousness over the ten years after 1898 occurs on three different levels: at the top, among AFL leaders, the move toward conservatism comes quickly, the symbolic affirmation being Gompers's notorious antisocialist speech at the Boston AFL convention in 1903.[33] On the next level, that of full-time trade union

---

For engineering, see BLS, *Bulletin,* no. 77, pp. 37–38, 82–83; *ibid.,* no. 604, pp. 282, 305.

For printing, see BLS, *Bulletin,* no. 77, pp. 5, 55, 110–11; *ibid.,* no. 604, pp. 353–54, 358.

Column (3)—Whitney Coombs, *The Wages of the Unskilled in Manufacturing in the United States, 1890–1924* (New York, 1926), p. 119.

Column (4)—Paul H. Douglas, *Real Wages in the United States 1890–1926* (Boston, 1930), p. 175. Ralph Hurlin's data (for average weekly earnings) are gathered from manufacturing, agriculture, construction, and railroads. Consequently, his index is probably superior to that of Coombs.

The use of a certain amount of wage rate data from 1907 in Column (2), rather than earnings as used in Columns (1), (3), and (4), would seem, on the face of it, to cause problems of compatibility. Wage rates are hardly influenced at all by business depressions, while earnings (calculated by dividing the total amount earned by the hours or weeks worked) are bound to fall because of short-time working and unemployment. This may account for some of the skilled workers' differential that emerges following the depression of 1907, but any longer-term errors are self-correcting. The depression was short-lived, unemployment declined, and consequently earnings would accelerate faster than wage rates—yet the gap between Column (2) and the rest shows no sign of narrowing, quite the contrary, which suggests that more fundamental, underlying forces were at work.

officials, the signs of rigidity, while never as absolute, come somewhat later, probably by 1906–7.[34] The shift in perspective of the craft rank and file is hardest of all to evaluate; certainly, as real wages increased dramatically and the craft differential widened, it could be expected on *a priori* grounds that the political outlook would move rightward. Particular crafts did slip into increasing conservatism, although others, notably the machinists and the journeymen tailors, ran against the trend. All that can be said with certainty is that the process was by no means complete even as late as 1917.

Unlike Germany, the United States had now passed through the major nineteenth-century crisis of industrialization without a social democratic party successfully imbedding itself; future attempts were bound to be fraught with even greater problems, since, by the twentieth century and in some cases well before, the working classes of the advanced Western world had come to accept the existence of the industrial system. To break with this established state of affairs sufficiently to create a viable labor party in the United States would in the future require a tremendous jolt to the system at all levels, such as experienced by Britain as a result of rising foreign competition in world markets and, more specifically, from the shattering effects of World War I. In the United States no such jolt occurred.

NOTES

I wish to express my appreciation for the helpful suggestions given at various stages during the completion of this paper by Peter Brooker, Mike Haynes, Bob Zieger, Marianne Debouzy, Herbert Gutman, David Brody, Alan Dawley, Alfred Young, Peter Shergold, Loretta Valtz-Mannucci, and Bo Öhngren.

1. Frederick Jackson Turner, *The Frontier in American History* (New York, 1920); Werner Sombart, *Why Is There No Socialism in the United States?* (1906; reprinted, London, 1976); Stephan Thernstrom, *The Other Bostonians* (Cambridge, Mass., 1973); Selig Perlman, *A Theory of the Labor Movement* (New York, 1928); John H. M. Laslett and Seymour Martin Lipset, eds., *Failure of a Dream?* (New York, 1974); Louis Hartz, *The Liberal Tradition in America* (New York, 1955); Gerald Rosenblum, *Immigrant Workers* (New York, 1973).
2. Eric J. Hobsbawn, *Labouring Men* (London, 1964), pp. 272–315.
3. Social democracy is here given its contemporary usage as embodied in the Second International (1889–1914); that is, it combined within itself such disparate political views as reform socialism, syndicalism, and revolutionary socialism. On the nature of the movement and its particular weaknesses, see George Lichtheim, *A Short History of Socialism* (Glasgow, 1975), pp. 239–54; Julius Braunthal, *History of the International 1864–1914,*

1 (London, 1966):195–320; Carl Schorske, *German Social Democracy 1905–1917* (New York, 1955); G. D. H. Cole, *A Short History of Socialist Thought,* 3, pt. 1 (London, 1956):1–103.

4. We must rescue the concept of the labor aristocracy from its misleading association with conservatism and class collaborationist politics. The labor aristocracy, far from acting as a stalking horse for bourgeois interests and ideals, made particular demands of its own that at key points ran contrary to the economic and political interests of the employing middle class and, to a lesser extent, the remainder of the working class. The earlier and one-dimensional treatment of the labor aristocracy has in recent years given way to an approach that recognizes the complex and often contradictory influences acting upon skilled workers. For two examples of this new approach related to nineteenth-century Britain, see Robert Q. Gray, *The Labour Aristocracy in Victorian Edinburgh* (Oxford, 1976), and Geoffrey Crossick, *An Artisan Élite in Victorian Society* (London, 1978).

5. For recent accounts that deal in some manner with preindustrial artisan culture, see Bruce Laurie, " 'Nothing on Impulse': Life Styles of Philadelphia Artisans, 1820–1850," *Labor History* 15 (1974):337–66; Alan Dawley, *Class and Community: The Industrial Revolution in Lynn* (Cambridge, Mass., 1976); Eric Foner, *Free Soil, Free Labor, Free Men* (New York, 1970); David Montgomery, *Beyond Equality: Labor and the Radical Republicans, 1862–1872* (New York, 1967). On the persistence of preindustrial social and cultural patterns within the working class, see Herbert G. Gutman, "Work, Culture and Society in Industrializing America, 1815–1919," *American Historical Review* 78 (1973):531–88.

6. For evidence that the working class in this period formed a significant portion of the labor force (52–62%) and that it was growing, albeit slowly, see Lewis Corey, "Problems of the Peace," *Antioch Review* (Spring 1945), p. 69; Harry Braverman, *Labor and Monopoly Capital* (New York, 1974), p. 379; Alba M. Edwards, "A Social-Economic Grouping of the Gainful Workers of the United States," *Journal of the American Statistical Association* 28 (1933):383.

7. For an account of the emergence of craft consciousness out of an artisan mentality, from an essentially institutional perspective, see Philip S. Foner, *History of the Labor Movement in the United States,* (New York, 1955): 78–88, 157–160; Gerald Grob, *Workers and Utopia* (Evanston, Ill., 1961), pp. 37–59, 138–42; Norman Ware, *The Labor Movement in the United States 1860–1895* (Gloucester, Mass., 1959).

8. As David Montgomery has suggested in "The 'New Unionism' and the Transformation of Workers' Consciousness in America, 1909–1922," *Journal of Social History* 7 (1974):509–29, employers, using such weapons as Taylorism, sought to deskill the crafts. But the impact of scientific management upon skilled workers should not be overstressed, especially in the period before World War I; often the application of new methods hit the day laborer to an even greater extent. If economic and technological forces had been pushing the skilled and the unskilled closer together in terms of shop-floor experiences, we would have expected to see the emergence of a much more potent working-class political movement in the years before World War I. That the skilled workers were able to strengthen their position during a period of rapid change clearly contradicts the prevailing wisdom. For a more extensive treatment of the impact of innovation upon

particular skilled occupations, see Andrew Dawson, "The Paradox of Dynamic Technological Change and the Labor Aristocracy in the United States, 1880–1914," *Labor History* 20 (1979):325–51.

9. The characteristics of such social barriers can be determined from social mobility studies. Even though Thernstrom asserts that the American working class merges gradually with the middle class, his own evidence does not unambiguously support this. Upwardly mobile semiskilled and unskilled workers were underrepresented in the skilled stratum, more being found in the lower middle class. Similarly, the skilled stratum, in relation to its obviously advantageous position, was underrepresented in the middle class, compared with the two other manual categories. Thernstrom, *Other Bostonians,* pp. 67, 89, 93–94; Laslett and Lipset, *Failure,* pp. 519–21.

10. *Journal of Proceedings of the Pattern Makers' National League of North America* (Chicago, 1891), pp. 86–87.

11. M. P. Carrick, "Illustrated History of the Origin, Rise, Growth and Present Condition of the Brotherhood of Painters Decorators and Paperhangers of America," *Official Journal* 17 (1903):533. For further examples of aristocratic consciousness, see the preamble to the *Constitution of the Pattern Makers' National League of North America* (1896); "Constitution on the Plan of the Cigarmakers," *Tailor* 11 (1900):1; and the preamble of the AFL constitution, *Report of Proceedings of the Tenth Convention of the American Federation of Labor* (Detroit, 1890), p. 3.

12. IAM, *Constitution* (1903), p. 2.

13. Michael Rogin, "Voluntarism: The Political Fucntions of an Anti-Political Doctrine," *Industrial and Labor Relations Review* 15 (1962):521–35, sees voluntarism as additionally fulfilling certain organizational needs of unionism in its battle with the state for the sympathy of the worker. For a criticism, see Gary Fink, *Labor's Search for Political Order: The Political Behavior of the Missouri Labor Movement 1890–1940* (Colombia, Mo., 1973), pp. 161–82.

14. For two recent studies of political action at the local level, see Thomas Gavett, *Development of the Labor Movement in Milwaukee* (Madison, Wis., 1965), and Fink, *Labor's Search.*

15. Rogin, "Voluntarism," pp. 530–34.

16. *American Federationist* (Dec. 1896), quoted in Lyle Cooper, "Organized Labor and the Trusts," *Journal of Political Economy* 36 (1928):727.

17. *Report of Proceedings of the 19th Annual Convention of the American Federation of Labor* (Detroit, 1899), p. 149.

18. The point is worth underlining, for at the 1900 AFL convention a similar proposal for nationalization was modified out of existence. Cooper, "Organized Labor," p. 730. The tensions between, on the one hand, continued reliance on economic activity and, on the other, the political demands for nationalization were never resolved, nor in the nature of craft consciousness could they ever be.

19. *Journal of Proceedings of the Pattern Makers' National League of North America* (Cincinnati, 1894), p. 35.

20. *Platform and Constitution of the Socialist Labor Party* (New York, 1896), p. 5; *State Platform: Socialist Party of Massachusetts, 1917* (1917).

21. For a more detailed examination, see F. E. Wolfe, *Admission to American Trade Unions* (Baltimore, 1912); Herbert Northrup, *Organized Labor and the Negro* (New York, 1944); Sterling Spero and Abram Harris, *The Black*

Worker (New York, 1931); and Philip S. Foner, *Organized Labor and the Black Worker 1916–1973* (New York, 1976), pp. 64–102.

22. Socialist Party of America, *Proceedings of the National Convention* (Chicago, 1908), pp. 98–100.

23. SPA, *Proceedings of Socialist Unity Convention* (Indianapolis, 1901), pp. 102–7, 109–13, 361–75, 444–46.

24. *Report of Proceedings of the Fourteenth Annual Convention of the American Federation of Labor* (Denver, 1894), p. 15.

25. *Report of Proceedings of the Seventeenth Annual Convention of the American Federation of Labor* (Atlanta, 1897), p. 30.

26. *Journal of Proceedings, Eighth Regular Session, Pattern Makers' National League of North America* (St. Louis, Mo., 1898), p. 6.

27. *Machinists' Monthly Journal* 11 (1899):253.

28. Clarence Long, *Wages and Earnings in the United States 1860–1890* (Princeton, N.J., 1960), p. 97.

29. For additional evidence of widening wage differentials, see Dawson, "Paradox."

30. Hobsbawn, *Labouring Men*, pp. 300–303.

31. "A. F. of L. Campaign Programme," *American Federationalist* 13 (1906): 530.

32. Foner, *History of the Labor Movement*, 3 (New York, 1964): esp. 136–73.

33. *Report of Proceedings of the Twenty-third Annual Convention of the American Federation of Labor* (Boston, 1903), pp. 196–98.

34. During the period 1906 to 1907, from a fairly wide interest in political and social questions, a number of craft journals narrowed their scope to include only trade union matters. See, among others, the respective organs of the tailors, printers, cigarmakers, pattern makers, and painters and decorators. There are, of course, dangers in overemphasizing these tendencies: first, because not all crafts made the transition during the dates suggested, and secondly, because some subsequently returned to a more overtly radical position. In reality the watershed of 1906–7 represents only a general tendency.

7

The German Immigrant Working Class of Chicago, 1875–90: Workers, Labor Leaders, and the Labor Movement

HARTMUT KEIL

On 14 January 1886 the *Chicago Daily News* announced that it would present "some facts" on the socialists' activities in the city, for "it is well for the public to know what these vagabonds are about." Rather than giving the facts, however, the opinionated article assured its readers that

> there is one rock which all the theory and threats of socialists may be expected to beat in vain—the rock of the equality of every American citizen. . . .The opportunities for making money, for attaining position, for securing fame, for happiness, are equal in this country. And it is this which constitutes the difference between the civilizations to which these socialists have come and that they have left. It is this difference that makes socialism such a dark and sickly growth in America. . . . Socialism in America is an anomaly, and Chicago is the last place on the continent where it would exist were it not for the dregs of foreign immigration which find lodgement here.

After the Haymarket incident the alien nature of those involved was described in even more vituperative language. The socialists were "savages . . . not lifted out of their Apache nature, . . . the loafers, the idle and vicious cranks, the physically, morally, and mentally depraved," "leprous barbarians," and "scabs that have been scraped from the sores of society in the old world."[1]

Of course, this well-known reaction to the events of 1886 has always been read for what it really was: the interpretation of a hostile and hysterical middle-class press. Why, then, take the issue up once more? Because this obviously biased view of socialist immigrants as unacquainted with, and alien to, American traditions has had important repercussions on traditional labor historiography and its evaluation of the impact of socialism on the American labor movement. Thus traditional wisdom has drawn a sharp line between political and economic activity, attributing marginal importance to the former and praising the latter as the true mode of organization for American workers. Young Selig Perlman even went so far as to claim that "trade-unionism . . . in this country originated and grew up in perfect independence of any socialist influence."[2]

This article intends to question the rigid dichotomy of political and economic orientation by looking at the activities of German socialist leaders. These have usually been viewed as a theoretically oriented intellectual elite raised in the dogmatic German socialist tradition and lacking a pragmatic perspective. Since ample proof exists that numbers in the socialist parties were limited and that membership was confined along ethnic lines, the conclusion was drawn that these leaders lacked a following and operated in a vacuum. In order to reassess their role, however, one has to go beyond party organization and look at the local level. This article will focus on Chicago as a midwestern city with a substantial German working-class population and as a center of the American labor movement during the period under consideration. Underlying the argument is the hypothesis that a change of perspective, including economic as well as political activities, is needed in order to arrive at a balanced evaluation of the role of German workers and labor leaders in the Chicago labor movement. The article attempts to demonstrate that (1) there was a substantial German working class that supported, and was in turn affected by, working-class institutions and the leaders who headed them, and its condition and experience were such as to make for radicalism and class consciousness. (2) German labor leaders reflected the condition of the Chicago German working-class community, which witnessed a high influx from Germany and at the same time the beginnings of consolidation or integration into American society. Thus leaders were shaped both by their German experience and by the emerging Chicago working class. (3) In contrast to the traditional view of the preponderance of the political movement for German labor leaders, these leaders saw it as their primary task to organize the Chicago working class on an economic basis. Their role as labor union organizers, and not as socialist party leaders, is the more significant one in terms of the impact of German immigrant workers on the American labor movement.

Chicago's industrial as well as its population growth during the second half of the nineteenth century is representative of the rapid expansion of midwestern cities during that period, when they increasingly attracted large numbers of immigrants. By 1850, when the Midwest emerged as the major destination of German emigration to the United States, reports on Chicago's enormous economic potential and on its fluid social structure had already reached European emigration districts. The city gradually became the center of German urban settlement in the Midwest.[3] In 1850 Germans accounted for over 5,000 of Chicago's 30,000 inhabitants. In June 1884 the school census recorded a population of 617,000, one-third of whom were first- or second-generation German immigrants. These figures led the city's German working-class daily, *Chicagoer Arbeiter-Zeitung*, to run the bragging headline "A German City in America," pointing out the fact that there were only five cities in Germany with a larger German population than that of Chicago. When in 1890 the population of the city had passed the one million mark, German-born residents, comprising 35.6% of the foreign-born, still contributed the largest immigrant element.[4]

During the same period industrial employment, standing at somewhat less than 5,400 workers in 1860, witnessed an unprecedented growth as a result of the expansion of major industries, such as the meat-packing, iron and steel, construction, clothing, printing and publishing, agricultural and other machinery, furniture, and brewing industries. The most spectacular rise occurred from 1880 and 1890. While the city's population doubled during this decade (the German-born element increasing from 75,000 to 161,000), the relative increase of the number of industrial workers was even greater (from 92,000 to 208,000). At the same time, both rapid mechanization and the introduction of new technologies caused structural changes in the industrial sector, where more and more unskilled labor, largely recruited from among the immigrants, was employed. In this key formative period of American industrial society, artisans, small businessmen, and skilled workers were thus caught up in fundamental processes of displacement.

By 1890 the ethnic composition of Chicago's working class and the occupational structure of Germans in particular were as follows. Only one-third of all workers were native Americans; the remaining two-thirds were foreign-born (as compared with 41% foreign-born of Chicago's total population).[5] Germans contributed 22.5% to the industrial labor force (47,000 in absolute numbers). Not only were Germans the largest immigrant element of the working class of Chicago, but the majority (i.e. more than 55%) of all Germans gainfully employed were artisans or worked in the industrial sector in skilled and unskilled occupations.

What was the situation of Chicago's working class at that time?[6] The general trend toward an increase in wages after the severe depression years 1873–77 was reversed again by the depression of 1883. From 1882 to 1886 wages declined 5.7%. But structural changes as well as cyclical fluctuations were responsible for this decline, which affected both unskilled workers in large units and skilled workers like cabinet makers or shoemakers whose wages were depressed by the introduction of new machinery.[7] P. H. McLogan, president of the Chicago Trades Assembly, appearing before the Blair committee in August 1883, gave an example of the displacement of skills in the former trade:

> We find that in the various wood-working departments of trade there are thousands of children employed. Take cabinet-making, for instance. Formerly a boy went into a cabinet-maker's shop and learned the trade, but since the introduction of labor-saving machinery the cabinet-makers will take boys from twelve to sixteen years of age, and will put them into the cabinet shop to do a certain part of the work that they can easily learn to do in a short time . . . that is, they learn to do a certain little piece of the work by means of labor-saving machinery, and there they remain from year to year making that same little piece. . . . The same rule applies in . . . almost all the other branches of mechanical industry.[8]

To a substantial degree, German artisans and skilled workers were affected by this process. Wages for bakers, brickmakers, butchers, carpenters, cabinet makers, carriage and wagon makers, coopers, metal workers, toolmakers, furniture workers, i.e. in trades where Germans were strongly represented, fell below the average wage per year of $569.

This reduction was aggravated by the high degree of unemployment. In October of the slack year 1884 the number of unemployed in Chicago reached 30,000 and caused a hopeless overburdening of municipal and private relief agencies. In "normal" times about 15% of the workers were unemployed.[9] But more characteristic of the Chicago labor market was seasonal or temporary—rather than permanent—unemployment. Only 20% of the workers were employed all year, whereas 33% were idle more than six months. The average length of employment per year was 37 weeks. Earnings were more decisively depressed by seasonal unemployment than by the reduction of wages. Both were responsible for the fact that many working-class families could not make ends meet. Of the 78 German working-class households in Chicago that the State Labor Bureau included in its 1884 investigation of working-class families in Illinois, more than 40% reported higher expenses than incomes—despite the fact that in one-third of the cases several family members worked and contributed to the income (the comparable figure for German working-class families in the state of Illinois was 18%).

Whereas more than one-third of trade union members owned a

house in Illinois (excluding Chicago), in the city of Chicago only few workers were able to realize this dream.[10] Whether they succeeded in acquiring property depended on kind and degree of skill; significant differences with regard to house ownership existed within the working class. A greater proportion of artisans, skilled workers, and workers with an income higher than average owned a house, but among this group of skilled workers and artisans construction workers surpassed all other trades.

Of the German working-class families in Chicago whose condition the Illinois Labor Bureau affirmed to be representative of other German working-class households and therefore described in detail in its 1884 report, none owned a house. However, a few artisans or skilled workers (one trunk maker, two upholsterers, one cigarmaker) lived in well-furnished rented houses and in "healthy location." The families were described as well dressed and "intelligent"; the men were union members. In one case the report even concluded, "On the whole, they are a happy family." But the economic and social situation of all the other families was not nearly so good. A blacksmith, his wife, and five children lived in decent and clean circumstances, but in a four-room apartment in a tenement house; he had been able to find work for only 25 weeks, and they "are not satisfied with their condition." A cigarmaker's family of eight occupied a three-room house and paid an exorbitantly high rent of $20 a month. The house was depicted as "scantily and poorly furnished, no carpets, and the furniture being of the cheapest kind." It was located in an unhealthy neighborhood and kept in filthy condition; the children were sick "at all times." The husband belonged to the union but found work only every now and then; therefore, the family depended upon additional income earned by the wife and the oldest son. A laborer's family was even worse off: they lived in "filthy condition," "in a block of miserable frame tenements," were badly dressed and undernourished, sick and "exceedingly illiterate." As a consequence of the long hours of work, a streetcar driver saw his children only when they were already asleep. A conductor, hardly better off, was permanently employed, but because of a sixteen-hour workday did not even have time to read the paper; he complained that "the company is grinding [me] and all the others down to the starvation point."[11] Similar complaints about increasing mechanization and speed of work, about strict work discipline and the imposing of fines for singing and talking during work hours, were often made in the Chicago working-class press.

These poor or even miserable conditions invited comparison with life in Germany. In the winter of 1883 Paul Grottkau, editor of the

Chicagoer Arbeiter-Zeitung, who had emigrated to the city from Berlin in 1878, accompanied a committee of the Citizens' Association on its inspection tours of Chicago's tenement districts. Michael Schwab, one of the convicted Haymarket anarchists, describes in his autobiography Grottkau's reaction upon his return to the office: "By his friends, G. is considered a cynic. When he came back he was deadly pale, greatly excited, he was not feeling well. He said that he never would go out to see such terrible things again. He knew a good deal of Berlin and her misery, but such a condition of affairs did not exist there, not even in the poorest quarters."[12] Schwab took Grottkau's place as reporter and confirmed his impressions. Those Haymarket anarchists who had immigrated from Germany all refer in their autobiographies to their own experiences when contrasting the two societies. Thus Georg Engel, having failed as a small businessman in Germany, wanted to climb the ladder of economic success in the "free and glorious country." He, as well as Schwab and Oskar Neebe (who was born in New York City as a son of German immigrants but was apprenticed in Germany), soon realized that the displacement of artisans and skilled workers in America's industrial centers had progressed as far as in Germany. The wages of bookbinders, observes Schwab, who himself had learned the bookbinder's trade, if measured against the cost of living, were lower in Chicago than in Germany. August Spies comes to the conclusion that conditions were about the same, but he adds: "I never saw there such real suffering from want as I have seen in this country. And there is more protection for women and children in Germany than here."[13]

Faith in uninhibited personal and political freedom, seen to be the most noticeable distinguishing characteristic of American society by newly arrived German workers, was gradually eroded. Even before the Haymarket tragedy Chicago had established a tradition of reckless violation of workers' rights through police brutality, denial of the right of freedom of assembly, and election frauds.[14] It was during the railroad strike of 1877 that the Chicago police for the first time indiscriminantly used brutal force against workingmen. Philip Van Patten, then secretary of the Workingmen's party, was badly clubbed and barely escaped with his life, while a German worker was beaten unconscious and received severe injuries. The next day a business meeting of the Furniture Workers Union in Turner Hall was raided by wildly shooting and clubbing policemen who killed one of the workers.[15] Police violence was also used to break strikes in succeeding years, and after Haymarket it was also leveled against innocent individuals, as increasing reports on such incidents in the labor press illustrate. One victim, after relating his experience in an open letter, concluded: "In America workingmen are outlawed, being on a level with pariahs."[16]

Election frauds made an equally lasting impression. After election day the German working-class papers often pointed out the tricks politicians had played on the workingmen's vote, like confiscating election tickets—which at that time had to be distributed by party members to its prospective electors—chasing away or even arresting these ticket peddlers, changing the voting places overnight without notice so that workers were prevented from voting before going to work and closing them before the workday was over, using intimidation in the shops, and stuffing ballot boxes. As early as 1874 the *Vorbote* spoke of "most cunning election frauds," after tickets for the Labor party of Illinois—later the Socialist Labor party (SLP)—had been torn up and votes suppressed. A bigger scandal happened in the spring election of 1880, when Frank Stauber, socialist candidate for alderman in the 14th ward, was counted out several days after having been declared elected. Although the socialists went to court and were able to prove that this reversal was the result of shameless ballot-box stuffing, the two election judges responsible were acquitted because they had acted "in good faith." "We are fully justified in saying," wrote the *Vorbote*, commenting on the former incident, "that the holiest institution of the American people, the right to vote, had been desecrated and become a miserable farce and a lie."[17]

Both socioeconomic conditions and political abuses had a sobering effect on German immigrant workers, who increasingly turned to labor organizations. Although sporadically (and with differing success) workers in Chicago, especially the German element among them, also formed and supported labor parties, it was the trade union movement, not the political movement, that proved to be the permanent mode of organization with significant and lasting effects for Chicago labor. When in the early 1880s the labor movement in the United States advanced markedly, Chicago became the center of the organizing drive that culminated in the eight-hour movement of 1886. Of the 352,000 workers participating throughout the country, almost one-third lived in Chicago. In June 1886 the city's labor organizations reported a membership of 60,191, the trade unions comprising about twice as many members (41,800) as the Knights of Labor (18,350).[18] As Table 1 shows, German workers, measured against their proportion of the total working class (about 22.5%), were overrepresented: they contributed almost one-third of the membership of all Chicago labor organizations. Whereas only one-fifth of the Knights of Labor membership was German (Americans comprising about 34%), the

Table 1. *Ethnic Distribution of Chicago's Organized Workers, 1886.*

	Trade Unions	Knights of Labor	All Labor Organizations
Native Americans	16.1%	33.9%	21.6%
Germans	35.8	20.7	31.2
Irish	18.9	14.4	17.5
Scandinavians	13.4	4.9	10.8
English	5.0	6.8	5.5
Bohemians	1.8	9.0	4.0
Poles	2.1	4.6	2.8
Scots	1.6	0.2	1.2
Italians	0.8	0.2	0.7

Figures were computed from the tables in the *Fourth Biennial Report,* pp. 172ff., 186ff., 224ff.

figure for the trade unions was 35.8% (14,910). Germans were therefore the largest ethnic group even before native Americans. In 27 of 100 trade unions, the proportion of German workers exceeded this average, sometimes extraordinarily so. Table 2 specifies those ten trade unions in Chicago with the highest absolute numbers of German members.[19]

But not only because of their absolute numbers were German workers an important factor in the Chicago working class; they also decisively helped to set the tone of its political and cultural activities.

Significant credit for the vitality and organizational involvement of the German working class of Chicago must be given to its labor leaders. It is difficult to characterize them as a group, for there were basic differences of background and personality, and a high degree of fluctuation occurred over the years. Leaders in this respect were representative of the composition of the German working-class community. Most were first-generation immigrants from various parts of Germany, often staying in the city for only a limited number of years and then moving on to different places in the United States. Yet despite individual differences and rapid turnover, they also had a common characteristic that provided for basic continuity of their work in Chicago: they had all been prominently involved in the German labor movement before leaving the country for political reasons, were steeped in its socialist tradition, and continued to show deep dedication to the labor movement. At the same time the beginnings of a transition toward a more Americanized leadership can already be made out in those few leaders who had immigrated at an early age and who, while

Table 2. *Trade Unions in Chicago with Highest Absolute Numbers of German Members, Spring 1886.*

Trade Union	Number of Germans in Trade[a]	Percentage of Germans in Trade[a]	Number of German Members in Union[b]	Percentage Germans of Total Membership[b]	Percentage Germans in One Trade Organized
Metal workers	3.032	19.5	1.815	60.0	59.0
Lumbermen's laborers	—[c]	—[c]	1.545	80.4	—
Furniture workers	3.260[d]	34.0[d]	1.458	60.0	44.7[f]
Hod carriers	—[c]	—[c]	1.200	34.3	—
Carpenters and joiners	3.586	24.8	1.160	68.1	32.3
Bricklayers and stonemasons	1.266	32.0	1.015	25.4	80.1
Bakers	970	46.3	814	84.8	83.9
Butchers	1.355	34.2	700	58.3	52.4
Brewers and maltsters	321[e]	58.8[e]	600	60.3	—
Brick makers	608	49.0	600	51.1	98.6

[a]Figures were computed from *Tenth and Eleventh Census: Statistics on Population*, pp. 870 and 650 respectively.
[b]Figures were computed from the tables in the *Fourth Biennial Report*, pp. 172ff., 186ff., 224ff.
[c]No figures available.
[d]Figures for 1890 only.
[e]Figures for 1880 only.
[f]This figure has heuristic value only, for the base years are not the same. It would be higher if the number of Germans in the Furniture Workers Union had risen from 1886 to 1890, and vice versa.

based within the German working class, purposely reached out beyond ethnic confines to the Chicago working class as a whole. These
different backgrounds can be illustrated through the biographies of
two of these labor leaders, Paul Grottkau and George A. Schilling.

Paul Grottkau, son of a fairly well-to-do Prussian noble family, was
born in 1846. In order to become an architect, he had to acquire
practical skills as a mason, thus coming into contact with the labor
movement in Berlin. In 1871 he was already on the board of the
General German Workingmen's Association and served as an organizer for the Lassallean movement. Known for his brilliant oratorical
gifts, Grottkau concentrated his abilities on the trade union movement, becoming president of the German Bricklayers and Stonecutters Union in the same year and advocating a national federation of
trade unions after the political movement had been unified at Gotha
in 1875. Being also a gifted journalist, Grottkau contributed the bulk
of articles to the *Grundstein,* organ of the Bricklayers Union; he later
became an editor of the social democratic *Berliner Freie Presse.* For his
union and political activities, he had to serve several jail sentences for
a total of at least 15 months. When early in 1878 the Prussian police,
intensifying its persecution of social democrats, wanted to jail Grottkau again, this time in his capacity of editor-in-chief, he preferred to
escape to the United States, going directly to Chicago. There he took
over the editorship of the *Chicagoer Arbeiter-Zeitung* and *Vorbote* and
dedicated himself to the organization of trade unions. Because of his
strong labor union bias and his principled socialism, he twice came
into conflict with the supervisory board of the papers and, breaking
with the anarchist movement of Chicago in 1884, went to Milwaukee
in 1886, where he both edited the local German labor paper and
organized the Central Labor Union. During the eight-hour movement of that year Grottkau was indicted for his role in the so-called
Bay View Riots, but because of a hung jury he was not convicted. Back
in Chicago in 1888, he again wrote for the German labor papers
before going to San Francisco in 1890, where he edited the *California
Arbeiterzeitung.* Grottkau died in 1898 while visiting Milwaukee during
an agitation tour for Debs's social democracy.[20]

Three years before Grottkau, George A. Schilling had arrived in
Chicago. By that time, however, he had already worked throughout
the Midwest at the cooper's trade and in railroad construction, having
come to the United States with his parents as an infant from the
province of Nassau in the early 1850s and grown up in Ohio. After
joining the Workingmen's party in 1876, he helped establish its English-
speaking section and became one of the leading socialists in Chicago,
often serving as intermediary between German and native American

workers, ceaselessly campaigning during election times, and sometimes running as a candidate himself. At the same time he was a
member of the Knights of Labor and himself organized unions, like
the coopers' union whose first president he became. Acting on the
principle that "those seeking economic progress must shape their
conduct in accordance with the traditions and environment of the
country in which they live,"[21] Schilling during the 1880s pursued
several channels to promote a strong and uncorrupted labor movement. Thus he prominently participated first in the Socialistic Labor
party and after 1885 in various coalition labor parties. He also served
on several central labor bodies and as Master Workman of District
Assembly 24 of the Knights of Labor, which under his leadership
seceded from the parent organization in 1889 as a result of Powderly's
opposition to the eight-hour movement and his condemnation of the
Chicago anarchists. In the late 1880s Schilling became a friend of
John Peter Altgeld, in whom he found an ally for Chicago labor
within the Democratic party. As one of the leaders of the defense
association for the Haymarket anarchists, it was Schilling who rallied
support from various elements of the Chicago working class for Altgeld and who, working from his new position in Springfield as secretary of the state Labor Bureau, was instrumental in obtaining the
governor's pardon for Neebe, Schwab, and Fielden in 1893.[22]

It took Schilling several years after his arrival in Chicago in 1875
before he was firmly based in the working-class community and
emerged as one of its leaders. For the rest of his life he remained in
the city and thus retained his local roots. Why, by contrast, were
outsiders like Grottkau immediately accepted by the German constituency of the Chicago labor movement? Two reasons may be suggested
here. These leaders were usually well known among the German
working-class community, because even before emigrating to the United
States workers themselves had often participated in the labor movement in Germany and had closely followed developments in their
home country through the Chicago labor papers. Therefore, new
arrivals, especially the more prominent ones, were greeted as people
of their own kind and as valuable reinforcements. These strong trans-
Atlantic ties were thus more than adequate as a substitute for familiarity with the local community. Equally as important, however, was
the availability of, and access to, an established German labor press as
the most important institution of the community. It was only through
this means of communication that German labor leaders were able to
exert their considerable influence. As a rule, the position of editor of
the labor press, regardless of the individual concerned, entailed multiple additional tasks. The editor would be invited to address mass

public meetings, speak at rallies and picnics, give the keynote address at working-class festivities, agitate in labor union and political party meetings, rally Turner societies to the support of labor, help educate children in Sunday free schools, and advance labor's demands before legislative bodies. Thus listing the editors of the *Vorbote, Chicagoer Arbeiter-Zeitung,* and *Fackel* is almost equivalent to enumerating Chicago's outstanding German labor leaders of the period.[23] On the other hand, for those leaders not in editors' positions it was vital to gain access to the press, even at the cost of establishing rival labor papers. At a time when the leading German labor publications in Chicago pursued a course adverse to coalition politics, a group of Lassalleans led by Karl Klings founded the *Sozialist* (later named *Chicagoer Volkszeitung*) in 1877. Again, when the Chicago anarchists, under the leadership of August Spies, had secured complete control over the papers, the socialists of the city, led by the venerated Julius Vahlteich and by Gustav Belz, ventured the short-lived *Illinoiser Volkszeitung* in 1884. Even George Schilling, who had other means of access to his fellow workers at his disposal, had connections with the German labor press (e.g. as agent for the labor organizations and as advertising agent) and thus maintained his close institutional ties to the German working-class community.

The key role of the labor press is made even more evident by looking at the fate of editors who vacated their positions. Paul Grottkau's resignation in the summer of 1879 is a case in point. To make a living, he opened a "Fancy Quilt Manufactory" on the North Side in a German section of Chicago, but apparently failed to attract working-class customers in sufficient numbers. In advertisements inserted in the *Chicagoer Arbeiter-Zeitung* shortly before Christmas, he openly criticized the lack of solidarity on his behalf, sarcastically asking whether "the real friends will come or rather go shopping in strangers' stores," and complaining that while sacrifices on the part of individual socialists of "money, time, and energy" were taken as a matter of course, the community failed in its duty to support those same individuals when they themselves were in need. He was therefore dependent upon the middle class and could not afford to antagonize these potential customers by continuing to agitate for the labor movement.[24] It seems as if solidarity was extended only to those who ran into difficulty in their official role as representatives of the working class, but not as private individuals. Thus, when Grottkau was indicted in Milwaukee as the leader of the eight-hour movement in May 1886, Chicago collected money for his defense, although at that time the burden on the community was a heavy one because enormous funds had to be raised for the Haymarket victims and their families. Likewise, sufficient contributions were made to enable Gustav Belz, who had contracted tuberculosis, to go first to California to a healthier climate and then back home. When Belz died soon afterward, an obituary in the *Vorbote*, praising his indefatigable dedication to the cause of labor, could not refrain from remarking that "only a few persons appreciate the work done, the mass forgets him as soon as he is out of sight."[25]

And yet, even if these leaders retained their positions for only relatively short periods and then moved on to different places where they would serve in similar capacities again, their work in Chicago is characterized by a high degree of continuity. It is claimed here that both kinds of leaders, as represented by Grottkau and Schilling, were consistent in their goal of uniting German workers and other groups—ethnic and native—of the Chicago working class. In Schilling's case it is easier to detect outward signs of this purpose. He was bilingual, as a rule addressed workers in English, and frequently organized English-speaking and other elements of the working class. He also had extensive connections to American middle-class reformers and was even accepted by the business community as a spokesman of labor. Grottkau, on the other hand, had a bad reputation as a troublemaker, anarchist sympathizer, and uncompromising Marxist. He was a brilliant speaker only in his native tongue and therefore valuable for agitation among fellow Germans alone. During his trial in Milwaukee he had to depend on an interpreter.

With regard to the substance of their intentions, however, both men were strikingly similar. Schilling as well as Grottkau, according to traditional interpretation, should be classed as belonging to the "political wing" of the labor movement, for Schilling was one of the leading exponents of political action in the late 1870s, and Grottkau was a Lassallean who therefore should have been completely opposed to economic organization. If, instead, one looks at the record of both men, these prejudices do not stand up. Thus it is quite remarkable that Grottkau was one of the leading proponents of trade unionism even in Germany.[26] While president of the Bricklayers Union, in 1873–74 he wrote a series of agitation letters to German bricklayers that, if compared with his later outlook and activities, reveal a striking consistency of approach. In these letters he convincingly argued for the priority of economic organization in much the same way that the Internationals had done. He conceded that political emancipation was necessary but maintained that economic exploitation of men by men was the fundamental evil. Moreover, "since trade-union organization is a result of present economic developments, it would be ridiculous to dismiss it off-hand." Every worker of a trade should be admitted without regard to his political convictions; solidarity must be learned as a consequence of common conditions and experiences. As the best means of furthering the organization of trade unions, Grottkau proposed agitation for the reduction of the workday, giving all the well-known arguments that had been brought forth repeatedly in the American labor movement.[27]

Once in Chicago, he continued to emphasize this approach with even more justification, since political freedom, which workers still had to fight for in Germany, had been constitutionally granted for almost a century in the United States, without at the same time visibly improving the economic condition of workers. In his first article written in the *Vorbote*, Grottkau therefore concluded: "Political freedom in the face of economic dependence and servitude does not make sense. Political action of the workers without a strong organization and without real means of power in this country is equal to fighting windmills."[28] Given this perspective, it is not surprising to see him lead German workers in the Chicago eight-hour movement of 1879, argue in editorials for its necessity, and appear as one of the main speakers during the climactic July picnic days of the SLP along with Ira Steward and J. P. McGuire.[29] Throughout the 1880s Grottkau zealously continued to write and agitate for the eight-hour day, using whatever means were at his disposal and, while based in Chicago, working especially as organizer for the Furniture Workers Union. After his break with the Chicago anarchists he twice toured the country in 1885 and in early 1886 to prepare the eight-hour movement of that year, meeting with enthusiastic reception wherever he went. In addition, he was the principal organizer of the movement in Milwaukee. And once again in 1890, he spoke in all the industrial centers of the country, this time as an officially appointed organizer of the AFL.

Schilling's priorities, if they inclined more to the political side before 1880, took a decided turn shortly afterward. While he did not completely repudiate political action in later years, it is equally clear that even when he was known as a political activist, he continually urged economic organization, dedicating himself almost exclusively to this field in the 1880s. This is not to say that Grottkau and Schilling experienced a conversion of the Samuel Gompers or Adolph Strasser kind. Rather, they pursued "short-range labor-union goals as the precondition of the radical alteration of present-day social institutions."[30] It was therefore not at all inconsistent for Schilling to ally himself with Altgeld, or for Grottkau to work for the AFL.

The prevalence of labor union orientation in the face of substantial variations of political activity is further illustrated by the fact that labor leaders either had to accommodate themselves to this basic objective or were likely to be ignored by the working-class constituency.

The fates of some other Chicago labor leaders are representative of these alternatives. Karl Klings, the first editor of the *Vorbote* in the winter of 1874, was replaced by Conrad Conzett within two months when his editorial policy turned out to be strictly opposed to labor unions. Conzett, following the guidelines set by the First International, succeeded in firmly establishing the new paper in the German working-class community. Gustav Lyser, on the other hand, had learned the hard way to adapt himself to American conditions by the time he took over the editorship of the *Fackel* in Chicago: he had been dismissed from his editorial position on the *New York Social-Demokrat* because of his hostile attitude to economic organization. Similarly, W. L. Rosenberg's fall came after he had left Chicago where he had pursued a friendly course toward unions in line with the obligations resulting from his role as editor of the labor paper. When as secretary of the SLP he began to attack unions, he, together with other members of the executive, was removed in 1889 by persons closely cooperating with, and encouraging the organization of, unions. In the case of the Chicago anarchists, the story goes that they were reluctant to join the eight-hour movement of 1886 and did so only because of immense pressure from within the working class.[31] While this version seems open to doubt,[32] the record of their activities, regardless of the motives involved, from the fall of 1885 to the May days of 1886, impressively proves their thorough dedication to concerted economic action. It is thus by no means a matter of chance that German labor organizations were firmly united behind the demand for a shorter workday, and that in Chicago they and their leaders were in the forefront of the organization drive of 1886.

This look at the German working-class community of Chicago and its leaders suggests that the notion of supposedly alien ideas intruding upon an already existing native working class with specifically American characteristics should be reconsidered. For one thing, the American working class during the period under consideration was itself undergoing fundamental changes. It would therefore be more adequate to characterize it as a class in a process of reorganization to which immigrants overwhelmingly contributed and during which, in terms of composition, skills, outlook, and tradition, quite diverse elements were incorporated.

Saying this, one has to concede at the same time that little is known yet about these processes of incorporation. The careers of labor leaders offer some glimpses into which working-class traditions were brought along and how these were maintained or transformed. But were their careers representative of immigrant workers' experiences?

What, for instance, was the impact of artisan culture and German social democracy on the masses of immigrant workers from Germany? How exactly did the processes of adaptation to the new societal and cultural context develop, and which were the important factors influencing them? How can we weight elements of continuity, discontinuity, and transformation, and what was the long-range direction of change of the German working-class community in Chicago?[33] Answers to these questions can contribute valuable insights into the specific character of the American working class. What from a later perspective was claimed to be the typical mode of organization of American labor might very well turn out to be to a significant degree an expression of the needs and interests of immigrant workers. Thus elements of institutional and cultural continuity might play a larger part than has been generally assumed in shaping working-class life and, more specifically, organized labor in America.

NOTES

1. Unidentified Chicago newspaper clipping, 25 May 1886, in "Chicago History, 1872–1914," scrapbook no. 88, Chicago Historical Society Collection. For more examples of newspaper reaction to the Haymarket tragedy, see Henry David, *History of the Haymarket Affair* (Chicago, 1963), pp. 178–89.

2. Selig Perlman, "History of Socialism in Milwaukee, 1893–1910" (B.A. thesis, University of Wisconsin, 1910), p. 19; see also his "Upheaval and Reorganization," in John R. Commons *et al.*, *History of Labour in the United States*, 2 (New York, 1918):195–331. For a general discussion of the impact of socialism in the United States, see pt. 1 of John H. M. Laslett and Seymour Martin Lipset, eds., *Failure of a Dream? Essays in the History of American Socialism* (New York, 1974), as well as the lucid and concise discussion by Peter Lösche in his *Industriegewerkschaften im organisierten Kapitalismus* (Opladen, 1974), pp. 183–202. See also Herman Schlüter's statement that the positive effect of agitation by the IWA, SLP, and Socialist party on the trade union movement has not been acknowledged, in *Die Internationale in Amerika* (Chicago, 1918), pp. 399, 511.

3. For the regional and ethnic distribution of immigrants in cities, see David Ward, *Cities and Immigrants: A Geography of Change in Nineteenth Century America* (New York, 1971), pp. 78–79. The chart shown there demonstrates that the percentage of Germans in Chicago was typical of that in other midwestern cities. Even in 1850, 5% of the German immigrant population of the states of Illinois, Wisconsin, Iowa, and Minnesota lived in Chicago. This figure increased to 13% by 1880. Cf. Ulf Beijbom, *Swedes of Chicago* (Växjö, 1971), p. 116. For Chicago's industrial development, see Bessie L. Pierce, *History of Chicago*, vols. 2 and 3 (Chicago, 1940 and 1957), and Alfred Pred, *The Spatial Dynamics of U.S. Urban Industrial Growth, 1800–1914* (Cambridge, Mass., 1966).

4. *Chicagoer Arbeiter-Zeitung* (hereafter cited as *ChAZ*), 30 Aug. 1884. These and the following population figures are from *U.S. Census on Population* for the years 1870, 1880, and 1890; Pierce, *History*, 2:482–500, 3:516–18; Thomas Bullard, "Distribution of Chicago's Germans, 1850–1914," ms. in the Chicago Historical Society (Apr. 1969).

5. The ethnic character of the Chicago working class becomes even more apparent if it is remembered that almost two-thirds (63.5%) of native American workers were second-generation immigrants. The following table breaks down the working class along ethnic lines:

Americans	34.5%
native parents	12.5
foreign parents	22.0
Germans	22.5
Irish	9.8
British	5.0
Scandinavians	11.3
Others (especially Poles, Italians, Bohemians)	13.8

Black Americans and Canadians are not included in the table. Source: *Eleventh Census: Statistics on Population*, pp. 650–51.

6. The situation of Chicago's working class in the mid-1880s can be partly reconstructed by computing the relevant figures for Chicago from the detailed statistics compiled by the Illinois Labor Bureau on the condition of workers in Illinois for the years 1884 and 1886. This procedure also allows for comparisons between Chicago and small and medium-sized towns in Illinois. Unless otherwise indicated, the following figures were obtained from "Earnings, Expenses and Condition of Workingmen and Their Families," in Illinois Bureau of Labor Statistics, *Third Biennial Report* (Springfield, Ill., 1884), pp. 135–414, and "Trade and Labor Organizations," in *Fourth Biennial Report* (Springfield, Ill., 1886), pp. 145–463.

7. Weighting structural and cyclical causes on the basis of existing figures raises some problems. Woytinski observes a considerable increase of wages for the 1880s, but that applies especially to the second half of the decade. These facts point to cyclical causes. W. S. Woytinski *et al.*, *Employment and Wages in the United States* (New York, 1953), pp. 47–48. On the other hand, figures given by the Illinois Labor Bureau that show the development of wages from 1882 to 1886 are very detailed. Information is given on 114 occupations and branches of industry; in 17% of these cases wages had remained the same, in 20% they had risen, and in 63% they had fallen. Analysis of occupations where wages had been reduced more than average shows that especially affected were large production units like cloak, shoe, and watch factories (mainly as a result of the switch to female labor), and steel mills, as well as traditional craftsmen and skilled workers like bakers, carpenters, cabinet makers, and shoemakers. "Wages for a Series of Years," in *Fourth Biennial Report*, pp. 335–61. That the development of wages in these trades had in fact long-range structural causes is confirmed by comparing the figures for wages over two decades (1871–91) in U.S. Department of Labor, *History of Wages in the United States from Colonial Times to 1918*, Bureau of Labor Statistics Bulletin no. 604 (Washington, D.C., 1934). Similar developments were traced by Bruce Laurie *et al.* for Philadelphia for the period 1850–80, in "Immigrants and Industry: The

Philadelphia Experience, 1850–1880," *Journal of Social History* 9 (1975–76):219–46.

8. "Relations between Labor and Capital," Senate Committee on Education and Labor, 47th Cong., 1st Sess., 1 (Washington, D.C., 1885):568. The evil effects of mechanization were repeatedly referred to in testimony by workers and businessmen, e.g. testimony given by Samuel Gompers, Adolph Strasser, Adolf Douai, R. Heber Newton, and George Blair. In 1879, when the Wright committee visited Chicago to investigate business and labor conditions, McLogan had already brought forth similar arguments and had been seconded by other labor leaders, e.g. C. F. Kenyon and Thomas J. Morgan, both speaking on behalf of the Trade and Labor Council. "Investigation by a Select Committee on Depression in Labor and Business Relative to the Cause of the General Depression in Labor and Business . . . ," 45th Cong., 3d Sess., House Misc. Doc. 29 (Washington, D.C., 1879), pp. 116–42.

9. The figure 30,000 is the mean of the figures given by Pierce, *History,* 3:269, and *ChAZ,* 27 Oct. 1884. An average unemployment rate of 15% is given by the *Fourth Biennial Report* for the spring and summer of 1886 (p. 193). This percentage refers to 104,000 members of labor organizations in Illinois, of whom 85% were reported as being "employed" by their unions. After careful weighting of various possible sources of error, the report concludes that the figures given correctly represent the condition of the working class in Illinois (pp. 193–94).

10. The figures given in the *Fourth Biennial Report*—42% for Illinois and 23% for Chicago—are definitely too high. Since they refer to trade union members only, they tend to leave out laborers as well as unorganized workers at large, whose average yearly earnings were $40 below those of organized workers. Moreover, the figures relate to married union members only; projecting them on to the total number of trade union members reveals 11% house ownership for Chicago. This figure approaches the specifications given by the Illinois Labor Bureau in 1884, when only 7.5% of the interviewed working-class families in Chicago owned a house. McLogan, in his testimony before the Blair committee in 1883, estimated that even among the best-paid skilled workers, the printers, only 5% owned houses (p. 586).

House ownership is a problematic indicator for measuring real living conditions and changes of social status. Title-deed as sole criterion does not say anything about house quality, mortgages, and liabilities. In addition, the assumptions mobility studies often tend to make—presupposing a prevalent aspiration for house ownership among workers and inferring a change of class orientaton from house ownership—seem to be unfounded and open to doubt. Despite these caveats, comparison with the figures for Illinois excluding Chicago can at least illustrate the special conditions in that city.

11. These details were compiled from the extensive descriptions of individual working-class households in the *Third Biennial Report,* pp. 358–91.

12. Autobiography of Michael Schwab in *Chicago Knights of Labor* (hereafter cited as *ChKL*), 18 Dec. 1886; for descriptions of housing conditions see the reports in *ChAZ,* 28 and 31 Jan., 3, 5, 7, 14, 22, and 28 Feb., 1883.

13. Autobiography of August Spies in *ChKL,* 6 Nov. 1886. The autobiographies of Adolph Fischer, Georg Engel, Michael Schwab, and Oskar

Neebe appeared in *ChKL*, 20 and 27 Nov., 18 Dec. 1886, 30 Apr. 1887. See also Philip S. Foner, ed., *The Autobiographies of the Haymarket Martyrs* (New York, 1969). This book also contains Louis Lingg's autobiography, which originally appeared in *Alarm*, 29 Dec. 1888, 5 and 12 Jan. 1889.

14. See the history of the Chicago labor movement as related in the *Vorbote*, 4, 11, 18, 25 May, 1, 8, 15 June 1887. This account strongly conveys the sense of outrage and frustration that must have been prevalent in the German working-class community.

15. See affidavits given by Philip Van Patten at Hot Springs, Ark., 11 Apr. 1893, and by Fred Korth at Chicago, 15 Apr. 1893, in Illinois State Archives, Springfield, Ill. These and other affidavits that relate further incidents of police brutality against striking workers were collected by George A. Schilling, then secretary of the Illinois Labor Bureau, to supply arguments for Governor John Peter Altgeld's pardon of the jailed Haymarket anarchists in 1893. For Schilling's part in the pardon, see Harry Barnard, *Eagle Forgotten: The Life of John Peter Altgeld* (Indianapolis, 1962).

16. *ChAZ*, 7 Dec. 1886; see also *ibid.*, 10 and 22 Dec. 1886 and 2 May 1889, where the Chicago police was declared to be even more brutal than the Russian police.

17. *Vorbote*, 7 and 28 Nov. 1874. For other examples of accounts of and comments on election frauds, see *ibid.*, 6 June 1874, 30 Jan. 1875, as well as the history of the Chicago labor movement, May and June 1887; *ChAZ*, 20 Feb. 1880, 18 Feb 1885, 15 Apr., 7 June 1887. George Schilling evaluated the effect of the election fraud of the spring of 1880 as follows: "This circumstance did more, perhaps, than all the other things combined to destroy the faith of the Socialists in Chicago in the efficiency of the ballot." "History of the Labor Movement in Chicago," in Lucy E. Parsons, ed., *Life of Albert R. Parsons*, 2d ed. (Chicago, 1903), p. xxviii.

18. The proportion of organized workers to the total number of workers in Chicago can be established only by indirect means. The number of workers employed in industry, trade, and transportation for the year 1886 is estimated at 150,000, which means a degree of organization of about 40%. This estimate was arrived at by the following method. Added to the figures under "Manufacturing, mechanical and mining industries" of the census of 1880 were the figures given under "laborers" and "transportation." Figures for the respective occupations in the census of 1890 were calculated, and then the average yearly increase from 1880 to 1886 was computed. See *Tenth* and *Eleventh Census: Statistics on Population*, pp. 870 and 650 respectively. The percentage of organized workers was probably greater. The *Fourth Biennial Report* points out that because of the rapid increase of the Knights of Labor in 1886, only half of the Knights of Labor assemblies were listed in its statistics (p. 221).

19. For those occupations specifically listed in the published censuses of 1880 and/or 1890, figures and percentages were computed for comparative purposes. These should, however, be read with caution, since their degree of reliability cannot readily be established.

20. Biographical data from *Geschichte der deutschen Arbeiterbewegung: Biographisches Lexikon* (Berlin, 1970), pp. 173–74; Dieter Fricke, *Die deutsche Arbeiterbewegung 1869–1914* (Berlin, 1976), pp. 76, 116, 123, 641; Eduard Bernstein, *Die Geschichte der Berliner Arbeiterbewegung*, 1 (Berlin, 1907):224ff.; Werner Ettelt and Hans-Dieter Krause, *Der Kampf um eine marxistische Ge-*

werkschaftspolitik 1868–1878 (Berlin, 1975), pp. 427ff.; Franz Mehring, *Geschichte der deutschen Sozialdemokratie,* pt. 2 (Berlin, 1960), pp. 410, 738; Annemarie Lange, *Berlin zur Zeit Bebels und Bismarcks* (Berlin, 1976), pp. 160ff.; Fritz Paeplow, *Zur Geschichte der deutschen Bauarbeiterbewegung* (Berlin, 1932), pp. 242ff. Biographical material for the time after Grottkau's emigration was compiled from *ChAZ, Vorbote,* and *Fackel,* and from the obituaries in *Wisconsin Vorwärts,* 4 June 1898, and *Fackel,* 5 June 1898. See also Thomas Gavett, *Development of the Labor Movement in Milwaukee* (Madison, Wis., 1965), and Frederic Heath, "Landmarks of the Labor Movement in Milwaukee," clippings from the *Social Democratic Herald* in Milwaukee County Historical Center.

21. George Schilling to Lucy Parsons, 1 Dec. 1893, George A. Schilling Papers, Illinois State Historical Society, Springfield, Ill.

22. Biographical material was compiled from *ChAZ, Vorbote,* and *Fackel;* Schilling, "History of the Labor Movement in Chicago"; Barnard, *Eagle Forgotten;* Eugene Staley, *History of the Illinois State Federation of Labor* (Chicago, 1930); Barbara Newell, *Chicago and the Labor Movement* (Urbana, Ill., 1961); Ralph W. Scharnau, "Thomas J. Morgan and the Chicago Socialist Movement 1876–1901" (Ph.D. dissertation, Northern Illinois University, 1969); George A. Schilling Papers, University of Chicago and Illinois State Historical Society; Thomas J. Morgan Papers, University of Chicago and University of Illinois at Urbana.

23. The following leaders, in addition to Grottkau and Schilling, were connected with the German labor papers during the time under consideration: Karl Klings (1874, 1877–79), Conrad Conzett (1874–78), Jakob Franz (1879–80), Gustav Lyser (1878–79), August Spies (1880–86), W. L. Rosenberg (1881–84), Julius Vahlteich (1884–85, after 1900 with *ChAZ*), Joseph Dietzgen (1886–88), Gustav Belz (1886–88), Jens L. Christensen (1887–90), and Simon Hickler (1889–90).

24. Advertisements in *ChAZ,* 14 Sept., 5 Oct., 16 and 19 Dec. 1879, and letter of 25 Mar. 1880.

25. *Vorbote,* 24 Oct. 1888; see also the exhortation in *ChAZ* to contribute money for Grottkau's defense, 21 Dec. 1886. The trial was reported in detail in *ChAZ,* 1–13 Dec. 1886.

26. Another leading trade unionist was the Lassallean Friedrich Wilhelm Fritzsche, who organized the cigarmakers in the 1860s and, together with Grottkau, strongly advocated the centralization of trade unionism. He also emigrated to the United States in 1881 after having toured the country as a representative of German social democracy. *Geschichte der deutschen Arbeiterbewegung: Biographisches Lexikon,* pp. 141–42.

27. "Unterhaltendes in 12 Briefen zusammengestellt an die Mitglieder des Allgemeinen deutschen Maurer- und Steinhauer-Vereins und Solche, die es werden wollen," first and second letter reprinted in Paeplow, *Geschichte,* pp. 687–705.

28. *Vorbote,* 2 and 9 Mar. 1878.

29. See reports in *ChAZ,* 5–7 July 1879.

30. Grottkau in *Vorbote,* 9 Mar. 1878.

31. See, for instance, David, *History of the Haymarket Affair,* pp. 148–50.

32. Thus, in its history of the Chicago labor movement, the *Vorbote* not only claimed that 75% of all Chicago unions had actually been founded by socialists, while the other 25% were founded at their instigation, but main-

tained that the success of the eight-hour movement in Chicago was entirely due to the extraordinary efforts of the Central Labor Union and the IWPA. *Vorbote*, 4 and 25 May 1887.

33. A research project presently being carried out at the Amerika-Institut of the University of Munich under the direction of the author, funded by the VW Foundation, deals with some of these problems. It aims at a social history of the German workers of Chicago between 1850 and 1910.

8

Yugoslav Immigrants in the U.S. Labor Movement, 1880–1920

IVAN ČIZMIĆ

Immigration from the region of Yugoslavia to the United States was sporadic up until the last decade of the nineteenth century. In that phase of early immigration the first immigrants came singly and then later in small groups from the Yugoslav coast. They moved to California, a land that, because of its climate and other similar characteristics, drew the immigrants from the coast. Larger concentrations of immigrants in the period of early migration were established near the delta of the Mississippi River, along the northern Pacific coast, and in the city of New York. To a large extent the first Yugoslav immigrants were sailors, fishermen, and farmers and, as they were small in number, not a significant group within American society. Because they were widely scattered, the immigrants, in the first phase of their migration to the United States, were not organized to any great extent, nor did they take part in social or political activities in their new surroundings. Up to the 1880s there existed only two organizations, both of which were local in character. In 1857 the Slavonic Illyrian Mutual and Benevolent Society was founded in San Francisco, and in 1874 the United Slavonian Benevolent Society in New Orleans.[1]

The period of mass migration from Yugoslavia began toward the end of the nineteenth century. The last period of free immigration to the United States was between 1890 and World War I. During that period Yugoslav emigration became an integral part of the strongest immigration movement in the history of the United States.

It cannot be said with certainty how many Yugoslavs emigrated to the United States up to World War I. In Austro-Hungary there existed a principle of free movement and emigration so that statistically it was not possible to gather precise information regarding emigration. I examined relevant statistical sources such as the *Annual Reports of the Commissioner General of Immigration* in the United States and also a book by Emily G. Balch, *Our Slavic Citizens*. I looked up ships' registers of companies that had transported the immigrants. I analyzed statistical data concerning immigration collected by Josip Lakatoš, one of our statisticians.[2] On the basis of all the above mentioned sources, I came to the conclusion that in the United States there had lived about 700,000 immigrants from the territory of present-day Yugoslavia (approximately 450,000 from Croatia, 150,000 from Slovenia, and the rest Serbs and others).

A great number of South Slav immigrants did not intend to emigrate permanently. They went to the United States with the idea of spending only a few years there in order to earn enough money to solve their financial problems on their farms back home. The objective factors influencing them in the United States, and the difficult economic situation back home, resulted in the majority of them never leaving the States.

Until World War I the target of the emigrants was almost exclusively North America, specifically the United States. The main flow of migration began in New York, which was the location of the immigration transportation center, and moved toward the most industrially developed American states: Pennsylvania, Ohio, Illinois, and Indiana. The Yugoslavs, however, moved to other areas of the United States as well, especially to California, where they were united with the earlier settlers.

It was the highly industrially developed state of Pennsylvania that most attracted the immigrants, as it offered the possibility of a good income in the numerous coal mines, steel mills, and nearby railway and road construction.[3] Another important center was Cleveland, Ohio, where the steel and machine industries were also concentrated. In that city there was already a population of several thousand Yugoslavs by 1890. The immigrants were also attracted to Chicago because, as one of the largest commercial and industrial centers in the United States, it offered the possibility of employment in the developed industries of steel, leather, electrical appliances, chemicals, and food. In Chicago were situated world-famous abattoirs, which offered a good possibility of employment for the unskilled worker.[4]

What were the living conditions like for the Yugoslav immigrants in their new surroundings? At first life was difficult for almost all, but later on, many factors were to decide individual fates. Except for some merchants, bankers, and saloon proprietors, Yugoslavs were not completely freed from economic difficulties during their stay in the United States. They lived in a continual struggle for existence. For many, any hope of returning home slowly became unrealistic. Their status in society improved only gradually. Besides all these difficulties, they felt a great longing for their homeland and in many cases for their own families, which they had left behind. They had to earn enough to satisfy both sides, that is, so that they could live their own lives and still send something back to their relatives in Yugoslavia.[5]

Until then the United States had had very little welfare legislation, and no insurance protection for the workers in case of accidents, sickness, death, or unemployment, especially not for foreigners, let alone unskilled workers who worked at the hardest, most dangerous, and worst-paid occupations. The union movement was only just emerging and at that point comprised only certain "elite" fields largely occupied by local workers; therefore the unskilled immigrants, especially those of Slavic descent who belonged to the so-called New Emigration, were burdened with even more prejudices. It was because of this that they were in the least favorable position in American society at that time. Special bourgeois reactionary organizations (vigilantes) in the settlements spread hate and contempt toward those immigrants, mockingly calling them, "Honky," "Slav," and so on.

Exposed to pressures from various sides, the Yugoslavs found it very difficult to adapt themselves to their new lives. People who had up till then been peasants, inexperienced and uneducated, and many who were illiterate and without knowledge of their new surroundings, were forced to live in isolation within narrow circles of acquaintances and countrymen. Highly discriminated against and without any particular social or cultural life at the beginning, they spent their immigrant days under very difficult conditions. The working day lasted ten to twelve hours, sometimes even more, and all the time they were subject to intense supervision and pressure from "foremen" and "superintendents," so that without any safety measures accidents were an everyday occurrence.

On top of the hard working conditions, their private lives were also full of privations. In the immediate vicinity of factory or construction site, the companies would erect accommodations for the immigrants. The houses in which the immigrants lived were all similar, made of wood covered in soot from the smoke of the factory and packed close to one another. They were popularly called "boarding houses." They did not have running water, electricity, or any other comforts. In the courtyard there would be a pump and around that a bench with washbasins. The house would have six rooms, three on the first floor and three on the second. On the first floor was the proprietor's room, the dining room, and the kitchen. In each room there would be three iron beds, and in each bed two men.[6]

Owning a hotel, which was popularly called a "saloon," was at the time the most profitable and surest way to prosperity. The person who chose that occupation was given a chance to acquire great influence among his fellow countrymen, so that the hotels soon become important centers in the private lives of the immigrants. These proprietors were, by the way, also agents for the American companies, supplying them with new manpower from the recently arrived immigrants. Some of the "saloon" proprietors were also engaged in the banking field and served as mediators among the American authorities, courts, and immigrants. The saloon proprietors were able to obtain American citizenship much more easily than their fellow countrymen. They were active on committees of immigrant benevolent and church organizations. As a knowledge of English was essential in the performance of this occupation, they were the first to learn the language among the immigrants.

Today there is some controversy about the influence that the "boarding houses" and "saloons" had upon the lives of the immigrants. Some described them as places where the immigrants spent their earnings on alcohol and gambling.[7] It must be pointed out, however, that along with their negative aspects, the boarding houses and saloons also played a positive role in the lives of the immigrants. They were, especially in the earlier periods, the scenes of great gatherings of immigrants. There they exchanged their immigrant experiences and gave one another advice. It was here that they would receive the most recent news of events in their homeland, especially of political events. They were also places of political agitation among the immigrants, since many saloon proprietors, as we have already mentioned, were the creators and functionaries of the immigrants' political and benevolent organizations.[8] The so-called *šifkartaši* (ticket agents from shipping companies) or bankers, who played an important role in the life of the immigrants, were also to be found in the saloons. They sold tickets to the immigrants and were the intermediaries in sending the immigrants' money home for them.

The proprietors of the boarding houses and saloons, together with the *šifkartaši,* were active in establishing settlements or colonies of Yugoslav immigrants. With the increasing number of immigrants the settlements provided quarters where the immigrants were able to continue in many ways their old style of life and keep up the customs of their old country.

In the history of South Slav immigration a major role was played by the clergy and their parishes. In all the larger immigrant colonies churches were built, parishes created, and clergymen brought out from the home country. Among the South Slavs the Church played an important role in the cultural, educational, organizational, and national fields. Near the churches schools where the language was taught were built. Often the churches were the only place where the immigrants could gather, so they became centers for political and cultural manifestations. Up to World War I the Croatian immigrants in the United States had created 33 Croatian parishes. From this it appears that their efforts to satisfy their religious needs were successful. The Slovene immigrants also built churches and created parishes in their larger settlements. In some instances the Slovenes and the Croats had the same parishes and priests. The Serbs' churches were of the Orthodox faith, and therefore there was no contact between them and those of the Croats or the Slovenes. The Church, while providing community centers, formed a strong barrier to the spreading of socialist ideas among the South Slavs. This was not the case, as we shall see, with the benevolent societies.

While the people of other nationalities with a long tradition of immigration, for example Italians, Greeks, Poles, Czechs, Jews, etc., were able to found their own ethnic organizations that could offer help in emergencies, the Yugoslavs did not have such organizations, so that their situation, especially in the case of accidents at work, was difficult. In order to fulfill their own needs, the Yugoslav immigrants began to create their own benevolent organizations and by the end of the nineteenth century, in larger immigrant settlements at any rate, were able to involve themselves in the fraternal movement in the United States.

In 1868 John Upchurch, a railway worker, organized a society called "The Ancient Order of United Workmen." The main aim of this society was to offer the workers better conditions and security than those offered by the unions. Upchurch's initiative became more popular, and the organizations formed on these lines became more successful and more competitive. The idea of fraternal protection became acceptable to the general public. Workers who were members of the fraternal organizations enjoyed protection under very desirable conditions of pay.

In 1886 the Order of United Workmen invited representatives of the various fraternal organizations to a meeting held in Washington. At the meeting an association of the relief organizations to be known as the National Fraternal Congress was formed. The reason behind the formation of this association was the need for more successful leadership in the struggle against the insurance companies.

There was disagreement within the National Fraternal Congress when in 1900 the "force bill" was introduced under which some of the younger fraternal organizations had to pay their share on a much higher scale than the older organizations. The association broke up and another organization, the Associated Fraternities of America, was created. But this schism did not last long, and at the joint meeting in 1912 in New York they united as the National Fraternal Congress of

America. After that the American fraternal movement began to grow, and immediately prior to World War II there were 182 national relief organizations in the United States with government permission to operate. Their membership consisted of 6,465,240 adults and 1,034,194 young adults. This membership was spread out among 99,048 departments. The total assets of all the relief organizations amounted to over $1,331 million and the value of protection or bonds amounted to almost $661 million.[9]

During the period of the mass South Slav migration, the Slavs gradually adopted the principles of American fraternal unions for mutual aid, life insurance, and the development of humane, social, and cultural activities within the boundaries of their abilities and in the spirit of brotherly and friendly relations in their own settlements. This is how, in all of their settlements, the benevolent and fraternal societies began to grow. They also established clubs, homes, and halls for meetings, and organized conferences, discussions, and a wide range of other activities among the immigrants.

The benevolent societies united so that they could be more effective in offering aid to their members. They thought that social activities could not be practiced in the limits of smaller or bigger settlements around the mines and factories. Rather, they had to think of a larger and wider formation of a national character, yet still preserve the ideas of fraternal and mutual work so that they would always develop in the spirit of brotherhood. With this thought in mind in 1894 the Croatian National Union was formed in Pittsburgh out of six existing fraternal societies. Soon, many other benevolent societies from the other settlements also began to join. In addition to the formation of the Croatian National Union in the United States, twelve similar organizations were founded. Up to the period of World War II all of these were united under the umbrella of the Croatian Fraternal Union.[10]

In Gary, Indiana, in 1922 a Croatian Catholic Society was formed, also a fraternal organization. Its creators were Croatian clergymen in the United States who did not agree with the progressive and leftist politics of the Croatian National Union. This organization has remained independent up to the present day and is still under the influence of the Croatian clergy in the United States.

The Slovenes and Serbs also formed their own benevolent societies. In the United States twenty benevolent and relief societies were registered in 1920, of which seven were Croatian, nine Slovene, and four Serbian. These immigrant organizations had 3,500 lodges, a membership of about 200,000, and $7 million in ready cash as well as movable fixed assets.[11]

The creation of strong fraternal organizations was a turning point in the life of the South Slav immigrants in the United States. In these organizations they found the possibility of reciprocal aid and cultural improvement and of collective action for alleviating the difficult conditions of life in a strange land. Their broad, humane, and fraternal outlook on the social and economic processes of America, their organizational system composed of separate departments for the young and old, and their provision of quarters for the promotion of social activities all resulted in the South Slav fraternal societies becoming the main promoters of almost all the cutural activities of immigrants in the United States. Under the patronage of their departments, courses in English for the immigrants and in the mother tongue for their offspring born in America were held. The various departments of the societies were also the initiators of committees and societies for the promotion of education, of various artistic groups, and for the development of tamburica and orchestral music.

Although the South Slav fraternal societies in the United States were primarily insurance organizations, they nevertheless developed and are still developing, within the extent of their abilities, the cultural side of their work. They were also the base for the political activities of South Slav immigrants who wanted to help their people in their home country in their fight for freedom.

The fraternal organizations were also very active in propagating socialist ideas among the South Slav immigrants, doing their best to explain the concepts of the class struggle. I would like to show here how the National Croatian Society helped the Croatian workers in times of strikes.

Under the very difficult living and working conditions of the American workers, it was natural that they resorted to strikes and other forms of protest in the struggles for higher wages, shorter working hours, better working conditions, and the recognition of workers' unions. The Yugoslav immigrants were very active in these strikes, but they and other recent immigrants also suffered the most in the suppression of the strikes. Factory owners organized special campaigns against these immigrants, spreading rumors against them in an attempt to frighten them and separate them from the American workers, hoping in this way to destroy the unity of the strikers. Such an example is the strike of 1884 in Connellsville, Pennsylvania, when the local newspaper attacked the Croatian strikers, abusively calling them "Huns" and Slavs. The National Croatian Society made a statement in a local German newspaper there, denying the accusations against the Croatians.[12]

Croatian immigrants also took part in the coal miners' strike of

1902 in Pennsylvania. The National Croatian Society gave the strikers $500 in aid. The president of the United Mine Workers of America, John Mitchell, thanked the society for its help.

There was a large strike in 1909 at the Pressed Steel Car Corporation in McKees Rocks, Pennsylvania. The president of the corporation was at the same time the president of the German National Bank in Pittsburgh, in which the National Croatian Society and other Yugoslav immigrants kept their money. As a sign of solidarity with the strikers they all withdrew their money from that bank.[13]

Strikes followed year after year and the Yugoslav workers became increasingly more active in them. The strike in Calumet, Michigan, remained in the memory of the immigrants for a long time. It began with the founding of the union known as the Western Federation of Miners. Among the organizers was the young Croatian Toni Maleta, who spoke English well, which was at that time a rarity among immigrants. He organized the Croatians and the Slovenes. During the time of the strike they printed a newspaper in the Croatian language. At the same time the newspaper *Hrvatski radnik* (The Croatian Worker) emerged, which also helped to unify the miners. The miners' wives and daughters took part in the preparations for the strike and, under the leadership of the young Slovene Anne Clemenc, created a women's organization that actively took part in the strike and helped the miners in every way.

In July 1913 the miners' union submitted its requests to the company. They were rejected, and 15,000 miners then went out on strike. Then began a long and difficult struggle that lasted over six months. The owners of the coal mines mobilized their private mounted police, which every day terrorized, provoked, and frightened the strikers in attempts to break their solidarity and thus end the strike. But the strikers remained firm and disciplined. The Yugoslav immigrant newspaper wrote much about the Michigan strike and organized aid for the strikers.[14]

In 1914 the miners struck at Ludlow, Colorado. This time the strike led to bloodshed. The miners had been working fourteen hours a day for very low wages. In September they submitted requests to Rockefeller's Colorado Fuel and Iron Company for a 10% increase in wages, the lowering of the number of working hours to eight hours a day, and the recognition of their union. Many members of the National Croatian Society participated in the strike. The housing of those taking part was deliberately destroyed by fire so that many lost all their possessions.[15]

In the strike of 1915 in West Virginia a large number of Yugoslav immigrants took part. In a struggle during the strike a deputy sheriff was killed. As a result, 26 Yugoslav miners were accused of his murder. The National Croatian Society arranged for two Croatian lawyers living within the United States to defend those accused. These two lawyers achieved some success, as many of those accused were freed and the rest were given light sentences.[16]

As a result of the difficult living and working conditions, around the turn of the century a strong workers' movement began to develop among the American working class, among the immigrants in particular. Many Yugoslav immigrants were active participants in these movements. They were mostly apprentice workers who had brought with them socialist ideas and experience of activities in the labor movements. I shall mention here some of the most active. Josip Ječmenjak was elected president of the Shoe and Bootmakers Union in Zagreb in 1893. Tomo Bešenić was an active member of the Tailors' Union of Croatia. Milan Glumac was a reporter and the secretary of the Social Democratic party in Slavonia and Srijem; the Yugoslav Socialist Club extended an invitation to him and in 1908 he arrived in Chicago, where he became the editor of the newspaper *Radnička straža* (The Workingmen's Guard).[17] Juraj Mamek completed his tailor's apprenticeship in Zagreb and became a member of several workers' unions and collaborated in the *Radničkom glasniku* (The Workers' Voice). He was among the first instigators of the workers' movements in Croatia. Etbin Kristian and Jože Zavertnik were prominent in the social democratic movement not only in Slovenia but in the whole of Austro-Hungary. On their arrival in the United States all these men took part in the workers' movements, especially in the Yugoslav immigrant workers' movements.

The American Slovenes were among the first Yugoslavs in the United States to develop the socialist movement. The first Slovene socialist club in America was founded on 2 February 1900 in Chicago. After this the Slovenes, and then the Croats and Serbs, formed their own clubs and began publishing newspapers in their own languages.

However, the Yugoslavs in America did not have any significant successes in the first years of their participation in the socialist movement. The socialist clubs were divided and their activities uncoordinated, so that they were not able to develop; in fact, they often collapsed soon after they began. As a result of this, the Yugoslav socialists did not have a significant effect in the early years on the lives of the Yugoslav immigrants. They were also inactive in the political and economic struggle of the American proletariat. In an effort to remedy their inadequacies, *Radnička straža*, the publication of the Croatian socialists, wrote: "Our belief is that the Yugoslav movement will be powerful and successful only if the organizations unite into a single

Yugoslav Socialist Union. Instead of the present day vacillating and meagre mutual aid (which is manifested in the single occasion of a gathering and entertainment) it is necessary to enter into unlimited mutual aid, a common direction, and systematic activities."[18]

The first initiative in the creation of a unified organization of Yugoslav socialists—Južnoslavenskog Socijalističkog Saveza, the South Slavic Socialistic Federation of America—was made at the assembly of socialists in June 1909 in Pittsburgh. However, it was decided then, as a result of the still small number of socialist organizations, insufficient means, and widespread unemployment, to defer the creation of the union to a later stage. In December 1909 a conference of South Slavs associated with *Radnička straža* was held in Chicago. Also present was a deputy from the Slovene socialist organization, Josip Zavrtnik. At the conference it was unanimously decided to unite to form the South Slavic Socialistic Federation. For this purpose a committee of three people was elected, which, with the consent of the representatives of the Croatian, Serbian, Slovene, and Bulgarian socialists, would within six months convene the first South Slavic Socialistic Congress, and there propose the creation of a league. In accordance with the conclusions of the conference, all four South Slav organizations in Chicago (Slovenes, Croatians, Serbs, and Bulgars) proposed the election of a special inter–South Slavic committee for the convocation of the congress. After much discussion the committee extended invitations and proposals to all South Slav socialist associations in America. They pointed out that the four Chicago organizations had accepted the idea of a united South Slav proletariat in the field of the socialist struggle. This would encompass the struggle for the economic and political freedom of the proletariat, the struggle for cultural and national advancement, and the national freedom of all peoples. In the invitation and suggestions it was also pointed out that the ideal of the class-conscious worker in Chicago was the creation of the South Slavic Socialistic Federation, an organization through which socialist activities would be organized.

In the need for the creation of a unified organization of South Slavs in America, circumstances in the homeland at that time under Austro-Hungary were also a factor. The annexation of Bosnia and Hercegovina and the general threat of war in the Balkans considerably affected the decision about the unification of the Yugoslavs in America. Immediate motives for the unification were the South Slav conference in Ljubljana in 1909 and the Balkan conference in Belgrade held the same year.

In December 1910 a South Slav Socialist Congress was held in

Chicago. Present were 28 delegates representing all the South Slav organizations in America. Tomo Bašenić was elected president of the congress, and Ivan Masten and Frank Petrić its secretaries. The congress began with a report of the state of the Yugoslav socialist movement in America. Further discussion was held regarding the immigration of South Slavs to America, and this led to the acceptance of the following resolution:

I. Yugoslav emigration originated in the ranks of the petit-bourgeoisie [peasants, apprentices, small merchants, etc.] and the working class. II. Reasons for the emigration of the Yugoslavs from Europe to America lie in the lack of economic development of the Yugoslav countries; on one side the petit-bourgeoisie was forced to join the ranks of the proletarians, and on the other side, the development of the already impoverished working class was thrown into even more upheaval in its efforts to rid itself of its difficult circumstances and the working class saw migration to America as one means of escaping those conditions. III. As a result of their own slow cultural development, ignorance of the English language, and great isolation, let alone the impossibility of their taking up some sort of position in production ensuring them a better material existence, the Yugoslav workers, despite their large numbers, were exposed to the worst exploitation and poverty.[19]

In discussing the position of the South Slavs in the working-class movement in America, the congress was faced with a dilemma. Should the South Slavic Socialistic Federation be included in the Socialist party or in the Socialist Workers' party? After lengthy and heated discussion, it was established that the Socialist party had achieved greater success, while the Socialist Workers' party was continually declining. The intolerant attitude of the latter toward the trade unions alienated the American working class from its ranks, while the Socialist party, with its sincere attitude and activities, won over the large trade unions. Because of this it was decided that the South Slavic Socialistic Federation was to recognize the program and principles of the Socialist party of America.

At the congress, relations between the South Slav socialist movement in the United States and the South Slav social democrats in Europe had to be defined. Even though it was thought that their most important obligations were to educate and organize the South Slav working class in America, it was the opinion of the congress that they should not alienate themselves from the South Slav socialist proletariat in Europe. They had to pay attention to events in the Balkans as they were already being reflected among the South Slav working class in America. At the congress the position that nationally oppressed peoples were not even able to develop socialistically was unanimously agreed upon.

The most important reason for the convocation of the congress and its greatest success was the founding of the South Slavic Socialistic Federation. It was based on the principles of international socialism and it recognized the program and constitution of the Socialist party of America. Its sphere of activity extended across the United States, Canada, and Mexico. The headquarters of the federation was in Chicago, Illinois. The purpose and object of the federation was the organization of American South Slavs into socialist groups and organizations and to convey to them by systematic enlightenment the concepts of socialism.

Any person over the age of eighteen who was willing to recognize the principles of socialism could become a member of the federation. Local organizations could be founded wherever there was a minimum of five members. Every local organization was called the Yugoslav Socialist Association. All the external and internal affairs of the federation were dealt with by the Executive Committee in Chicago, which consisted of twelve members. Each nation—Slovenes, Croats, Serbs, and Bulgars—was represented by three members on the Executive Committee.[20] An even narrower body within the structure of the Executive Committee was the National Central Committee, in which there was one member from each nation in the Executive Committee and two elected members from the Chicago socialist organization. The National Central Committee independently, but in agreement with the Executive Committee, dealt with the campaigns and organizational activities. It also operated a newspaper under the supervison of the Executive Committee.

The South Slavic Socialistic Federation in America played a significant role in the workers' movement of the Yugoslav immigrants. According to the statements of Frank Petrič, a secretary of the federation for many years, at the time of its peak there were over 4,000 active members in the federation. But after World War I, during which the South Slav immigration movement had been very active in its desire for freedom and unity, the federation suffered its worst crisis and ceased activities after 1917. That year, at the congress in St. Louis, the Socialist party decided on its antiwar stand. This stance of the Socialist party led to an open split in the South Slavic Socialistic Federation and caused even more misunderstanding among the socialist immigrants. The Croatian section of the federation accepted the decisions of the congress, while the Slovenes and Serbs were opposed to their ideas and left the party.[21]

In the middle of 1917 the American government introduced step-by-step censorship of the press. In June of the same year the Chicago City Council accepted a resolution by which all criticism by Chicago citizens regarding the conduct of the war was forbidden. According to the law of 6 October 1917, all foreign newspapers either had to have special permission to write freely about the war or world politics, or all news pertaining to the war had to be translated into English. After those decisions, which affected many of the South Slav newspapers in America, the *Workingmen's Guard* completely changed its format, containing only very short political articles in English. The considerable remainder of the paper was filled with general and educational articles. However, in its last issues the *Workingmen's Guard* reprinted articles from American newspapers that favored the October Revolution in Russia and in this way demonstrated without ambiguity the stance of the Croatian sector toward that revolution. Because of difficulties stemming from the American laws of censorship, the *Workingmen's Guard* ceased publication shortly after the beginning of 1918. The Slovenian newspaper *Proletarac* continued to be issued, but by the end of the war it was the real voice of another political organization, the Slovenian Republican Association. After the congress of St. Louis, the activities of the Yugoslav socialists no longer had any marked effect upon South Slav immigrants in America.

NOTES

1. For Croatian immigration to the Mississippi River delta, see Otokar Lahman, "Naši iseljenici oko ušća Mississippija" (Our immigrants around the mouth of the Mississippi), *Geografski glasnik XI-XII* (Zagreb, 1950). Californian immigration is described by Adam S. Eterovich, *Yugoslav Survey of California, Nevada, Arizona and the South, 1830–1900* (San Francisco, 1971).

2. Josip Lakatoš, *Narodna statistika* (National statistics) (Zagreb, 1914).

3. In Pennsylvania the largest groups of settlers were in Allegheny City, Aliquippa, Ambridge, Bethlehem, Bennett, Blairsville, Braddock, Breensburg, Brownsville, Cannonsburg, Cokeburg, Conway, Donora, Etna, Latrobe, Lucerna, McKeesport, McKees, Midland, Millvale, Nonaca, Morrisville, Philadelphia, Pittsburgh, Rankin, Reading, Rochester, Slovan, Steelton, and Uniontown.

4. Apart from Chicago, a large number of immigrants lived in the following places in Illinois: Arlington, Canton, Danville, Joliet, Kewanee, Lincoln, Livingstone, Matherville, North Chicago, Springfield, Staunton, Taylorville, and Taylor Springs.

5. In 1907 Sirovatka calculated that on average every Yugoslav immigrant in the United States after three years of work saved about $500. Sirovatka's conclusion was: "Don't think of America if you are needed for work on your farms. Only if you have a surplus of men will it pay for one or two to seek employment there." Hinko Sirovatka *"Kajo je u Americi i komu*

se isplati onamo putovati?"—*How It Is in America and for Whom It Makes Sense to Travel?* (Zagreb, 1907).

6. The way of life of the immigrants in boarding houses and saloons is described by Kraja Josip in "Narodna borba prvih hrvatskih useljenika u USA" (The national fight of the first Croatian immigrant in the United States), *Hrvatska revija* (Buenos Aires, 1963), p. 3.

7. Sirovatka, *"Kako je u Americi,"* p. 42.

8. See George J. Prpić, *The Croatian Immigrants in America* (New York, 1971), p. 158.

9. *Radnički kalendar* (Workers' almanac) (Pittsburgh, 1941).

10. For the founding and role of the National Croatian Society, see *A Short Historical View of the "Croatian Fraternal Union"* (1894–1949) (Pittsburgh, 1949), and for the Slovenian National Benevolent Society a book by Jože Zavertnik, *American Slovenes* (Chicago, 1925), p. 302.

11. "Jugoslaveni u Americi," *Večernja pošta* (Evening Post) (Sarajevo, 1925), p. 3.

12. *Short Historical View,* p. 95.

13. *Ibid.,* p. 95.

14. S. Lojen, *Uspomene jednog iseljenika* (The memories of one immigrant) (Zagreb, 1963), p. 71.

15. *Ibid.,* p. 68.

16. *Ibid.,* p. 74.

17. *Narodni glasnik* (National Herald) (Chicago), 16 Oct. 1957.

18. *Radnička straža* (Workingmens' Guard) (Chicago), 6 June 1910.

19. *Ibid.,* 12 Dec. 1910.

20. The Bulgars quickly withdrew from the Yugoslav Socialist Association and acted independently of the other South Slavs.

21. See Ivan Čizmić, *Jugoslavenski iseljenički pokret u USA i stvaranje jugoslavenske države 1918* (The Yugoslav emigrant movement in the U.S.A. and the creation of the Yugoslav state in 1918) (Zagreb, 1974).

PART III

Immigrants

Labor history and immigration history have frequently been separated, though contemporaries from the 1820s onward complained of connections between immigration and urban poverty, the latter meaning unemployment or starvation wages. Of course, immigrants did go west but many stayed in the cities or on construction jobs. During the period of the "Old Immigration" from 1820 to 1880 more than 10 million immigrants arrived; of these the Irish, i.e. about 28% stayed in the cities. Of the almost 26 million "new" immigrants arriving in the period 1881 to 1924, most became urban workers. The proletarian mass migration of the turn of the century still has many unexplored aspects. It existed within Europe before expanding to trans-Atlantic scale. British artisans shuttled back and forth over the Atlantic, while Austrian agricultural laborers worked in Europe and South and North America following the harvest. There was also permanent remigration: up to 40% of Italian immigrants returned to Italy. What we have at this time is in fact an international working class. Both the Marxist London-based First International and the reformist American National Labor Union concurred on this point and corresponded about whether the NLU should publish a report on American working and living conditions to be circulated in Europe to destroy illusions about the "unlimited opportunities." American workers knew that employers frequently attempted to hire immigrant workers at lower wages or to break strikes. European activists realized that class solidarity and discontent were being reduced by the draining off of the protest potential inherent in the emigrants. Industrialization meant moving millions of workers to wherever they were needed with little regard for their old community ties.

The Irish, so the common notion is, preceded industrialization, were pushed out by hunger. David Doyle talks of a different Irish migration, that of the years after 1880. What did their arrival mean to second-generation Irish-Americans? What did the expectation of departure mean to those still at home? Arriving in America, did they join the advanced labor market position of some of their early-coming kinsmen? Swedish immigrants came from a society that in many respects was similar to U.S. class structures. Lars-Göran Tedebrand asks how workplace and plutocratic social conditions shaped migration decisions. Sune Åkerman and Hans Norman describe the conservative character of other Swedish workers on the American side who accepted paternalism as natural. Auvo Kostiainen's Finnish emigrants, who came from the same lumbering district background as many Swedes, were fiercely militant, so much so that later a Finnish mass emigration from the United States to the Soviet Union developed. Which cultural and economic forces shaped such widely different reactions?

It is obvious that the following essays can touch only on a few of these questions. Immigration history in recent years has become much more sophisticated, and it is time that labor and immigration historians cooperate to provide answers to questions that still remain about remigration, multiple migration back and forth, migration in stages; the community content of hall socialism, the class content of coffeehouse meetings, the interdependence of social and political life; and the interaction of the economic exigencies of the workplace and traditional cultural norms.

9

Unestablished Irishmen: New Immigrants and Industrial America, 1870–1910

DAVID N. DOYLE

The fields of labor history, of continental immigration to America since 1870, and of the study of U.S. radicalism continuously throw forth casual and conflicting images of the Irish. The Irish appear as a second-generation labor establishment, or as union leaders born in Ireland but matured as young men in America: both generations inseparable in attitudes. Only British and Russian Jewish immigrants produced more foreign-born labor leaders than did the Irish, but neither's descendants equaled the role of between 90 and 115 American-born leaders of Irish parentage or ancestry over the years 1830–1970, as David Montgomery has shown. Between 1900 and 1920, 50 of 110 American Federation of Labor unions had Irish-stock presidents or senior officers, when the Irish-born and their sons constituted but one-thirteenth of the total male work force. Antiradical in the Lawrence mill strike, pre-eminently political in the San Francisco earthquake aftermath in California, militant organizers in the anthracite fields in 1900 and 1902, theorists of industrial government or union/management cooperation on the one hand (John Lynch of the Typographers) and virtual protagonists of armed conflict on the other (the McNamara brothers of the anti–U.S. Steel dynamite campaign): Irish-stock leadership cannot be classified facilely in its key decade of 1900–1910. It reflected the extraordinary range of their working-class experiences in America and the increasing complexity of their wider Irish-American society, a society rather than an inhibiting community.

   This has been obscured by the focus of Irish-American studies on a single central trajectory. It deals with the massive famine migration and its aftermaths. Scholars have tended to assume a progression from pre–Civil War arrival and initial urban impoverishment, through post–Civil War breaches of the skilled trades, to the emergence of a political and middle semi-establishment around 1900 at the apex of an ordered and hierarchic community, largely consisting of skilled industrial and transportation workers and white-collar workers earning decent competence rather than high status. Irish historians have emphasized this in their studies of the outflow, as Americans have in their studies of the immigrant city before 1880. Others, including myself, have emphasized the third stage, that of relative establishment after 1890, with some finding it anticipated earlier on the West Coast and lesserly in Milwaukee and Detroit between 1870 and 1880. It is perhaps ironic, however, that this schema is largely the product of historians who in their family histories are offspring of exceptions to it; even Oscar Handlin, its progenitor, went to grade school with the poorer recent Irish of Manhattan depicted by Ronald Bayor. Perhaps had we pooled memories rather than nineteenth-century census data, our reservations might have attained earlier documentation.

The classic trajectory discounted major anomalies and real polarities, and assumed a coherence among Irish-Americans that did not exist. It led us to assume that Irish newcomers were easily and readily assumed into the craft, status, and social networks of their American-born cousins, beneficiaries both of the latter's advances and of an increasing behavioral and educational modernization in Ireland that enabled new immigrants to take advantage of what these cousins might offer. It was a reasonable belief: almost all immigrants after 1900 went to related "Yanks" or to Americanized aunts and uncles who had migrated as young singles a generation before. Lawrence McCaffrey and Emmet Larkin have stressed the effect of universal primary schooling in English on these migrants. What more natural than that cousins influential in labor unions or in precinct Democratic party connections would assure them jobs, apprenticeships, or union cards? Certainly the outlines of an order could be seen in the community, not merely in labor structure or class ranking. It was the age of the Irish urban bosses, increasingly reformist and inclined to organize new immigrants (as did Charles Murphy in New York), yet never in such a way as to jeopardize their own power or disturb their subordinate but meaningful relationship to the political and business status quo. Again, as churchmen, whether conservative or liberal, the Irish were committed to the Americanization of all newcomers, despite tactical concessions to temporary ethnic organization. Over 6% of Irish-born males and their sons were in professional, executive, or business ownership situations; another 14% were lower white-collar workers or small businessmen (grocers, saloon keepers); almost 10% were farmers. The cautious reformism of their elites among churchmen and politicians was thus firmly based.

Less clear is whether they in fact ordered their whole community. Just 363,950 middle and lower middle-class male breadwinners of a total number of 1,800,000 workers of Irish birth or parentage did indeed shape the ostensible Irish-American pyramid toward the native American norm, as did 162,800 Irish-American farmers. In 1900 Irish-Americans were thus peculiarly well structured to give an Americanizing face to urban politics, Catholic life, and even labor bureaucracy. But the tasks and circumstances of these people did not always place them in contact, much less in sympathy, with the 1,275,000 Irish laborers and industrial workers. Indeed, the unusual concentration of over 25% of Irish professionals, manufacturers, and executives in New York's cities tended to absorb them in abrasive competiton with their native-stock counterparts, and in a bid for leadership of a nationally oriented Catholic subculture. Elsewhere, disproportionate middle-class elements were to be found in western and midwestern states, where optimism about the Irish and Catholic social situations, and fairly favorable social pyramids, even among the immigrant generation, likewise turned middle-class concern away from realistic concern with the total Irish-American situation.

For there were still 181,700 Irish-born laborers in the United States in 1900, working everywhere from farms to construction sites, and another 187,400 men of Irish parentage similarly engaged: 25% of the first and 17% of the second generation. This was a marked change from the mid-nineteenth-century norm of over 40% in eastern cities, but its persistence, given the attainment of relative parity with native America at professional and white-collar levels, requires explanation. As late as 1904 the Irish provided a higher proportion of the nation's paupers than any other group, as well as figuring disproportionately (as well as visibly) among these casual laborers. Scores of thousands of Irish lived cheek-by-jowl with Italians and Russian Jews in the slums of New York, Chicago, and Philadelphia. The vast body, of course, were in industrial employment, with heavier second-generation dominance in skilled trades (20% of the nation's plumbers and steam fitters, 15% of its rubber operatives), but with unusual continuities between generations in industries such as textiles, carpet making, and rubber making. In short, the Irish shared both the high-status achievements of British immigrants and the low-status situations of Italians and Hungarians. Indeed, a half-century ago Isaac Hourwich and Nicholas Nolan drew attention to this anomaly among immigrant groups and ethnic stocks: the widest occupational distribution of any group in the United States. It was hardly a finding commensurate with any reassuring image of a close-knit ethnic community, its members helping one another along at every opportunity: the "Irish mafia" of American common speech.

The origins of such a wide dispersal of the Irish-American "community" are many. I wish to show the extent to which the Irish quasi-establishment of 1890–1920, its roots in the prosperity of the Gilded Age, was unable to cope with the problems posed by a vast continuing Irish influx or those presented by Irish-Americans cycled in poverty, especially during the 1873–77 and 1893–97 depressions. It lacked the power, the knowledge, and sometimes the will to alter the logic of either situation. That logic determined, as harshly as it did for Hungarians and Croats, that those without influential connections, those without industrial skills, those with inadequate command of English, were forced to take what they could in a fluctuating, chaotic, and at times overcrowded labor market. No one depicted this better than the young Finley Peter Dunne in Chicago during the depression of the 1890s, an experience which so seared him that he never again attempted direct portrayal of the Irish working-class Bridgeporters after the ambiguous good fortune of a war offered him fame, readership—and superficiality.

Biographical evidence confirms this picture. The father of the poet Padraic Colum worked as a common laborer in New York, c. 1880, after unemployment in Colorado, although in Ireland he was a workhouse master and later (on return) a railway station master. The future revolutionary Tom Clarke, despite Clan-na-Gael patronage, was likewise forced into laboring and unemployment in New York in 1899. Micky Gowan, after varied menial jobs from farm laboring to quarry work in both East and Midwest, took "the hard road to the Klondyke" to try his luck vainly on the gold diggings. The brother of Blasket Islander Tomás Ó Crohan returned a broken man shortly before, hardly clothed and without "a red farthing in his pocket . . . though he had not had a day out of work all those long years." Future agrarian leader Michael Davitt refused to follow many of his fellows from among the Lancashire Irish to America in the 1870s because he realized that, without connections, the certainty was hardship. James Connolly, despite his great gifts and although cautious in revealing his views, was unable to secure permanent and decent employment in New York City, in Troy, and in New Jersey during his American years from 1903 to 1909. His unknown contemporary, Seamus Moriarity from West Kerry, worked as a copper miner in Butte after 1906, but soon turned to San Francisco to earn his living as a park gardener, when blacklisted by employers for writing home to discourage others from Montana. Seán Ó Gormáin wrote back in Irish of the contem-

porary mill girls from Kerry in Massachusetts "destroyed" by their
labors:

> Their knees are broken and there's no strength in their backs,
> Their heads are empty of sense and their ears are deaf,
> From continually standing and tying knots
> Until they lose their minds and run amuck.

Belfast immigrant Frank Roney encountered harrowing insecurity
and poverty in several states in the early 1870s, better revealed in his
San Francisco diary of 1875–76 than in his accurate but softened
memoirs. Seán Ruiséal disliked western mining as much as Moriarity
and Roney: "It's a miserable way to earn a living / For any strong
vigorous fellow," while Eóin Ua Cathail in Michigan described a laborer's regimen in 1902 little unchanged from mid-century: intermittent employment, poverty, open-air hardship, endless work.

Such individual instances were broadened by the thousands to create whole communities of the deprived. Sam Bass Warner has pointed
out that the Irish-born of Philadelphia were more concentrated
in 1930 than in 1860 in the largely lower-class neighborhoods and
parishes along the Delaware River their forerunners had inhabited
80 years before. Kate Claghorn's contemporary research for the
Industrial Commission revealed that New York's gigantic (399,348)
population of Irish birth or parentage was still disproportionately
concentrated in poorer areas, notably the Lower East Side in 1890.
Thirty-one Irish folk shared the notorious "Big Flat" in Mott Street
with 368 Jews and 31 Italians in 1886. The death rates among the
New York Irish, despite vast intervening improvements in tenement
and living standards, were still exceptionally high, reminiscent of the
antebellum rates. In the state as a whole it was 25.9 per thousand in
1910, against the Italian of 12.9 and the Russian (including Jewish)
of 13.1. An Irish-American doctor, examining the figures for the city
itself, found the Irish death rate to be 34.0 in 1915, an increase over
that of 1877 (at 24.5) and twice that in Ireland (at 16.5). Children
were swept away by infectious diseases, adults by tuberculosis and
pneumonia, diseases in which Irish children and womenfolk were
citywide leaders, and the men almost so. He agreed with the finding
of John Spargo, the reformer, that ignorance and unhygienic practices of Irish mothers was responsible for high infant mortality (in
contrast to the exceptionally low infant mortality rates of the Jews
who shared the same areas). In fact, these rural newcomers lacked
the genetic immunity against tuberculosis and gastroenteritis partially
possessed by European and American town dwellers: indeed, the west

of Ireland had been all but free of these illnesses, so that subsequent devastation earned for tuberculosis the title "the Irish disease" in 1920s Manhattan, and in Connacht the title "the American sickness" (it was introduced by infected returnees and spread through certain families).

Additionally, Ireland's male-dominated culture presaged the New York disease ratios by giving turn-of-century Ireland a uniquely Asiatic distinction in Europe: higher female than male death rates. Nonetheless, the American work chosen by men—dockwork, carting, warehousing, and laboring—was open-air work ravaged by health disorders, as Irish-born dockers Patrick Powers and Dennis Delaney told the Industrial Relations Commissioners around the same time. They were also jobs which enhanced male camaraderie at the expense of domestic affection, and promoted alcohol consumption between cargoes or carting stops, exacerbating past Irish patterns. The Irish slum in 1900, as 50 years before, was still characterized by chronic alcohol morbidity (leading New York City); unsurprisingly, Irish women accounted for the largest group of the city's paupers and insane: the abandoned victims of this culture at its worst.

All this took place, as stressed, against a background of general improvement for Irish America viewed as a whole. It clearly raises the question, can Irish America be treated as a whole at all? At the same time as Father Peter Yorke was championing the Irish newcomer laborers of San Francisco, Father John Keogh was fighting drunkenness and wife beating in Philadelphia, and Humphrey Desmond was asserting that the only hope of Irish-Americans lay in group endeavor through the radical progressivism of his friend Robert LaFollette in Milwaukee, there were Irish visitors who chalked up the successes. Douglas Hyde, founder of the Gaelic League and future president of Ireland, used his prestige to gain an entrée to the homes of the new Irish-American elite during two tours before and after 1900. He could visit such people all over the country: James J. Roche, the editor, in Boston; John Quin, the wealthy corporate lawyer and arts patron, in New York; Count Creighton, the Omaha financier. His second orbit, in 1905, was notably higher than his first, in 1891, consonant with his own rising status. On the first he visited the ethnic middle class: its publishers and editors and writers like Patrick Ford and Louise Guiney, its house politicians like O'Donovan Rossa. On the second he was entertained by wealthy Americans who happened to be proudly Irish, leading politicians, likewise Irish, and leading Catholic prelates: Senator James Phelan, Charles Murphy, the archbishops of Philadelphia, Minneapolis, and San Francisco, among many others. Around the same time the Nationalist and Catholic mayor of Waterford, Sir James A. Power, visited America, to enjoy an even more remarkable circuit: he was made an honorary member of eight of New York's social clubs, including the Manhattan and the Republican; in six of these instances his introduction was by one of their Irish members.

Between the world of the clubs and the sweat of the slums, a vast gulf intervened. It was filled by an Irish population represented at every social level: one-fifth middle class or lower white collar, one-half properly working class, 15% each agricultural or dependent on casual laboring. This pyramid is a composite of first and second generations, as were the details on New York. In the second generation the pyramid swelled at the middle levels somewhat and diminished at the bottom; in the first generation it swelled at the bottom levels more considerably and shrank somewhat at the upper and middle levels. Nonetheless, it is important to stress that both generations spanned the entire social experience of Irish America. The picture as a whole cannot be explained only in terms of intergenerational mobility: the children of the famine and postfamine migrants made good, the newcomers were depressed and unskilled (see Tables 1 and 2). Major and unstudied changes in the background of continuing Irish migration are at least equally important, and perhaps more so. They certainly prepared some Irishmen to enter American life in relatively favored positions, but they also and more usually drew from new populations in Ireland immigrants as vulnerable to an industrial America of increasing sophistication and competitiveness as the postfamine migrants had been to the more rudimentary America of their time. In short, the spread of "modernized" patterns of education and material expectation in Ireland triggered massive migration from new areas and from among new social classes, but the new education—skeletal and shallow—was inadequate for a society where "modernization" had been ever accelerating.

Before 1870, with the exception of the famine exodus itself, emigration from Ireland's western seaboard counties was fitful rather than continuous, and insufficient to counteract still traditionally high marriage and birth rates. Likewise, emigration to America from among farm laborers, domestic servants, and the poor generally was limited. Earning from 6d to 9d a day, often only at ploughing, planting, and harvest times, meant that laborers simply could not afford the passage; nor could servants, who earned a few pounds a year, which they as often as not sent to their parents, since their keep was provided. Similarly, many on the western seaboard were too isolated, too poor, and too conservative to think in American terms. By the 1880s all this had changed. Elsewhere, too, migration from Ulster before the famine had been largely Protestant; in the latter part of the century it

Table 1A. *Occupational Distribution of Emigrants from Ireland, Selected Years, 1877–1901, 1904–13.*

	MALES						FEMALES			
Year	Professional	Clerks	Farmers[a]	Shopkeepers	Laborers	Others and Unstated	Milliners	Mill workers	Servants	Others and Unstated
1877	85	589	320	157	12,001	9,677	545	387	9,476	7,988
1880	42	546	1,994	117	36,688	20,802	420	130	30,304	14,814
1883	31	742	2,914	193	35,819	15,694	647	100	30,651	22,125
1886	17	718	1,240	182	24,561	5,423	226	29	22,073	8,947
1889	42	808	1,406	244	26,260	7,687	623	18	24,416	9,296
1892	8	373	802	169	19,588	4,631	576	108	18,944	5,801
1895	20	590	945	33	16,586	3,398	852	57	21,058	5,395
1898	29	569	598	7	10,859	3,203	325	28	14,075	4,172
1901	69	807	658	41	13,359	3,408	452	45	15,638	5,392

	MALES					FEMALES			
Year	Professional	Middle Class	Shopkeepers and Artisans	Laborers and General Service	Unspecified	Middle Class and Professional	Artisans and Shopkeepers	General/Service	Unspecified
1904	50	3,776	1,370	10,349	1,979	406	787	14,114	4,584
1907	88	4,020	2,010	13,133	2,255	470	954	11,334	5,298
1910	69	3,005	2,057	11,486	1,496	749	904	10,201	2,956
1913	72	3,003	1,426	10,499	1,727	815	1,006	9,697	3,094

Source: Registrar General, *Emigration Statistics of Ireland, 1877–1913.* Compiled by Nolan, 1933.
[a] From 1903 farmers were reclassified as either "independent" (professional), middle class (educated sons of larger farmers), or general service class (smallholders and their sons).

Table 1B. *Comparative Occupational Distribution of Select Immigrant Nationalities as Percentage of All Immigrants.*

| | ETHNIC GROUP | | | | | | | |
	Hebrew	Scotch	German	South Italian	Irish	Magyar	Polish	Lithuanian
Skilled	34.6%	31.7%	30.6%	12.4%	5.4%	5.0%	4.0%	3.0%
Unskilled	11.3	19.5	15.7	59.4	80.2	65.8	60.3	70.8
Unspecified	54.1	48.8	53.7	28.2	14.4	29.2	35.7	26.2

Source: U.S., *Reports of the Industrial Commission*, vol. 15: *Immigration* (1911), p. 304.

was increasingly and predominantly Catholic. These changes meant that the whole character of Irish emigration to America was changing: emigrants were recruited more and more from among those classes and districts where traditional patterns of thought, together with the constraints and effects of poverty, were most deeply concentrated. We shall look at each of these aspects in turn.

Before 1870 the southern province of Munster dominated emigration: in 1861–70, 42% of recorded and specified emigration was from that province, against a similarly estimated 15.5% from the western province of Connacht. Afterward, from 1891 to 1900, for example, 41% was from Munster and 27% from Connacht. There was considerable decline in the eastern province of Leinster, from 20% in 1861–70 to 12% in 1891–1900, and a smaller decline for the northern province of Ulster. These figures, however, are only broadly indicative. Within Ulster and Munster there was a shift westward geographically and downward socially: both provinces have western seaboards, from which emigration had previously been unusual. These trends have been noted already by L. Paul-Dubois, a contemporary, and more recently by S. H. Cousens, as by N. Nolan in 1935. The full significance is being illuminated by the research of Kerby Miller of the University of Missouri. The western region broadly coincided with two major culture patterns: before the famine it had been overwhelmingly Irish-speaking, frozen into an isolated but then still vigorous traditional world view. Thereafter Irish declined, and the pace of its decline roughly coincided with the "contagion" of emigration fever (as two scholars aptly dubbed it). Second, this area was mired in deep poverty, unalleviated by the fact that in many subsectors population continued to increase down to 1880, and in isolated areas (such as parts of Donegal) until almost 1900. Regional self-perception changed dramatically in the period 1870–1900, from a self-contained and genuine acceptance of things to rejection and ambition: rejection of des-

titution, ambition for change. This alteration was linked to, and then
accelerated, the decline of the Irish language, the coming of railroads,
the material improvement at earlier dates throughout the rest of the
country (to which westerners migrated as harvesters) and the desire
to emulate it, the spread of schooling in English, and the rise of
political propaganda and agrarian agitation. More minute factor analysis of so protean and elusive a change would be impossible: its effects
varied from area to area.

The western regions were largely classified as "Congested Districts,"
eligible for special governmental aid, by a British parliamentary act
of 1891. A strange juxtaposition of beautiful scenery and crowded
impoverishment was the region's hallmark, from Kerry in the south
to Donegal in the north. Tiny farms or gardens, cultivated by hand
(often by the women), fringed empty moorlands and occasional es-
tates on the coast. Inland, in areas such as east Mayo, Sligo, and
Roscommon, hillsides and poor soils were often crowded, while cattle

Table 2. *Occupational Distribution of Irish Americans, 1900: Numbers and
Percentage of Breadwinners in Key Occupational Concentrations.*

Occupation	Male Immigrants		Male Second Generation	
All occupations	714,222	100.0%	1,090,103	100.0%
Professions	13,910	1.9	179,499	16.5
Manufacturers and officials	7,905	1.1	12,160	1.1
Merchants and dealers	20,574	2.9	31,302	2.9
Agents and salesmen	14,853	2.1	43,251	3.9
Bookkeepers, clerks, etc.	15,403	2.2	67,879	6.2
Building trades (skilled)	41,851	5.9	74,840	6.9
Carters, teamsters, etc.	30,569	4.3	49,809	4.6
Iron and steel workers	20,013	2.8	27,350	2.5
Miners and quarrymen	22,892	3.2	28,421	2.6
Blacksmiths	11,697	1.6	13,604	1.2
Machinists	9,471	1.3	24,918	2.3
Railroad employees	31,188	4.4	47,876	4.4
Saloon keepers, barmen, waiters, servants	25,646	3.6	29,868	2.8
Farmers, planters, overseers	67,036	9.4	95,766	8.8
General laborers	158,933	22.3	110,960	10.2
Agricultural laborers	22,805	3.2	76,478	7.0

Table 2. (*continued*)

Occupation	Female Immigrants		Female Second Generation	
All occupations	245,792	100.0%	388,108	100.0%
Professions (teaching)	3,735	1.5	31,538	8.1
Merchants and dealers	3,992	1.6	2,716	.7
Bookkeepers, clerks, etc.	2,185	.9	22,537	5.8
Stenographers, typists	825	.3	11,587	3.0
Saleswomen	2,990	1.2	24,099	6.2
Textile mill operatives	18,302	7.4	40,512	10.4
Needle trades	18,428	7.5	69,637	17.9
Shirt, collar, and cuff makers	1,249	.5	6,535	1.7
Servants and waitresses	132,662	54.0	62,159	16.0
Boarding housekeepers, etc.	13,463	5.5	12,704	3.3
Laundresses	15,925	6.5	11,338	2.9
Nurses and midwives	6,300	2.6	6,391	1.6

Source: U.S. Immigration Commission, *Reports*, vol. 28: *Occupations of Immigrants* (1910), pp. 75, 163.

multiplied in the ill-kept and ill-drained pastures of graziers, increasingly favored by landlords for the rents they could produce. The men had furnished agrarian labor to much of the rest of Ireland, and to Scotland and England, in the past. With mechanization, a shift from cereal cultivation in the wake of American competition, the demand for these wandering cottiers and *spailpíns* declined rapidly after 1850, even as their families increased. Ireland abandoned the tradition of spade cultivation; if tillage declined less than has been believed (by one-seventh from 1871 to 1911), laborers declined by one-half in the same period. With the spade, too, had disappeared the Irish plough, which had required two or three men to use it. The decline in laborers was mirrored in the contraction of the cottier and *spailpín* economy in the west, despite the naive conviction of even Charles Stewart Parnell that it had a future. Where the growing sons of the past had migrated, those after 1870 emigrated. The impressive researches of Sam Clark indeed suggest that the great concentration of antilandlord agitation in the west (mapped by David Fitzpatrick) represented not merely a conscious effort to outflank this central crisis but was largely the effort of older men: younger men, determined to emigrate, often held aloof

from the Land League of 1879–80. Peasant rents were to be frozen
at low levels shortly after, and dismantled with the spread of govern-
ment-assisted land purchase after 1903: a trend already anticipated
in the west by the Congested Districts Board and to be facilitated by
its grants and loans. But as William Rooney noted around 1900, psychic
modernization (which he termed "anglicization") had ensured that
"no agrarian agitation can effectually solve the emigration question.
Though every acre of Ireland were rent-free to the occupiers, emigrants would still go, for the day has passed when a farm can support
in perpetuity an average Irish family"; he should have said, "can
support in terms of modern expectation."

By 1910 a quarter of Ireland was classified as "congested." From
the seven leading counties involved came 35% of Irish emigrants
from 1881 to 1910. From the west as a whole came over 60% of
emigrants to America between 1890 and 1910. Indeed, the region has
never recovered. The hearings of the Congested Districts Commission, gathered under royal warrant throughout the region in
1906–8, as had the earlier parliamentary Select Committee on Colonization from Congested Districts (1889–90), presented graphic evidence of the pathology of the region, of the spread of emigration as
the antidote to its ills and (via money remittances) the prop of its
remaining inhabitants, and, above all, of the rarity with which its small
farmers, priests, and shopkeepers could face the root of the alienation
of the young, even when (as was usual) they accepted the immediate
necessity of the emigration of some of their children. Scattered evidence is especially revealing: the Sligo farmer who would have liked
his sons to remain with him but knew, "Of course when they come to
any sense or perfection and see they cannot live at home, they go
away," or the north Antrim farmer, John Byrne, who noted that vast
profits of towns enabled them to pay higher wages than farmers could
afford, and to richly endow education and thus "starve the intellect in
the country." As for the many priests who testified, one senses the
tension between their genuine compassion for the poverty they encountered and the dislike they felt at the spiritual malaise (as they saw
it) partly fueling the new discontent with poverty: a theme made
explicit in clerical spokesmen, from the west Cork pastor and novelist
Canon Sheehan at the time to the dissenting report of Bishop Lucey
of Cork to the Irish Commission on Emigration in 1954.

The spread of education was the key to much of the "malaise" of
the young, as Canon Sheehan endlessly worried. This had been pre-
dicted by the Cork landlord W. Bence Jones on the eve of the change:
"One thing at least is certain, that the spread of education and intelligence that has made the Munster peasant glad to emigrate any-

where, and even marry a Chinese, will produce the same effect in Connaught, as soon as it reaches the same point there." Only a decade later the Local Government Board Inspector Major Ruttledge-Fair told a House of Commons committee: "if you go into one of the national schools any day, and ask a child to write an ordinary letter for you, the letter is invariably written to some friend either in the United States, or Canada, or Australia, asking the person to send a ticket to take them out. That is the ordinary letter that would be written in 99 national schools out of 100 . . . it is perfectly marvellous how universal [the desire to go] is." As the English language swept into the west, it brought not a new culture but only the intimation of one: the hope or dream of America. A generation later Padraic Colum would write of the poorest subregion: "Either Connemara or America. There is no third place within their range of vision." The networking of the west with railroads, particularly after 1880, with branch coastal lines authorized under an act of 1890, hastened the flow, so much so that the Vice-Regal Commission on Irish Railways (1909) recurrently dealt with the matter of whether they accelerated regional depopulation, concluding that it would have occurred anyway. Graphically, the Australian priest John T. McMahon would later describe the final phase of this movement, how in August 1927 the Sligo-Ennis line seemed to him a "Via Dolorosa," so public and uninhibited were the sights of grief at station after station through four western counties as the train picked up emigrants for White Star liners from Cork to New York: only the hardened young "returned Yank" was embarrassed by it all.

What sort of emigrants were these people? W. Bence Jones was mistaken: the people of the west had not attained the intelligence of the wider world to be found in much of central Munster. All the concurring evidence is that people from the Congested Districts were, at best, ill equipped for life in industrial America, particularly as it was developing after 1880. The Irish-language culture of prefamine Cork and Kilkenny and Tipperary had been intelligent, often well schooled, shared by farmers and laborers, and, if not outward-looking, yet broadly provincial and acquainted with wider worlds. The Irish- and post-Irish-language culture of seaboard Connacht and Donegal was notably more limited and parochial, scarred by the general poverty of the region, and the transition into English was faltering and isolated (where in the south there had been a rich gentry and clerical culture, and urban centers, to enrich the transition).

The warmest friends of the new emigrants were alarmed by their character and incapacities. An Irish-speaking Cork priest, Monsignor M. B. Buckley, met Connemara immigrants just off the boat in New

York in 1871, and was convinced that men so remote from city life would be sorely exploited. Charlotte Grace O'Brien worked forcefully in Ireland and America for the well-being of these people, and was partly moved by the same thought. She scrutinized the faces of young single emigrants awaiting embarkation at Queenstown in 1881: "Poverty was written there—ignorance, weakness, too, and indecision . . . with a hopeless submission to daily want. They were faces needing to be hardened, welded and ground; not dull, far from it, but inapt, tremulous, long-suffering." The U.S. consult there at the time, and his wife, John and Sarah Piatt, agreed and were also concerned. Miss O'Brien was particularly moved by those who had only Irish and no English:

> Speechless! ay, speechless, for their Gaelic tongue
> Is dead; as wanderers from some far-off age
> They strike against the shores of human life, to wage
> A too unequal fight with toil and wrong.

The English official Sir Henry Robinson, closely connected with the Connacht people at the beginning of the migration, worried likewise: "How these boys and girls, many of whom could barely speak English, who had never been farther from their own homes than the nearest market town . . . how they managed . . . to catch the night train, and to embark with their belongings at Queenstown, and stand the sea journey, and get suitable work right away, was always a marvel to me—they were childishly ignorant of life beyond their own homes." Yet clearly these witnesses underestimated the emigrants, though they are corroborated by all testimony as to the profound simplicity of the western people in modern terms: they assumed that to function in the new society, it would be necessary to understand it. Their contemporary observer, J. M. Synge, the dramatist who studied the west so closely, noticed that such people could work for years in America, their essential character unchanged. Most were young, and did change.

Few doubted the efficacy and necessity of the migration. There was no alternative, despite the panaceas of politicians (peasant proprietorship and land redistribution), short of social revolution, as only the Land League leader Michael Davitt really understood. The distress that prompted the Land League, the near famine of 1879–80 with partial repetitions in 1890 and 1898–99, caused even some priests to break ranks and promote the flow: as the parish priest of Clifden in west Galway put it, "I wish to God half the people of this barren territory would emigrate somewhere. Penal servitude would be a paradise to many of them compared to their present condition." As a result, emigration was initially organized. Under the Arrears of Rent

Act (1882) and the Tramways Act (1883), £133,173 made in government grants enabled 54,283 people to emigrate by 1891. Small numbers were also assisted under the poor rates under an act of 1849. Vere Foster of Belfast spent much of his inherited wealth placing 20,000 girls in American homes between 1880 and 1887. The *New York Herald* ran a fund to bring whole familes from the west out, and the English Quaker J. H. Tuke acted for another group of philanthropists in the same way. Irish-Americans in the Midwest, notably John Sweetman and Archbishop John Ireland, acquired land for colonization by established Irish and other Catholics in eastern states, and by new immigrants from Ireland. Most were successful, at Avoca, Graceville, and Clontarf in Minnesota, but the 309 "Connemaras" who were introduced directly to the colonies in 1880 were to prove wretched failures as frontier farmers: most drifted into apathetic and impoverished dependence upon established Irish-American farmers. There was to be no more dramatic indication of the gulf between the old and new Irish-Americans. The archbishop later confided that the whole incident "was the greatest grief of his life," and he determined to hear the cry of Connemara distress no more. Yet even direct Irish immigrants from the more prosperous County Meath were to prove that, while western immigrants melodramatized the gulf by their incapacities, they did not create it alone. Despite the severe blow to the *amour propre* of America's comfortable Irish, a blow so strong that some sought immigration restriction on the Irish at this time, most agreed with U.S. Consul Piatt, for whom the combination of Irish poverty and American opportunity made for its own humanitarian imperative:

> O landless, shelterless
> Sharp-faced with hunger, worn with long distress—
> Come hither finding home.

Soon the migration was self-generating. The initial grants had functioned as supplementary seed money. Once a member of a family was out in America, he began the chain of prepaid passages that linked siblings and then generations. Within ten years officials were saying that the Congested Districts Board would have no need to assist emigrants, as the family mode was quite adequate.

Emigration from the west was complemented by a great depopulation throughout the country at the lower ends of the social scale. Overwhelming proportions of emigrants reported themselves as single laborers (males) and servants (females). Since so many became these in the United States, these statements might be regarded as declarations of intent rather than description. But in fact they prob-

Table 3A. *Changing Occupational Structure of Irish Provinces of High Emigration Levels, 1861–1911.*

	1861	1881	1911
MUNSTER			
Male			
All occupations	484,221	400,187	326,852
Farmers, graziers	89,096	82,636	74,975
Farmers' sons, etc.[a]	—	41,619	41,776
Agricultural laborers[b]	135,164	63,550	35,558
General laborers[c]	95,471	41,237	37,996
All servants[d]	11,185	31,930	23,500
Female			
All occupations	211,379	193,881	83,806
Farmers, graziers	6,266	10,732	11,213
Laborers[e]	28,110	5,907	361
Farm servants[f]	—	6,200	1,175
Domestic servants, etc.[f]	—	[74,155]	—
Domestic servants, corrected[g]	—	49,437	35,157
Other servants[f]	—	[35,565]	—
Other servants, corrected[g]	—	23,710	—
All servants, corrected	68,667	79,347	36,332
ULSTER			
Male			
All occupations	598,615	524,079	488,618
Farmers, graziers	171,530	144,277	117,362
Farmers' sons, etc.	—	66,158	51,590
Agricultural laborers	112,950	52,824	39,782
General laborers	99,532	35,003	47,671
All servants	10,248	40,418	22,752
Female			
All occupations	329,812	316,837	189,796
Farmers, graziers	9,953	23,904	18,906
Laborers	14,299	6,216	786
Farm servants		5,898	719
Domestic servants, etc.		[61,868]	
Domestic servants, corrected		40,945	34,089
Other servants		[44,670]	
Other servants, corrected	68,304	29,780	
All servants, corrected	68,304	76,623	34,808

[a]This category, of relatives working the farm, was largely included with agricultural laborers in 1861, but many were not listed.

[b]Including ploughboys, separated in 1861 but not thereafter.

[c]"The majority of whom may be assumed to be agricultural laborers although not returning themselves as such." Regular statement in the printed statistics.

[d]These were not distinguished in 1861. Thereafter they combine "farm servants":

ably reflected the reality and are consonant with Irish occupational patterns. As Karl Marx early noted, as Charles Booth emphasized in 1886, and as C. H. Oldham developed in 1913, the rationalization of Irish agriculture, and the decline of productive but nonfarm employ-ment as British industrial products filled Irish markets, meant that the nonproductive and indeterminate sectors of quasi-employment and unemployment were continuously expanding. In short, Irish op-portunity was contracting even more rapidly than Irish population in the period 1861–1911. This was despite the improving qualities of such opportunities in agriculture and trade for those could link their lives to the process of rationalization: stronger farmers, merchants, and the associated service and professional people. The sober and scholarly Booth and Oldham were thus later to concur with those insights of Marx in *Capital* that the increasingly polemical German never developed but later dissipated in his further discussions of Ire-land: "The revolution in agriculture has kept pace with emigration. The production of relative surplus population has more than kept pace with absolute depopulation." To Marx, this was intimately linked to what appeared to be the worsening condition of agricultural labor-ers in Ireland: increasing wages were continuously outflanked by de-clining employment, by the decline of customary and nonmonetary support for that class, and by the growing reluctance of improving farmers to grant their laborers plots and cabins on their land—con-ditions he found confirmed in the contemporary John Nicholas Mur-phy's distillation of the reports of official inspectors.

In 1894 the Royal Commission on Labour was to send an offical team to investigate these conditions throughout Ireland and discover them to vary widely from province to province and area to area, yet broadly confirm that analysis. This was despite intervening rises in wages and considerable reduction in numbers (Table 3). To general-ize, conditions were worst where local laborers were usually supple-

---

the all-purpose "boy" retained largely for year work and occasional laboring, as well as other domestic, demense, and other servants.

eCombines both agricultural and general (effectively agricultural). The decline in this category, confirmed in Irish Folklore Commission reminiscences, represents the most marked evidence of changing thought about the place of women.

fThese categories were not separately listed in 1861. Since they widely overlap, the original reluctance to distinguish them was soundly based, and was revived in 1911.

gThe corrected figures represent a calculation to bring the 1861 and 1881 figures into line with the 1911 statistics. From 1891 onward relatives (wives, daughters) working domestically in their own home were excluded from the designation "serv-ant," but most, if not all, were included through 1881. It has been estimated that around one-third of those in the earlier numbers were such relatives, and I made the adjustments accordingly.

mented or replaced by incomers from the western districts during harvest or ploughing: in dairying south-central regions, where men came over from Kerry; in northwest Cork; and in the midlands, where meadows were seeded and mown by Connacht and Donegal men. Intense localism distorted the sense of justice to enable farmers to exploit such "outsiders." On the other hand, conditions were usually better among the permanent laboring class traditionally employed locally: in the southeast tillage area, in County Dublin and parts of Ulster, for example. Here, too, laborers were more likely to concert their efforts, as in Kanturk in Cork and Mountmellick in a peculiar midland district: they were English speakers and better educated. Irish speakers from the west were thereby disadvantaged, given attitudes in richer, English-speaking zones. By this period the terms for such men, *spailpín* and *slábhaí*, had derogatory and demeaning overtones in midland and eastern districts, although not in the west.

But there is evidence that perhaps the status (as well as material security) of all laborers was declining steadily. Related to it was the similar decline in the status of servants. On both these subjects much research must be done: my own findings are fragmentary and hence tentative. The enormous decline in the number of cottiers throughout the country, from 182,000 (1841) to 88,000 (1851) to 62,000 (1910), and the virtual elimination of men with plots of under one acre (135,000 in 1841), removed the intervening social strata between those absolutely dependent on others for employment and those with viable holdings (farmers over five acres). Only in the west did the under-five-acre holding survive broadly. Whereas in the past culture patterns, family connections, language, and the chance of getting a smallholding (or marrying one) had linked laborers and servants with cottiers, now they confronted a calculating farmer class determined to distance their employees and diminish the hold of custom on increasingly economic relations. Yet whereas the number of laborers declined continuously from 1851 onward, the number of servants at first rose slowly until 1881, then declined fairly rapidly. The first resulted as farmers made work for the growing unemployed and saw the cheapness with which servants could be hired before around 1880; the decline had many causes, but not least was the response, hitherto delayed, to the great contraction of marriage possibilities consequent upon the shrinkage of the pool of cottiers and laborers (Table 3).

Much points to these changes. Despite average wages that rose from 4s 8d in 1845 to 7s 10d in 1870 to 10s 0d in 1895 for a man without keep (for "boys" with keep, teenagers usually, they were lower), the rising expectations of laborers led to deep and widespread discontent. The hovels in which they traditionally raised families were by the time of the 1894 commission generally regarded as intolerable, a view that had been spreading since around 1870. Yet the laborers' cottages authorized for construction under government aid after acts of 1883-85, which by 1900 housed 16,000 or about 5%, while a vast improvement and one that freed the men involved from taking what their meager wages could get them or what farmers would grant them in the form of a hut, nonetheless epitomized in their design the status to which the class was consigned, and were usually built apart from both farms and streets of independent townsmen. The general discontent of laborers was scarcely mollified.

Gerald Fitzgibbon, a strong farmer himself, noted in 1868 how smaller farmers now increasingly relied on themselves and their families to do the work of their holding, although laborers were in fact

Table 3B. *Changing Structure of Three Congested Counties in Connacht and in Ulster.*

	1861	1881	1911
Galway			
Farmers (m.)	20,377	24,639	22,490
Laborers (m.)[a]	41,309	16,700	7,523
Farmers' sons, etc.	—	13,614	13,629
Servants (f.)[a]	10,461	14,409	2,879
Farmers (f.)[a]	985	3,384	4,039
Mayo			
Farmers (m.)	24,395	27,375	25,525
Laborers (m.)[a]	41,719	9,490	6,784
Farmers' sons, etc.	—	15,102	15,074
Servants (f.)[a]	7,990	13,509	2,246
Farmers (f.)	990	3,906	3,676
Donegal			
Farmers (m.)	27,679	24,281	21,095
Laborers (m.)[a]	29,093	8,957	6,993
Farmers' sons, etc.	—	12,433	11,718
Servants (f.)[a]	7,087	11,726	3,385
Farmers (f.)	1,007	3,811	3,485

[a]The social structure of the western seaboard defied all the efforts of Victorian census takers to classify it; the overlap of smallholder and laborer was everywhere apparent, and almost all master-servant (or laborer) relationships were partly confounded by kin connections. The figures stand uncorrected, and are merely indicative.

Source: *Census of Ireland, 1861, 1881, 1911*, Summary and County Occupational tables.

more comfortable with such types in the past: they "work with a will for the poor man, when they will not work for the rich man one jot harder than they consider necessary to avoid dismissal." Andrew Kettle (1836–1916), like Fitzgibbon a Dublin area farmer, recalled an intimate and paternalistic little commonwealth on the farm of his childhood: "a woman carding wool, a girl spinning yarn, an old woman knitting, the carter mending harness, the thrasher soleing his brogues, the boy platting a straw hat," all together on a winter's evening in the 1840s. By the 1880s Kettle himself ran a more efficient and commerical farm than his father, and was a strict disciplinarian to his laborers. Mary Carberry recalled of her childhood on a wealthy Limerick dairy farm in the transition period, the 1860s and 1870s, a regimen of strong discipline, of the separation (at meals) of ploughboys and dairymaids on a modernizing farm, but the community was still large. By around 1881 a ballad lamented "the good olden times/When the servants and masters together all dine," and contrasted it with the present, when now better-off farmers "snug in bed they can stay . . . [while] at four in the morning to work we must go/To reap mow and harrow and follow the plough," work well into the evening, and feed on "parridge rea' hot," while the servant girls for their part "must scour, milk and churn, and work I tell you/When the days work is over must polish the shoes."

As the living standards of farmers rose, and the gulf between them and their help widened with the disappearance of the cottiers, resentment spread in the countryside ("envy" to the conservative Fitzgibbon). Social differentiation was increased by the tendency of many farmers to deny their servants the better diet now available—tea, eggs, bacon, bread—and instead continue to feed them on stirabout (or porridge), potatoes, and milk. The memories of aged farm laborers such as Patrick Williams of Wexford, or Richard Denihan of Limerick, children in the 1870s, and of others collected by the Irish Folklore Commission, sharply recall grievances about food as well as pay and accommodation. The widespread resort to the "tally-stick" (whereby both farmer and worker notched matching sticks for each day worked, to prevent cheating in payment), and later the keeping of notebooks as literacy spread, indicated the mistrust involved. The classic routine, of work from dawn to dusk, was increasingly seen as unjust: an imposition when a servant boy never saw whether his master's house was thatched or slated, since he was free only after dark. Servants (laborers and domestics) exchanged stories of ill-treatment; farmers cocooned their hardening attitudes by likewise telling stories of the stupidity and incapacities of their workers. Granting the tendency of the commission's aged respondents to telescope events, and to attribute changing attitudes to the wrong periods, the evidence is that past unity of mind about the nature of service (itself very problematic) was *seen* to have largely broken down by the 1880s, certainly by 1900. Part of this was unquestionably due to landlord propaganda, which sought to embarrass the Land League's farmers by rousing the laborers in certain areas beneath them; part of it was connected with the depopulation of, and changing attitudes in, the English and Scottish countrysides, to which so many Irish migrated seasonally. Much of it was elusive: even so highly traditionalist a girl as Peig Sayers, in a remote Irish-speaking district in west Kerry, who believed unquestioningly in the relation of master and servant, and brought very filial presuppositions to the relationship in the 1880s as a girl of eleven and twelve, nonetheless entered a made marriage rather than return to domestic service: "when I was the mercy of strangers." She recalled her second service: "The minute I entered the house it was as if the darkness of the world came down over me for I knew that once again I was going into slavery" (*Autobiography*, Dublin, 1973).

It is not surprising, then, that America laced the daydreams of Peig Sayers as the image of a real deliverance: unfortunately, her kinswoman who had emigrated and promised the fare never sent it. The relationship between the increased independence and assertiveness of laborers and servants and the mobility offered by America was widely understood:

> The servants of Ireland are all going away
> They are going to america as you may understand
> You must give them all wages or give up your land.

An Athea man later said local servants dropped from 150 to nine owing to emigration. As early as 1856 farmers had recognized this connection, when they protested on Drogheda quay against Vere Foster's earlier emigration work: "Many of the farmers were mad at me for reducing the supply of laborers and servant girls; and alternate entreaties, threats and force were used to prevent many of my party embarking. . . ." By the end of century the connection, however, had been reinforced: both by providing an economic alternative, and by feeding back a new social outlook, America was helping subvert the assumption of deference upon which old Irish rural society had rested.

J. F. Costello wrote to family in Limerick in 1883, "There are no Gentlemen here. If a farmer in Ireland made 3 or 4 thousand dollars in a year you couldn't walk the road with them." Monsignor Buckley, the Cork visitor of 1870–71, who at first had deep misgivings about the emigration, given the harshness of work and lack of rich social life in America, had his mind changed by emigrant poor from Cork who emphasized the effect of equality: "everyday I spend in this country the more I appreciate the democratic character of the people, the apparent equality of intercourse that exists between them, and the more absurd appears to me the aristocratic spirit at home, the lines of demarcation between the different ranks of society, and the cringing respect with which those in the lower rungs . . . regard those above them." The east Cork laborer Daniel Cashman in the 1800s hoped that Clan-na-Gael would scotch the fortunes of the Irish Parliamentary party back in Ireland, because he saw the latter as representative of the power and social pretension of farmers.

Such attitudes, carried back, changed the social climate: men still deferred publicly, from fear of loss of employment, but the acceptance of rank itself, the internalized repression of self, was going, especially in Munster: "the strength and independence begotten of American thought is to-day springing like new blood through the veins of Ireland," wrote Cork woman Charlotte O'Brien. "The country is permeated by American ideas . . . far more lasting than any Fenian conspiracy," Scottish official George Campbell had noted in 1869. Among men the effects of these ideas were social and political, among girls, domestic and personal. "Every servant-maid thinks of the land of promise, where . . . husbands are thought more procurable than in Ireland," a Cork paper noted in 1860. It was to be two decades later that the general revolt against subordination turned into a full-scale flight. Its harbinger, noted a Frenchman, was the returned "workman-politician," discontentedly going back to America: Ireland had no status for him.

The social customs governing both laboring and service, when coupled with rising wages, acted to facilitate this flight. Girl-servants and laborers were hired at "hiring fairs" or hirages, for a period of eleven months usually, renewable thereafter, apart from those hired only for the harvest. Both servants and semipermanent or yearly boy-laborers lived on the farms where they worked and were fed by their masters. When wages were minimal (before 1870), little was probably saved; after 1870, with rising wages, it was possible to put aside the wages and within a year or two make up the passage money to America. This pattern was soon pervasive. In areas of Tipperary different agricultural workers came in every year from south Kilkenny, saved and emigrated, to be replaced by a new batch the following year. In Kildare laborers said that they would go to Australia as readily as a duck would swim, except that the wages would not cover the cost. Once members of laborers' families were out, of course, they too would tend to send back passage money for brothers and sisters. Higher wages, however, now made possible the initial migration to America among families that had previously migrated their members to Britain. Poorer families in the west sent laboring sons first to Scotland, who, "as soon as they have earned sufficient to earn their way, cross over to New York." In south Ulster, around Newry, a class of "firemen" emerged who plied the opportunities of unskilled work along the Atlantic sea routes and in their ports, from Liverpool to New York, Glasgow to Boston, sometimes settling in America. Other laborers, too, went via the English harvests.

Were these emigrants—westerners, laborers, and servants—aware of what awaited them in America? To a considerable extent, they were. Arnold Schrier and Kerby Miller have shown how by the 1880s the letters from emigrants back to their families were realistically descriptive about working and living conditions for people of their class in America: the slum tenements, periodic unemployment, harsh mechanical work in factories, fierce competition with other nationalities for employment, prejudice against their accents and manners by other Americans. Yet the effect of remittances and prepaid passages, coupled with the revolt against poverty in Ireland, was sufficient to turn emigration into a self-sustaining "habit" (as contemporaries L. Paul-DuBois, William Rooney, and William O'Brien called it around 1900). It seems to have been a collective determination that relativized all evidence to the contrary: west Kerry knew broken and returned emigrants, and received harsh letters from Seamus Moriarty, Seán Ruiséal, Sean Ó Gormáin, and others graphically describing the hardships of industrial Massachusetts and of laboring out West: yet still the flow went on. Only the extent of the awaiting mortality (for emigrants and their children) does not seem to have been properly communicated. Charlotte O'Brien stressed this in a letter to the Dublin *Freeman's Journal* in 1882: "seventy-five per cent of the children born in New York among the poor Irish die. . . . I believe the vast number of those who wish [to emigrate with state aid] . . . do so, thinking to benefit their children. I tell them, their children will have a better chance of life, starving and barefoot at home. . . . They are well dressed, well cared for, sapless, lifeless, pale. '*It would keep you poor burying your children,*' said one woman to me." Even she agreed that, while no land of gold but of toil, America represented real hope for the young, "especially for women." The real engine of the migration was thus less narrowly material than the search for active and self-respecting life, against a backdrop of poverty, inertia, and subordination.

The very tenacity of family ties reinforced it, as was widely noted: social and family life was soon so densely re-created in America as to

counteract homesickness among social groups and classes who identified less with a generalized Ireland than with their own locality.
Everywhere this trend was reported to investigating commissions: the
girls of the Glens of Antrim, it was said, felt as strange in Belfast 50
miles south as in Boston, the men of Sligo only ten miles from their
own farms. Hence it was easier to cross to a knot of relatives in America than to migrate within Ireland. The contrast with Ireland's better
farmers, who would place their children in the police, in trade, or
whatever, or the contrast with mobile townsmen, was widely noted.
Put bluntly, the poorer emigrants sought out a livelihood among those
who cared about them. This resulted in a parochialism that distressed
observers like Monsignor Buckley: "in America, the Irish are extremely 'clannish.' The Northerns look down on the Southerns, and
both dislike the Connaught-folk. . . . [All] admit how baneful these
distinctions are, but all alike act in accordance with them." American
lecturer Henry Giles explained it in a manner that makes its continu-
ance in industrial America understandable in our terms, although he
addressed wealthy American Catholics:

> When we consider how local and restricted laborious life is . . .
> native associations are of great value. . . . Whatever the poor man
> can glory in, after his conscience, lies near him. The sphere of his
> life . . . is that of immediate neighborhood. Beyond that he is not
> known, and away from that he loses consequence. *There* . . . there
> are witnesses to his integrity . . . and the habits which expose him
> elsewhere to mockery, are, where he was born, the habits of associ-
> ates . . . it is poverty which compels him to emigrate, and poverty
> has manifold disadvantages. Even the outside of it is often read by
> the most benevolent as they would read a bill of indictment. Poverty
> is not comely, and, like an idiot in the family, the tolerance of it is
> local [*Lectures and Essays on Irish and Other Subjects,* New York, 1869].

The reconstitution of networks of familiarity in American cities
among those in Ireland too disadvantaged and too poorly treated to
enter the race of rising prosperity and hardening calculation, so well
shown by recent scholars, created a rich resource for the whole American working people. The full development of this theme would take
another paper. And certain themes can only be indicated. By bringing
a vast new immigrant population into America of the same nationality
as the majority of trade union leaders and political bosses in the
northeastern cities, the migration of the "unestablished Irish" helped
to involve the embarrassed, somewhat distant, but still concerned
American-born Irish in the problems of poverty, slums, factory welfare, and human improvement generally: to function as a connection
between the problems of all new immigrants and the American estab-

lishment to whom they acted as stewards. In many cases, such as Frank Walsh's sympathetic chairmanship of the Industrial Relations Commission, Bourke Cockran's long defense of Tom Mooney, Cardinal James Gibbon's paternalistic but concerned attitude toward labor, John Mitchell's opening of the resources of United Mine Worker authority to Slavic interests, and so on, the resultant activity was fully genuine. Of course, full community did not ensue. But were the impoverished Irish thereby estranged (by a leadership that cared too little for them) from their proper socialist destiny? Albeit, those impelled by the demands of humanity within the constraints of existent society were not about to detach their power and conscience from the suffering they saw among their co-religionists of their own national origin. What is to be regretted is that they did not do more. Second, more ironically, the existence of hundreds of thousands of "new" Irishmen among the Slavic, Jewish, and Italian mine workers, textile workers, and factory operatives of the American city after 1890 created strange tensions and misunderstandings among them. Not least has been the tendency of certain historians of "new immigrant" origin, such as Marc Karson, Melvyn Dubofsky, and others, to misinterpret the complex issues of Irish America, ascribing the passivity of newcomers to acquiescence in established clerical or political positions (essentially American) rather than to the highly peculiar social background, cultural poverty, and extreme consequent clannishness that these new Irish exhibited. Related is the tendency of "social mobility" scientists like Thernstrom and Hershberg to ignore completely such crucial distinctions among the Irish: for immgrants from the anglicized eastern provinces, and from more privileged and better educated social sectors (the extra children of stronger farmers, for example) had also continued to come in throughout our period. Indeed, a tabular breakdown of Irish immigration by class is not really possible (see Tables 1 and 4), for sons and daughters of both landless laborers and smallholders reported themselves as laborers and servants.

By recovering the reality of this whole migration, we find that at its heart lay people at once in flight from subordination and cultural isolation, from poverty and parochialism, yet a people who were still shaped by these forces, who strangely (as J. M. Synge, Stephen Gwynn, and others saw) owed much of the vitality they brought to lower-class America to these very things. They were partly insulated against the corruptions of a strenuous individualism by an intense familialism linked (unlike the analogous case of Sicilians) to an intense localist solidarity, expecially in the case of those of Gaelic background, and were given resilience and pyschic continuity by the religious convictions of what Engels once dubbed, with wry admiration, the *sacra*

Table 4. *Irish Emigration to the United States, 1871–1910.*

Years	Irish Immigration	Irish Born at End of Each Decade
1871–80	436,871	1,854,571
1881–90	655,482	1,871,509
1891–1900	403,496	1,615,459
1901–1910	339,065	1,352,251

Total Immigration, 1871–1910, 1,834,914

insula. Those who observed these immigrants most closely had little doubt that such associations and convictions underlay what spirit they brought to the American slum, although others would necessarily teach them how to fight back against it.

In Ireland the emigration and its feedback, via opportunity, rising wages, and American letters, brought about the unnoticed social revolution in the status of women. As emigrants, they might work excessively harshly in mills or as servants in American homes. But they could now choose the status of self-respecting "help" in American kitchens or restaurants, employees in plants there, as against the demeaning role of "skivvy" in an Irish townhouse or on a farm; their ambitions could help prompt their daughters toward teaching, typing, and clerical work in American towns. Relatedly, and ironically, the growing unavailability of help for Irish farmwives intensified their own burden, and may thereby have contributed to the collapse of the rural marrriage rate and the general flight of unmarried girls from the land, so well known to scholarship. Such trends were, of course, incomplete: perhaps there is no better illustration of the degree to which Irish emigrant women of this era stood between two worlds than the fact that, as late as 1916, the majority of *them* in America *opposed* the principle of the vote for women!

The feedback also affected the Irish political climate. The changes in Munster in the era of Fenianism, consequent on the growth of independent thought, were two generations later repeated in Connacht, the last redout of a publicly deferential society, obeisant to Britain, outside the Protestant North. Now its attitudes, too, had changed. As George Birmingham quoted his gardener, having watched this change spread: "The way of it is this. . . . It's our opinion that the time has come for us to be yous, and for yous to be us." "In that single sentence," continued the Mayo Anglo-Irishman, "he had, so it seemed to me, expressed the whole meaning of every revolution that ever was, or ever will be." The Irish War of Independence was more closely linked to the great emigration than Irish historians, focusing upon the activities of professional revolutionaries, have cared to concede.

Suggested Reading

Brown, Thomas N. *Irish-American Nationalism 1870–1890.* New York and Philadelphia, 1966.
Clark, Dennis J. *The Irish in Philadelphia: Ten Generations of Urban Experience.* Philadelphia, 1974.
Connell, K. H. *Irish Peasant Society.* Oxford, 1968.
Cousens, S. H. "Emigration and Demographic Change in Ireland, 1851–1861," *Economic History Review* ser. 2, 14 (1961):275–88.
———. "The Regional Pattern of Emigration during the Great Irish Famine, 1846–1851." *Institute of British Geographers, Transactions and Papers* 28 (1968):119–34.
———. "Regional Variations in Population Changes in Ireland, 1861–1881." *Economic History Review* ser. 2, 17 (1964):301–21.
Cowan, H. I. *British Emigration to British North America,* 2nd ed. Toronto, 1961.
Cronin, Bernard C. *Father Yorke and the Labor Movement in San Francisco, 1900–1910.* Washington, D.C., 1943.
Doyle, David N. "The Irish and American Labor, 1880–1920." *Saothar: Journal of the Irish Labour History Society* 1 (May 1975):42–53.
Ernst, Robert. *Immigrant Life in New York City, 1825–1863.* New York, 1949; reprint ed., 1965.
Faherty, William B. "The Clergyman and Labor Progress: Cornelius O'Leary and the Knights of Labor." *Labor History* 11 (1970):175–89.
Glazer, Nathan, and Daniel P. Moynihan. *Beyond the Melting Pot: The Negroes, Puerto Ricans, Jews, Italians, and Irish of New York City.* Cambridge, Mass., 1963.
Handlin, Oscar. *Boston's Immigrants 1790–1880: A Study in Acculturation.* Cambridge, Mass., 1941; revised ed., 1959.
Henderson, Thomas McL. "Tammany Hall and the New Immigrants, 1910–1921." Ph.D. dissertation, University of Virginia, 1973.
Jackson, John A. *The Irish in Britain.* London, 1963.
Kane John J. "The Irish Immigrant in Philadelphia, 1840–1880." Ph.D. dissertation, University of Pennsylvania, 1956.
Larkin, Emmet. *Life of James Larkin.* London, 1968.
McCaffrey, Lawrence J. *The Irish Question 1800–1922.* Lexington, Ky., 1968.
Niehaus, Earl F. *The Irish in New Orleans, 1800–1860.* Baton Rouge, 1965; reprint ed., New York, 1976.
O'Brien, W., and D. Ryan, eds. *Devoy's Post-bag, 1871–1928.* 2 vols. Dublin, 1948 and 1953.
Ó Crohan, Tomás. *The Islandman.* Oxford, 1963.
Paul-DuBois, L. *Contemporary Ireland.* Dublin, 1968 (transl.).
Pomfret, John E. *The Struggle for the Land in Ireland, 1800–1923.* Princeton, N.J., 1930.
Rodechko, James P. "Patrick Ford and His Search for America: A Case

Study in Irish American Journalism, 1870–1913." Ph.D. dissertation, University of Connecticut, 1968.

Roney, Frank. *Irish Rebel and California Labor Leader: An Autobiography.* 1913; reprint ed., New York, 1976.

Sayers, Peig. *The Autobiography of Peig Sayers of the Great Blasket Island.* Dublin, 1973.

Schrier, Arnold. *Ireland and the American Emigration 1850–1900.* Minneapolis, Minn., 1958.

Shannon, William. *The American Irish.* New York, 1963.

Synge, J. M. "The Aran Islands," in *Collected Works,* vol. 2: *Prose.* London, 1966.

Vinyard, Joellen McN. "The Irish on the Urban Frontier: Detroit, 1850–1880." Ph.D. dissertation, University of Michigan, 1972.

Ward, Alan J. *Ireland and Anglo-American Relations, 1899–1921.* London, 1969.

(I am grateful to Priscilla Metscher, Universität Oldenburg, for her help in compiling this list. —Ed.)

10

Strikes and Political Radicalism in Sweden and Emigration to the United States

LARS-GÖRAN TEDEBRAND

Joe Hill (Joseph Hillstrom = Joel Hägglund), executed on doubtful grounds in Salt Lake City, Utah, in 1915, is the best known of the Swedish immigrants who took part in the American labor movement. He was born in the Swedish town of Gävle in 1879 and emigrated to the United States together with his brother in 1902. In 1905 he first came in touch with the International Workers of the World (IWW), known for their struggle on behalf of nonskilled workers. Joe Hill became an agitator and organizer in the IWW, but he is nowadays mainly remembered as a successful singer and textwriter. The heroes in his suggestive songs are workers, including women like the "rebel girl" who loyally joined in the struggle against employers.[1]

To what extent were the radicalism and class-consciousness of Joe Hill atypical of the Swedish immigrant? Around 1880 the Swedes settled primarily in the Middle West, while around 1900 they were widely distributed in the industrialized states to the east, such as New York and Massachusetts, and in the lumber areas in the states of the West Coast.[2] Although there was a strong influx of Swedish immigrants to urban and industrial America after 1900, the ethnic and cultural "Swedish-America" has always had a clear middle-class bias, concentrated on the Middle West. Fear of "socialism" and trade unions is often said to characterize the bulk of Swedish-Americans. A general assumption is that a majority of Swedish-Americans have had a long-time Republican voting history, only broken by the Great Depression when they began to support Franklin D. Roosevelt and the New Deal.[3] This assumption is, however, not quite true, not even for the Swedes in the Middle West. Many Swedish-Americans were influenced by the Grange, the Farmers' Alliance, the populists, and the Nonpartisan League. The Swedish-born Minnesota congressman Charles A. Lindbergh, son of a former member of the Swedish parliament and father of the pioneer aviator, had established a reputation as a staunch Republican progressive prior to World War I.[4] The Swedish-born publisher Swan J. Turnblad, owner of *Svenska amerikanska posten* in Minneapolis, the largest Swedish paper in America, backed the Democratic party. It must also be mentioned that the so-called farmer-labor politics in Minnesota in the 1920s were backed by many Americans of Swedish descent.[5]

The early Swedish emigrants had an agrarian background and no experience of labor politics and unionism in Sweden. The aspirations of the immigrants were dominated by petite bourgeoisie standards. The class consciousness of the rural workers was also hampered by vertical ties in Swedish agrarian society. It is also well known that trade unions remained very weak in the United States throughout the nineteenth century, embracing not more than 1 or 2% of the total labor force and perhaps less than 10% of industrial workers. The participation of the many urban and industrial workers, who formed a large part of the later Swedish mass emigration in the main stream of the American labor movement, as well as in radical organizations, has so far been very little investigated. There is no counterpart to the studies of Finnish-American workmen's associations.[6] However, Swedish contributions to American radicalism have not been entirely rudimentary and are well worth studying.[7] A vitally important question is whether any contacts existed, through Atlantic migration, between organized labor in Sweden and America. Studies in the archives of the Swedish labor movement (Arbetarrörelsens Arkiv, Stockholm) do not reveal any such formal contacts.

The aim of this paper is not to discuss the contributions of Swedish immigrants to American labor history. Instead the purpose is to discuss the connection between labor unrest in Sweden and emigration to the United States. To what degree had immigrants experienced industrial life and labor market conflicts before leaving Europe? This problem is fundamental to the understanding of American labor history before World War I. However, even this topic must be seen in a broader context. The following aspects will be discussed:

(1) the socioeconomic transformation of Swedish society from 1860–1930 and emigration to the United States; (2) formation of a working class and the labor movement; (3) the image of America among organized labor. (4) channels of information about conditions in America and the character of information in the Swedish labor press; and (5) strikes and emigration (a typology based on some case studies).

The gross emigration from Sweden to North America (1851–1930) amounted to roughly 1.3 million people and was part of the so-called old emigration from western and northern Europe. In Europe only Ireland and Norway had higher emigration frequencies than Sweden.

Swedish mass emigration, which started later than in countries like Great Britain, Ireland, Germany, and Norway, culminated in the period 1879–93, when 487,754 persons emigrated to the United States (Table 1). At the outbreak of World War I nearly 90% of the transoceanic migration from Sweden and taken place.

The main background factors of Swedish mass emigration were overpopulation in the agrarian sector and a comparatively late urbanization and industrialization. In 1870, at the start of the mass emigration period to the United States, 72% of all gainfully employed persons in Sweden were active in farming, forestry, and fishing, whereas only 13% were active in industry and crafts. The urban population amounted to just above 10% of the total population. The industrial breakthrough in Sweden from 1870 onward was to a high degree a process of adaptation to events in the industrialized countries of Western Europe.[8] Only to a lesser extent was it an independent process of economic expansion. However, owing to multiplier effects, the growth of the export industry also resulted in an expansion in the consumer goods industry. In the 1870s the iron, steel, and mining industries were quite expansive, employing about a quarter of the industrial workers. Next came the timber products industry, which expanded rapidly in the 1880s. During the 1890s the timber products industry came to outstrip the iron industry, only to be outstripped in its turn by metals and engineering during the first decade of the twentieth century. However, according to European standards the industrialization and urbanization of Sweden were in 1913 still quite modest. In 1930, when mass emigration came to a halt owing to the depression in the United States, the farming population of Sweden had diminished to 38% whereas industry and crafts amounted to 33%.

The emigration frequency reached its peak in the 1880s at a time when more than half of the Swedish population was active in traditional sectors of the economy. In rough figures only a quarter of the

Table 1. *Registered Emigration from Sweden to the United States, 1861–1930.*

1861–65	9,420	1896–1900	61,568
1866–70	79,311	1901–1905	127,949
1871–75	41,280	1906–10	91,300
1876–80	59,895	1911–15	59,923
1881–85	146,543	1916–20	21,614
1886–90	177,742	1921–25	54,506
1891–95	138,956	1926–30	37,426

Source: Bidrag till Sveriges officiella statistik, Serie A, 1851–1900. Serie Befolkningsrörelsen, 1901–30.

emigrants came from cities. In proportion to its total share of the population, farming did not provide more emigrants than industry. Owing to deficiencies in official Swedish emigrant statistics, it is difficult to draw strict comparisons on the national level between emigrants from the agrarian and the industrial sectors during the further course of mass emigration.[9] Conditions also varied both geographically and chronologically. However, during the first two decades of the 1900s industry appears to have had a somewhat higher emigration frequency than agriculture, whereas the opposite was true during the 1920s.

There was a close connection between business cycles and industrial and urban emigration from Sweden.[10] The conditions in Sweden, with its rapid population growth and slow industrialization, created a latent push of emigration, while American business cycles gave rise to great variations in the emigration curve. Differences in emigration frequency between various industrial branches were rather small, and consequently the iron and metal-working industry accounted for a relatively large share of emigration.[11] This was especially true around 1880, when a large number of blacksmiths emigrated from different parts of Sweden. During the period from 1900 to 1930 emigration from the mechnical engineering industry was close to the national emigration average. An important emigrant group were the sawmill workers, the majority of whom came from the lumber areas in northern Sweden. Their emigration frequency was extremely high during the recurrent crises in the sawmill industry. The connection between emigration and strikes in the sawmill sector will be dealt with later.

The number of industrial workers in towns and rural industries increased very rapidly at the end of the nineteenth century. Numbers in industry, mining, and crafts mounted to 96,000 in 1870, to 189,000 in 1890, and to 400,000 in 1900. The accelerated transformation of Swedish society was a prerequisite for the establishment and growth of radical and socialist movements. In 1889 the Swedish Social Democratic Labor party was founded, and in 1898 the Landsorganisationen (the Swedish Confederation of Trade Unions) was established. Despite the numerical growth of the working class, the organizational structure of the labor movement remained weak in Sweden before World War I. The number of organized workers did not pass 100,000 until after the turn of the century. It is symptomatic that the great general strike in 1909 resulted in a defeat for the laborers. A good deal of the mobilization of the masses in the growing cities and industrial areas was channeled into the so-called popular movements (*folk-rörelser*), such as the temperance movement and the free churches.[12]

These voluntary associations had more than 300,000 members in 1900. Owing partly to voting restrictions for the workers, the Social Democrats were for a long time sparsely represented in the parliament (the Riksdag), and during the main part of the era of mass emigration Sweden was ruled by Conservatives. Not until 1905 did Sweden get a Liberal government. The Social Democrats participated in a government for the first time in 1917 (Liberal-Socialist coalition), and in 1920 they formed an exclusively socialist cabinet. On the local level, in many towns and industrial areas, however, the influence of the Social Democrats was already considerable at the turn of the century.[13]

Organization of the industrial workers made only slow progress, partly owing to the animosity of the employers against organized labor, partly to the spread of industrial units, and also to the rural background of the early industrial labor force.[14] Many workers, organized in the free churches, also showed animosity toward the young socialist labor movement, which was considered to be atheistic. However, the class consciousness of the workers soon increased in the new industrial areas and in the growing cities. The crises in the export industries during international depressions and the struggle for higher wages, better working conditions, and the right to organize led to more than 3,000 registered strikes in Sweden from the 1870s up to World War I, with a culmination in the general strike in 1909 when 220,000 workers participated. Table 2 shows the number of strikes in Sweden during the period 1873–1909.

The arithmetical rise in the number of strikes over the years is a good measure of the growing tension between the Swedish working class and the upper sector of the plutocratic society before World War I. In this tense situation emigration became a politically important question and a royal commission on emigration (Emigrationsutred-

Table 2. *Strikes in Sweden, 1873–1909.*

1873	11	1882	4	1891	64	1900	135
1874	7	1883	5	1892	26	1901	118
1875	3	1884	6	1893	53	1902	139
1876	1	1885	10	1894	44	1903	142
1877	3	1886	28	1895	65	1904	215
1878	1	1887	16	1896	102	1905	189
1879	7	1888	41	1897	114	1906	290
1880	3	1889	38	1898	163	1907	312
1881	10	1890	105	1899	105	1908	302
						1909	138

Source: Förliknings—och skiljenämndskommitténs betänkande, 1901; Kommerskollegii avdelning för Arbetsstatistik, 1909–11.

ningen) was appointed to study the causes of emigration.[15] The labor movement regarded emigration as a symptom of the inability of the class society to take care of its citizens.[16] This leads to the question of the organized labor movement's image of America during the mass emigration era.

To understand the image of America in Sweden during the era of mass emigration, it is important to define various sectors of opinion. The Swedish bourgeoisie, especially its leading strata, was oriented toward Wilhelminic Germany at the end of the nineteenth century and was critical of many tendencies in American society. This negative attitude soon disappeared, and the free enterprise and vitality of American capitalism must be considered to have been an ideal for the Swedish bourgeoisie during the twentieth century. In many rural areas the ties with "Swedish America" have remained strong and a positive attitude toward America has dominated.

When discussing opinions among laborers, it is important to keep the time aspect in mind and to distinguish between judgment of the possibilities of the American labor market and wages on the one hand, and judgment of the power and superstructure of American society on the other. The old "liberal" picture of America as a land of political liberty, justice, and religious tolerance faded under the influence of developments that took place in the United States and Sweden.[17] The beginning of the twentieth century was marked by the political and economic advancement of the working class in Sweden, which reduced the relative differences between Sweden and America. The political questions of parliamentarism and universal suffrage were solved at the end of World War I, when Sweden was on the verge of revolution.[18] As has already been mentioned, the socialists participated in a government in 1917. The political advancement of the working class was soon followed by legislation favorable to it. This included accident and old-age insurance and the eight-hour law (1919).

On the other hand, political and economic institutions in the United States were very stable. After the close of the 1880s a growing segment of the Swedish working class also acquired new standards by which to judge social and political conditions. The labor movement was theoretically under the influence of Marxism, and it displayed an outspoken aversion to the capitalistic form of society, of which America was considered to be the prototype. The emigrants after 1900 also encountered to a higher degree than before industrial and urban America with its restless activity and hard competition as well as its slums and corrupt big city politics. Especially after World War I organized labor in Europe regarded America with suspicion. In 1925,

Arthur Engberg, a leading Swedish publicist and socialist politician, wrote: "In our opinion, the American capitalism is one of the most ruthless systems to be found on this earth. As an observer from afar one cannot rid oneself of the impression that the capitalistic civilization in this huge country has inherited the crude and repulsive spirit of the primitive gold digger camps. It is a chase for dollars with the revolver in hand. And the proletariat's conditions of life are simply dreadful."[19]

It is well known that public revulsion in the 1920s reached a dramatic climax when Sacco and Vanzetti were executed in Boston in 1927. This aroused indignation and bitterness among workers in Sweden as well as in the rest of Europe.[20] Over time, a change in attitude toward American society among organized labor in Sweden can thus be noticed. It is also important to distinguish between the laborer's view of the American superstructure and their view of the American labor market as a realistic and attractive alternative to a depressed Swedish labor market.

The decision to emigrate by industrial and urban workers was based on an evaluation of the different prospects on the Swedish and American labor markets. Information about conditions on the American labor market was spread orally by previous emigrants, through letters, and through the press. An often neglected form of information was personal man-to-man contact. The many returning emigrants during the later phase of mass emigration spread general information about urban and industrial America. (Remigration from America to Sweden totaled 19% of the emigration.)[21]

The influence of returning migrants on society in the various European countries, i.e. the transmission of technical and cultural impulses from America to Europe, is a complicated and important research topic.[22] It has been maintained that those remigrants who were disappointed with American capitalism were important to the radicalization of the Norwegian labor movement in the 1920s.[23] A corresponding effect can hardly be supported regarding Sweden. When discussing personal contacts, it must also be mentioned that the so-called yankees, who returned to Sweden for a few weeks during summertime, were of great importance as disseminators of information and as recruiters of additional emigrants.[24]

An important channel for information about the prospects of the American labor market was letters.[25] In fact, the "America letters" must be listed as one of the most important pull factors behind transoceanic emigration. There are no statistics concerning the number of letters from America to Sweden during the era of mass emigration.

However, if the Swedish emigrants were as eager to write letters as were the Danish, a couple of million letters would have reached Swedish addresses every year informing relatives and friends about wages and jobs in America.[26]

Thus returning emigrants, "yankees," and letters were important disseminators of information about America. It is, quite naturally, impossible to systematize the kind of information given through those channels, whereas it is easier to quantify the information given in newspapers, the fourth channel of information to be discussed. A case study of the information about America in the Swedish labor press around 1890, i.e. during some of the peak years of urban and industrial emigration, will be presented below.[27] The newspaper to be dealt with is *Socialdemokraten* (the Social Democrat), which began to be published in 1886. It was the main paper of the Swedish Social Democratic party. Circulation did not exceed 4,000 copies during the first years, but the newspaper's information was probably more widely spread among laborers, mainly in Stockholm, than circulation figures indicate: its information about the situation on the American labor market was spread by its readers in factories, hiring halls, and associations, especially the trade unions.[28] As far as information about America is concerned, the *Socialdemokraten* depended upon American newspapers and periodicals, America letters from emigrated party members, and, to a limited extent, on the newspaper's own correspondents in America.

The few reports in this newspaper from the years 1886–87 give on the whole a negative picture of the actual conditions in America: it was difficult to get a job and the wages were low. A few successful strikes were regarded as a positive factor. Nor during the following years, 1888–89, does the paper give a more attractive picture of the American labor market. It is to a great extent dominated by reports on a number of unsuccessful strikes, wage cuts, and extensive unemployment. In 1890, however, very little is said about unemployment in America. Special attention is paid to trade union activities, often leading to strikes, of which at least a few favored the workers. The information about wages and working time must have had a favorable impression on Swedish workers during that specific year. From 1891 onward reports about the American labor market are again pessimistic: unemployment, wage cuts, and violent labor conflicts dominate the news. The peak is quite naturally reached with the Homestead strike in 1892, which was noted in the *Socialdemokraten* with a lasting impression of the powerlessness of American labor organizations. The reports of an increase in mass unemployment are more and more frequent during the following year. In 1894 the picture of America as a country of bankruptcy and shutdowns is total, and industrial and urban emigration from Sweden symptomatically reached a low point that year. The Pullman strike especially raised many important issues. At stake was the right of industrial workers to organize unions, to declare boycotts, and to strike.

Some conclusions can be drawn from the foregoing, which underline what I said earlier about the image of America among organized laborers. The overall view of American society in the Swedish socialist press around 1890 was without illusions. The class struggle and repression of organized labor in America were stressed. However, the actual conditions on the labor market in Sweden were now and then judged to be worse, and in those situations the attractiveness of America increased even among workers within relatively strong trade unions and with socialist views. It was therefore considered important to inform potential emigrants among the readers in great detail about conditions in America; the high degree of realism of this information is striking.

In strong contrast to the realistic information in the labor press about prospects in America was the information given by foreign emigration agencies in connection with emigration to Brazil in 1891. Their propaganda offered a completely unrealistic future to immigrants. This particular emigration ended in disaster.[29]

Socialist politicians and publicists were restricted in their activity in the Swedish class society of the end of the nineteenth century. There are some examples of prominent socialist functionaries and publicists leaving Stockholm for America, and in at least one case (Erik Nordman) political activity was continued in America.[30] As far as trade unions are concerned, it has already been mentioned that many employers did not acknowledge freedom of association. There are examples of trade unions collecting money to help unemployed and blacklisted members to emigrate. Even some well-known trade union functionaries left Sweden for America. In a situation where alternatives were limited and a feeling of expulsion from Swedish society prevailed, emigration could thus be a solution for some labor functionaries.

When discussing the connection between strikes and emigration, some difficulties must be pointed out. During the whole era of mass emigration from Sweden it seems reasonable to assume that there were some connections between strikes and emigration. Controversies between strikers and strikebreakers among lumberers in northern

Sweden thus promoted emigration in 1923, the last peak of Swedish emigration.[31] The connection between strikes and emigration must, however, have been weakened over time.

It is also difficult to separate strikes from depressions as the direct cause of emigration. Our interest will be focused on some well-documented connections at the individual level between strike/emigration and socialist mass activity/emigration. Three conflicts will be discussed under these aspects: the Sundsvall strike in 1879, the Norberg strike in 1891–92, and the so-called Ljusne conflict in 1905–6. It is necessary to present and comment on these case studies extensively before presenting a typology.

The first big strike among industrial workers in Sweden occurred in the so-called Sundsvall district in the north in May-June 1879.[32] At the end of the nineteenth century this district was the largest sawmill area in Sweden, perhaps in the world. The most important cause of the strike was that the worker's wages had been lowered by the employers during the international depression of 1878–79. The strike affected about 5,000 sawmill workers and led to a complete defeat for the workers. The means of the working class in the struggle were still limited, and the repressive measures taken against the workers were massive: patriarchal employers and the state, represented by civil and military authorities, united against the industrial working class, which was still under formation.

The well-known journalist Isidor Kjellberg visited the Sundsvall district shortly after the strike had ended. He wrote: "If any plan for the future can be called common (in the Sundsvall district) it is that of leaving, the sooner the better, the present home for America, where many fellow workers—some say 2,000, counting wives and children—have already moved after the breaking of the strike. America is the thought for the day and the dream of the night." However, Kjellberg's figures are overestimated. Emigration from the Sundsvall district after the strike was not as high as he imagined.[33] In 1878 only two persons emigrated from the district as compared with 271 registered emigrants in 1879 (out of a population of over 15,000 people). In 1880, when there was no strike, 311 persons emigrated, in 1881 376 persons. However, the real number of emigrants must have been somewhat higher because many sawmill workers were seasonal workers; when they emigrated, they were registered as emigrants in their rural home parishes, not in the sawmill districts.

A connection between industrial depression and emigration can thus be established. There can also be no doubt of the close connection between strike participation and emigration: eight leaders of the strike were arrested in July 1879; four of them emigrated. Of the 236 persons who migrated from eight sawmills in the Sundsvall district in 1879, 179 emigrated.[34] Other migration alternatives were blockaded by the contemporary industrial depression in Sweden. It is also a well-known fact that emigration is a strong migration alternative for a labor force that has already participated in migration, in this case mostly from poor rural areas in eastern Sweden to the rapidly expanding lumber districts in the north.

In 1891–92 there were three strikes among miners in Norberg, an iron ore parish in the middle of Sweden.[35] The biggest strike started in November 1891 and lasted for almost six months. The striking workers were organized by the Norberg Miners' Union, founded in 1890, and they were supported by the Swedish Social Democratic party. The question in dispute was the workers' demand for the right to take part in negotiations about wages and other working conditions. Large subscriptions for the strikers' benefit were made from the whole country; contributions even came from the United States. The miners endured until the spring of 1892, but at the end of May the strike ceased and the trade union had to be dissolved.

The employers were reluctant to hire all those strikers they had previously employed. Especially the leaders or those who had in some other way compromised themselves in the employers' eyes had no chance of going back to work. Population registers and other sources show that immediately after the strike many miners migrated from Norberg to the newly opened iron mines in northern Sweden. Large contingents of workers also emigrated to America (80 in 1892 and 42 during the first half of 1893, while the number of emigrants did not even reach 20 in any other year in the 1890s). Among those who emigrated in 1892 were some who had played a prominent part as strikers or trade union leaders, e.g. the local union's former chairman Gustaf Stäckig.

After the turn of the century the Swedish sawmill industry went through a recession. In 1905 the sawmill company in Ljusne in northern Sweden decided to close the sawmill in 1907.[36] There existed strong animosity between the Young Socialists' Club, founded in December 1904 and numbering 217 members by June 1905, and the owner of the company, Count Walther von Hallwyl. The great wave of emigration from Ljusne in 1906 had two causes: the element of uncertainty resulting from the planned stopping of production, and the tensions arising between the politically conscious workers and the management. The core of the conflict was the right to organize, which was not recognized by the management in the context of political and trade union activity. Tensions also arose between older and better "adjusted" workers and their younger, radical mates. In 1906, 105 persons emigrated from Ljusne, of a total labor force of 1,200 members. It is noteworthy that the members of the Young Social Democrats' Association seemed to have had a noticeably greater tendency to emigrate than other settled workers (46 of the emigrants belonged to the club). A large number of the functionaries emigrated. Thus in the case of Ljusne there is a clear connection between socialist political activity and mass emigration.

The following can be concluded from these case studies. In a situation where a strike or socialist activity led to blacklisting, and a feeling of expulsion from the community existed among workers, emigration to America could be an attractive alternative. The strength of the emigration alternative depended upon the degree of repression exerted by the employers/society against the workers and upon the existence of a tradition to emigrate in the local community. The influence of the general situation in the Swedish labor market must also be stressed.

The general concept of the European immigrant to America as being almost illiterate and uprooted from traditionalist agrarian environment is one of the most long-lived myths in immigration history research. Many workers participating in late Swedish mass emigration had already experienced the tensions and repressions of the expanding capitalistic industrial state before leaving for America. The confrontation with industrial America was no shock for them; many were well prepared to take part in the struggles of the American working class.

NOTES

I am grateful to Andrew Dawson, Herbert Gutman, Harald Runblom, and Bo Öhngren for comments on this paper.

1. Gibbs M. Smith, *Joe Hill* (Salt Lake City, 1969).
2. Hans Norman, "Swedes in North America," in H. Runblom and H. Norman, eds., *From Sweden to America: A History of the Migration* (Minneapolis and Uppsala, 1976), pp. 228–300.
3. Bruce Larson, "Swedish Americans and Farmer-Labor Politics in Minnesota," in N. Hasselmo, *Perspectives on Swedish Immigration* (Minneapolis, 1978) pp. 206–24.
4. Richard B. Lucas, *Charles August Lindbergh, Sr.: A Case Study of Congressional Insurgency, 1906–1912* (Uppsala, 1974); Sten Carlsson, "Swedes in Politics," in *From Sweden to America*, pp. 291–300.
5. Larson, "Farmer-Labor Politics in Minnesota."
6. Auvo Kostiainen, *The Forging of Finnish-American Communism, 1917–1924: A Study in Ethnic Radicalism* (Turku, 1978), and the article by Kostiai-

nen in this volume. Cf. Paul George Hummasti, *Finnish Radicals in Astoria, Oregon, 1904–1940: A Study in Immigrant Socialism* (Eugene, Ore., 1975).

7. There was, for instance, an active Scandinavian section in New York within the Socialist Labor party called Skandinaviska Arbetarförbundet. The Swedish socialist pioneer Erik Nordman, who emigrated to the United States in 1888, was the first editor of the *Arbetaren* (the Worker), the newspaper of Skandinaviska Arbetarförbundet. Another radical newspaper in Swedish was *Svenska socialisten* (Swedish Socialist), founded in Rockford, Ill., in 1905. See Henry Bengston, *Skandinaver på vänsterflygeln i USA* (Stockholm, 1955).

8. Lennart Jörberg, "The Nordic Countries 1850–1914," in Carlo M. Cipolla, ed., *The Emergence of Industrial Societies 2*, Fontana Economic History of Europe (London and Glasgow, 1973), pp. 375–485.

9. Sten Carlsson, "Chronology and Composition of Swedish Emigration to America," in *From Sweden to America*, pp. 114–48.

10. For a theoretical discussion of the variations of Swedish mass emigration, see Sune Åkerman, "Theories and Methods of Migration Research," in *From Sweden to America*, pp. 19–75.

11. Carlsson, "Chronology and Composition."

12. See Sven Lundkvist, *Folkrörelserna i det svenska samhället 1850–1920*, Studia Historica Upsaliensia, no. 85 (Uppsala, 1977).

13. See Bo Öhngren, *Folk i rörelse: Samhällsutveckling, flyttnings mönster och folkrörelser i Eskilstuna 1870–1900*, Studia Historica Upsaliensia, no. 55 (Uppsala, 1974).

14. See Gösta Bagge, "Mackmyrakonflikten," *Social Tidskrift* 5 (1906), and Ragnar Casparsson, *LO under fem årtionden 1898–1923*. (Stockholm, 1947).

15. See Ann-Sofie Kälvemark, *Reaktionen mot utvandringen: Emigrationsfrågan i svensk debatt och politik*, Studia Historica Upsaliensia, no. 41 (Uppsala, 1972).

16. Harald Runblom, "Svensk reaktion mot utvandringen," *Historisk Tidskrift* 2 (1973): 284–90.

17. See Harald Elovson, "Den liberala amerikabilden i Sverige," in Lars Åhnebrink, ed., *Amerika och Norden* (Uppsala, 1964).

18. C.-G. Andrae, "Regeringen Swartz och den svenska revolutionen," *Historisk Tidskrift* 3 (1976):311–38.

19. *Socialdemokraten*, 25 July 1925.

20. J. S. Lindberg, *The Background of Swedish Emigration to the United States* (Minneapolis, 1930). Cf. R. Laurence Moore, *European Socialist Attitudes and the American Promised Land* (New York, 1970).

21. L.-G. Tedebrand, "Remigration from America to Sweden," in *From Sweden to America*, pp. 201–27.

22. See Nils Runeby, "Americanism, Taylorism and Social Integration," *Scandinavian Journal of History* 3 (1978):21–46.

23. B. J. Hovde, "Notes on the Effects of Emigration upon Scandinavia, *Journal of Modern History* 6 (1934):253–79.

24. See L.-G. Tedebrand, "Sources for the History of Swedish Emigration," in *From Sweden to America*, p. 90.

25. See Ingrid Semmingsen, "Utvandring og kontakt med Amerika," in Åhnebrink, ed., *Amerika och Norden*, pp. 65–74.

26. Kristian Hvidt, *Flugten til Amerika eller drivekraefter i massutvandringen fra Danmark 1868–1914* (Odense, 1971).

27. The study is based on Fred Nilsson, *Emigrationen från Stockholm till Nordamerika 1880–1893: En Studie urban utvandring* (Stockholm, 1970), pp. 206–29.

28. It must not be forgotten that many workers, even organized ones, read the Liberal press. A lot of workers also read the newspapers of the teetotallers' associations and the free church press.

29. Karin Stenbeck, "Utvandringen från Sverige till Brasilien 1868–1891," ms. (Uppsala, 1973).

30. Nilsson, *Emigrationen från Stockholm till Nordamerika*, p. 235.

31. Mats Rolén, unpublished paper (Department of History, Uppsala University, 1978).

32. See Tage Larsson, *Väckelsen och Sundsvallsstrejken 1879* (Motala, 1972), and N.-G. Hildeman, "Var Sundsvallsstrejken förberedd? *Historisk Tidskrift* 1 (1962): 1–34.

33. N.-G. Hildeman, "Swedish Strikes and Emigration," *Swedish Pioneer Historical Quarterly* 8 (1957): 87–93, and especially Anders Norberg, "Sundsvallsstrejken 1879—ett startskott för den stora Amerikautvandringen?" *Historisk Tidskrift* 3 (1978):263–82.

34. The information is based on Norberg, "Sundsvallsstrejken 1879."

35. Hildeman, "Swedish Strikes," and especially N.-G. Hildeman, *Norberg under industrialismens genombrottstid*, off-print from Norberg genom 600 år.

36. The study of the Ljusne conflict is based on Björn Rondahl, *Emigration, folkomflyttning och säsongarbete i ett sågverksdistrikt i södra Hälsingland 1865–1910*, Studia Historica Upsaliensia, no. 40 (Uppsala, 1972).

11

Political Mobilization of the Workers: The Case of the Worcester Swedes

SUNE ÅKERMAN and HANS NORMAN

Research regarding political mobilization in the last hundred years has been much occupied with basic economic and social changes while trying to connect them with political developments. Industrialization and its corollary urbanization especially have been scrutinized in this context.[1]

Geographic mobility or migration also ranks high as an explanatory factor. Thus it has been noticed that migrants tended to join voluntary associations more than others. Such associations as free churches, temperance organizations, and of course trade unions were active in the political sphere. The argument is that they played a crucial role in political mobilization in Sweden if not elsewhere.[2] They have been looked upon as training fields for politicians because of their organizational experience. In addition, these voluntary associations were directly active in politics. It started with the free churches. Later on the teetotallers and trade union people used their organizations to interfere with politics. As early as the 1910s these fairly militant groups had a strong overrepresentation in the Swedish parliament. The link between the trade unions and the Social Democratic party was especially strong. It is also well known that liberal political groupings had firm backing from different free churches and to some extent from the temperance people.

The industrialization process implied a higher migration rate, especially over long distances, than was the case earlier in a predominantly rural society with its few urban areas, which were also rather small. In the new in-migration areas voluntary associations took care of many social, religious, and cultural needs. Scholars of this research tradition have also pointed out the very important role of the free churches in this respect.

On an individual level the opportunity structure of the new labor market created quite different possibilities than before. A strong social circulation was the result, involving both upward mobility and skidding, which could facilitate political mobilization and protest movements. An important prerequisite was, however, a general improvement in education, which in most countries meant the creation of a compulsory school system.

In this article we intend to question some of the established truths of research into mobilization. We try to do so on the basis of our studies of a small but important part of the mass emigration to the United States from Sweden. The investigation area is Worcester, Massachusetts, and the group studied is its contingent of Swedish immigrants, who became one of the more important ethnic groups in the city.

Taken as a whole, Worcester had a very mobile population, with good opportunities for professional and social mobility as well as educational possibilities. The subject of our study is an immigrant group that had already been exposed to radical political thought before emigrating from Europe. To some extent this group had actively participated in the radical political movement, and, what is more, some of the migrants had been leaders of this movement back in Europe.

Of course there were striking differences between the American and the European scene. The size and structure of the U.S. political system, with its two big dominating parties, as well as the lack of a strong labor party were apparent. It is also well known that the American trade unions struggled to establish the right to organize in a more severe climate than in most countries, at least in Western Europe.[3] There were also dramatic tensions between skilled and unskilled workers when it came to organizing the unions. The multi-ethnic society, with its large-scale immigration of unskilled, often illiterate rural people from less developed parts of Europe, reinforced this situation.

In this context the link between voluntary associations and political mobilization may indeed seem questionable. Religious denominations and trade unions were more or less antagonistic, craft unions and industrial unions were fighting each other, and so on. In addition, union recruitment was still at a very low level at the turn of the century, and it fluctuated very much. Repression on the part of the employers and state or federal authorities had a detrimental effect on many trade unions but could at the same time foster political activities and organization. That is what happened in 1877–78, 1886, and 1892–94.[4]

One of the typical voluntary associations of the time, the producers' and consumers' cooperative, was also looked upon as a real alternative to political mobilization. To complicate things even more, several political factions in the United States were critical of trade unionism in general, for example, the Lasalleans. Others preferred direct political action to parliamentarism. It is also important to keep in mind that most new immigrants did not have the right to vote. As a matter of fact, the majority of the American working class must have been immigrants at the end of the nineteenth century.[5] At that time even in Europe most workers were excluded from the possibility of influencing society by voting. In this case income qualifications functioned as an obstacle that very few workers could get past.

Hence more or less the same basic conditions for mobilization seem to have existed on both sides of the ocean. The prerequisites for at least some political participation within and outside the national political systems were at hand. Therefore it seemed reasonable to try a comparative approach in the study that we intended to carry out. In this way the different outcomes of the development can be illustrated and the causal connections specified.[6]

Worcester is situated in the Boston region in Massachusetts, but from the 1840s onward the city developed fast enough to be able to act as a fairly independent local center.

From the point of view of internal migration and immigration it had a different structure from Boston.[7] While Boston's population according to censuses grew from 61,000 in 1830 to 178,000 in 1890, Worcester developed from 7,500 inhabitants in 1840 to 25,000 in 1860 and 85,000 in 1890. It passed 100,000 in the middle of the 1890s and reached 120,000 at the turn of the century. In 1960 the population amounted to more than 200,000. During our period of observation from the 1870s to the 1910s Worcester grew to the size of a small metropolis if compared with the situation in Sweden, but this of course meant only a middle-sized city from the American point of view.

An idea of the population mobility of Worcester can be gained from an indirect calculation based on the city directories for the 1880s (Table 1). It shows that the population grew from 58,000 to 85,000 during that decade and that the net migration was almost 20,000 in the same period. To get this net-migration increase there had to be an impressive total mobility.

Hence almost 230,000 migrants were necessary to create a surplus of less than 20,000. In migration-research circles this is by now a well-known phenomenon. It is no exaggeration to state that this urban population was rather volatile. This can also be illustrated by a persistence chart (Figure 1) that includes 300 persons who have been traced all through the 1880s.

Figure 1 shows that only 37% of the population under study remained in the city for a full ten-year period. Of course, this must have

Table 1. *Reconstruction of Worcester's Total Population Mobility in the 1880s.*

Year	In-migration	Out-migration	Net Migration	Total Population Mobility
1881	7,353	6,016	1,337	13,369
1882	13,046	8,214	4,832	21,260
1883	13,299	14,040	741	27,339
1884	13,624	14,181	557	27,805
1885	10,956	8,217	2,739	19,173
1886	15,692	9,415	6,277	25,107
1887	12,578	10,011	2,567	22,589
1888	7,790	6,970	820	14,760
1889	15,480	16,052	572	31,532
1890	13,790	10,792	2,998	24,582
Total	123,608	103,908	19,700	227,516

Source: Åkerman, "Stabilitet och förändring." The asumption is that the birth rate was in the range of 25-30 per thousand and the mortality 15-20 per thousand. In any case, the calculation must be looked upon as pure approximation.

had implications for the political and social life of the community.[8] Nothing suggests that the Swedes may have had a different mobility pattern from the rest of the population. Thus a small investigation shows that only 40% of the Swedish immigrants to Worcester stayed in the city for more than three to five years at the beginning of the

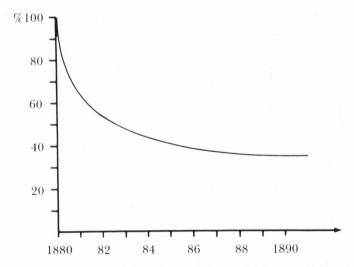

Figure 1. Persistence rate of a subpopulation in Worcester, 1880–90 (N = 300) (from Åkerman, "Stabilitat och förändring").

1880s. Far from being more stable than other ethnic groups or nationalities, the Swedes seem to have been fairly mobile. The high turnover must be connected with the fact that all these immigrants were newly arrived people who for the first few years after their arrival were supposed to have had great difficulty in getting a foothold in American society. Many of them moved on to other cities and industrial areas and others returned to Europe.[9]

Behind the strong and even population growth lay a rapid process of industrialization. By 1890 there were already about 900 large and small enterprises engaged in more than 100 different industries.[10] Unlike several other cities in Massachusetts, the textile industry played only a minor role in Worcester. Of more importance were the mechanical, machine, shoe and, to an increasing extent, the earthenware industries. During the first part of our study period Washburn & Moen was by far the most important firm in the city. It had been founded by Ichabod Washburn, who started his experiments in wire manufacturing in 1831. His efforts were to father the largest wire factory in the United States by 1880. Washburn & Moen, which by 1900 had 4,000 workers, produced material for hoopskirts in the 1860s and barbed wire for enclosing the plains of the West in the 1870s.[11]

The same is true of another Worcester firm, the Norton Company, which had originally produced pottery but had gone over to manufacturing emery wheels in the 1870s. This was, by the way, a Swedish invention, and Swedish management lay behind the changeover. From the turn of the century to the 1920s this industry underwent very strong expansion.[12]

Washburn & Moen and the Norton Company had a central position not only among the industries of the city but also for the Swedes. There were whole departments of the plants that were Swedish-speaking during our study period.

The most dominant among the nationalities of the Boston-Worcester area was the big Irish group. The Irish started their mass immigration to this area in the 1850s. They were followed by several other nationalities such as Germans and French-Canadians and, later, Italians and East European Jews. Normally the Scandinavians did not play an important role in the eastern states, but here in Worcester they were one of the big immigrant groups. Worcester was one of the biggest centers of the Swedes after Minneapolis, Chicago, and New York.

The Swedish immigration was mainly characterized by two distinct groups (see Figure 2). Immigration by the first of them started in 1869 when two potters from Höganäs in the southernmost part of

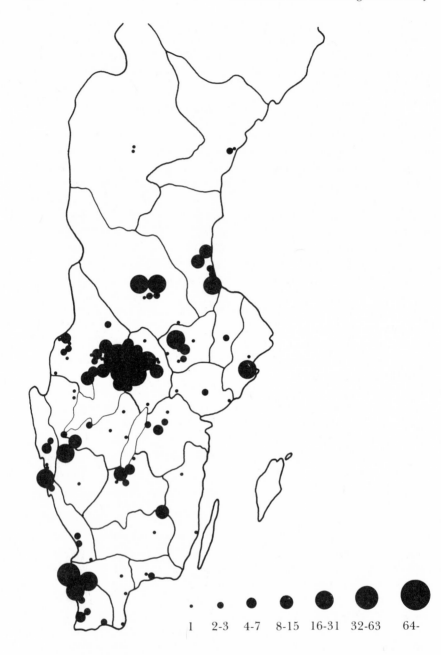

Figure 2. Areas of recruitment for Swedish immigrants to Worcester as based on notations in parishes of birth or emigration in *Kalender över Svenskarna i Worcester 1883* (from Norman, *Från Bergslagen*, p. 242).

Sweden arrived in Worcester. At once they got employment at the Norton pottery works. From then on there was a considerable flow of migration from Höganäs to Worcester, especially during the years of expansion from around 1900 to 1920. These immigrants seem to have been desirable manpower within the pottery industry, and many of them did well. Two of the pioneers from Höganäs, Sven Pålsson and John Jeppson, played an important role in the Norton Company's changeover to manufacturing emery grinding machines. Jeppson later became a shareholder and superintendent of the company. The company advanced to become an international concern, and for a long time Swedish immigrants constituted a considerable part of the labor force.[13]

The second group consisted mainly of iron mill laborers from Bergslagen, the mining district in central Sweden. During a study trip to Swedish ironworks there, one of the partners of the Washburn & Moen wire mill, Philip Moen, encouraged skilled workers to go to the workshops in Worcester. From the 1870s on there was a great demand for fences in the agrarian western states, and during the 1880s the mill had developed to become the largest in the United States. Thus workers from the central Swedish mining area for a long time dominated Swedish immigration to Worcester. They came chiefly from the ironworks in the Örebro and Västmanland *län* but also from Gävleborgs and Kopparbergs *län*.[14]

In 1876 the Swedish colony consisted of about 200 persons; by 1880 there were more than 1,000, according to the manuscript census. During the late 1880s there were about 5,000 Swedes. At the turn of the century, finally, Swedes of first and second generations were estimated to number more than 10,000, around one-tenth of the Worcester population.[15]

What was the social structure of the Swedes in Worcester?[16] According to the census of 1880 there were 463 skilled workers from Sweden in the city. At that time large-scale immigration of Swedes to this area had only just started. According to a city directory, the corresponding number had increased almost tenfold in 1907. This information about occupations and social groupings is surveyed below (Table 2). Reference to the social structure of the city of Örebro, a regional center in the southern part of Bergslagen, provides a relevant comparison.

It can be assumed that in 1880 only a small number of Swedes had managed to follow a professional career in Worcester. A handful of them belonged to the higher social groups. We find only one clergyman in Group I and some clerks in Group II. Consequently, Groups IV and V, i.e. skilled workers and craftsmen and unqualified workers

Table 2. *Number of Employed Persons of Swedish Origin in Worcester, 1880 and 1907, and the Total Population of Örebro in 1900, Distributed According to Social Groups.*

	I	II	III	IV	Va	Vb	N	% (Total)
Worcester, 1880	0.2	1.9	0.9	25.9	55.3	15.8	463	100.0
Worcester, 1907	1.5	12.6	0.3	33.2	52.1	0.3	4108	100.0
Örebro, 1900	4.6	18.6	1.0	24.3	46.7	4.8	6394	100.0

I   Owners of large business enterprises, landowners, higher civil officials, university graduates
II   Small-scale business entrepreneurs in trade and industry, master artisans, lower civil officials and clerks, school teachers, foremen
III   Farmers, tenant farmers
IV   Craftsmen and artisans below the rank of master, skilled workers
Va   Unqualified workers in industry and urban commerce
Vb   Farm workers, domestic servants
Sources: *U.S. Census 1880; Scandinavian City Directory 1907;* extracts from parish books, Central Bureau of Statistics, Stockholm (Norman, *Från Bergslagen,* p. 263).

respectively, are large. Together they amount to more than 80% of employed persons. The qualified group consists mainly of machinists, stokers, wire drawers, melters, and workers in the pistol factory as well as smiths and craftsmen. Already at this early stage of Swedish settlement in Worcester there was a relatively large number of skilled workers.

But the real social breakthrough came around the turn of the century. While only 2% of the population had attained middle-class status in 1880, this group amounted to 14% in 1907. At the same time the size of the skilled worker category increased considerably from a quarter to a third of that of the Swedish group. Hence this immigrant group had attained a social structure comparable with the total population of an *expanding* Swedish urban center (Örebro) at a corresponding point in time.[17]

What kind of political engagement can we find among the Swedes of Worcester, more specifically, what kind of radical engagement? Our general impression is that the Swedes were active everywhere else but in politics. From a history of the Swedes in Worcester printed in 1898, we quote: "From a political point of view the Swedes of this city like their countrymen in other areas have shown a rather unforgivable indifference. Politics has not attracted as much interest as it ought to and it is a deplorable fact that whenever we have tried to create a political coordination of our countrymen much time has not elapsed before this new interest has slackened. Hence the whole attempt has failed."[18] This statement could very well be supported by similar observations on Swedish immigrant societies in the United States.[19] Such an attitude, by the way, seems to be fairly common within other immigrant groups as well.[20]

Another source claims that the Swedes to a certain extent were able to assert themselves politically, but this seems mostly to have been wishful thinking. "In politics the Swedes in Worcester gain a hearing more and more. Several clubs have been founded during the last few years, but in most of the cases they have been of short duration."[21]

A survey of newspapers from the years after 1900 shows that the Swedes of Worcester seem to have ignored political activities and questions about labor conditions. But this does not mean that they were passive. On the contrary, they plunged into the social life of Worcester, participating with great enthusiasm in newly created ethnic associations like lodges, clubs, choirs, professional associations, etc. Like other immigrant groups, they also very soon founded their own religious congregations. At the turn of the century there were nine different Swedish churches in Worcester. These Swedish immigrants thus were busy reshaping their social and cultural neighborhood and not just accepting the limitations of the established host society.[22]

Why did the Swedes of Worcester prefer this type of activity to real political engagement? When we try to answer that question, we touch upon the often-discussed problem of the political engagement of the American worker. That is the problem of "the conservative worker."[23]

What are the basic elements of mobilization? How do they interact to articulate the interests of a group? How are such spontaneous groups created? How can they be maintained? How does the interplay between information-knowledge-aspirations and action take place? These are all questions that are relevant to our discussion.

Within communication sociology and linguistics rather than among political scientists, these crucial, elementary questions have been handled with some success. The big problem is to portray the *dynamic* aspect of mobilization—we are now talking of a general process, not just political mobilization. One very promising attempt is the concept of *the helix of cooperation* that has recently been constructed.[24]

The point is how an interplay is created "between action and communication in various ways, patterns, and functions." The result is an amplifying process. Hypothetically this takes place in four different dimensions that mutually enforce each other. The meaning of this basic mobilization process can be described as follows: The individual is enabled to *articulate* himself. The individual's basic need to *be together* with equals is satisfied. The individual is enabled to *obtain impor-*

tant information related to his position. The individual is enabled to
influence his environment.[25]

Figure 3 shows how a subpopulation moves in these four dimen-
sions, i.e. *identity, sense of community, knowledge,* and *action,* thereby striving for or reaching certain common goals in a growth process taking
the shape of a helix. Much can be said about conceptual construct,
but it has an undeniable pedagogical value that is striking. From this
angle of approach we can, for example, perceive why the vigor of the
multi-ethnic society is so strong when it comes to different kinds of
mobilization. In such social surroundings it is theoretically much easier to start such processes and for the individual to identify groups
with common interests and backgrounds.[26]

There is also reason not to comment upon the question of how
political mobilization takes place. Such discussions often start from
the assumption that the masses are for the most part passive. Thus
the problem is to activate them. We have remarked upon the fact that,
compared with the preconceived views, our study group was different
and all but passive, as were most other ethnic groups in Worcester.
There activities cannot be neglected when analyzing attitudes toward
politics and political organization. Hence we must observe that especially in the American setting a population that has disclosed organizational talent and energy constitutes quite a different basis for political
mobilization than a more inert mass of people.

Trade unionism rather than socialism is the result. Economic organizations like trade unions and cooperatives act *within* the framework
of the existing society. Even if they were not restricted to negotiations
about salaries, and ultimately to the use of the strike as a weapon,
their political horizons would be limited. They could work for political legislation about shorter working hours, industrial welfare, and so
forth, as well as support different political parties, thereby trying to
achieve limited goals of interest to their members.

This can be seen as one pathway to political mobilization, which
leads to reformist politics (see Figure 4). Our interpretation of the
part played by voluntary associations, then, is somewhat different
from the one mentioned in the introduction to this article. We consider the activities of the elite to be crucial here. This group of people
is not homogeneous, but they tend mainly to act through voluntary
organizations by guiding the anonymous membership, and to some
extent by channeling the reactions of their fellow members. It is most
important to notice here that spontaneous activities of this kind do
not automatically lead to political radicalism. This was early realized
by Marxist leaders.[27] Moreover, in the American case the ethnic com-

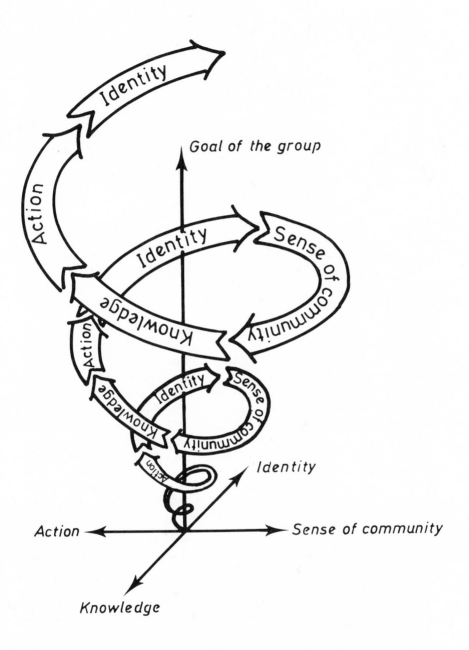

Figure 3. The helix of cooperation (from Thunberg *et al.*, *Samverkansspiralen*, p. 94).

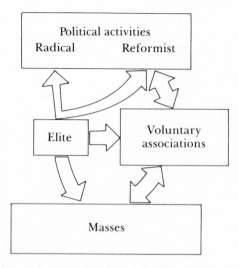

Figure 4. Alternative paths to political mobilization: A theoretical angle of
    approach.

plexity of the society basically determined the different mobilization
processes.

The choice of *the left path* means something quite different. In this
case the role of the elite is even more pronounced. This implies that
ideological antagonism stands out as most striking within the elite
group itself. The majority within this group will, of course, try to
preserve the status quo or accept and strive for modest changes along
the reformist line. From experience we know, however, that societies
characterized by inequality also produce more radical political groupings. Such groupings are recruited from an intelligentsia within the
elite. It is natural to think that these persons are outsiders as related
to the establishment.

It may very well be difficult to mobilize people along the *right path*
of our figure, but these difficulties are small compared with what is
waiting along the left path. The whole ideological and economic machine of bourgeois society hinders such a development. Radical efforts are faced with the fact that individuals have been exposed to a
long-standing and deep indoctrination by institutions like the family,
the church, and the school system (and in Worcester by no means
least of all the big companies). Hence the small radical elite has two
choices. The first one means influencing the masses through political
agitation. This implies an agitation from outside or above that will
make the laboring masses conscious of the realism of a socialist
analysis.[28]

Radicalism means a long perspective, while reformism aims at immediate economic and political goals, i.e. a short perspective. The latter will normally attract most people. Under these circumstances it will be tempting for the radical elite to try to achieve political power *directly* by militant action as has happened in many revolutionary contexts, for example, in Russia in 1917. In such a case the problem will be to legitimatize the coup d'état afterward. At least theoretically the power has to be based on the support of the people. This choice of strategy means great risks for democratic development. The Soviet Russian leadership has, for example, never been able to handle the interplay with the masses. Instead, they have developed an extreme form of guardianship on the right-hand path of our figure. Trade unions and other voluntary economic associates may interfere with representative democracy. Eventually strong corporate tendencies or even a corporate state will emerge.

The Swedes of Worcester emigrated from areas in their homeland that must be considered politically active. They also came from a country that had a fairly democratic political system and, more important, its political structure was in a process of change. Around the turn of the century a strong extraparliamentary suffrage movement leveled severe criticism against the established political order. Other voluntary associations like free churches, temperance societies, and trade unions pointed out other shortcomings caused by the social and economic order of the time.

As was indicated earlier, the immigrants came from two particular regions in Sweden, either from the central iron mill region or from Western Scania, i.e. the southernmost part of the country, as well as from other urban areas. Especially Western Scania was the scene of early and strong political activities, and the Höganäs area was characterized politically by the Scanian form of social democracy during the years after the turn of the century.[29]

An important background factor was the educational ordinance of 1842 that forced every Swedish parish to establish compulsory schooling. This did not mean any great change in literacy but made for a real improvement in writing ability among the masses. Reading ability was already fairly high in the late seventeenth century.[30]

As a matter of fact there were among the Swedish immigrants to Worcester quite a few with secondary school education and some who had acquired special training as engineers. Even a number of persons with academic backgrounds were attracted to Worcester.[31] The size of the Swedish group in Worcester also formed the basis for considerable merchant activities. The same is true of the ethnic printing industry. In general, there were good possibilities for social advancement in the Boston-Worcester area at this time of economic expansion. Stephan Thernstrom has pointed out in *The Other Bostonians* that the Scandinavians were able to compete successfully on the skilled workingmen level, although their upward social mobility could not be compared with that of the Yankee or Jewish population.[32]

It is worth mentioning that social mobility, upward and downward, was remarkably high even in the urban areas of the European countries, a fact that is often neglected by American scholars. Thus there were good opportunities for upward social mobility on both sides of the Atlantic, especially in urban areas.[33] During our study period around the turn of the century there was a great deal of turnover in the labor market at all social levels, with people shuttling back and forth across the Atlantic Ocean.[34]

This mobile Atlantic labor market was an excellent ground for the spread of political ideas. All the other factors mentioned might have prepared our study group for some kind of political engagement. The situation of the Swedes, with all their activities in voluntary associations and the organizational ability they showed, could have facilitated different activities in the field of politics. At least this might have been the case in the local community. As a matter of fact one political issue really did agitate the Swedes. Typically enough it was the liquor question. Every year a liquor referendum was held simultaneously with the city election. In this permanent tug-of-war between the prohibitionists and their antagonists, the Swedes sided with the antiliquor grouping. In 1888 the most fanatic advocates of temperance seem to have backed a special Prohibition party, which, however, received only 2% of the city's vote. Here the worker community of Quinsigamond stands out as an antiliquor precinct. It is symptomatic that the Methodists had a stronghold in this southern suburb of Worcester totally dominated by Swedes.[35]

It was, however, almost unrealistic and unthinkable for this political activity to have been linked with radicalism. The left-hand path of our figure was therefore excluded as an alternative. The American scene did not allow such a development. The working class that was to be mobilized was split into many ethnic groups, nationalities, and tongues with widely differing backgrounds. Hence it was in the long run difficult to anchor a radical policy in the masses of American labor. The same split and communication problems must also have existed within the potential leftist elite. It must be remembered that an essential part of the unskilled labor force looked upon itself as *Gastarbeiter*, foreigners, who never intended to stay in the United States for good.

One of the many difficulties that deserves to be mentioned was the size of the United States. To organize and keep together a political grouping covering all the states would have been an administrative masterpiece in itself. In spite of all this, some attempts were made to work along this line. The best example is probably the Industrial Workers of the World (IWW), who made desperate efforts to gather the many toilers and immigrants, *Gastarbeiter,* and labor migrants around a radical political program with the slogan "One big union." It was no coincidence that the political program of the Wobblies had a strong syndicalistic bent. The IWW stood up against capitalistic society as well as government authorities. The Wobblies also had to fight the hysterical nationalism that emerged during World War I, since they worked for labor solidarity across the borders and were consequently opposed to America joining the war.[36]

The inertia of the Swedes and their working-class community changed very logically into an active Republican stand in support of World War I. In 1916 the Republican party worked out a new strategy that aimed at undermining the Irish, Catholic, and working-class vote. In this strategy the Swedes were supposed to act as a wedge. After all that has been said, this political orientation of the Swedish workers is remarkable.[37] We cannot yet explain exactly how this came about. We would need a much more extensive set of data, especially in the form of interviews.

It seems possible, however, to combine our present knowledge to form a fairly reasonable explanation. Thus the dilemma of ethnic cleavage applies not only in general but of course specifically in the case of every ethnic group. The religious cleavages were as important as the ethnic tensions and prejudices and interwoven with them. These tensions are of the utmost importance in American society. In Worcester the religious and ethnic complexity rendered cooperation difficult between the Irish and the Scandinavians in the fields of common interest.[38]

Another aspect of great importance is that divisions appear even within ethnic groups. This is well known as regards the Italians in the United States. Among them we find a socialist-oriented group opposed to another grouping deeply rooted in the Catholic church. This was the case, for example, in Chicago.[39] In that city a similar division of the Swedes has been noticed.[40] There are good reasons to suspect that the same applies to Worcester.[41] Hence, when prominent representatives of the Swedish community of Worcester commented upon the modest political engagement of their countrymen, they were not talking about such radical positions as engagement in the Farmer Labor party or the Socialist party.

We also have to take into consideration the effects of social mobility.

Earlier we presumed that social circulation could facilitate political mobilization. On the contrary, there is reason to suspect that marked changes in social position would, rather, function as an alternative to political protest.[42] The labor market of Worcester seems to have been very favorable to the Swedes, and their general improvement may have contributed to their passivity. Their economic and social adaptation thus left them with restricted space for political action. Behind this suggestion lies the idea that upward social mobility costs a lot of energy. The same is true also of the general adaptation of an immigrant population.

When it comes to migration, we have to look a little closer into the effects. Even if it is quite possible for migration in general to act as a positive factor for mobilization, e.g. in the trade unions, we have to be cautious to avoid simplifications. The big geographic turnover that we found in Worcester—among the early Swedes just as much as among the others—must have been detrimental to efforts to unite the workers.[43] It seems fair to suggest that unskilled workers were most susceptible to a more radical political message. But they were also a very volatile part of the population. That may be one reason why the Socialist Labor party repeatedly failed to organize the Swedish workers, as we have noticed. A minimum of continuity is required for any organization to work. Thus the indications are that the mobility pattern strengthened the influence of the middle-class group of the Swedish colony. Consequently the working-class group was weakened in spite of its numerical strength. This may, of course, apply to every immigrant society in the industrial era.[44]

Thus it is not strange that old trade union leaders and socialists lost their political stamina in the new environment.[45] The right to organize was far from accepted by the big employers of Worcester. Both Washburn and Moen and the Norton Company reacted in a very primitive way to attempts to organize the workers, and they practiced a typical open-shop system.[46] The threat of being fired hovered over those who did not accept the policy of the employers. At the same time these big employers had a paternalistic attitude toward their workers. Such a policy could, of course, dampen the need for organizational achievements at least during good years.[47]

It is possible to substantiate our interpretation of the role of migration by introducing other information about the Swedish group in Worcester. Even as late as 1904 not even 2,000 members of the group were able to vote.[48] Hence a large section had not bothered to apply for citizenship. It is not far-fetched to think that the possibility of returning to Sweden was present for many, many years for the average immigrant.[49] Perhaps this is astonishing. The Scandinavians have been looked upon as easily assimilated in the United States, in contrast to most immigrants from the Mediterranean area or East-central Europe.

We have established that the Swedes were highly successful in various respects in the receiving country, at least in Worcester. But now we are considering the psychological dimension, and here the adaptation may very well have been far from complete. To our reasoning this is the most relevant thing to bear in mind. The party constellation in Worcester was not unfair to the Swedish immigrants. Before the large immigration to Worcester of the Irish, who almost always voted Democratic, Republicans dominated the political scene. They consisted mainly of older immigrant groups, in the first place the Anglo-Saxons.

The leading financial families had a strong influence on Worcester politics during this period. Through the immigration of the Irish the political balance shifted slowly to the Democratic party. When the Swedes, who, in the main, fitted best into the non-Catholic, Republican fold, came to Worcester, they were received with open arms by older-established Republicans. Because of the short period they had been in the country and because of language difficulties during this initial phase, it took some time before they could assert themselves in the party where the hierarchy was already well established. The Swedes therefore had to be satisfied with relatively modest political positions for quite some time.[50]

When we discuss political development and the level of political mobilization in the United States, it may be illustrative and practical to limit the study to one of the many ethnic groups or nationalities and try to find out about its experiences and reactions to the host society. We must remember, however, that even if most ethnic groups have had unique experiences of America, the most striking thing is the many common traits. That means that no single group is more interesting than the others and that they are interchangeable. Thus there is, of course, a call for more comparative research than has been performed hitherto.

We have chosen to study the city of Worcester in Massachusetts. The background of the Worcester Swedes was well known to us when we started our investigation. It is one area of study from the vast research that has recently been devoted to the mass emigration overseas of the Scandinavians.[51] Worcester seems to correspond to an expanding urban center and multi-ethnic community so typical of America at the turn of the century. Together with the Irish and the French-Canadians, the Swedes constituted a substantial part of the population of the city. Thus their opportunity to assert themselves politically seems to have been good, all the more so as they had made considerable progress in the American labor market. From a very modest start in the 1870s they had advanced to become one of the key groups among the skilled workers, especially within the metal and manufacturing industry. To some extent the Swedes also reached a position within the middle class. A sympathetic relationship emerged between the Swedish immigrants and the Yankee Republicans that extended "beyond politics and into the economic structure of the community." Here, of course, the Swedes could profit from the fact that they were a WASP group.[52]

Similarly to most other ethnic groups, the Swedes showed an astounding drive to organize different voluntary associations. New congregations were created and church buildings erected as well as other assembly premises, and they were filled with activities both religious and secular. We find economic organizations like cooperatives and savings and insurance associations, temperance societies, and other social and cultural activities within lodges, clubs, choirs, theaters, etc. To some extent parochial schools were established. Very early a Swedish press grew up in Worcester. Gradually the city became one of the leading publishing centers of "Swedish America."

Some basic results of recent Swedish research into voluntary associations have served as a framework of reference for our judgment of the sluggishness of the Swedes in mobilizing politically. This sluggishness can hardly be questioned. It is all the more remarkable as very favorable preconditions were at hand. Apart from the many voluntary associations, which have been looked upon—at least in Sweden—as the most important base for political activities and articulation, we have seen that the Swedish immigrants in Worcester originated from fairly radical areas in the home country. In addition, there were several immigrants who had been former leaders of local trade unions and Social Democratic party units. Yet we have seen that the trade unions had a very difficult start in Worcester.

On a more theoretical level we can suggest that an American city like Worcester could trigger off the collaboration process of identity, sense of community, knowledge, and action in the small group that has been described as the nucleus of democracy and social life (Figure 3). Far from being a hindrance to such a process, the multi-ethnic society must have been highly advantageous. This can be easily observed in the community life of other ethnic groups like the Irish or the French-Canadians as well.

Political mobilization, however, is not only a spontaneous drive to organize at the grass-roots level. The typical course involves an inter-play between elite and masses. The steering function of the elite is crucial. The interplay may take different forms and be more or less pronounced. It is likely that democratic development will be stabilized when political life to a great extent is based on voluntary associations and spontaneous political activities. But along this line no genuine and basic societal changes will arise. This will happen only if a radical elite group acts vigorously on both organizational and ideological levels. We have labeled this development the left path to political mobilization (Figure 4).

Here ethnic complexity tends to be a real problem aggravating the communication between different nationalities and elites. This is what, for example, the Socialist party of America experienced. Even an open and fairly undogmatic organization like the SPA had difficulty in uniting different sections of the party and reaching a broader audience. The sheer size of the country contributed, of course, to this situation.

Another obstacle was the fact that the working class of the United States consisted to such a great extent of immigrants. They struggled with the economic and social adaptation that was their primary goal. For the important group of immigrants who were successful in the new country, social mobility seems to have acted more or less as an alternative to political effort. One might suggest that these immi-grants and their children later on could act from their middle-class position within the framework of traditional U.S. politics. Supposedly their loyalty to their social origins had by then been drastically atten-uated. Compare the fact that parts of the new middle class in Sweden have constantly backed the Social Democratic party. Of course the structural changes in the middle class are relevant to our discussion. Hence it would have been appropriate to dwell more upon the inter-play as well as the hostility between blue-collar and white-collar work-ers, following Charles Wright Mills's analysis.

The general pattern of geographic mobility must also have in-creased middle-class influence in communities like Worcester. Cer-tainly all social groups were mobile, but the toilers were more mobile than the others.

Finally, the most important, American political institutions, espe-cially the two-party system, have not been able to adapt to and chan-nel activities and aspirations at the grass-roots level even if now and then strong efforts have been made to establish a third party. Thus the oldest formal democracy in the world has had obvious difficulties in incorporating the mass of immigrants and workers into a meaningful political process. That the workers are still alienated in the American form of democracy can be seen in their extremely low participation in recent elections.

NOTES

1. Stein Kuhnle, *Social Mobilization and Political Participation: The Nordic Countries 1850–1970* (Bergen, 1973); Samuel N. Eisenstadt and Stein Rokkan, eds., *Building States and Nations* (Beverly Hills, Calif., 1973), vols. 1–2.

2. Sven Lundkvist, *Folkrörelserna i det svenska samhället 1850–1920* (Voluntary associations in Swedish society 1850–1920) (Uppsala, 1977).

3. Selig Perlman and Philip Taft, *History of Labor in the United States, 1896–1932* (New York, 1935), vol. 4.

4. *Ibid.*, Philip S. Foner, *History of the Labor Movement in the United States* (New York, 1947), 3:36ff.

5. Perlman and Taft, *History of Labor*, pp. 3–4; Philip S. Foner, *American Socialism and Black Americans* (Westport, Conn., 1977), pp. 86–87; Don Divance Lescohier in John R. Commons *et al.*, *History of Labour in the United States, 1896–1932*, 3 (New York, 1935):15–28.

6. A comparative approach is lacking as yet in Swedish research. Occasional comparisons have been made in American research. See, e.g., Perlman's references to the conditions in Europe when dealing with American labor's distrust of government authority, in Perlman and Taft, *History of Labor*.

7. The text dealing with Worcester population and population turnover is based on Sune Åkerman, "Stabilitet och förändring i en medelstor stads migration: Fallet Worcester, Massachusetts" (Stability and change in the migration of a middle-sized city: A case study of Worcester), unpublished paper (Department of History, Uppsala University, Uppsala, 1971). Compare also Stephan Thernstrom, *The Other Bostonians: Poverty and Progress in the American Metropolis, 1880–1970* (Cambridge, Mass., 1973), and Kevin L. Hickey, "Geography and Leadership: An Interdisciplinary Evaluation of Worcester's Industrial Development," unpublished paper (Assumption College, Worcester, Mass., 1979), stressing the diversity and continuity of Worcester's economic growth.

8. Compare Peter Knights and Stephen Thernstrom, "Men in Motion" (M.S.S.B. Conference, Princeton University, 1972).

9. Margaretha Eriksson, "Emigrationen från Örebro län 1879–1882 till Nordamerika" (The emigration from Örebro County to North America 1879–1882), unpublished paper (Department of History, Uppsala University, Uppsala, 1971).

10. Hjalmar Nilsson and Eric Knutson, *Svenskarna i Worcester 1868–1898* (The Swedes in Worcester 1868–1898) (Worcester, Mass., 1898), p. 5.

11. C. C. Buell, "The Laborers," unpublished paper concerning the social situation in Worcester, 1850–80 (Northeastern University, Boston, Mass., 1971), pp. 2ff.

12. Nilsson and Knutson, *Svenskarna i Worcester*, pp. 121ff.; Steven Koblik, oral research report on the Swedes in Worcester (Uppsala, 7 Feb. 1979).

13. Nilsson and Knutson, *Svenskarna i Worcester,* pp. 17–18; Robert N. Beck, "Brief History of the Swedes of Worcester," *Swedish Pioneer Historical Quarterly* 10 (1959):105ff.; Harald Runblom and Hans Norman, eds., *From Sweden to America: A History of the Migration,* A Collective Work of the Uppsala Migration Research Project (Minneapolis and Uppsala, 1976), p. 255.

14. Hans Norman, *Från Bergslagen till Nordamerika: Studier i migrationsmönster, social rörlighet och demografisk struktur med utgångspunkt från Örebro län 1851–1915* (From Bergslagen to North America: Studies in migration pattern, social mobility and demographic structure on the basis of Örebro County 1851–1915), Studia Historica Upsaliensia, no. 62 (Uppsala, 1974), pp. 237–38; Beck, "Brief History," p. 107.

15. *U.S. Census 1880;* Runblom and Norman, eds., *From Sweden to America,* p. 255; Nilsson and Knutson, *Svenskarna i Worcester,* p. 121. It is quite possible that we might have reached somewhat different results if we had chosen other areas of investigation, e.g. Minneapolis's Sixth Ward or Brooklyn, New York. Compare Byron J. Nordström, "The Sixth Ward: A Minneapolis Swede Town in 1905," in Nils Hasselmo, ed., *Perspective on Swedish Immigration* (Minneapolis, 1978), and Per Olof Ödman, *De sista svenskarna: Om Svenskarna i Brooklyn, New York* (The last Swedes of Brooklyn, New York) (Helsingborg, 1976). The Swedish working-class community of Old Brooklyn and Bay Ridge consisted of 50,000 people in 1930.

16. The presentation of the social structure of the Worcester Swedes is based on Norman, *Från Bergslagen,* pp. 262–64.

17. See also Runblom and Norman, eds., *From Sweden to America,* pp. 264–66, where the social situation of the Chicago Swedes is discussed. For a further study of the Chicago Swedes, see Ulf Beijbom, *Swedes in Chicago: A Demographic and Social Study of the 1846–1880 Immigration,* Studia Historica Upsaliensia, no. 36 (Växjö, 1971).

18. Nilsson and Knutson, *Svenskarna i Worcester,* p. 140.

19. Sometimes this opinion could be maintained in a very naive ethnocentric way, as by the Swedish-American author Vilhelm Berger: "The Swedish-American is as awake and interested in general questions as the American himself or immigrants from other countries, but he does not throw himself into politics with his whole soul, he does not make politics into a means of support. He is an idealist, he prefers ideas to things . . ." (quoted in Biejbom, *Swedes in Chicago,* p. 315).

20. Influential persons among the different ethnic groups in America frequently called the attention of their countrymen to the importance of being politically active. This opinion was pointed out in the editorials of the papers. "Oscar Durante, owner and editor of Chicago's *L'Italia,* constantly urged newcomers toward the realization that economic advancement came after naturalization and participation in politics rather than before. . . . In America, he who does not vote does not 'get by.' " Humbert S. Nelli, *Italians in Chicago 1880-1930: A Study in Ethnic Mobility (New York, 1970), p. 88.*

21. Carl G. Norman, *Svenskarna i Worcester* (The Swedes in Worcester) (Prärieblomman, 1904), pp. 25-26. The author mentions that the engineer James Forsstedt was a member of the school board for several years, and John F. Lundberg was the first Swede to be a council member. During 1904 three Swedes were council members. The first to gain a federal position in Worcester was A. W. Ekström, who served as a deputy collector of internal

revenue, with his office in Worcester. Amandus N. Hagberg was the first Swede to have a position in the city hall at Worcester (sealer of weights and measures). Finally, two Swedes from Worcester had been members of the House of Representatives in Massachusetts. At this time the Swedish presence in Worcester dated back 30 years.

22. *Svea: Illustrerad veckotidning för svenskarna i Amerika, 1902* (Svea: Illustrated weekly magazine for the Swedes in America, 1902); Nilsson and Knutson, *Svenskarna i Worcester*, p. 26.

23. Eric Hobsbawm, *Labouring Men: Studies in the History of Labour* (London, 1971).

24. Anne-Marie Thunberg *et al.*, *Samverkansspiralen: Människan i informations- och kommunikations- samhället* (The helix of cooperation: Man in the society of information and communication) (Stockholm, 1978), pp. 80ff.

25. *Ibid.*, p. 84.

26. This approach explains neither the original cohesion of a subgroup especially in a more homogeneous population nor the reverse process that has happened so often, e.g. in the history of trade unions. There is no real discussion of how the goals are determined or how they may change over time. And what about the role of the local and national elite? The petrifying effects of formal organization, however, is mentioned in passing.

27. Lenin, *Vad bör göras?* (What has to be done?), *Valda verk*, 1 (Moscow, 1956):194; Rosa Luxemburg, "Sociala reformer eller revolution?" (Social reforms or revolution?) from *Ich war, ich bin, ich werde sein*, ed. Bo Gustafsson (Uddevalla, 1966), p. 76.

28. Lenin, *Vad bör göras*, p. 191.

29. Sten Carlsson, *Lantmanna-politiken och industrialismen: Partigruppering och opinionsförskjutningar i svensk politik 1890–1902* (Peasant politicians and industrialism: Grouping of parties and shifting opinions in Swedish policy 1890–1902) (Lund, 1953), pp. 19ff,; Leif Lewin, Bo Jansson, and Dag Sörbom, *The Swedish Electorate 1887–1968* (Uppsala, 1972), pp. 193, 198.

30. Egil Johansson, "The History of Literacy in Sweden in Comparison with Some Other Countries," *Educational Reports*, no. 2 (Umeå, 1973).

31. Thure Hanson, "Settlement, Growth and Progress of the Swedish People in Worcester," in *Swedish-American Souvenir* (Worcester, 1910). Compare also Nilsson and Knutson, *Svenskarna i Worcester*.

32. Thernstrom, *Other Bostonians*.

33. *Ibid.*; Sune Åkerman, "Swedish Migration and Social Mobility: A Tale of Three Cities," *Journal of Social Science History* 1 (1977): 178–209.

34. Frank Thistlewaite, "Migration from Europe Overseas in the Nineteenth and Twentieth Centuries," *Rapports*, vol 5, XIe Congrès International des Sciences Historiques (Uppsala, 1960).

35. Kenneth J. Moynihan, "Swedes and Yankees in Worcester Politics: A Protestant Partnership," unpublished paper (Assumption College, Worcester, Mass., 1979). The different political composition of the wards in Worcester is described by Moynihan on pp. 2–3.

36. James Weinstein, *The Decline of Socialism in America 1912–1925* (New York, 1967). The author also stresses the importance of the Socialist party of America.

37. Moynihan, "Swedes and Yankess," p. 8. The first real political question in which the Swedes became seriously engaged concerned public schools. The Irish and other Catholic groups within the Democratic party who

desired public financing of parochial schools were engaged in a dispute with the Republicans, who were against all religious interference in the tax-supported educational system. The Swedes, here, were mainly supporters of the Republicans. "The 'old parties' in this country have shown themselves, when forced by the situation, capable of a flexibility of one hundred and eighty degrees in their platforms, with extraordinary dexterity at 'stealing the thunder' and the votes of the new party." Perlman and Taft, *History of Labor*, 4:6–7; Koblik, oral research report.

38. A strong trade union could have changed this situation drastically, especially if introduced at the plants of Washburn & Moen, where so many Irish and Swedish workers were employed. On a nationwide scale labor's defeat in the struggle against the U.S. Steel Corporation in 1901 was decisive, since it helped to determine the fate of unionism in the metal manufacturing industries elsewhere. Perlman and Taft, *History of Labor*, p. 11. Apart from the difficulties in organizing the workers in the big plants of Worcester, the average size of the industries of the city was unfavorable to trade union work. Compared with other middle-sized cities like Fall River, Scranton, and Paterson, Worcester had very small industrial units. In 1890, for example, the average working force of Worcester was 20, compared with 62, 50, and 39 respectively for the other cities mentioned. John F. McClymer, "The Urban Context: A Tentative Framework for Studying Worcester, Massachusetts and Other Middle Sized Cities in Victorian America," unpublished paper (Assumption College, Worcester, Mass., 1979), p. 15.

39. Nelli, *Italians in Chicago*.

40. Beijbom, *Swedes in Chicago*, pp. 270ff.

41. Charles W. Estus, "A Swedish Working-Class Church: The Methodists of Quinsigamond Village, 1878–1900," unpublished paper (Assumption College, Worcester, Mass., 1979), p. 20.

42. Albert O. Hirschman, *Exit, Voice, and Loyalty: Responses to Decline in Firms, Organizations, and States* (Cambridge, Mass., 1970).

43. Compare the discussion about community continuity in Knights and Thernstrom, "Men in Motion."

44. Estus, "Swedish Working-Class Church," pp. 17–18, has noticed the stability of the religious leaders of the Methodist congregation of Quinsigamond, who were mainly skilled workers, foremen, or independent businessmen as well as house owners in the village. But he has not calculated a mobility rate for the unskilled workers who rented their homes or lived in the well-known "three-decker" of Washburn & Moen.

45. This point was stressed by the socialist agitator and trade union man Walfrid Engdahl (active in Minnesota in the 1910s and 1920s) in an interview with Sune Åkerman in Apr. 1971.

46. Koblik, oral research report.

47. Lescohier in Commons *et al.*, *History of Labour*, pp. 316ff. The author stresses that American wage earners have been peculiarly susceptible to control and stimulation through welfare and personnel programs established by their employers. His explanation is that a substantial percentage of the immigrants as well as the domestic labor supply came directly from the country.

48. Norman, *Svenskarna i Worcester*.

49. The same observation has been made by Charlotte Erickson for such

an easily assimilated group as the English, in *Invisible Immigrants* (London, 1972), pp. 64ff.

50. Koblik, oral research report; Moynihan, "Swedes and Yankess," p. 8.

51. Runblom and Norman, eds., *From Sweden to America*, pp. 335ff. See also Bo Kronborg, Thomas Nilsson, and Andres Svalestuen, *Nordic Population Mobility* (Bergen, 1977).

52. Moynihan, "Swedes and Yankeess," p. 12. See also Charles Nutt, *History of Worcester and Its People* (New York, 1919), vol. 1. The ethnic composition of Worcester is described in McClymer, "The Urban Context," p. 9.

12

For or against Americanization? The Case of the Finnish Immigrant Radicals

AUVO KOSTIAINEN

The socioeconomic background of Finnish immigrants arriving in America did not differ notably from that of other new immigrant groups. They were mostly peasants or agrarian workers coming from rural Finland. The specific features of the small Finnish immigrant group[1] were their language and culture, which shaped their immigrant community in the New World. A special characteristic of the Finns was that they had had to live under the Russification programs of the czarist rule until 1917. At the end of the nineteenth and the beginning of the twentieth century a good number of Finnish politicians escaped from Finland to America, among them several socialist leaders.

Finnish-Americans were employed like other new immigrants in mines, factories, building, fishing, farming, and forestry. Since they were unskilled, they were employed in the lowest paid and more dangerous jobs. However, within each immigrant group soon developed a special immigrant culture including different kinds of societies, literature, newspapers, etc. Among the American Finns the immigrant culture also flourished in a variety of forms and forums. More than 98% of the Finns were literate, and they were used to fairly democratic ways of handling issues in their autonomous home country, with its rich forms of cultural life. For example, the feudal system of landowning had never really taken root in the north of Europe. This was quite exceptional when compared with the low literacy rates and authoritarian political cultures of immigrants arriving from southern or eastern Europe.[2] A coherent cultural background helped the Finns to organize in numerous churches, temperance groups, and, from the 1890s on, in workers' associations. Many studies about Finnish-Americans emphasize the development of Finnish organizations in America and how the immigrants sought a better life through collective effort rather than through individual enterprise.[3]

This article examines one of these immigrant organizations, the Finnish-American workers' societies, and the attitude of Finnish radicals in America[4] toward the process of Americanization. What factors facilitated it? What factors retarded it? The study then proceeds with an examination of Finnish-American labor groups and their activities in the framework of Finnish-American "hall socialism," their activities in educating youth as Americans and internationalists, their attitude toward the environment in the workplace, and their aims in the naturalization process. The main sources for this study were materials produced by Finnish-American radical groups: proceedings, resolutions, and publications.

An effort will also be made to compare the Finnish-American workers' associations with other groups within the Finnish-American community as well as in the immigrant community as a whole. The term "Americanization" in this context means a consciously articulated movement during the period of World War I to strip the immigrant of his native culture and remold him in the form of an American along Anglo-Saxon lines. The term also describes a long-term process of integration of the immigrant worker into American society, primarily into the American working class.[5]

In the Finnish-American community the church was the most notable and influential institution, particularly in the late 1800s. It reinforced Finnish nationalistic sentiment by keeping contact with parishes in the "old country" and by emphasizing and maintaining contacts with the Finnish church.[6] This can also be seen in the name of the largest Finnish church in America, the Suomi Synod (Finland Synod). Contacts with the church in Finland were frequent, but in the twentieth century, with the polarization of the Finnish immigrant community between the churches and the socialists, the church started increasingly to stress loyalty to the United States. This became apparent especially during the time of the great strike waves of 1907 through the establishment of the antisocialist leagues, and during and after World War I, when "loyal Finnish-Americans" made an effort to emphasize contacts with the American community and accused the radicals of un-American revolutionary activities when these wanted to give their support to the ideals of the Russian Bolshevik Revolution.[7] John Wargelin, the president of Suomi College, for example, dedicated his book *The Americanization of the Finns* to this cause.[8]

Yet the Suomi Synod was not completely an Americanizing institution. An important analysis by Taisto John Niemi of efforts of the Book Concern of the synod to promote Americanization through its publications finds that these efforts were mainly indirect. The Book Concern was primarily interested in improving the ability of Finns to understand English, yet an overwhelming portion of the literature published by the Book Concern in 1901–50 was in Finnish and dealt not with American society but mostly with religious and ethical questions.[9]

Set apart from the church and temperance groups stood the Finnish-American labor movement. It was actively supported by about one-fourth of the Finns in America, or about the same number as those actively supporting the churches. The temperance group was notably smaller than those mentioned above, and members of it were usually also members of churches or workers' associations. Those Finnish-Americans who did not belong to any of these three groups were either organizationally inactive or belonged to certain less significant groups.

The most important organizational stages in the development of the Finnish-American labor movement were the creation of the Finnish Socialist Federation (Yhdysvaltain Suomalainen Sosialistijärjestö) (FSF) in 1906, and its subsequent affiliation with the Socialist party of America; and the radical split in 1913–14, when about 3,000 members quit the FSF when its membership was at a peak of 13,500 and joined the syndicalist Industrial Workers of the World (IWW). Following the Russian Bolshevik Revolution in 1917, the communist movement began to emerge, and in 1919–21 the majority of the FSF became communist. In the early 1920s the Finns accounted for almost one-half of the membership of the legal communist party, the Workers party of America.[10] When tracing the reasons for the Finns' activities in the radical groups, the old-country background has frequently been referred to: the rising socialist movement in Finland, the effect of "industrial immigrants" from southern Finland, the Finnish labor leaders who moved to North America, and so forth. The effect of the American environment with its labor conflicts and need for associational life has also drawn attention, as well as the influence of the international labor movement deriving its force from Europe and, especially after the Russian Revolution, from Soviet Russia.[11]

There are several ways to look at the attitude of the Finnish-American radicals toward Americanization. In studies of the Finnish-American working-class movement, a general conclusion has been put forward that its most important aspect was "hall socialism."[12] This term indicates a large mix of social and political activities carried on in Finnish workers' halls in North America. For example, in 1912 a report of the Executive Committee of the FSF listed information from

189 Finnish socialist branches with the following subgroups: 86 agitation committees, 12 women's clubs, 107 theater groups, 23 glee clubs, 28 bands, 91 sewing circles, and 53 athletic clubs. In addition, the activities included English courses, summer and Sunday schools for children, and buying, selling, and publishing literature. The branches also provided libraries and reading rooms for the members.[13] The workers' associations often owned buildings of their own where activities took place, and which especially in smaller communities served as public meeting places.

When historians claim that the Finnish-American workers' movement was hall socialism, they argue that it expressed a generalized class consciousness within the framework of workers' associations, which also served the immigrants as important ethnic institutions. John I. Kolehmainen says that they never lost that basic orientation and were far richer in social, educational, and cultural uplift than in political achievement.[14] This way of thinking emphasizes the sociocultural functions within the Finnish-American labor movement and the concentration of these activities around the Finnish-American community. The Finns worked almost exclusively within their own nationality, and thus hall socialism helped to preserve the old-country background and traditions in the new environment. In other words, hall socialism was ethnocentric and worked against Americanization, assimilation, and the international workers' movement.

The opinion presented above was a major concern of the growing Finnish-American labor movement from its very beginning. When the first Finnish workers' societies in the United States were formed in the 1890s, the question of their relationship to the American and Finnish labor movements was raised. The first of the societies, Imatra of Brooklyn, New York, has always been accused of being a representative of bourgeois reformism relying heavily on Finnish nationalistic ideas. Still, its by-laws provided for contacts with American workers' associations.[15] The developments that led to the formation of the Finnish Socialist Federation in 1906 were a result of the growing influence of the supporters of international socialism, which meant above all contacts with American workers and ultimately affiliation with the Socialist party of America. This kind of attitude was seen in, for instance, the resolution accepted at the conference of Finnish workers' associations in Cleveland, Ohio, in 1904, which stated that "only by joining the Socialist Party the Finnish-American labor movement will have the opportunity to have an effect on the development of the socialist movement in America."[16]

In the following decades contacts with American labor were a frequent topic of discussion. Thus in 1912 the convention of the FSF urged all branches to cooperate in agitation work with the English-language party branches, particularly during elections, although it was recognized that the language difficulties might pose great problems.[17] The culmination of demands to "Americanize" (or to integrate) the Finnish-American working-class movement occurred in communist circles. From the early 1920s this aspect was continuously emphasized, and references were made to the Third International, established in 1919 in Moscow to unite the workers of the world in a fight against capitalism. The International, better known as the Communist International or Comintern, flooded workers in other countries with information and demanded international solidarity of them. In the case of America this meant above all that the ethnic minorities should become a part of the larger American society. It was understood that internationalism in America would be achieved through Americanization. Cooperation among ethnic groups was a sign of international solidarity, but according to Comintern orders this was not the final aim. The purpose was to achieve contact with the large American working class, i.e. with English-speaking workers. When all the workers in America were amalgamated into one united working class, they could affect the course of American history and take power. Then they would be able to overpower capitalism; the next step would be the gradual unification of the workers' states of the world and, according to Marxist theory, the dissolution of separate states.

The Comintern also sent occasional messages specifically to Finnish workers in America. They urged the Finns to give up the "nationally concentrated activities" that had been carried on in the Socialist party, a tradition that was continued in the communist ranks.[18]

In 1924–25 a strong campaign of Bolshevization was conducted by the Comintern to purge the communist ranks of bourgeois elements. One of the primary aims in this campaign was to tighten control of the communist groups in all countries and get them under closer supervision of the Comintern. In the United States Bolshevization meant the move from ethnic-based organization to multinational, or international, party organization, where all the different nationalities could work together and at the same time become Americanized. However, in this process many Finnish-American communists left the party because they did not want to give up the rich social and cultural activities maintained by the Finnish communist branches. Only about one-third of the former FSF (from 1923 called Workers Partyn Suomalainen Järjestö, the Finnish Federation of the Workers party, FFWP) joined the international cells. Contact with those members who had left was re-established in 1927 when a new Finnish Workers Organization (Suomalainen Työväenjärjestö) was formed and they again were subservient to the American communist movement.[19]

Finnish-American communism, however, was still not American enough after these organizational changes. A new crisis was born in the late 1920s, which was connected with the "right-wing deviations" in the Finnish-American radical cooperatives. "Help" was received from the Comintern after a visit of American and Finnish-American communist leaders to Moscow in the winter of 1930. The Executive Committee of the Comintern sent a letter to the central organs of the American Communist party regarding the Finns. It paid special attention to hall socialism and the form it took among Finnish-Americans. On the one hand the Finns were given credit for good organizational ability, but on the other hand hall activities were seen by the Comintern as proof of an inability to get rid of national limits and to assimilate into American society.[20] Therefore, contacts with Americans should be established on a more solid basis. The Comintern stated:

> Away with national isolation! For that purpose organized contact and brotherhood with other American workers should be established, it should be made a point of honor for the Finnish Federation to take part actively and in large numbers in the class struggles and class organizations of the American proletariat. Special attention has to be paid to the American-born generation to make it active in the proletarian struggle. Finnish workers must necessarily become a part of the revolutionary movement of the American working class. Americanization is for them the most important step in order to become real internationalists.[21]

Finnish-American communists were thus urged to become part of the American and international working class. However, it is obvious that the purpose was not to become an integral part of the American capitalist system but to prepare for the future American socialist society.

But how legitimate actually were the claims of negative attitude toward American society and Americanization by Finnish immigrant workers? It seems that the isolationist tendencies of the hall activities have generally been overemphasized. First, we have to consider that one of the basic themes in the organized socialist movement is internationalism, and a great majority of the Finnish-American workers' organizations saw themselves as part of the American and even the international working class from the very beginning. This tendency was seen in their first efforts to organize in the late 1800s. For this purpose they joined the American socialist and communist ranks and the Industrial Workers of the World.

The fact also remains that, although Finnish-American workers' organizations were supposed to be in close contact with the rest of society, their functions greatly concentrated on the activities around the Finn halls. But we have to remember that in the halls and in Finnish workers' organizations generally there were several aspects that pushed the members toward American society. The immigrant papers were always a means to make the readers acquainted with the new society. They included news from Finland in varying degrees as well as news dealing with immigrant society. The characterization by P. George Hummasti of the nature of the Finnish-American working-class newspaper is valid for the functions of all the immigrant press in America:

> It helped them [the immigrants] retain important contact with Finland and with other Finns in America, while at the same time introducing them gradually to American mores and politics and to American material goods. Thus it, in connection with other immigrant institutions, made possible their gradual and sane acculturation to a new society and saved them the bewildering, and often crushing, experience of having to adapt to a myriad of new situations simultaneously. Even the working class newspaper, which from the *Amerikan Työmies* in 1900 on stressed the rapid assimilation of its readers into at least the political and economic life of America, served as a brake on this process by providing these same readers with a source of information and contact within the cultural substance of their Finnish heritage.[22]

The organization of the Finnish-American workers' movement generally required the participation of the Finns in party activities at many different levels in addition to their own branches. They had to participate in city and district organizations as well as at national conventions, where they could not use Finnish. Here they had contacts with workers of other nationalities, as well as in celebrations held to honor certain international workers' holidays like May Day or the Russian Revolution. In addition, festivities were organized to support workers in different countries or, for instance, to help Soviet Russia recover from the civil war and the famine years.[23] In these kinds of activities the feeling of internationalism formed an important ideological basis.

The foregoing makes it clear that the indictment of Finnish-American radicalism, with its attendant hall socialism, as isolated from the rest of society, and from other workers' groups, is indeed one-sided. Actually hall activities were a suitable means of keeping immigrants' cultural and intellectual life alive in a strange environment. It made it easier to adjust to a new language, customs, government, and workplace. It prevented anomie and the loss of worker consciousness. In this way hall socialism prepared a kind of "soft landing" for Finnish immigrant workers in America, and it contributed notably to the Americanization process. Hall socialism also played its part in radicalizing Finnish-American workers. The functions around the halls provided a financial basis for ideological work; without those forms of activity, socialism, communism, and the IWW would hardly have gained so many supporters among American Finns. All three causes derived great strength from Finnish "hall socialism."

During the course of the Finnish-American labor movement the education of young people to be Americans has always held a very important position. As early as 1909 the FSF convention gave a general recommendation to the locals to found young socialist leagues.[24] As a sign of growing interest in the education of socialist children in 1912, a resolution was accepted by the FSF that in summer and Sunday schools education of children based on class consciousness should be increased.[25] Emphasis was always laid on the fact that the language in young people's and children's organizations should be English, and they should join English-language organizations. Quite early in the Finnish-language socialist papers special sections were reserved for youngsters and children, and the language used there was always English.

F. J. Syrjälä, the Finnish-American social democratic leader, summarized well the ideas of his group about the class education of second-generation immigrants: "In spite of its international basis, socialism in America must have an American interpretation. No Finnish, German or Russian form of socialism will ever have a success in the American working class. Only the American form of socialism, whichever it will be, shall complete that noble ideology in this country. . . . It is not possible to think that the youth which is born and educated here and gained its experience here, would be the supporter of a Finnish-American working class movement."[26]

In the 1920s the communist FSF (or FFWP) strongly urged second-generation Finnish-Americans to cooperate with the American communist movement proper. In 1924 the convention of the FFWP proclaimed that special attention should be paid to these sections, and financial and other kinds of assistance would be offered by the branches and by the federation itself to the communist Young Workers League. In addition, the children's and youngsters' clubs should use English, if possible.[27] These activities among second-generation Finnish-Americans were so successful that Finnish-Americans constituted a large proportion of the Young Communist League. In 1929 it was estimated that about one-third of the league's members were Finns, the second largest nationality group after the Jews.[28] In later decades American-born Finns were to gain an even more notable position in the leadership of the Communist party of the United States,[29] most prominently the American Finn Gus Hall, who was a presidential candidate in the U.S. presidential election in 1976.

Finnish-American workers were in frequent contact with American society through employment. At workplaces they met with other nationalities and came into contact with trade unions and their representatives. Usually the contacts thus established were more intense during times of conflict, as during the strikes of 1907 and 1916 in the Mesabi range in northern Minnesota, in 1913–14 in the copper country of northern Michigan, or in the great steel strike of 1919. In these conflicts the class consciousness of the immigrant workers was raised, and ultimately Finnish-Americans did join American trade unions in large numbers. Their participation in the American trade union movement remained notably above the average union membership of American workers,[30] and also the second generation seems to have been at home in the unions. Many of them held leadership positions during the organizational campaigns of the 1930s and in the AFL-CIO.

A concrete example of the attitudes of Finnish-American radicals toward Americanization may be seen in their attitudes toward naturalization. When the immigrants arrived in America, a large number of them planned to stay for only a few years, perhaps somewhat longer, but usually they dreamed of returning to the old country to establish their homes on a solid basis there after having saved some money. However, about 75% of them remained permanently in America.

Those who stayed in the United States were soon faced with the question of naturalization in order to establish their position in the new society and to vote. Generally American Finns seem to have been quite passive in this respect. For example, in 1910, 45.6% of all foreign-born adult males[31] were citizens, while 30.6% of all Finnish immigrants were naturalized. In 1920 the percentages were 47.8 and 39.2 respectively.[32] During that ten-year period the number of naturalized Finns had grown notably, but they were still less active in seeking citizenship than foreign-born males in general.

William Carlson Smith has observed that ignorance of language is an important barrier to assimilation.[33] Because Finnish differs totally from English and other Anglo-Saxon languages, Finnish immigrants faced abnormally great difficulties in acquiring necessary skills in English.[34] It also seems that the rank-and-file immigrant knew little about the naturalization process and the requirements connected with it. This became evident, for instance, in the war years when hundreds, perhaps thousands, of immigrants went to Canada to avoid military service in the U.S. Army, among them many Finnish-American radicals. A great number of radicals and aliens were arrested because they were ignorant of the duties involved with military service or did not want to go into the Army.[35]

For those willing to become naturalized, federal and state programs offered courses that taught the necessary skills. But the immigrants themselves also actively worked toward this goal. John Wargelin says that the Finns in general were "very anxious" to become naturalized, particularly during World War I, when they founded and actively participated in many organizations working toward this goal.[36] When we examine the Finnish-American workers' organizations, we find that the question of naturalization was raised for the first time at the 1909 convention of the Finnish Socialist Federation. At that time a general resolution was adopted that each Finnish socialist branch should form a naturalization committee to help persons willing to become naturalized. The resolution grew out of a discussion based on the proposal by a certain A. Pekkola, who demanded that each member of the FSF should become a citizen in order to go to the polls.[37]

It seems that interest grew as the naturalization statutes and requirements were made known to Finnish workers in America.[38] In 1906, 11.2% of the members of the FSF were U.S. citizens, in 1912, 19.9% of the members, and in 1920, 22.4%; in the communist FFWP in 1923 the percentage was as high as 36.1.[39] The questionnaires the foregoing numbers are based on were not returned by every branch and thus the percentages must be interpreted with caution. However, they show the same tendency as that presented above in regard to foreign-born Finnish adult males. It is probable that the fast growth in the willingness of the radicals to become naturalized was largely due to the period of World War I, when the pressure against radical and alien elements was growing in intensity. Antagonism against these groups culminated in the famous "red raids" under Attorney General A. Mitchell Palmer, when thousands of radicals were arrested and many of them deported from the United States.[40] This and the drive for restrictions on immigration[41] embodied in the laws of the early 1920s further pushed radical Finns toward naturalization.

As practically no new blood was entering immigrant communities, contacts with American society increased with the growing second generation of Finnish-Americans. This happened in the great majority of Finnish-American communities, from the far left to the far right. Table 1 shows at which time a sample of foreign-born Finns in the United States was naturalized. It is divided according to the three

Table 1. *Timing of Naturalization for Foreign-Born Finns.*

Citizenship Received after Residence of	"Church" %		"Labor" %		"Other Groups" %		Total %	
10 years or less	50	(27.3)	59	(26.1)	28	(25.9)	137	(26.5)
11 to 20 years	42	(22.9)	79	(35.0)	30	(27.8)	151	(29.2)
21 years or more	55	(30.1)	56	(24.8)	25	(23.1)	136	(26.3)
Year unknown	28	(15.3)	15	(6.6)	15	(13.9)	58	(11.2)
No citizenship	8	(4.4)	17	(7.5)	10	(9.3)	35	(6.8)
Total	183	(100.0)	226	(100.0)	108	(100.9)	517	(100.0)

major groupings in the Finnish-American community, the "church Finns," the "labor Finns," and "others" prior to 1939.[42]

In the sample there were 274 women and 243 men, which reflects an unusual division of sex, apparently owing to the greater mortality of men, since males were generally dominant in Finnish emigration. A total of 43.7% of the persons were counted as "Labor," while 35.4% were counted as "Church" people.[43]

A. William Hoglund has argued that Finnish-American socialists tried to become naturalized as early as possible in order to be able to go to the polls.[44] When we examine Table 1, we find that about one-fourth of the immigrants were naturalized within ten years of their arrival in the United States. A total of 27.3% of the "Church" people became naturalized prior to ten years of stay in the country, while 26.1% of the "Labor" were naturalized within the same period. However, when we look at the first twenty years, we find that 61.1% of the "Labor" were naturalized compared with 50.2% of the "Church" people.[45] It seems that notably fewer of the "Labor" people were naturalized after 21 years or more of stay in the United States than of the "Church" people. These numbers seem to give only weak support to the Hoglund thesis of the readiness of the radicals to become naturalized early.

The question of why there are more "Labor" than "Church" people who did not become U.S. citizens at all still remains. Most of these persons arrived in the country before 1900–1920, but after more than 40 years they were still Finnish citizens. Probably some of them had a kind of emotional attachment to their mother country and decided never to become citizens of other countries. On the other hand, there were language problems that made it difficult to become naturalized, since quite a number of older immigrants had lived for decades in ethnic communities where English was not "necessary." In addition, when we consider Finnish-American radicals, they were perhaps persons so strongly opposed to the American capitalistic system that they never wanted to become citizens within that system. This attitude is reflected by the mass movement of Finnish-American radicals to the Soviet Union in the late 1920s and particularly in the early 1930s, when they wanted to leave the "rotten capitalistic world" and to build a new "labor republic" in the Soviet Union.[46]

Finally, we can state that there is discernible a certain difference when we compare the process of Americanization in church circles with that in the labor movement: the so-called church Finns were largely "compelled" to assimilate. They were basically nationalistic, but the decision to favor "loyalism" forced them to become more American. At the same time they faced a situation where the younger generation was becoming assimilated, and the Finnish-American church would sooner or later become "American." In the church the transition to the use of English lessened its nationalistic features, and this process was finally completed in the 1960s when major Finnish churches merged with American churches.[47]

Within organized labor the Americanization process proceeded in different ways. Finnish participation in the IWW diminished clearly in the 1920s with the fading importance of the movement. Douglas J. Ollila states that "the syndicalist Finns Americanized very rapidly because the IWW was a completely American organization."[48] The core of Finns in the IWW was foreign-born, as was the case for the supporters of the Socialist party of America, who finally during the period of World War II decided to quit all political parties in order to wait for the creation of an "influential political labor movement."[49] The social democrats thus seem to have preserved most of the tradition of hall socialism when they stayed out of political parties and directed their attention more purely to their ethnic institutions.

The communist group appears to have been perhaps best assimilated. A great number of them—excluding those who were ousted because of ideological disputes—became members of American radical groups. In the 1940s Finnish-American communists become integrated into the American Communist party, although some degree of ethnic functions still persisted thereafter.[50]

In the socialist- and communist-dominated cooperative movement, which had a very strong foothold among the American Finns, Americanization also proceeded rapidly. From the beginning the cooperative movement emphasized contacts with international and American cooperative movements. From the 1920s the use of English became more common, and particularly after World War II Americanization proceeded swiftly. Finnish-American cooperative stores gradually merged with the other American stores.[51]

Some general conclusions may be drawn from the discussion presented above. First, it has to be stressed that the international labor movement in its various forms exercised a strong effect on Finnish-Americans and their willingness to become Americanized. As was pointed out earlier, internationalism was one of the central themes in their minds from the beginning of the organized labor movement. It led them to join American radical organizations and to participate in them, and it made the communist-minded Finnish-Americans obey orders from the Communist International. Consequently, we may state that radical workers' organizations clearly pushed their members toward Americanization and assimilation. Behind this kind of behavior lay two ways of thinking: immigrant workers should be able to take advantage of the economic opportunities offered by America, and at the same time they should become eligible to go to the polls, which would be the way to influence and change the future course of American society.

On the other hand, the human desires of individuals in many cases slowed down the Americanization process. For example, inability to learn English, contacts with and longing for the old country, or dislike of the American capitalist system often became the final obstacle to naturalization. It is difficult, however, to examine these factors in detail.

But how do the facts that have been presented in the foregoing actually fit in with the general theory of American ethnicity and immigrant culture? Traditionally American history writing stressed the concept of the American melting pot, but in recent decades a growing number of historians have stressed America's cultural pluralism.[52] Timothy L. Smith has attacked the pluralist ideas and claimed that assimilationists still persist. Rather than being victims of a coercive Americanization policy, the immigrants pursued assimilation as a means of advancing their fortunes and those of their children, he argues.[53]

It is not possible, however, to agree completely with Smith, nor with the cultural pluralist theorists. This special group of immigrant workers pursued Americanization and assimilation notably because of their own will and ideology when preparing for the future socialistic America. But their positive attitude toward assimilation was also affected by coercive Americanization: U.S. immigration policy, the question of loyalty, and the attitudes of the mass media and the school system.[54] Additional pressure was exerted by employment policy, which dealt with the immigrant workers unfavorably.

The above discussion sheds additional light on the complex process of Americanization of immigrant workers. In this connection we have to remember that Finnish-American radicals were part of a small immigrant group, the fate of which is always somewhat different from that of a large ethnic minority, like the Italians, Poles, and Jews. Also, the radical Finns were unusual in the sense that they were exceptionally active in the political labor movement, although their activities stressed ethnic social functions in addition to political ones. It made it easy for them to adopt attitudes different from those of other workers, who organized only in the "conservative" trade unions or who did not organize at all.

NOTES

1. The number of Finnish immigrants to North America prior to 1930 was about 350,000. At its peak in 1920 the number of Finns living in the United States was about 150,000. *Fourteenth Census of the United States*, "Population 1920" (Washington, D.C., 1922), 2:689.

2. Ingrid Lehman has compared the background of the Finns and the Italians more carefully. She has also analyzed the factors influencing the willingness to participate in the radical movements of the United States. See Ingrid Lehman, "Ethnicity and Class Consciousness: Towards a Theory of Immigrant Radicalism in the United States" (M.A. thesis, University of Minnesota, 1974), esp. p. 87.

3. A. William Hoglund, *Finnish Immigrants in America, 1880–1920* (Madison, Wis., 1960); John I. Kolehmainen and George W. Hill, *Haven in the Woods: The Story of the Finns in Wisconsin* (Madison, Wis., 1965).

4. The term "Finnish radicals in America" is used here to describe those who were members of radical political organizations (socialist, communist or syndicalist-oriented Industrial Workers of the World), or were sympathetic to them.

5. For an extensive discussion of the meaning of Americanization, assimilation, and acculturation, see Milton M. Gordon, *Assimilation in American Life: The Role of Race, Religion and National Origins* (New York, 1964), esp. pp. 60–83.

6. See, e.g., Douglas J. Ollila, Jr., "The Finnish-American Church Organizations," in Vilho Niitemaa *et al.*, eds., *Old Friends—Strong Ties* (Vaasa, Finland, 1976), p. 169.

7. See Elis Sulkanen, *Amerikan suomalaisen työväenliikkeen historia* (The history of the Finnish-American labor movement) (Fitchburg, Mass., 1951), pp. 140–43; S. Ilmonen, *Amerikan suomalaisen sivistyshistoria: Johtavia aatteita, harrastuksia, yhteispyrintöjä ja tapahtumia siirtokansan keskuudessa, Jälkimmäinen osa* (The cultural history of the Finns in America, pt. II) (Hancock, Mich., 1931), pp. 11–17.

8. (Hancock, Mich., 1924), pp. 103–5.

9. Taisto John Niemi, "The Finnish Lutheran Book Concern, 1900–1950: A Historical and Developmental Study" (Ph.D. thesis, University of Michigan, 1960), esp. the list of published works, pp. 306–18.

10. For a general survey of the history of the Finnish-American labor movement, see Auvo Kostiainen, "Finnish-American Workmen's Associations," in *Old Friends—Strong Ties*, pp. 205–32.

11. For a discussion of the background of Finnish-American radicalism,

see, e.g., Auvo Kostiainen, *The Forging of Finnish-American Communism, 1917–1924: A Study in Ethnic Radicalism,* Annales Universitatis Turkuensis, ser. B. pt. 147 (Turku, 1978), esp. pp. 32–37; see also Reino Kero, "The Roots of Finnish-American Left-Wing Radicialism," *Publications of the Institute of General History University of Turku Finland,* no. 5 (Turku, 1973), pp. 45–55.

12. This view is seen in, e.g., the works by John I. Kolehmainen, the pioneer of Finnish-American history writing. See, for instance, John I. Kolehmainen, *From Lake Erie's Shores to the Mahoning and Monongahela Valleys: A History of the Finns in Ohio, Western Pennsylvania and West Virginia* (New York Mills, Minn., 1977), pp. 179–212.

13. *Suomalaisten sosialistiosastojen ja työväenyhdistysten viidennen eli suomalaisen sosialistijärjestön kolmannen edustajakokouksen Pöytäkirja 1–5, 7–10 p. kesäkuuta, 1912* (FSF Proceedings, 1912), ed. Aku Rissanen (Fitchburg, Mass., n.d.) pp. 53–55.

14. Kolehmainen, *Lake Erie's Shores,* p. 212. However, it should be borne in mind that, in this connection, Kolehmainen refers only to the Finns in Ohio, western Pennsylvania, and West Virginia.

15. See, e.g., F. J. Syrjälä, *Historia-aiheita ameriikan suomalaisesta työväenliikkeestä* (History of the Finnish-American labor movement) (Fitchburg, Mass., n.d.), pp. 56–57.

16. Quoted from *ibid.,* p. 60.

17. FSF Proceedings, 1912, p. 310.

18. For a more detailed discussion of these developments, see Kostiainen, *Forging of Finnish-American Communism,* esp. pp. 150–60.

19. See Auvo Kostiainen, "The Finns and the Crisis over 'Bolshevization' in the Workers' Party, 1924–1925," in Michael G. Karni, Matti E. Kaups, and Douglas J. Ollila, Jr., eds., *The Finnish Experience in the Western Great Lakes: New Perspectives* (Vammala, Finland, 1975), esp. pp. 182–85.

20. See *Taistelu oikeistovaaraa vastaan: Kominternin opetuksia amerikansuomalaiselle työväelle* (The Communist International on the right-wing danger) (Superior, Wis., n.d.), p. 18.

21. *Ibid.,* p. 32.

22. P. George Hummasti, " 'The Working Man's Daily Bread: Finnish-American Working Class Newspapers, 1900–1921," in Michael G. Karni and Douglas J. Ollila, Jr., eds., *For the Common Good: Finnish Immigrants and the Radical Response to Industrial America* (Superior, Wis., 1977), p. 180.

23. For the organizational position and duties of the Finns in, e.g., the communist movement, see Kostiainen, *Forging of Finnish-American Communism,* pp. 152–58.

24. *Kolmannen amerikan suomalaisen sosialistijärjestön edustajakokouksen pöytäkirja, Kokous pidetty Hancockissa, Mich. 23–30 p. Elok., 1909* (FSF Proceedings, 1909), ed. F. J. Syrjälä (Fitchburg, Mass., n.d.), p. 245.

25. FSF Proceedings, 1912, p. 310.

26. Syrjälä, *Historia,* pp. 219–20.

27. *"Workers partyn suomalaisen järjestön maaliskuun 3, 4, 5 ja 6 päivinä 1924, pidetyn edustajakokouksen pöytäkirja"* (FFWP Proceedings, 1924), *Työmies,* 3 Apr. 1924.

28. "Hyne's Exhibit No. 16, D (The Results of National Registration, July–August, 1929, of the Young C.L. of the U.S. of America)," *Investigation of Communist Propaganda. Hearings before a Special Committee to Investigate Communist Activities in the United States of the House of Representatives,* 71st Cong., 2d Sess. (Washington, D.C., 1930), pt. 5, 4:805.

29. Kostiainen, *Forging of Finnish-American Communism*, p. 193.

30. At the end of 1911 a total of 27.3% of the members of the FSF belonged to a union. FSF Proceedings, 1912, p. 54. In 1923 the respective number for the communist FSF was 22.1. "Suomalaisen sosialisti järjestön yhdeksännen edustajakokouksen pöytäkirja. Laadittu Chicagossa, Ill., helmik, 28 p.—4 p. maalisk., 1923 pidetyssä S. S. Järjestön edustajakokouksessa" (FSF Proceedings, 1923), *Työmies*, 8 Apr. 1923. In 1924 it was estimated that 32.1% of the members of the Workers party of America were union members. See *The Fourth National Convention of the Workers (Communist) Party of America* (Chicago, Ill., n.d.), pp. 40–41. In 1930 11.6% of the total of 29.4 million nonagricultural employees in the United States were union members. *Historical Statistics of the United States, Colonial Times to 1970, Bicentennial Edition*, pt. 1 (Washington, D.C., 1975), p. 178.

31. Not until 1920 had all the states in the United States ratified the Nineteenth Amendment, which proposed women's suffrage.

32. Hoglund, *Finnish Immigrants*, pp. 112–14.

33. William Carlson Smith, *Americans in the Making* (New York, 1970), pp. 147–49.

34. See Jouni Ekonen, "Amerikansuomalaisen työväenliikkeen suhtautuminen Yhdysvaltain presidentinvaaleihin vuosina 1908–1920" (Finnish-American labor and the American presidential elections) (M.A. thesis, University of Turku, 1973), p. 28; cf. Wargelin, *Americanization*, pp. 103–5.

35. See, e.g., Douglas J. Ollila, "Defects in the Melting Pot: Finnish Immigrants and the Loyalty Issue, 1917–1921," *Turun Historiallinen Arkisto* 31 (1976):398–99, and Wargelin, *Americanization*, p. 171.

36. Wargelin, *Americanization*, pp. 171–72; cf. Ollila, "Defects."

37. FSF Proceedings, 1909, p. 247.

38. For instance, *Köyhälistön nuija* 2 (1908):155–75.

39. Information is based on the returned questionnaires. The numbers are from T.H. (Taavi Heino), "Katsaus liikkeeseemme" (Our Movement), *Köyhälistön nuija* 1 (1907):40–41; FSF Proceedings, 1912, p. 12; *Suomalaisen sosialistijärjestön seitsemännen edustajakokouksen pöytäkirja. Laadittu Waukeganissa, Ill. 25–31 P. Jouluk., 1920 pidetystä S. S. Järjestön edustajakokouksesta* (FSF Proceedings, 1920), ed. Aaro Hyrske (Superior, Wis., 1921), p. 25; FSF Proceedings, 1923.

40. For more on this period, see, e.g., William Preston, Jr., *Aliens and Dissenters: Federal Suppression of Radicals, 1903–1933* (New York, 1966), pp. 208–37.

41. For instance, John Higham, *Strangers in the Land: Patterns of American Nativism 1860–1925* (New York, 1973), esp. pp. 300–30.

42. The information is derived from the questionnaires returned to the Department of History, University of Turku, in 1968. The first 1,000 questionnaires were examined for this study, 517 of which included data about immigrants arriving in the United States. A total of 439 (84.9%) of them had arrived in the country prior to 1920. The classification of the persons according to "Church," "Labor," and "Other" groups was accomplished by considering the societies they belonged to and were or had been active in, and the papers they subscribed to, such as the "churchly" *Amerikan Suometar*, "liberal" *New Yorkin Uutiset*, socialist *Raivaaja*, socialist and later communist *Työmies*, and syndicalist *Industrialisti*. The sample included several persons who could not be counted as clearly "Church" or "Labor" and they

were included in "Others." Thus the division in Table 1 is not on a social basis. Had we used social status as a criterion, almost every person would have been included in the "Labor" group.

43. The proportions mentioned are very different from those given at the beginning of this article, which stated that about one-fourth of the Finns belonged to "Church" and one-fourth to "Labor." The difference is apparently due to the timing of the question: after a long stay in America most Finns had at some time belonged to some organization, even for a shorter period. The same was true with newspaper subscriptions. Most Finns had at some time ordered Finnish-language newspapers. These factors made the proportions belonging to "Church" or "Labor" high, but it is assumed that this does not give a wrong impression in regard to the naturalization problem.

44. Hoglund, *Finnish Immigrants,* pp. 113–14.

45. The reports of the Immigration Commission of 1910 show that Finns were quite active in becoming naturalized. For example, the report states that 65.7% of foreign-born male Finns 21 years of age or over at the time of coming to the United States were fully naturalized after 10 or more years in the country. The respective number for all immigrants was 56.9%. The Finns also appear to be close to the top among the new immigrant nationalities in seeking citizenship. *Reports of the Immigration Commission,* Abstracts of Reports of the Immigration Commission (New York, 1970), 1:485–87.

46. It is estimated that about 10,000 Finns from the United States and Canada left for the Soviet Union in the early 1930s. See, e.g., Reino Kero, "Emigration of Finns from North America to Soviet Karelia in the early 1930's," in *Finnish Experience,* p. 215.

47. Ollila, "Finnish-American Church," pp. 170–71.

48. Ollila, "Defects," p. 411. However, Ollila's statement appears to be an oversimplification, since the IWW also had a strong immigrant basis and the IWW-Finns had abundant ethnic functions in their halls and particularly around their paper *Industrialisti* until its death in the 1970s.

49. Sulkanen, *Historia,* p. 254.

50. Kostiainen, "Finnish-American Workmen's Associations," esp. pp. 230–31.

51. It has been suggested that promoting and developing the cooperative idea was perhaps the most important contribution by Finnish-Americans to the United States. For a general developmental study of Finnish cooperatives in America, see Arnold Alanen, "The Development and Distribution of Finnish Consumers' Cooperatives in Michigan, Minnesota and Wisconsin, 1903–1973," in *Finnish Experience,* pp. 103–30.

52 For a bibliographical survey of the developments of the melting pot and cultural pluralism theses, see Rudolph J. Vecoli, "European Americans: From Immigrants to Ethnics," in William H. Cartwright and Richard L. Watson, Jr., eds., *The Reinterpretation of American History and Culture* (Washington, D.C., 1973), esp. pp. 82–89.

53. Timothy L. Smith, "New Approaches to the History of Immigration in Twentieth-Century America," *American Historical Review* 71 (1966): 1265–79.

54. See Smith, *Americans in the Making,* p. 298.

About the Authors

SUNE ÅKERMAN began his work with studies of the political pressure groups formed by Swedish iron mill owners in the 1830s and of Swedish experiments with a progressive income-tax system from 1810 to 1812. From political and economic history he moved into the field of demographic studies and was head of the Migration Research Group, 1966–73. He has edited a volume of essays, *Chance and Change*, on the social, economic, and demographic development of the Baltic area in a 300-year perspective (together with H. D. Johansen and D. Gaunt) and is working on a monograph on population mobility.

BRUNO CARTOSIO, of the University of Milan, developed his interest in American history during the 1960s. It was a consequence of the effort to understand, and respond to, the many questions that social movements— particularly the black movement—posed to young militants on the left everywhere. He moved along two main lines of research: one going back to slavery—its origins, its development, and its relations with the growth of European capitalism and African impoverishment—and the other aimed at achieving an understanding of the development of the American working class. His publications include "Note e documenti sugli Industrial Workers of the World," *Primo maggio* (1973); "American Labor Movement," in *Il mondo moderno* (1978); *Dentro l'America in crisi* (1980), a book on the current economic and political situation in the United States; and translations of as well as introductions to three books by George P. Rawick, Martin Glaberman, and Herbert G. Gutman.

IVAN ČIZMIĆ was professor of the history of state and law at the University of Split and since 1964 has worked as adviser in the Croatian Matica Home, collecting material on emigration and on the life of his people abroad. He has published a book, *Yugoslav Emigrant Movement in the USA and the Creation of the Yugoslav State in 1918* (1974), and essays on individual emigrants, emigration from specific districts, Yugoslav-American volunteering during World War I, and the founding and work of the Yugoslav Socialist League, 1911.

ANDREW DAWSON is lecturer in social and economic history at Thames Polytechnic, London, Great Britain. His interest in the history of the working class can be dated from the period of political turmoil during the late

1960s. Reading for a degree in economics, he reacted to the then all-pervasive acceptance of neoclassical economic theory. Here the working class—when it was recognized as such—was treated as the pliant object of technological and market forces rather than as a group conscious of its own social position and capable of seeking redress. At Thames Polytechnic he centered upon examining ideology, cultural formation, and consciousness in modern Western societies and attempted to forge links between the processes of technological change, craft workers, and ideology. In his analysis of the changing impact of Selig Perlman's major work, in "History as Ideology: Fifty Years of Job Consciousness," *Literature and History* 8 (1978), he has argued that outside the factory gates the historians of the "history-from-below" approach busy themselves among crowds and communities, while inside the traditional labor historians, latter-day supporters of Perlman and Commons (and there are more than we care to think), continue to produce further paeans to the American industrial system.

MARIANNE DEBOUZY's work in American studies began with an interest in American literature and society. Her thesis dealt with "social protest in the American novel, 1875–1915." In the late 1950s and early 1960s her experience as a teacher of American literature made her increasingly dissatisfied with the way literary studies were taught and organized in language departments. Her growing interest in social history, linked to her political interest in social change and the role of the working class, made her shift from American literature to American labor history, and since the experimental University of Vincennes was created after the May 1968 student uprising she has held a teaching position in its history department. Her numerous publications include *Le capitalisme 'sauvage' aux Etats-Unis, 1860–1900* (1972); "Le problème de l'immigration et l'histoire des Etats-Unis," *Annales (E.S.C)* (1972); *"La New Economic History,* splendeurs et misères d'une 'Nouveauté,' "* Politique aujourd'hui* (1975) (with Jacques Debouzy); and contributions to the collective works *Histoire mondiale de la femme* (1966) and *Histoire générale du socialisme* (1974 and later).

DAVID N. DOYLE, lecturer in American history at University College, Dublin, Ireland, has concentrated on Irish America: patterns of emigration, class stratification, and occupational distribution in the United States, community organization, and politico-social activity. He says that since 80% of eighteenth- and nineteenth-century Irishmen at home were impoverished, the underlying assumption of certain studies of the Irish rise to "intermediacy" (M. Barron's phrase), viz., that people only become meaningful when successful, leaves him somewhat cold. For most of its development the Anglo-Atlantic economy used the Irish rather than advanced them: he is currently working on a study of the 100,000 native Irish indentured servants imported to prerevolutionary America. The manner in which the Irish community in Ireland and in the United States developed an ideology acceptive of the politics and law of that world, and of the inevitability of their own class stratification on its terms, yet one which retained a measure of consciousness of the collective situation of the Irish and hence of the need (even among established Irish) for an aggressive strategy of group improvement, needs fuller study. In his words, "The Irish were underneath the Anglo-Atlantic economy for so long, that, even granting their subsequent power and upward mobility, how else can they be studied?" His publications include *Irish Americans, Native Rights and National Empires, 1890–1901: Structure, Divisions and Attitudes of the Catholic Minority* (1976) and an article, "The Irish and American Labour, 1880–1920," *Saothar: Journal of the Irish Labour History Society* (1975). He is co-editor with L. J. McCaffrey, J. Walsh, and M. Conners of *The Irish-Americans*, 42 vols. (1976), and with O. D. Edwards of *America and Ireland, 1776–1976*, a volume of reinterpretative essays (1979).

FERRUCCIO GAMBINO teaches the sociology of labor and industry at the Istituto Scienze Politiche of the University of Padua. His interests in the study of contemporary U.S. society arose in the late 1960s, focusing on the international aspects of working-class self-activity. In his essay on Ford of Britain in the collective work *Operai e stato* (1972), he argued that not only is the working class internationally influenced by the movements of capital but also that the latter are dependent on the state of organization of the workers in all its forms. In his essay on U.S. direct investments abroad and class composition, in Luciano Ferrari Bravo, ed., *Imperialismo e classe operaia multinazionale* (1975), he extended the analysis to post–World War II changes in working-class composition both in the United States and abroad vis-à-vis capital's mobility in the last 30 years. This has led to a reconsideration of specific issues of the working-class movement in the United States, in particular the black proletarian movement within black nationalism. He is presently doing research on U.S. working-class composition of the 1950s and 1960s. His publications include essays in *Imperialismo e classe operaia multinazionale* (1975) and *Operai e stato* (1972).

HARTMUT KEIL is the director of the "Chicago Project" at the Amerika-Institut of the University of Munich. His interest in German immigrant workers was aroused by two factors: the historiography on German immigration has focused on the middle and upper classes, whereas the mass of immigrant workers has been totally neglected; also, traditional American labor history almost completely disregarded the impact of the German element within labor's ranks. He began his research with an emphasis on the second aspect, dealing with the impact of socialist emigrants from Bismarck Germany, during the time of the antisocialist laws (1878–90) in the United States, on both the emerging labor parties and union movements. Directly related to this endeavor is his projected publication of the correspondence of Friedrich Adolph Sorge, eminent German-American socialist and for a time general secretary of the First International. The ambitious "Chicago Project"—a cooperative effort—intends to reconstruct the social history of German immigrant workers in Chicago from 1850 to 1910, including the question of ideology and its relative importance in different social contexts. His publications include "Elemente einer deutschen Arbeiterkultur in Chicago zwischen 1880 und 1890," in *Geschichte und Gesellschaft* (1979) (with Heinz Ickstadt).

AUVO KOSTIAINEN teaches general history at the University of Turku, Finland, and became involved in the emigration history research project, particularly Finnish-American culture and society. He has now concentrated on the history of the Finnish-American labor movement, especially the communist group, since this ideology gained notable support among American Finns during the interwar period. His purpose is to investigate different sides of Finnish-American radicalism, major emphasis being on the organizational-ideological aspects. One of the primary goals in his research has been to put the Finnish-American ethnic community in its proper place as a part of the larger American environment and at the same time to look at developments in the international background, because Finnish immigrant radicals always strongly posed internationalism in their ideology. He is author of *The Forging of Finnish-American Communism, 1917–1924: A Study in Ethnic Radicalism* (1978) and *Santevi Nuorteva—kansainvälinen suomalainen*, the biography of an international Finn (in press) and co-author of *Toholammin väestön muuttoliikkeet amerikansiirtolaisuuden alkuvaiheissa (1870–1889): Yhteispohjoismaisen muuttoliiketutkimuksen suomen osa* (Population mobility in Toholampi in the early period of the American emigration, 1870–1889) (1978).

HANS NORMAN, of the Avdelningen för Amerikansk Historia, Uppsala University started his research on emigration from Örebro County in Sweden to North America. As the work advanced, it was natural to broaden the study to include Swedish immigrants settling in America and their situation there, both in rural pioneer areas in western Wisconsin and in industrializing Worcester, Mass. He then expanded the scope of his work again, dealing with migrational movements in general and their causes, social mobility, colonization settlements, and the social and demographic patterns of immigrant populations. Together with Harald Runblom, he has edited the final report of the Uppsala Migration Research Project, *From Sweden to America: A History of the Migration* (1976).

HUBERT PERRIER teaches American civilization at the University of Nancy. He was one among many to rediscover America in the mid-1960s when the insurgency of the ghettos as well as the campuses challenged the prevailing notions that the United States had stranded itself in the dull waters of the death of the Left and the "End of Ideology." He had a keen interest in the revival of American radicalism and, consequently, its origins, history, and traditions. Impressed by the efforts of Herbert Gutman, David Brody, and others to reshape traditional views on the identity and role of workers in the context of industrializing America, he carries over some of their methodological and conceptual advances to the study of socialism in the same period—the Gilded Age—to learn something new about: (1) the workers and other diverse men and women who at one time or another were attracted to the SLP; (2) the real contribution of socialists of all backgrounds and ranks to shaping the political and social orientations of the American working class; (3) the American version of the dilemma, common to all socialists at the time of the Second International, about the "correct" link between minimal and revolutionary goals.

PETER R. SHERGOLD teaches at the University of New South Wales, Kensington, N.S.W., Australia. He takes a comparative noninstitutional approach to American labor history. Continuing research on history "at the bottom" has led to a concern with the manner in which manual workers expended their discretionary income and time during the formative period of American unionism in the late nineteenth and early twentieth centuries. He is currently writing on working-class budgetary behavior, response to debt, and access to leisure facilities. He has published several articles, among them "Immigration and White American Fertility 1800–1860," *Australian Economic History Review* (1974), "Relative Skill and Income Levels of Native and Foreign Born Workers," *Explorations in Economic History* (1978), and "The Loan Shark: The Small Loan Business in Early 20th Century Pittsburgh," *Pennsylvania History* (1978).

LARS-GÖRAN TEDEBRAND has taught at the Historiska Institutionen of Uppsala University since 1969. He is now professor of historical demography at the University of Umeå. In his dissertation he dealt with migrational processes and social change during the industrialization of the lumber areas in northern Sweden, with emphasis on emigration to the United States and Canada. Concerned on the one hand with demographic stability and change within the young Swedish working class during the industrial revolution and with small-town demography, he is preparing a study of social and demographic behavior among iron foundry workers in Sweden in 1800–1870. Interested on the other hand in international labor migration between Sweden and North America before 1930, he asks to what degree America was an alternative to the Swedish labor market for the great bulk of the Swedish working class at the end of the nineteenth and beginning of the twentieth centuries. His publications include *Västernorrland och Nordamerika 1875–1913: Utvandring och återinvandring* (Emigration from Västernorrland County to North America and re-immigration) (1972).

About the Commentators

DAVID BRODY, University of California at Davis, emphasizes the role of the workplace in the formation of class consciousness. He is on the editorial board of *Labor History*. In his publications he has traced the decline in bargaining power of skilled workers in the steel industry and has edited several anthologies on the labor movement and industrial America.

ALAN DAWLEY teaches at Trenton State College. His book *Class and Community*, on the life and work of Lynn shoemakers in the nineteenth century, is one of the best recent examples of a cultural history of the working class. With Paul Faler he has co-authored an article in the *Journal of Social History*.

CHARLOTTE ERICKSON is on the faculty of the London School of Economics and Political Science, which was founded in 1895 with the support of the Fabian Society. She teaches American economic and social history. Among her publications are *American Industry and the European Immigrant 1860–1885* (1957) and *Invisible Immigrants; The Adaptation of English and Scottish Immigrants in Nineteenth-Century America* (1972).

HERBERT G. GUTMAN of the City University of New York has published numerous books and articles on the American working class, the role of immigrants, the persistence of family structures under slavery, and the use and misuse of statistics by historians.

WILLIAM H. HARRIS teaches American labor history at Indiana University, Bloomington. He spent a year at the University of Hamburg as a Fulbright scholar. His publications include *Keeping the Faith: A. Philip Randolph, Milton P. Webster, and the Brotherhood of Sleeping Car Porters, 1925–1937* (1977).

DANIEL J. LEAB of Seton Hall University, New York, is editor of *Labor History* and contributing editor to the *Columbia Journalism Review*. He has published articles on the unemployment movement in the United States during the 1930s. His books include *Union of Individuals: The American Newspaper Guild 1933–1936* (1970) and *From Sambo to Superspade: Black Experience in Motion Pictures* (1975).

GÜNTER MOLTMAN teaches at the University of Hamburg. His publications include *Atlantische Blockpolitik im 19. Jahrhundert—Die Vereinigten Staaten und der deutsche Liberalismus* . . . (1973) and—as editor—*Deutsche Amerikaaus-wanderung im 19. Jahrhundert* (1976). He is past president of the Deutsche Gesellschaft für Amerikastudien and is now engaged in a project on German emigration to the United States.

BO ÖHNGREN teaches in the Department of History, Uppsala University. He has been studying the political behavior of voluntary associations including the trade unions, the political mobilization of different social strata, Swedish engineering workers, and urbanization in *People on the Move* (1974).

LONGIN PASTUSIAK of the Research Institute on Contemporary Capitalism in Warsaw has just finished an essay on the origins of the working-class movement in Chicago during the second half of the nineteenth century. He is now working on a survey of the U.S. labor movement to be published by the institute as part of a fundamental work on trade unions in capitalist countries.

TIHOMIR TELIŠMAN is director of the Zavod za Migracije i Narodnosti (Institute of Migration and Nationalities) in Zagreb. He has published a statistical compilation about emigrants from Croatia and a survey of emigrant studies in Yugoslavia. He is now engaged in research on "The Role of the Croatian Fraternal Union in the Life of Croatian Migrants in the U.S.A."

ARNALDO TESTI teaches at the University of Pisa. He has published essays on Richard Hofstadter's history between conflict and consensus, on Italian socialists' image of the United States from 1886 to 1914, and on the New Deal. His book *American Socialists in the Progressive Era: The Social-Democratic Party of Wisconsin, 1900–1920* has been published recently.

LORETTA VALTZ-MANNUCCI teaches at the University of Milan. She has published books on the black and student movements in the 1960s (1968); on blacks in the 1940s as compared with the period of World War I and the Depression (1975); on the roots of American ideology, 1763–1803, with Roberto Petrolini (1979). She is now working on a study of ideological adaptation to industrialization between 1880 and World War I.

RUDOLPH J. VECOLI teaches at the University of Minnesota. He is director of the Immigration History Research Center. His publications include *The People of New Jersey* (1965) and numerous articles in the field of immigration and ethnic history. His research has focused especially upon Italian immigration to the United States, e.g. "The Coming of Age of the Italian Americans: 1945–1974," *Ethnicity* (1978), and he is currently writing a history of the Italian labor and radical movements in America.

ALFRED F. YOUNG teaches at the University of Northern Illinois. He has published a book and essays on *The Democratic-Republicans of New York* (1967) and has edited two volumes of *Explorations in the History of American Radicalism* (1968, 1976), which served as a model for this volume's essays. He is now working on a study of artisan culture in the early republic.

Index

Abolitionism, 46
Acculturation, 108-9, 178-83, 215-18,
  241-43, 259-66; political involvement,
  242-54 *passim*
Adams, H.C., 28-29
Altgeld, John Peter, 166, 169
American Bureau of Industrial
  Research, 34
American Economic Association, 17,
  30-31, 34
American Federation of Labor, 9, 35-
  36, 48, 107, 114-15, 117, 121, 122,
  126-28, *passim*, 143, 144, 145, 147,
  151, 169, 193; AFL-CIO, 5, 267. *See
  also* Congress of Industrial
  Organization, unions
American sickness, 197-98
Americanization. *See* Acculturation
Arbitration, 22, 29
Artisans, 137, 158
Assimilation, 123. *See also* Acculturation
Associated Fraternities of America, 181
Associated Press, 144
Association for Labor Legislation, 17
Austro-Hungary, 177

Balkan conference, 1909, 186
Bellamy, Edward, 114
Black, blacks, black workers, 5, 18, 43-
  58, 145-46; Nation of Islam, 44;
  Niagara Movement, 46-47; Pan-
  African movement, 48-49, 51;
  professionals, 45-46; proletariat, 44-
  58 *passim;* strikebreakers, 49;
  Tuskegee Institute, 45-46; unions,
  146. *See also* National Association for
  the Advancement of Colored People
Boarding houses, 179-80
Boycott, 115, 117
Business unionism. *See* Unionism

Capital, 21, 33, 44, 47-48, 53; and
  wages, 58; in New York, 116
Capitalism, 32, 35, 145, 148, 226
Central Labor Federation, 112, 114-
  23
Central Labor Union, 114, 117

Chicago, 44, 50, 113, 156–76, 178, 196;
  Citizens' Association, 161; police, 11;
  railroad strikes, 1877, 61, 70, 72–73;
  steel strike, 1919, 49; Trades
  Assembly, 159–60
Chicagoer Arbeiter-Zeitung, 158, 161, 165,
  167
Chicanos, 5
Citizenship. *See* Naturalization
Civil War, 46, 54, 148
"Civil war," 70, 73
Class consciousness, 135–38, 157–59
Class, ruling, 73–74. *See also* Middle
  class; Working class
Class struggle, 232; blacklisting, 232;
  collective initiative, 71; crowd action,
  62–65; guerilla warfare, 62, 72;
  revolution, 35–36, 49, 129; sabotage,
  71–72; shop floor action, 120. *See also*
  Unions
Clergy: role of, 180–81
Colonialism, 48–49
Comintern. *See* International, Third
Commons, John, 8, 18, 34–37, 84
Communism, 261–71 *passim*
Communist party, 264, 267, 270, 271
Congress of Industrial Organizations,
  43
Contract: freedom of, 28
Cooperative movement, 32–33, 115,
  118, 236, 270
Cost of living: Birmingham and
  Pittsburgh, 85–101
Craft consciousness, 135–55 *passim*
Crafts, 137
Croatian National Union, 182
Croats. *See* Immigrants, Yugoslav

De Leon, Daniel, 111, 113, 115, 126,
  127, 128
Debs, Eugene, 147, 165
Depressions, 18, 124, 126, 147, 196,
  225, 230–31; Great Depression, 43–
  44, 221
Detroit, 43–44, 50, 115, 144
Douai, Adolf, 21
Du Bois, W. E. B., 18, 43–58

East St. Louis: strikes, 50, 64–65, 66, 67–68
Economic history, 31
Economics, science of, 25–37 *passim*
Economy: political, 27, 30–31
Eight-hour movement, 22–23, 167, 169
Elites, 253
Ely, Richard T., 8, 22-37 *passim*
Ethnic Heritage Act, 7
Ethnicity, ethnic diversity, 5, 108, 117, 121–22, 156–58, 181, 191, 195, 236, 239, 244, 251–52, 271–72
Exclusivity, 139–46 *passim*

Fabian Society, 17–18
Fackel, 167, 170
Farmer Labor party, 249
Finnish-American workmen's associations, 222, 260-72 *passim*
Finnish Socialist Federation, 261–63, 266, 268
Finnish Workers Organization, 264
France, 145; glassworkers, 11; labor organizations, 17; Paris Commune, 17, 32–33
Fraternal societies: Yugoslav, 181–83

Gaelic League, 198
Garvey, Marcus, 50–51
Gastarbeiter, 249
General German Workingmen's Association, 165
Germany, 107–8, 145, 151, 161, 165, 171, 223; economists, 27; Kathedersozialisten, 3, 29; labor organizations, 17; recent labor historiography, 61; U.S. historians trained in, 25–30 *passim*, 44
Ghetto, 44–45, 58, 199; revolts, 50
Gompers, Samuel, 35–36, 48, 107, 114–15, 124, 147, 149–50
Government, 147, 162; elections, 162, 237. *See also* Labor, legislation; U.S. Army
Government ownership. *See* Nationalization
Great Britain, 145, 148, 151; Birmingham labor, 80–101; British observers on American labor, 23; historiography, 5, 37; labor organizations, 17; Manchester school, 26; union movement compared to U.S., 135–40; workers' education, 17–18
Grottkau, Paul, 160–61, 165–68

Hall, Gus, 267

Haymarket massacre, 11, 23, 156, 161
Hewitt, Abram S., 21–22
Hill, Joe, 221
Hillquit, Morris, 146
Historiography, 51, 75, 79, 194; comparative, 3, 4, 11, 17, 18; Du Bois, *Black Reconstruction*, 43–58; immigration history, 6; Johns Hopkins school, 35; labor historiography, 3, 8, 10–11, 17, 18, 19–37 *passim*; "old labor history," 9; "Old Left," 5; operarist approach, 10; Wisconsin school, 3, 17, 34–37; working-class history, 5, 6, 8
Holding company, 107

Illinois Labor Bureau, 159, 160
Immigrants, 107–9, 121–23; Bulgarian, 5; East European, 84, 122–24; Finnish, 192, 259–75; German, 108, 113, 121–22, 156–76; Greek, 5; Irish, 121, 191–92, 193–218, 239; Italian, 84, 108, 121; Jewish, 121–24; Scandinavian, 122; Swedish, 108, 192, 221–58; Yugoslav, 5, 108, 177–90. *See also* Acculturation
Imperialism, 50
Industrial democracy, 145
Industrial evolution, 28
Industrial violence, 7, 12, 19–23 *passim*, 32, 61–75, 165, 236; Pinkertons, 11. *See also* Police; U.S. Army
Industrial Workers of the World, 7, 9, 47–48, 221, 249, 261, 264, 266. *See also* Unions
Internationalism, 47, 263–71
International, First, 191; Third, 263, 271
Ireland: Congested Districts, 202–9; land league, 203–4, 206; wages, 210, 218; mentioned, 193–218
Italy: recent labor historiography, 61

James, C. L. R., 52
Job consciousness, 119

Kathedersozialisten, 3, 29
Knights of Labor, 17, 22, 31–35, 69, 117, 162–63. *See also* Unions

Labor: aristocracy, 82–84, 136; Catholic reaction, 17; education, 17–18; European organizations, 17, 29; leadership, 112–29, 163–71, 236; legislation, 22–23, 25, 28–29, 115, 147; migratory, 5, 11, 20, 47, 50, 145–46; movements of the

Labor (*continued*)
  unemployed, 20; "the other labor
    movement," 8, 9; semi-skilled, 139;
    skilled, 81–85, 135–55, 241–42;
    statistics, 23–25 *passim;* unskilled, 90–
    100, 139, 241–42; wages and income,
    79–101. *See also* Historiography;
    Working class; Workers
Labor party of Illinois, 162
Labor theory of value, 12
Laissez faire, 23, 26–27, 33
Lassalleans, 17, 165, 237
"Liberty, equality, and fraternity," 74

McGuire, J. P., 169
McNamara brothers, 193
McNeill, George E., 17, 21, 22, 23, 24,
    33, 34
Marx, Marxists, 12, 17, 48–49, 57, 129,
    168, 191, 208, 226, 244
Massachusetts Bureau of Statistics of
    Labor, 21
Mayo-Smith, Richmond, 24–25
Middle class, 137, 158, 195, 221, 226,
    242
Migration, 237–38; and business cycles,
    224; information by letters, 228; in
    stages, 215; migration frequency,
    224; return, 227; self-generating,
    207, 215; temporary, 178, 267
Militarism, 49
Mobility: social, 217, 248
Mobilization, 120, 235, 254
Modernization, 199, 223
Muhammad, Elijah, 44
Municipal socialism. *See* Socialism

National Association for the
    Advancement of Colored People, 43.
    See also Blacks
National Civic Federation, 35
National Croatian Society, 183–85
National Fraternal Congress, 181
National Labor Union, 191
Nationalization, 144
Naturalization, 250, 267–70
New Deal, 51, 221
New York City, 20, 177–78, 196;
    Central Labor Federation, 112, 114–
    23; Central Labor Union, 114, 117;
    socialists in, 111–34
Nordic Emigration History Project, 11
Norway, 222–23

Oliver, Henry K., 23–24

Palmer, A. Mitchell, 268

Paris Commune, 17, 32–33
People, 116, 119, 121, 122, 123
Perlman, Selig, 8, 37, 157
Petrić, Frank, 186
Philanthropy, 45
Pittsburgh, 61, 62, 65, 67, 69–70, 80–
    101, 182
Planning: central, 145
Police, 45, 62, 71, 118, 120, 161;
    German, 165
Populism, 44, 144, 221
Powderly, Terence V., 166
Producing class, 136
Progressives, Progressive Era, 44, 47,
    127, 143

Racism: mentioned, 43–57
Railroads: strikes, 61–75
Reconstruction period: mentioned, 43–
    57
Reformism, 146, 194, 247
Revolution. *See* Class struggle
Ricardo, David, 26
Rosenberg, W. L., 113, 170
Royal Commission on Labour, 209
Russia, 259; revolution, 260–61, 265;
    Russification, 259; Soviet Russia, 247,
    265, 270

Sabotage, 71–72
St. Louis: strikes, 61, 62
Saloons, 179–80
Sanial, Lucien, 113–14
Schilling, George A., 165–69
Schwab, Michael, 161
Scientific management, 4, 101;
    efficiency and unions, 145
Seligman, E. R. A., 29, 30
Serbs. *See* Immigrants, Yugoslav
Settlement House movement, 3
Slavery, 46, 52–53. *See also* Blacks
Slave trade, 44, 48
Slavonian benevolent societies, 177
Slovenes. *See* Immigrants, Yugoslav
Smith, Adam, 26–28
Social Darwinists, 44
Social democracy, 135, 165, 171
Social justice, 145
Socialism, 17, 107–8, 244; Fabian, 145;
    German, 156–71 *passim;* hall, 261–66;
    in New York, 111–34; labor
    historians and, 35; municipal, 144;
    utopian, 17
Socialist Labor party, 19, 111–34 *passim,*
    162, 250
Socialist party of America, 144, 187,
    249, 253, 261–62

Socialist Trade and Labor Alliance,
111–29 *passim*
Socialist Workers' party, 187
Socialists: Christian, 17, 28; Fabian
Society, 17; Finnish, 259–72 *passim*;
Kathedersozialisten, 3, 29
Sociology, 31, 44; and social reform, 17,
31; and social research, 25
South Slavic Socialistic Federation of
America, 186–88
Sumner, Graham, 21
Steward, Ira, 169
Strasser, Adolf, 21
Strikes, 19–23, 117, 184–85, 244; as a
dynamic process, 63–66; of black
students, 51; cloak makers, 107;
committees, 61–75 *passim;* defense of
values, 74; Lawrence mill strike, 193;
McKees Rock, 1909, 184; Pullman,
1894, 229; railroad, 1877, 17, 18, 19,
32, 61–75, 161; steel, 1919, 49; in
Sweden, 225
Sweden, 221–34; Social Democratic
Labor party, 224; Confederation of
Trade Unions, 224; Royal
commission on emigration, 225–26;
strikes, 229–32
Syndicalism, 35

Taft, Philip, 37
Taylorism. *See* Scientific management
Technology, 80, 117, 137, 158
Temperance movement, 224, 247, 248,
259
Trade unions. *See* Unions.
Trusts, 143
Tuskegee Institute, 45–46

Unemployment benefits, 126, 159
Unionism, 139, 244; "Bread and
Butter," 9; "pure and simple," 23,
116, 126
Unions, 22, 80; business, 142; black,
50; Brotherhood of Locomotive
Engineers, 69; Brotherhood of
Painters, 140; democracy, 61;
Furniture Workers Union, 161, 169;
Garment Workers Union, 143;
International Association of
Machinists, 141; new trade unionism,
112, 121; Pattern Makers' League,
140, 147; Trainmen's Union, 69;
United Mineworkers of America,
184, 217; Western Federation of

Miners, 184; German Bricklayers and
Stonecutters Union, 165, 168;
Swedish, 229ff.; West German, 6. *See
also* Labor
United Hebrew Trades, 117, 124
U.S. Army, 71, 268
U.S. Bureau of Labor, 22, 24
U.S. Congress, 143
U.S. Department of Labor, 3
U.S. government and labor, 23, 26
U.S. House of Representatives:
committees on labor, 21
U.S. Industrial Relations Commission,
198, 217
U.S. National Guard, 19
U.S. Senate: committees on labor, 22,
159
Universal Negro Improvement
Association, 50

Van Patten, Philip, 161
Voluntarism, 142
Vorbote, 162, 165, 167, 168, 169

Wages, 79–101, 146, 149, 158–59;
relative real wages, 90–101; family
income, 98–100
Washington, Booker T., 45–46
Wilson, Woodrow, 49
Women workers, 5, 145–46
Work: hours of, 147, 179; minimum
hours, 143; seasonal, 159; working
conditions, 101
Workers: agricultural, 51; black and
white, 52–58; rank and file, 61, 117,
267; railroad, 61–75. *See also* Labor;
Working class
Workers party of America, 261, 263
Working class: autonomy, 61;
composition of, 158; direct action, 12,
29; mass worker, 10; self-
organization, 18, 61–75, 120;
socialism, 112; solidarity, 62, 122–23,
227, 263; standard of living, 78, 159–
60, 178; structure of, 135–52. *See also*
Class struggle; Labor
Workingmen's party, 69, 161
Workmen's Advocate, 114, 116
World War I, 47, 145; African roots, 48
Wright, Carroll D., 21, 22, 27

Young Communist League, 266
Young Workers League, 266
Yugoslavia: mentioned, 177–89